# NAVIGATING THE MICROSOFT NETWORK

Ned Snell

201 West 103rd Street
Indianapolis, Indiana 46290

*To Nancy, José, and John*

# Copyright © 1995 by Sams.net Publishing

FIRST EDITION

International Standard Book Number: 0-672-30778-2

Library of Congress Catalog Card Number: 95-70882

98  97  96  95      4  3  2  1

Interpretation of the printing code: the rightmost double-digit number is the year of the book's printing; the rightmost single-digit, the number of the book's printing. For example, a printing code of 95-1 shows that the first printing of the book occurred in 1995.

Composed in AGaramond and MCPdigital by Macmillan Computer Publishing

Printed in the United States of America

# Trademarks

**President, Sams Publishing** *Richard K. Swadley*

**Publisher, Sams.net Publishing** *George Bond*

**Managing Editor** *Cindy Morrow*

**Marketing Manager** *John Pierce*

**Publishing Manager**
*Mark Taber*

**Acquisitions Editor**
*Carla Randolph*

**Development Editor**
*Fran Hatton*

**Production Editor**
*Alice Martina Smith*

**Technical Reviewer**
*Donald Doherty*

**Editorial Coordinator**
*Bill Whitmer*

**Technical Edit Coordinator**
*Lynette Quinn*

**Formatter**
*Frank Sinclair*

**Editorial Assistant**
*Carol Ackerman*

**Cover Designer**
*Beth Guzman*

**Book Designer**
*Alyssa Yesh*

**Production Team Supervisor**
*Brad Chinn*

**Page Layout**
*Carol Bowers, Charlotte Clapp, Terrie Deemer, Louisa Klucznik, Steph Mineart, Tina Trettin*

**Proofreading**
*Georgiana Briggs, Mona Brown, Michael Brumitt, Jeanne Clark, Paula Lowell, Brian-Kent Proffitt, SA Springer*

**Indexer**
*Greg Eldred*

**Production Analysts**
*Angela D. Bannan*
*Bobbi Satterfield*

# Overview

| | Introduction | xii |
|---|---|---|
| Part I | **Setting Up The Microsoft Network** | **1** |
| 1 | Signing Up, Signing In, and Signing Out | 3 |
| 2 | Maintaining Your MSN Account | 29 |
| 3 | Member Rules and Etiquette | 45 |
| Part II | **Navigating The Microsoft Network** | **59** |
| 4 | Basic Navigation Techniques | 61 |
| 5 | Reading and Contributing to Bulletin Boards and Newsgroups | 81 |
| 6 | Hanging Out in Chat Rooms | 107 |
| 7 | Downloading and Uploading Files | 121 |
| 8 | Composing, Sending, and Receiving E-Mail | 141 |
| 9 | Viewing and Operating Titles | 157 |
| Part III | **Taking Control of MSN** | **167** |
| 10 | Finding Anything on MSN | 169 |
| 11 | Advanced Configuration Options | 181 |
| 12 | Trimming Time Online | 191 |
| 13 | Power E-Mail | 199 |
| 14 | Speeding Up MSN | 219 |
| Part IV | **Navigating the Internet Through MSN** | **233** |
| 15 | Understanding the Internet | 235 |
| 16 | Browsing the World Wide Web | 249 |
| 17 | Browsing Gophers | 281 |
| 18 | Downloading Files with FTP | 297 |
| 19 | Advanced Internet Techniques | 313 |
| Part V | **References** | **331** |
| A | Go Word Directory | 333 |
| B | Web Highlights | 343 |
| | Glossary | 353 |
| | Index | 361 |

# CONTENTS

**Introduction**                                                                                                                                        **xii**

**Part I    Setting Up The Microsoft Network                                                                                                               1**

**1    Signing Up, Signing In, and Signing Out                                                                                                             3**

Signing Up ..................................................................................................... 4
  Preparing to Sign Up................................................................................ 5
  "Pro" Sign-Up (for the Brave and Eager) ........................................... 12
  Signing Up ................................................................................................. 12
Signing In ...................................................................................................... 21
Signing Out ................................................................................................... 27
What Now? ................................................................................................... 28

**2    Maintaining Your MSN Account                                                                                                                        29**

Changing Settings....................................................................................... 30
  Access Numbers ..................................................................................... 31
  Dialing Properties .................................................................................. 33
Changing Your Password .......................................................................... 34
Changing MSN Options ............................................................................ 35
  The Folder Tab ....................................................................................... 35
  General Tab ............................................................................................. 36
Working with Billing .................................................................................. 38
  Billing Information ................................................................................. 38
  Online Statement and Subscriptions ................................................. 39
Contacting MSN Support ......................................................................... 41
  Help .......................................................................................................... 41
  Member Assistance ................................................................................ 41
  Telephone Support ................................................................................ 42
What Now? ................................................................................................... 44

**3    Member Rules and Etiquette                                                                                                                          45**

About MSN and "Cybersleaze" ............................................................... 46
  How MSN's Content Is (and Is Not) Controlled ............................. 47
Member Guidelines .................................................................................... 50
Netiquette ..................................................................................................... 52
  Watch Your Language ........................................................................... 53
  Avoid "Capital" Offenses...................................................................... 53
  Curb Quoting .......................................................................................... 53
  Be Discreet .............................................................................................. 53
  Keep Cool ................................................................................................ 54
  Communicate Efficiently ..................................................................... 54
  Post No Bills ........................................................................................... 54
Internet Shorthand ..................................................................................... 55

Emoticons ................................................... 56

What Now? ................................................. 58

**Part II    Navigating The Microsoft Network**                                    **59**

**4    Basic Navigation Techniques**                                           **61**

Understanding Windows 95 Concepts ................................. 62

Understanding MSN Concepts ...................................... 64

New Terms ................................................. 65

The "Content Tree" .......................................... 68

Browsing The Microsoft Network ................................... 69

Climbing Down the Content Tree .............................. 71

Climbing Up the Content Tree ................................ 73

Getting Back Home (MSN Central) ........................... 74

Browsing with Windows Explorer ................................... 75

Making a Beeline for Anything on MSN .............................. 76

Your Favorite Places Folder .................................. 76

Go ......................................................... 77

Opening Files ................................................... 78

What Now? ..................................................... 80

**5    Reading and Contributing to Bulletin Boards and Newsgroups**              **81**

Finding and Opening a BBS ....................................... 83

Reading Messages ................................................ 86

Organizing Messages in Views ................................ 87

Reading a Message ........................................... 90

Learning More About the Author .............................. 92

Writing Messages ................................................ 93

Composing and Posting a New Message ........................ 93

Posting a Reply ............................................. 94

Replying and Forwarding by Mail ............................. 95

Finding and Opening a Newsgroup .................................. 98

About Newsgroups ........................................... 99

How MSN Organizes Newsgroups ............................. 102

Getting Access to All Newsgroups ............................ 103

What Now? .................................................... 105

**6    Hanging Out in Chat Rooms**                                            **107**

Finding and Entering a Chat Room ................................ 109

Understanding How Chats Are Run ................................ 112

Participating in a Chat .......................................... 113

Advanced Chatting .............................................. 116

Saving and Clearing the Chat History ........................ 116

Hiding Spectators .......................................... 116

Chat Options ............................................... 116

Chatting Only with Certain Members .............................................. 117
Learning More About a Participant ................................................ 119
Learning More About Chat ................................................................ 120
What Now? ......................................................................................... 120

7    **Downloading and Uploading Files**                                    **121**
First Files to Download ..................................................................... 123
Viewers and Players ......................................................................... 125
Compression/Decompression .......................................................... 127
Decoding Newsgroup Files .............................................................. 128
Downloading a File from a BBS or Library ..................................... 128
Basic Downloading ........................................................................... 129
Downloading Options ...................................................................... 131
Uploading a File to a BBS ................................................................. 134
Downloading a File from a Newsgroup ........................................... 136
Saving the Message File ................................................................... 138
Decoding the File ............................................................................. 139
What Now? ......................................................................................... 140

8    **Composing, Sending, and Receiving E-Mail**                         **141**
About E-Mail ..................................................................................... 143
The Anatomy of an E-Mail Message ............................................... 144
About Exchange ................................................................................ 146
Have You Received E-Mail? .............................................................. 148
Receiving E-Mail ............................................................................... 148
Using Embedded Links and Shortcuts ........................................... 150
Composing and Sending a New Message ........................................ 150
Formatting Messages ........................................................................ 152
Replying and Forwarding .................................................................. 153
Addressing Mail Beyond MSN ........................................................ 154
What Now? ......................................................................................... 156

9    **Viewing and Operating Titles**                                        **157**
Identifying Titles .............................................................................. 159
Title Types ......................................................................................... 160
Using Titles ....................................................................................... 162
Using a Guidebook ........................................................................... 163
Using a Magazine-Style Title ........................................................... 164
What Now? ......................................................................................... 166

Part III  **Taking Control of MSN**                                         **167**

10   **Finding Anything on MSN**                                            **169**
Finding Services ................................................................................ 171
Phrasing Search Terms ..................................................................... 174

Finding People ....................................................................... 176
Finding It on the Internet ...................................................... 179
What Now? .............................................................................. 180

**11    Advanced Configuration Options                                    181**
Registering File Types............................................................. 182
Registering a File Type .................................................. 183
Editing a Registered Action .......................................... 184
Changing Languages ................................................................ 185
Filling in Your Own Member Properties ............................... 187
Setting Up Multiple Accounts ............................................... 189
What Now? .............................................................................. 190

**12    Trimming Time Online                                              191**
Creating and Using Shortcuts ................................................ 192
Creating an MSN Shortcut ........................................... 192
Using MSN Shortcuts .................................................. 193
Linking and Embedding MSN Content ................................. 194
Using MSN Help Offline ....................................................... 195
Saving E-Mail Minutes .......................................................... 195
Composing Mail Offline ................................................ 196
Reading Mail Offline ..................................................... 196
What Now? .............................................................................. 197

**13    Power E-Mail                                                      199**
E-Mail Options ....................................................................... 200
The Read Tab .................................................................. 200
The Spelling Tab ............................................................. 201
The Send Tab .................................................................. 202
The Services Tab ............................................................. 204
The Addressing Tab ....................................................... 204
Using Your Personal Address Book ....................................... 204
Adding an MSN Member or Non-Member Offline........................ 206
Adding an MSN Member from the Member Directory .................. 207
Addressing E-Mail from Your Personal Address Book ..................... 209
Creating and Using a Personal Distribution List ................................ 210
Attaching Files to E-Mail Messages ...................................... 212
Inserting a File ............................................................... 213
Inserting an Object ........................................................ 214
Sending MSN E-Mail from Windows Applications ............................. 216
Combining MSN E-Mail with Other Services ...................................... 217
Sending Faxes Through MSN .................................................. 218
What Now? .............................................................................. 218

**14    Speeding Up MSN**                                                    **219**

Tuning MSN ............................................................................. 221

    Hardware Choices ............................................................. 221

    Work Habits ..................................................................... 223

Tuning Windows 95 Performance ..........................................225

    Memory Management ...................................................... 226

What Now? ............................................................................. 232

**Part IV    Navigating the Internet Through  MSN**                          **233**

**15    Understanding the Internet**                                         **235**

What "Internet Access" Really Means on MSN ..................... 236

How to Sign Up for Internet Access ........................................237

    Using the MSN Sign-Up Program .....................................237

    Adding Internet Access after Sign-Up .............................. 238

    Using the Internet Wizard ................................................ 238

    Connecting to the Internet ............................................... 240

    Managing Your Configuration through
      the Internet Control Panel ........................................... 240

About Internet Access ............................................................ 241

    Understanding Internet Addresses ....................................242

    About Internet Tools........................................................ 243

How to Choose Client Software for Internet Services .......................... 244

More About the Internet ........................................................ 246

What Now? ............................................................................. 247

**16    Browsing the World Wide Web**                                       **249**

About the World Wide Web..................................................... 251

    Hypertext and Hypermedia .............................................. 251

    File Viewers ...................................................................... 256

    Home Pages ..................................................................... 257

    Links to Other Resources ................................................. 257

Navigating the Web ................................................................ 259

    URLs ............................................................................... 259

    Toolbar Tools ................................................................... 261

    Bookmarks ....................................................................... 262

Using Popular Web Browsers.................................................. 263

    Internet Explorer ............................................................. 263

    Mosaic 2.0 ....................................................................... 265

    Netscape .......................................................................... 267

Finding It on the Web ............................................................ 269

    Starting Points ................................................................. 269

    Web Directories ............................................................... 272

    Web Spiders ..................................................................... 277

What Now? ............................................................................. 280

**17    Browsing Gophers                                        281**

Who's the Gopher? ............................................................. 282

Multimedia Gophers ......................................................... 284

How to Use a Gopher Client ............................................. 284

   Setting Up a Gopher Client ........................................ 285

   Navigating Gopherspace ............................................ 285

   All the Gopher Servers in the World ........................... 287

   Moving Through Menus .............................................. 288

   Configuring a Gopher+ Client .................................... 289

Cool Gopher Sites for Windows Users ............................... 290

How to Search for Gophers ............................................... 292

   A Veronica Search ..................................................... 294

   Search-Term Options ................................................. 295

What Now? ...................................................................... 296

**18    Downloading Files with FTP                             297**

About FTP ....................................................................... 298

   Text Files Versus Binary Files ..................................... 300

Important FTP Sites for Windows Users ............................ 300

How to Use a Web Browser for FTP ................................. 300

How to Use Windows 95's FTP Client .............................. 301

   FTP Command Syntax ............................................... 302

A Third-Party FTP Client ................................................. 305

How to Find FTP Files ...................................................... 305

   Using Archie ............................................................. 307

What Now? ...................................................................... 312

**19    Advanced Internet Techniques                           313**

Telnet .............................................................................. 314

   Connecting and Logging In ....................................... 315

   About Terminal Emulation ......................................... 316

   Using Windows 95's Telnet Client .............................. 317

Internet Relay Chat (IRC) ................................................. 318

   Choosing a Channel .................................................. 319

MUDs .............................................................................. 322

   MUD Rules ............................................................... 323

   Finding a MUD ......................................................... 323

   Playing a MUD ......................................................... 324

Mailing Lists .................................................................... 325

   Where to Find Lists ................................................... 326

   Subscribing to a List .................................................. 327

   Confirming Your Subscription ..................................... 328

   Using Your Subscription ............................................. 329

   Unsubscribing ........................................................... 330

What Now? ...................................................................... 330

**Part V    References**                                                                 **331**

**A   Go Word Directory**                                                              **333**

Arts & Entertainment (Go Word = Entertainment) ............................ 334

Business & Finance (Go Word = Business) ......................................... 335

Chat World (Go Word = ChatWorld) ...............................................335

Computers & Software (Go Word = Computing) ................................ 335

Education & Reference (Go Word = Education) ................................. 336

Health & Fitness (Go Word = Health) ................................................336

Home & Family (Go Word = Home) ....................................................337

Interests, Leisure, & Hobbies (Go Word = Interests) ...................... 337

Internet Center (Go Word = Internet) ................................................ 337

MSN Passport (Go Word = Passport) .................................................338

News & Weather (Go Word = w) .........................................................338

People & Communities (Go Word = Community) .............................. 338

Public Affairs (Go Word = Public) ....................................................339

Science & Technology (Go Word = Science) .................................... 339

Special Events (Go Word = Events) ..................................................340

Sports & Recreation (Go Word = Sports) ......................................... 340

Member Lobby (Go Word = Lobby) ....................................................340

**B   Web Highlights**                                                                 **343**

Internet Directories and Search Tools ...................................................344

Business Pages ........................................................................................ 344

    Starting an Internet Business ........................................................... 344

    Economic/Financial Data ................................................................. 345

    Advertising ........................................................................................ 345

Education Pages ...................................................................................... 345

    General Education Resources .......................................................... 346

    K–12 Resources ................................................................................ 346

    Post-Secondary Resources ............................................................... 348

Entertainment and Leisure Pages .......................................................... 348

    Shopping ........................................................................................... 348

    Entertainment ................................................................................... 349

    Sports ................................................................................................ 350

Miscellaneous Interesting Stuff ............................................................. 351

**Glossary**                                                                           **353**

**Index**                                                                              **361**

# ACKNOWLEDGMENTS

My deepest thanks to all those who conceived, guided, nurtured, prodded, nudged, reassured, impelled, corrected, fixed, tailored, toned, polished, decorated, embellished, constructed, and otherwise yanked this book screaming into the world, especially:

Carla Randolph, Alice Martina Smith, and Mark Taber.

# ABOUT THE AUTHOR

**Ned Snell** is an award-winning computer journalist and author. Ten years ago, after a brief career as a teacher, Snell entered the software industry as a documentation and training specialist for several of the world's largest software companies. He then moved into the computer trade magazine business, where he served as staff writer and eventually as editor for several national publications.

In 1991, he became a freelancer so that he could pursue his dual professions: computer journalist and actor. Since then, he has written for international publications such as *Datamation* and *Software Magazine* and has also developed documentation and training materials for diabetes management software. At the same time, he has acted in regional professional theatres, commercials, and industrial films. Snell is the author of these Sams titles: *Souping Up Windows, Curious About the Internet*, and *Navigating the Internet with Windows 95*; he is a co-author of Sams' *Windows 95 Unleashed*. He lives with his writer and translator wife, Nancy Gonzalez, and their two sons in New Jersey, until they can think of a better place to live.

# INTRODUCTION

Nothing in this world is quite so scary as writing about a cultural revolution. Having no crystal ball and no dough for calling 1-900-PSYCHIC, a writer must make the most reasonable projections he or she can about the likely shape of the future as implied by the events of the present. History teaches that's a pretty stupid thing to try.

As I consider writing about where I think The Microsoft Network (MSN) may lead, I can't help remembering those who wrote that talkies would never draw a crowd, that DEWEY DEFEATS TRUMAN, that rock & roll was a quick fad, that CDs would never replace vinyl, that fat grams matter more than calories, or that there would be a PC in every American home by the late 1980s. (Microsoft chairman William Gates himself predicted that last one. You *wish*, Bill.)

And yet, the debut of MSN may signal a turning point. There have been commercial online services for at least a dozen years and widespread consumer use of the Internet for half a decade. But only with the debut of Windows 95 has the software required for accessing the online world been a standard component of a personal computer operating system. The MSN software does more than access online resources; it makes the resources provided by MSN appear like files and folders on your own PC. That constitutes a new PC paradigm: It's no longer a single machine that acts on its own contents; it's a member of a collective, with access to collective resources, by design.

What does it all mean? That depends on your own personal cynicism quotient. High-level cynics would say, "It means Microsoft wants to leverage its ownership of the world's most popular operating system to cash in on surging consumer interest in online services and the Internet." And the big cynics would be absolutely right! But aside from an analysis of Microsoft's motives, there's another meaning, one that low-level cynics, and even dreamers, may appreciate.

It means that access to *cyberspace* (for lack of a less overused term) is fast becoming a part of everyday life and is no longer a special privilege of the technological elite. The bundling of MSN software and Internet software in Windows 95 is a recognition that a modern, general-purpose PC operating system must have built-in online access, just as any new house must have plumbing, power, and phone lines. Note that Windows 95 contains not only built-in MSN software, it also has the necessary software for accessing the Internet *exclusive of* MSN. Sure, Microsoft wants a cut of the online trade. But the message of Windows 95's support for online communication holds true even if you choose to pay somebody other than Microsoft for the privilege.

Of course, there's other evidence for the shift, not the least of which is the upswing in coverage of online content by the news media. The other day, I read a report that the Amish people of Pennsylvania—the *Amish!*—now have their own Internet site. My local paper in New Jersey reports that I can use the Internet to reserve a tee-time at any Northern New Jersey golf course. On the national news the other night, I learned that I can use the Internet to find out where all the speed traps are on U.S. interstate highways. This is hardly technically oriented stuff; it's the application of online resources to everyday needs.

MSN is too new for its own content to grab much attention—although the debut of the service itself has been widely covered. Whether MSN will rival or exceed the popularity of king-pin online services America Online, CompuServe, and Prodigy is impossible to know. But even if MSN itself fails to catch on, the Internet access provided through MSN will almost certainly establish Microsoft as a major Internet provider. That means the revolution is here to stay, whether MSN flies or falls.

In this book, I won't attempt to sell you on MSN or to offer comparisons between MSN and its competitors. I'll assume that you wouldn't have picked this book up if you weren't already committed to the idea of MSN as your online service or Internet provider.

What I will sell you is that the full value of the journey you're about to take does not depend on the success of MSN. This book is about establishing your presence in the online world and moving within it. The vehicles demonstrated herein are MSN and the Internet *through* MSN. Over the years, however, MSN may come or go, but the Internet will inevitably grow and mutate, and the cyberspace of 2006 will undoubtedly look quite different from the cyberspace of today. The skills you acquire in this book equip you to participate fully in today's cyberspace; from there, you'll easily adapt to what comes. The *medium* of your journey is relevant at the moment, but not for the long haul.

So come with me into MSN and the Internet and let me teach you not only what you can do there, but how you can do it with efficiency, power, and style. I'm glad to have you.

And should the future fail to unfold *exactly* as I've described, have a giggle on me. I told you it would happen.

# Who This Book Is For

This book is written for people who have Windows 95 and intend to sign up for The Microsoft Network. It assumes that you have a general knowledge of your Windows 95 environment, but it also explains many Windows 95 concepts as they come up because Windows 95 is new to just about everybody.

Although the book explains MSN simply enough for newcomers to online services, it is by no means a "dummy's" or "compleat idiot's" treatment of the topic. Advanced configuration options, power e-mail techniques, and a variety of other advanced topics are covered in addition to the basics.

The goal of this book is not simply to get you started on MSN and the Internet, but to provide a complete guide to setting up, controlling, navigating, and exploiting MSN and the Internet. The book features techniques and tips that offer value to online novices, intermediate net-surfers, and full-blown hackers alike.

# How This Book Is Organized

This book is divided into five parts:

◆ The chapters in Part I, "Setting Up The Microsoft Network," provide complete instructions for setting up MSN on your PC, establishing an account, connecting to MSN, customizing and maintaining your MSN configuration and billing information, and observing MSN's member rules and other online customs.

◆ The chapters in Part II, "Navigating The Microsoft Network," detail every basic MSN resource (those accessed through the MSN software, not those you access through Internet client software). This part of the book begins with a complete tutorial in moving around on MSN. Subsequent chapters cover each of the major MSN services in detail.

◆ The chapters in Part III, "Taking Control of MSN," describe optional, advanced techniques for navigating, customizing, and exploiting MSN services. Techniques include methods for reducing time online to save money, speeding up MSN's online responsiveness, creating and using MSN shortcuts, and using MSN's Find utilities for locating MSN services and members.

◆ The chapters in Part IV, "Navigating the Internet Through MSN," cover in detail everything you can do using MSN's Internet access and your selection of Internet client software. The section opens with a full overview of how MSN's Internet access works, the software you need to use Internet services, and Internet concepts you need to understand and effectively operate Internet services. The four remaining chapters detail how to use each type of Internet resource.

◆ Appendix A provides a directory of Go words, key words that enable you to jump easily from place to place within MSN. Go words make getting around in MSN quicker and easier. (See Chapter 4, "Basic Navigation Techniques," to learn about Go words.) Appendix B offers directions to some of the most useful, entertaining, or weird places to visit on the Internet's World Wide Web. (See Chapter 16, "Browsing the World Wide Web," for more about the World Wide Web.) Following the appendixes is a complete Glossary and Index for reference.

PART

# SETTING UP THE MICROSOFT NETWORK

Signing Up, Signing In, and Signing Out    3

Maintaining Your MSN Account    29

Member Rules and Etiquette    45

# CHAPTER 1

# SIGNING UP, SIGNING IN, AND SIGNING OUT

Signing Up

Signing In

Signing Out

What Now?

To get as many Windows 95 users into the fold as possible, Microsoft has taken pains to make setting up The Microsoft Network (MSN) simple. For the most part, Microsoft succeeded; the process isn't quick and it involves quite a few steps, but the steps are logical and a Windows 95 Wizard leads you through them clearly.

If you're like many experienced Windows users, you may find that you can dive right in and sign up for MSN with no guidance from me. Or you may want a complete guide to signing up for MSN, which you'll find in this chapter. Either way, a little preparation before starting the sign-up procedure can ensure a smooth, no-fuss setup.

In this chapter, you learn how to do the following:

◆ Prepare your PC and yourself for setting up MSN

◆ *Sign up* for MSN, including choosing your member ID, password, and billing options

◆ *Sign in* to MSN—start the MSN software and connect to the MSN network

◆ Identify the choices on the MSN home page (also called MSN Central) and MSN Today, the two windows that appear when you first sign in to MSN

◆ *Sign out* of MSN—disconnect from the MSN network and close the MSN software

# Signing Up

A Windows 95 Wizard orchestrates your entire MSN sign-up, start to finish. The Wizard's icon appears on your desktop and in your Accessories menu, labeled *Sign Up for The Microsoft Network*. (If you don't see the Wizard on your desktop, refer to "Software Requirements," later in this chapter.) To sign up, you open the Wizard and follow its prompts. During the sign-up procedure, the Wizard accomplishes three things:

◆ It collects information about you—name and address, billing information, and your choice for an MSN member ID and password—and transmits this information to the *MSN data center*, the group of server computers at Microsoft that manage the MSN network and store most of the data you find on MSN.

◆ It selects *access numbers* for you, based on the most recent list of access numbers stored on MSN. Access numbers are the telephone numbers your PC dials to connect to MSN.

◆ It installs the *MSN client* software on your PC. The MSN client is the program that connects you, through the MSN network, to the MSN data center and then manages all your activity on MSN by interacting with server computers in the data center.

When the Wizard closes, an icon labeled *The Microsoft Network* appears on your desktop, and a choice for The Microsoft Network appears in your Programs menu. You can use either of these options to open the MSN client software and connect to MSN whenever you want to.

# Preparing to Sign Up

Before starting the Sign-Up Wizard, it's a good idea to do the following:

- ◆ Make sure that your PC and Windows 95 are properly outfitted for MSN
- ◆ Choose your member ID, password, and method of payment
- ◆ Learn about MSN access numbers and how they're chosen

## Software Requirements

On both CD-ROM and floppy disks, Windows 95 includes all the software required for using MSN: the Sign-Up Wizard, the MSN client software, the Microsoft Exchange e-mail application, and Windows 95's built-in communications facilities. However, the Wizard, MSN client, and Exchange are not always automatically installed during Windows 95 setup.

In general, these facilities are installed during Windows 95 setup if you choose the setup type Typical or Portable. (If you set up using either of these options, a dialog box appears, asking whether you want to install MSN, Microsoft Mail, or Microsoft Fax.) If you choose the Custom setup type, you must specifically choose to install MSN from the Components dialog box. If you choose the Compact setup type, MSN and Exchange cannot be installed during Windows setup and must be installed after setup as described later in this section.

If you don't see the Sign Up for The Microsoft Network icon on your desktop or in your Accessories menu, you must install the MSN software from your Windows 95 CD-ROM or floppy disks. To install the required MSN software, follow these steps:

1. Open your Start menu and choose Settings.
2. From the Settings menu, choose Control Panel and then open Add/Remove Programs.
3. Click the Windows Setup tab; scroll to the bottom of the Components list and look for an entry for The Microsoft Network (see Figure 1.1).
4. Select the checkbox next to The Microsoft Network and click OK.

Windows prompts you for your CD-ROM or a particular floppy disk and installs the MSN Sign-Up Wizard and MSN client software on your PC. If Exchange has not already been installed on your PC, Windows installs it automatically when it installs MSN.

When the installation is complete, the Wizard's icon appears on your desktop and in your Accessories menu, with the label *Sign Up for The Microsoft Network*. Another icon, with the label *Inbox*, also appears on your desktop. (The Inbox icon is part of the Exchange e-mail program; see Chapter 8, "Composing, Sending, and Receiving E-Mail.")

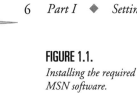

**FIGURE 1.1.**

*Installing the required MSN software.*

In addition to the MSN software, your modem must be installed and configured in Windows 95. If your internal modem was already installed in your PC or your external modem was already attached to your PC *before* you installed Windows 95, it was configured during Windows 95 setup and is ready for use. If you install a modem *after* configuring Windows 95, you must configure the modem by opening Add New Hardware in Control Panel (unless you have a Plug-and-Play-compatible modem and PC, in which case the modem is configured automatically in Windows 95).

For more information about installing and configuring a modem in Windows 95, see Windows Help or your Windows 95 documentation.

## Access Numbers

To understand access numbers, you must first understand how the MSN network works.

Throughout North America, Microsoft has aligned with local and regional communications services companies, sometimes called *access providers*. These companies provide local telephone numbers, called *access numbers*, for connecting to their computers (*communications servers*) in their areas. Each of the servers is connected, in turn, by high-speed communications lines to the MSN data center in Washington state. (Microsoft plans to eventually have many data centers located around the world to provide better service.) International MSN communications are a little more complicated, but the principle is the same. International members don't connect directly to the MSN data center; they connect to a server close to them, which is itself connected through international high-speed telecommunications lines or satellite links to the MSN data center.

Because MSN is new and evolving, the list of access numbers is constantly growing and changing. Microsoft's goal is to provide at least one access number within every local calling area in the United States. That would make dialing MSN a local call for every United States member. Not only does that approach save members from incurring long-distance charges while on MSN, it also makes MSN connections faster and more reliable. The connection between your PC and the local access provider is the "weakest link" of the communications chain—it's generally slower and less reliable than the connection between the access provider and the MSN data center. The greater the distance between your PC and the access provider, the more relays and other communications equipment your signal must pass through to reach the server. And the more complicated the communications, the greater the chance of trouble or failure.

All lines between access providers and the MSN data center operate at 28,800 bits per second (bps) or faster. Depending on limitations in access providers' equipment, some access providers may provide 28,800 bps access between your PC and their servers but others may supply only half that speed: 14,400 bps access (mostly outside major cities). Microsoft plans to eventually offer 28,800 bps access from anywhere in the United States.

During the sign-up procedure described later in this chapter, the Sign-Up Wizard connects to MSN through the nearest access number it already knows about and downloads from MSN an updated list of access numbers for your area. The Wizard then selects for you two numbers:

◆ A *primary* access number, the number always used first for dialing MSN.

◆ A *backup* number, a second number automatically dialed in the event that the primary number fails (as it would if a server or modem failed at the access provider).

The Wizard attempts to choose local numbers for both the primary and backup number; if it cannot, it displays a list of nonlocal numbers from which you can select a number in your area code.

You can change your access numbers whenever you want. For example, if you move or take your PC on the road, you can switch to a local access number for the area to which you've traveled. To learn about changing access numbers, see Chapter 2, "Maintaining Your MSN Account."

## Hardware Requirements

The official minimum hardware requirements for MSN are as follows:

| | |
|---|---|
| Modem | 2,400 bps |
| PC | Minimum Windows 95 configuration (386 processor, 4M of RAM, 16-color VGA display) |

*Tip*

You can use MSN on a notebook PC as long as the notebook meets or exceeds the same processor speed, RAM, and modem speed requirements for desktop PCs using MSN.

Unfortunately, like most *minimum* requirements, these are not *practical* requirements.

First, MSN is a processor-intensive, communications-intensive environment. In operation, it demands a great deal of system RAM and must transfer hundreds of kilobytes through your modem connection in the course of even the simplest tasks.

The MSN client software on your PC is a 32-bit, multitasking, multithreaded Windows 95 application. That design provides certain advantages—such as the ability to browse MSN and download a file simultaneously—but it also requires a robust, well-equipped PC for reasonable performance.

◆ Any 386 processor offers unacceptably slow MSN performance because of the 386 processor's limited ability to handle 32-bit operations.

◆ Any 486 processor is up to MSN's 32-bit design, but those slower than 66 MHz deliver poor performance because of MSN's massive processing load.

◆ Any Pentium processor delivers acceptable MSN performance, although slower Pentiums (75 MHz or less) may not deliver noticeably better MSN performance than the less-costly 486 DX2s.

During many activities, the MSN client must open additional applications on your PC, such as WordPad for viewing documents, Exchange for e-mail, or MSN's Online Viewer for viewing MSN's multimedia titles. The extra applications make additional demands on the PC, which is probably already struggling under the burden of the MSN software itself. The inevitable result is excessive *paging*—frequent exchanging of real memory and Windows 95's *virtual memory* (disk space used to mimic RAM when the PC lacks sufficient memory to manage the applications it's running). Paging slows down any task because your PC accesses data in RAM much more quickly than it does data on disk.

In addition, the fact that all MSN access numbers support modem speeds of at least 14,400 bps should tip you off that MSN is designed for fast modems—in fact, it *depends* on them. A 2,400 bps modem, although supported by all MSN access numbers, is simply too slow to provide reasonable responsiveness from MSN. Even a 9,600 bps modem—the state of the art only a few years ago—is insufficient.

Most importantly, the *combination* of a slow modem (9,600 bps or slower) and an underpowered PC (50 MHz 486-class or slower) makes MSN perform so slowly that it is functionally unusable.

Finally, many of the graphics that appear in MSN are 256-color graphics, which still show up on a 16-color display but don't look very good. Windows 95 (and by extension, MSN) runs best with a 32-bit or 64-bit accelerated graphics adapter with at least 1M of RAM (2M is better). These adapters support "high-color" graphics modes that supply from 16,000 to 16 million colors, but MSN never displays more than 256 colors at a time. Some graphics, such as photos displayed in MSN *titles* (see Chapter 9, "Viewing and Operating Titles"), appear slightly smoother and more realistic in high-color mode. Still, foregoing the high-color modes for 256-color mode delivers the best overall MSN performance.

The bottom line? The *practical* minimum MSN hardware configuration is as follows:

| | |
|---|---|
| Modem | 14,400 bps or faster |
| PC | 66 MHz 486 DX2 or faster, 8M of RAM or more, 32-bit or 64-bit accelerated SVGA display running in 256-color mode |

If your system doesn't meet these requirements, you can still sign into MSN and get started as long as your system meets the official minimums listed earlier. But you'll soon find the MSN experience tiresome. If, after trying out MSN on your current hardware, you expect to use MSN regularly, put a system upgrade at the top of your Christmas list.

## Member ID and Password

During the MSN sign-up procedure, you choose your own *member ID* and *password*.

◆ Your *member ID* is your all-purpose name and address on MSN; it's the name that appears on e-mail you send and messages you post on bulletin boards. It's the name that appears next to comments you contribute to chats. It's also the name other MSN members use to address e-mail to you. Your member ID is your MSN identity and personality; once you choose it, you can't change it except by canceling your MSN account and starting a new account.

◆ Your *password* is a secret word, known only to you, that you enter to sign in to MSN. Because your member ID is widely known, you need this secret word to prevent others from using your MSN account. As long as you don't reveal your password to anyone, you needn't worry about whether someone is surreptitiously using your account. You can change your password at any time.

> If you use a username and password to log on to Windows 95 or on to a local network, you can use the same name and password for your MSN member ID and password. However, Windows does not "pass along" your Windows or network logon information to MSN. Even if you use the same ID and password, you must enter them to log on to Windows 95 and enter them again to connect to MSN.

*Note*

It's a good idea to give some thought to your member ID and password *before* beginning the sign-up procedure; trying to dream them up when prompted for them during sign-up—when you're "under the gun," so to speak—may cause you to make choices you don't like later or choices you will find difficult to remember.

Your member ID can be any set of from 3 to 64 characters. You can use any uppercase or lowercase letter characters, any numeral, hyphens (–), and underscores (_). You cannot use other punctuation characters or spaces. To use a full name as your member ID, you can use any of the following IDs:

```
FredoCorleone
Fredo_Corleone
Fredo-Corleone
```

However, you cannot use this ID (no spaces allowed):

`Fredo Corleone`

Your member ID does not have to resemble your real name, but it can. A popular, no-nonsense approach is to use a first initial and then the last name; for example, `nsnell` or `bclinton`.

Others like to give themselves new names based on their alter-egos. Names like `Wild-Thing` or `Superman` are common. Note that your member ID must be unique; it cannot be the same as someone else's. Be prepared with a second (and even third) choice in case your favorite member ID has already been taken by another MSN member. (I tried to use `Godzilla` and found that another member had beaten me to it!)

In MSN, your member ID appears to others in the exact combination of uppercase and lowercase letters you type when you create it during sign-up. If you enter `MonkeyMan` as your ID, that's the way it appears to others online.

However, MSN doesn't really care about capitalization when you sign in. `MonkeyMan` can sign in as `MONKEYMAN` or `monkeyman` and the sign-in will succeed. All e-mail addressed to `MONKEYMAN` or `monkeyman` reaches the correct member. The same applies to uniqueness; if another MSN member is already using the name `SusanB`, MSN does not permit you to choose that name, regardless of capitalization—`SUSANB`, `susanB`, and `sUSANb` are all judged "already taken" by MSN.

Finally, note that capitalization doesn't matter for passwords, either.

Your password can be any combination of from 8 to 16 letter characters or numerals, hyphens (–), or underscores (_). No spaces or other punctuation characters are allowed.

You cannot use your member ID as your password; your password cannot include your whole member ID. For example, for my member ID (`nsnell`), I cannot use passwords such as `nsnell01`, `thensnell`, or `kingnsnell`. However, if I delete or change at least one character from the member ID, I can use it in a password: `nsne1001` or `thesnel1` is an acceptable password for member `nsnell`.

If you want to keep your MSN account secure, you really shouldn't use any variation of your name or member ID as a password. In fact, you shouldn't use any recognizable word as a password. Computer theft experts have long known that a nonsense jumble of characters such as `32xcg21p` is more difficult to crack than an actual word (although a nonsense password is also easier to forget). Passwords constructed from your birth date, anniversary, Social Security Number, or other "discoverable" number also aren't a good idea for the same reason.

Remember *WarGames*? In that film, Matthew Broderick brings the world to the brink of thermonuclear war all because the supposedly brilliant computer scientist who designed America's nuclear defense computer system used his son's name, Joshua, as his password. Be more careful than that scientist or you may find Ferris Bueller running up your MSN bill.

## Payment

Speaking of bills, MSN supports a variety of *subscription plans*, different ways MSN can count your time online and charge you for it. These are certainly subject to change; during sign-up, you are given a chance to review the options then in force. But as of this writing, you can choose from the following options:

◆ **Frequent User Monthly Plan:**

$19.95 per month; includes 20 hours of usage per month; each additional hour is $2.00.

◆ **Standard Monthly Plan:**

$4.95 per month; includes 3 hours of usage per month; each additional hour is $2.50.

Note that full Internet access is included in both plans. Even if you choose not to accept Internet access, the charges are the same (as of this writing).

Obviously, if you expect to use MSN infrequently, you may save some money by opting for the Standard Monthly Plan. But monitor your usage carefully. If you expect to use MSN for more than nine hours each month, the Frequent User Plan is a better buy. Nine hours on the Standard Plan adds up to $19.95—which is what you pay for 20 hours on the Frequent User Plan. Twenty hours on the Standard Plan is a whopping $47.45!

Although 20 hours online may seem like a lot, it's not—especially when the enticing riches of the Internet are available. An hour online each day, five days a week, adds up to 22 hours each month. A mere half-hour a day, five days a week, adds up to 11 hours—making the Frequent User Plan preferable even for half-hour-a-day users. Most new users of online systems under-estimate the time they'll spend online and end up paying through the nose for a "bargain," low-use subscription plan.

To learn how to check the number of hours you spend online, and to change your subscription plan after signing up, see Chapter 2, "Maintaining Your MSN Account."

To learn how to save money by minimizing your time online, see Chapter 12, "Trimming Time Online."

*Tip*

Whenever Microsoft changes pricing or subscription plan options, you'll receive e-mail informing you of the change.

## "Pro" Sign-Up (for the Brave and Eager)

The MSN Wizard prompts you through each step of the sign-up procedure. Once you understand the basics of MSN hardware and software requirements, member ID and password selection, payment methods, and access numbers, you may choose to dive right in and sign up for MSN without reading the detailed sign-up instructions that follow. If you've become reasonably comfortable with Windows 95, you can probably do so without running into any serious problems.

If that's your inclination, go to it. Double-click the Sign Up for The Microsoft Network icon and do whatever the Wizard tells you to do. *Vaya con Dios*.

But if you do run into trouble...

◆ Click the Cancel button on any dialog box during sign-up to abort the sign-up procedure.

◆ Consult the detailed procedure that follows, or the preparation steps covered earlier in this chapter, to solve your problem.

◆ Start the sign-up procedure over, from the top.

## Signing Up

The sign-up procedure typically takes from five to seven minutes (add an extra eight to ten minutes if you plan to read the entire Member Agreement during sign-up). The procedure involves moving through a series of screens on which you make simple selections or enter information about yourself. Twice during the sign-up procedure, the Wizard connects your PC to MSN—so make sure that your phone line is ready and available before you begin the sign-up procedure.

At any time during the sign-up procedure, you can click Cancel to abort the sign-up procedure. After canceling, you can start the sign-up procedure again from the beginning, whenever you want.

To sign up for The Microsoft Network, follow these steps:

1. Click the Sign Up for The Microsoft Network icon on your desktop or open the Start menu and choose **P**rograms, Accessories, Sign Up for The Microsoft Network. A screen like the one in Figure 1.2 appears.

2. Make sure that the checkbox at the bottom of the screen is *not* selected and then click OK. A screen like the one in Figure 1.3 appears. The Wizard uses the information on the screen shown in the figure to select a nearby access number to connect to MSN.

**FIGURE 1.2.**

*The opening screen of the Sign-Up Wizard.*

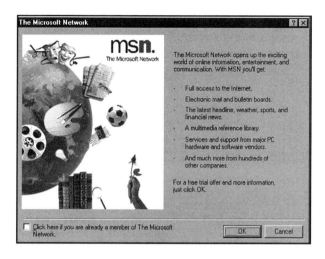

**FIGURE 1.3.**

*Entering your area and exchange codes so that the Wizard can locate a nearby MSN access number for you.*

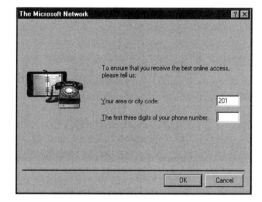

3. Although the area code has already been filled in for you, you can change it if it is incorrect. Then enter the first three digits of your phone number (the three digits that follow the area code) and click OK. A screen like the one in Figure 1.4 appears.

The area code that automatically appears in the screen shown in Figure 1.3 was copied from the Dialing Properties dialog box (accessed from the Connection Settings dialog box). If the area code is incorrect, change your Connection Settings as described in Chapter 2, "Maintaining Your MSN Account." You can enter the correct area code and complete your MSN sign-up now and then edit the Connection Settings later.

**FIGURE 1.4.**

*Preparing to connect to
MSN to collect an updated
access number list.*

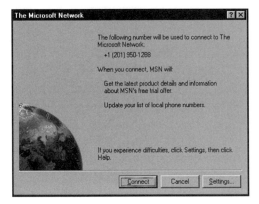

4. Click **C**onnect. The Wizard dials the access number it selected in step 3 and connects to MSN for a few moments to collect the most up-to-date list of access numbers for your area and the latest information about services offered on MSN.

   After transferring this information to your PC, the Wizard disconnects from MSN and displays a screen like the one shown in Figure 1.5.

**FIGURE 1.5.**

*Collecting member
information.*

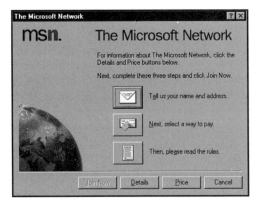

5. From the screen shown in Figure 1.5, you click each of the three buttons in the center of the screen to display a new screen, supply MSN with required information, and then close the new screen to return to the screen in Figure 1.5. When you return, the button whose task you have completed will have a checkmark next to it. You must complete all three buttons—the envelope, the bank check, and the page—before you can complete the sign-up procedure.

Two optional buttons appear at the bottom of Figure 1.5:

◆ Details displays a document containing the most up-to-date information about MSN services (this document was transferred from MSN during step 4). The document is hardly relevant at this point; if you've come this far, you've already made up your mind to join. But if you want to learn more about MSN before completing the sign-up, click Details.

◆ Price displays descriptions of the current subscription plans available (see "Payment," earlier in this chapter).

6. To begin, click the top button (the envelope) to display the screen shown in Figure 1.6. Enter your name, address (up to two lines), and home phone number where indicated; click OK to return to the screen shown earlier in Figure 1.5.

**FIGURE 1.6.**

*Entering your name and billing address.*

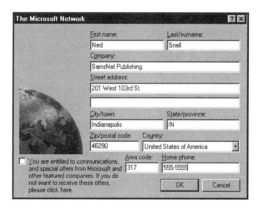

In the lower-left corner of the screen shown in Figure 1.6 is a checkbox. Select this checkbox if you want to deny Microsoft the right to use your member information to pitch direct-market products to you or to provide your member information to other companies for marketing purposes. If you leave this box deselected, your name, address, and home phone number will inevitably wind up in direct-marketing lists at Microsoft and at many other companies who will use it to send you junk mail and to telemarket you.

Unless you select this checkbox, you give Microsoft permission to use this information when you accept the MSN Member Agreement in step 8. The Member Agreement spells out Microsoft's rights to use your information.

7. Click the bank check button (it's on the screen shown back in Figure 1.5). A screen like the one in Figure 1.7 appears, requesting information about the credit card to which your MSN fees and online purchases are to be charged.

   Select a credit card by clicking its picture or by choosing it from the list. Enter the name of the issuing bank (usually printed on the back of the card), the card number, the expiration date, and the name printed on the card. (***Note:*** The bank and card number typed in Figure 1.7 are both phonies, so don't get any ideas.) When finished, click OK to return to the screen shown earlier in Figure 1.5.

**FIGURE 1.7.**

*Selecting a payment method.*

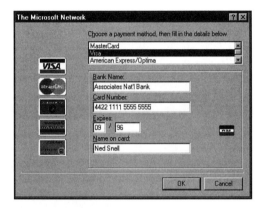

8. Click the third button, the page, to display The Microsoft Network Member Agreement in a dialog box that has two buttons: I **A**gree and I **D**on't Agree. You're supposed to scroll through and read the entire Member Agreement and click I **A**gree (if you click I **D**on't Agree or don't click anything, you can't complete the sign-up procedure).

   After you click I **A**gree, you return to the screen shown earlier in Figure 1.5. If you've successfully completed all the tasks accessed by the three buttons, checkmarks appear next to the buttons and the **J**oin Now button becomes available at the bottom of the dialog box.

9. Click **J**oin Now. A screen similar to the one shown earlier in Figure 1.4 appears, announcing that the software will connect to MSN again to send (and verify) your billing information and finalize the sign-up procedure.

10. Click **C**onnect. After a few moments, a connection to MSN is established and the screen shown in Figure 1.8 appears.

## The Member Agreement: The Brutal Facts

Okay, let's be *completely* honest…

The entire MSN Member Agreement, printed single-spaced in 10-point type, is 5.5 pages long (over 3,700 words). You know, I know, and Microsoft knows that 99.9 percent of MSN subscribers will not read the whole thing (if any of it).

But that's not the point; the point is limiting Microsoft's liability. Whether you actually read the agreement or not, by clicking I **A**gree, you pretty much abrogate all rights to sue Microsoft for anything that happens to you online and assume complete liability for any mischief you may commit while on MSN. That's OK with me. If it's not OK with you, you can't use MSN. Go to the library.

By clicking I **A**gree, you agree, among other things, not to use MSN to distribute obscene or defamatory material or material to which you do not own the copyright—all of this jargon protects Microsoft from being sued by persons who may be offended, insulted, or violated if you do any of these things. Of course, should you discover on MSN material that defames you or material you think obscene, the Member Agreement protects Microsoft from your outrage; you have to sue the person who put it there. (The particulars of an online service's liability are still being worked out, even in the Supreme Court, so there very well may be circumstances under which Microsoft *is* liable. But the Member Agreement is an attempt to protect Microsoft as much as possible, within the law.)

The Member Agreement also explains the conditions under which Microsoft can sell your member information to other companies for direct-marketing purposes. Finally, you agree that Microsoft has the absolute right to change the rules whenever it wants to—which makes everything else you've agreed to sorta pointless.

The Member Agreement also lists some of the rules of online behavior you are expected to observe. But these rules are buried in so much legalese that you're better off learning about them in another way; for example, by reading Chapter 3, "Member Rules and Etiquette." For now, simply remember that, when you sign up for MSN, you promise to play by the rules and accept that Microsoft is responsible only for keeping MSN running—not for what you find or do there.

If, in the future, you want to read the Member Agreement again (okay, for the *first* time), you can access it on MSN in the Member Assistance folder.

**FIGURE 1.8.**

*Choosing a member ID and password.*

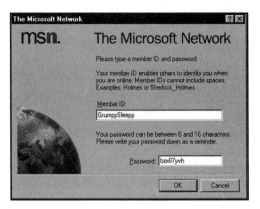

11. Enter your member ID and password. Use any uppercase or lowercase letters, any numerals, hyphens (–), or underscores (_). No other punctuation marks, special characters, or spaces are allowed. Your member ID can contain from 3 to 64 characters; your password can contain from 8 to 16 characters.

**Warning**

When you enter your password on this screen, it appears as you type it in the **P**assword box (see Figure 1.8). A passerby or snoop can see your password during this step. Be careful to perform this step when you are alone or when you are among those from whom you have no secrets. (By the way, the member ID and password shown in Figure 1.8 are phonies, so forget about using them to sign into MSN and order a stereo on my credit card.)

Later on, if you're concerned that your password may have been discovered, you can change it in MSN. See Chapter 2, "Maintaining Your MSN Account."

12. Click OK. If the member ID you entered is not already used by another member, the screen shown in Figure 1.9 appears. (Otherwise, a message appears telling you the ID is already in use. Click OK to clear the message and then enter a different member ID.) After you choose your member ID and password successfully, the Wizard disconnects from MSN.

13. In the dialog box shown in Figure 1.9, you choose whether you want Internet access or not. Make your selection by clicking a radio button and then click OK. The screen shown in Figure 1.10 appears.

    In this screen, the choices shown for your primary and backup numbers are the MSN access numbers closest to where you live (as determined by MSN and the Wizard). MSN is pretty smart about choosing these access numbers for you; it's unlikely that you'll want to change anything on this screen. However, you *can* change your access numbers, now or at any time. To learn how, see Chapter 2, "Maintaining Your MSN Account."

**FIGURE 1.9.**
*Choosing Internet access.*

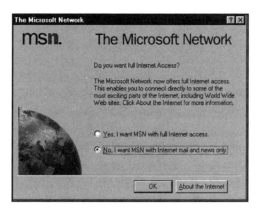

For a brief description of the Internet, click the **A**bout the Internet button at the bottom of the dialog box shown in Figure 1.9.

*Tip*

## Internet or Not?

In step 13 of this sign-up procedure, you choose whether or not you want Internet access.

If you choose No, you have access to all the regular MSN content, including BBSs, chat rooms, titles, and all other activities described in Parts II and III of this book (Chapters 4 through 14). Note that non-Internet MSN accounts nevertheless include two Internet tools: Internet e-mail and Internet newsgroups (described as *Internet mail and news* in Figure 1.9).

If you choose Yes, you have full access to all MSN content, plus other Internet tools such as the World Wide Web and Gopher.

Other than the content differences, the only other important difference between Internet and non-Internet accounts is that they require different access numbers. In fact, you can switch from non-Internet access to Internet access, and back again, merely by changing access numbers as described in Chapter 2, "Maintaining Your MSN Account."

Note that, at this writing, there is no pricing difference between Internet and non-Internet access—you save nothing by foregoing the Internet and lose plenty because the content of the Internet is far richer than MSN's alone.

For more about Internet access, see Chapter 15, "Understanding the Internet."

**FIGURE 1.10.**
*Choosing access numbers.*

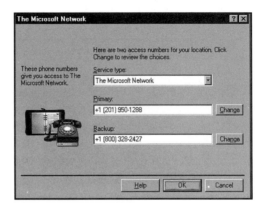

14. Click OK to accept the access numbers. A screen like the one in Figure 1.11 appears to inform you that your sign-up was a success.

**FIGURE 1.11.**
*Sign-up complete.*

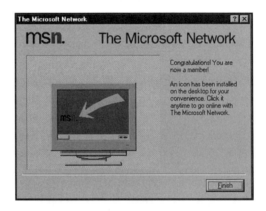

15. Click **F**inish to close the Wizard.

The Microsoft Network

When the Wizard closes, an icon labeled *The Microsoft Network* appears on your desktop. In addition, a choice for The Microsoft Network appears in your Programs menu. Use either of these options to open the MSN client software and connect to MSN whenever you want to.

*Note*

> You cannot move the MSN icon from your desktop, although you can create a shortcut to the MSN client and put it in any folder you want. See Chapter 12, "Trimming Time Online."

# Signing In

To connect to MSN, double-click the MSN icon on your desktop. Alternatively, open your Start menu and choose Programs, The Microsoft Network. The next screen you see is the Sign In dialog box (see Figure 1.12).

Actually, there are several ways to initiate a connection to MSN. In later chapters, you learn how to do the following:

◆ Create shortcuts that start MSN automatically

◆ Start MSN from Exchange, your e-mail program

◆ Start MSN from the Find utility

But no matter which way you start the connection process, the first thing you see is the Sign In dialog box shown in Figure 1.12.

**FIGURE 1.12.**

*Connecting to MSN.*

On the Sign In dialog box, a checkbox appears for **R**emember my Password. If you enter your password and select this box, the MSN Sign In dialog box remembers your password the next time you sign in—and all subsequent times—until you deselect the box. Sign in will be a simple matter of double-clicking the MSN icon and then clicking **C**onnect from the Sign In dialog box.

This checkbox is a nice convenience (I use it) but it entails two risks of which you should be aware. If you select the Remember my Password checkbox, the following may occur:

◆ Anyone with access to your PC (co-workers, kids, smart pets) can easily sign in to MSN without your permission or knowledge. The usurper's actions and behavior appear to all other MSN members to be yours; the usurper's online time or (*ouch!*) online purchases are billed to you.

◆ Because you won't regularly *type* your password, and won't *see* your password on the Sign In dialog box (where it always appears as asterisks), you may eventually *forget* your password.

Click the **S**ettings button on the Sign In dialog box to display a dialog box from which you can edit your Connection Settings (including your access numbers, your dialing properties, and more). To learn how and when to edit your settings, see Chapter 2, "Maintaining your MSN Account."

Your member ID appears automatically in the **M**ember ID box, so you need only enter your password. Type your password carefully because you can't see what you type; whatever you type for a password appears as a series of asterisks so that a snoop can't learn your password by peering over your shoulder when you sign in.

After typing your password, click **C**onnect. Your MSN client dials your primary access number, connects to the MSN network, and checks out your member ID and password to make sure that you're you. If all goes well...

◆ The Sign In dialog box disappears.

◆ The Microsoft Network icon appears next to the modem icon in the far-right corner of your taskbar to indicate that you are connected to MSN.

◆ The MSN *home page* appears (see Figure 1.13). The home page—which is also known on MSN as MSN Central—is your starting point for most MSN activities.

**FIGURE 1.13.**

*MSN Central, your "home page" or MSN jumping-off point.*

✦ MSN Today appears to inform you about special events of the day (see Figure 1.14). When you close MSN Today, the home page is revealed behind it. You can also display MSN Today any time by clicking MSN Today on MSN Central, the home page. (You can reconfigure MSN so that MSN Today does not appear automatically; see Chapter 2, "Maintaining Your MSN Account.")

✦ If MSN has new e-mail waiting for you, a message box pops up, telling you mail is waiting for you. Click Yes to open Exchange and retrieve your e-mail; click No to close the message box and retrieve your e-mail later. (For more about e-mail, see Chapter 8, "Composing, Sending, and Retrieving E-Mail.")

**FIGURE 1.14.**
*MSN Today.*

Even on a fast PC using a fast modem, MSN is a relatively slow application, especially at startup. You can easily wait 30 seconds or more from the time you click **Connect** until MSN Today appears.

MSN does not always show you the hourglass pointer when it is busy completing a task, as other Windows applications do. This can be especially disconcerting at startup; often, there is a pause of 5 to 20 seconds between the time the Sign In dialog box disappears and the home page (MSN Central) begins to appear. During this time, no activity appears on your desktop, and the regular cursor (not the hourglass) appears. (You can see activity in the modem status button on the toolbar, but only if you don't use the Windows 95 auto-hide feature for the taskbar.) During this lag, it's not uncommon for new MSN members to think that the MSN connection has failed—but it hasn't. It just takes awhile to warm up.

*Note*

> If you're accustomed to highly-responsive Windows applications, you should downscale your expectations when working with MSN. When in doubt, wait a few seconds and see what happens. MSN usually comes through.

Each of the choices on MSN Central takes you in a different direction:

MSN TODAY

**MSN Today**—Clicking MSN Today displays the MSN Today page (shown in Figure 1.14), which describes any special events of the day, such as scheduled chats with experts or celebrities (see Chapter 6, "Hanging Out in Chat Rooms"). The MSN Today page also provides *links* (described in Chapter 4, "Basic Navigation Techniques") to any events it describes; the page has a regular set of links along the left edge to popular MSN categories and online magazines.

One such link is Calendar of Events. If you move your pointer close to the words *Calendar of Events*, the pointer arrow turns into a pointing finger. Click to display the Calendar of Events (see Figure 1.15). The Calendar appears as an actual calendar, with the day's highlight filled in for each day. To see the complete list of events for any day, click the date number. A screen like the one in Figure 1.16 appears. The icons along the left edge (in the *Where* column) are shortcuts to the events described; click one to navigate directly to the event.

**FIGURE 1.15.**
*The Calendar of Events.*

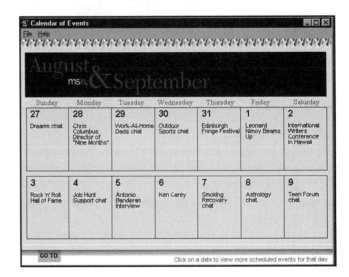

**FIGURE 1.16.**

*The event list for one day, featuring shortcuts to scheduled events.*

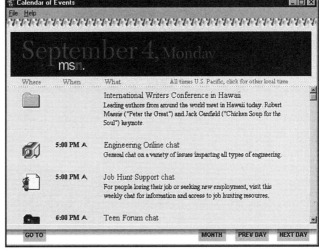

## MSN Is West Coast-Centric

In Figures 1.15 and 1.16, observe that the times for events are shown in Pacific time: Pacific Daylight Time (PDT) during the summer, Pacific Standard Time (PST) during the rest of the year. You'll find times listed in Pacific time throughout MSN because Microsoft and the MSN data center are located in Washington state.

I lived in Indiana for a few years, which is a very confusing place because (among other things) most of the state does not observe daylight savings time. Indianapolis is the same time as New York and three hours later than Los Angeles—except in the summer, when suddenly Indianapolis is an hour earlier than New York and two hours later than Los Angeles (get it?). While I lived there, I developed a highly efficient time-zone converter in my brain that automatically calculated the time where I currently was from any time shown in another time zone. It works in New Jersey, too.

If you don't have this converter in your brain, click any time that appears in MSN with an up arrow next to it (refer to the times shown in Figure 1.16). A small box pops up, showing what the selected time is in other time zones (see Figure 1.17).

Don't pick on Microsoft for being Pacific-centric. For most of its history, the United States has been New York-centric where time is concerned. (For example, TV shows broadcast live in the East are shown later, on tape, to the West). If the new frontier of online communications is emerging from the West, it's the East Coast's turn to figure out the time.

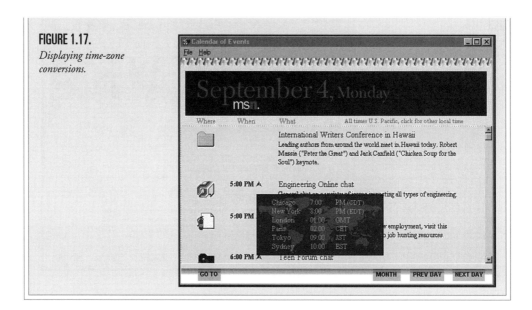

**FIGURE 1.17.**

*Displaying time-zone conversions.*

**E-Mail**—Clicking E-**M**ail does not take you anywhere in MSN. Instead, it opens Microsoft Exchange on your PC. You can then use Exchange to check for any new e-mail you've received or to compose and send new e-mail to MSN members and to the Internet. (For more about e-mail, see Chapter 8, "Composing, Sending, and Receiving E-Mail.")

**Favorite Places**—Clicking F**a**vorite Places opens a folder containing any Favorite Places shortcuts you've created (see Figure 1.18). Each Favorite Places shortcut contains the instructions for navigating to a folder, file, or service somewhere on MSN. When you double-click a shortcut, you jump directly to the MSN location recorded in the shortcut, saving the steps required to navigate there manually through folders. You learn how to create Favorite Places shortcuts later in Chapter 4, "Basic Navigation Techniques."

**Categories**—Clicking **C**ategories opens the Categories folder, which contains the top-level folders, called *categories* in MSN, that contain within them most of the folders and activities of MSN. Until you develop your own set of shortcuts, you'll begin your browsing sessions by clicking **C**ategories and then choosing any of the folders within it. (For more about the Categories folder, see Chapter 4, "Basic Navigation Techniques.")

**FIGURE 1.18.**

*Ned's Favorite Places folder. (Your own Favorite Places folder will be empty at first. Later, it will contain shortcuts you create to your Favorite Places.)*

**Member Assistance**—Clicking Member Assistance opens the Member Lobby folder, which contains folders, documents, and other useful items for learning more about MSN and answering questions about your MSN account. (For more about Member Services, see Chapter 2, "Maintaining Your MSN Account," and Chapter 3, "Member Rules and Etiquette.")

# Signing Out

*Signing out* from MSN does three things: It informs MSN that you've left, it "hangs up" the modem connection, and it closes the MSN client program.

*Tip*

By default, MSN signs you out automatically after 20 minutes of inactivity. To learn how to change the number of minutes MSN waits before signing you out automatically, see Chapter 2, "Maintaining Your MSN Account."

You can sign out in several ways:

◆ Choose **F**ile, Sign Out from any menu in MSN.

◆ Close all open MSN windows, using the × close button or by choosing **F**ile, **C**lose.

◆ Click the Sign Out button on any toolbar. The button looks like a modified hashmark: two horizontal lines intersected by two diagonal lines.

◆ From within Exchange (your Windows 95 e-mail program), choose **F**ile, E**x**it and log off. (See Chapter 8, "Composing, Sending, and Receiving E-Mail.")

◆ Double-click the MSN button in the taskbar.

◆ Right-click the MSN button in the taskbar and choose Close.

Whichever of these methods you choose, a dialog box like the one in Figure 1.19 appears. Click **Y**es to sign out; click **N**o to remain connected. When you want to sign out, click **Y**es.

FIGURE 1.19.
*Signing out.*

Tip

If you close all MSN windows before you disconnect and then choose **No** when prompted by the message in Figure 1.19, you remain connected to MSN, but the MSN windows do not reappear on your desktop. The MSN icon and modem status icon remain in the right end of your taskbar, indicating that you are still connected.

To resume working in MSN, double-click the MSN icon on your desktop to redisplay the MSN home page.

To sign out, double-click the MSN button on the taskbar and then choose **Yes** when prompted by the box in Figure 1.19.

# What Now?

Congratulations! You've not only signed up for The Microsoft Network, you've also grounded yourself in the basics of how MSN works and where and how MSN journeys begin and end.

The next two chapters cover techniques for maintaining and modifying your account and for understanding and observing the rules and customs of the MSN culture. These chapters prepare you to take control of your MSN account and to make a smooth, painless transition to the world online.

You may feel eager to begin exploring MSN right away. If so, skip to Chapter 4, "Basic Navigation Techniques," to learn your way up, down, and around the MSN "content tree." But be sure to return to Chapters 2 and 3 soon to round out your MSN education.

# CHAPTER 2

# MAINTAINING YOUR MSN ACCOUNT

Changing Settings

Changing Your Password

Changing MSN Options

Working with Billing

Contacting MSN Support

What Now?

In principle, MSN is maintenance free. As long as you don't change your hardware, change your phone number, move, max-out your credit card, or blurt your password in a spastic fit among untrustworthy Windows 95 users, you'll probably never *need* to modify your MSN account.

Still, there are circumstances under which you'll want or need to alter your billing information, password, modem settings, or other configuration details. More importantly, there are several ways you can modify the online behavior of MSN to suit your tastes or needs.

In this chapter, you learn how to do the following:

◆ Change your MSN access numbers

◆ Edit your name, address, and billing options

◆ Change your password

◆ Stop the MSN Today page from appearing automatically

◆ Contact MSN support

This chapter covers the basic maintenance techniques most likely to be required by the majority of MSN users. However, there are more ways to modify how MSN behaves. For example, you can change MSN's default choices about which application to open when you want to view or play a certain type of file or document obtained online.

For information about this and other advanced configuration techniques, see Chapter 11, "Advanced Configuration Options."

# Changing Settings

From the Connection Settings dialog box shown in Figure 2.1, you can change your access numbers, modify the way your modem dials, or change your modem's configuration settings. You can display the Connection Settings dialog box in one of three ways:

◆ When offline, right-click the MSN icon on your desktop and choose Connection Settings.

◆ When offline, double-click the MSN icon to open the Sign In dialog box and then click the Settings button.

◆ When online, choose **T**ools, **C**onnection Settings from any menu bar.

The descriptions to the right of each command button show the current settings for that option.

**FIGURE 2.1.**

*The Connection Settings dialog box.*

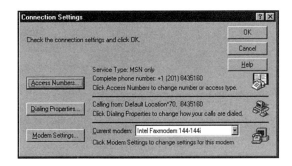

| Option | Description |
|---|---|
| **A**ccess Numbers | The current primary access number for MSN. |
| **D**ialing Properties | The exact number to be dialed to access MSN (including or excluding the area code, and including any special numbers required for accessing an outside line). |
| **M**odem Settings | The installed modem that Windows uses to access MSN. |

The modem settings, which you can edit by clicking the **M**odem Settings button, control your modem configuration and do not require modification unless you experience problems with your modem.

If you experience problems with your modem, consult your modem's documentation or Windows 95 Help.

## Access Numbers

Click the **A**ccess Numbers button on the Connection Settings dialog box to display the screen shown in Figure 2.2. The **S**ervice Type drop-down list has two choices: The Microsoft Network or Internet and MSN. The selection for Service Type matches the type of MSN service to which you have subscribed (MSN plus Internet or just The Microsoft Network); generally, there is little reason to change this setting, although you may decide to change it under certain special circumstances. See Chapter 11, "Advanced Configuration Options."

**FIGURE 2.2.**

*The Access Numbers*
*dialog box.*

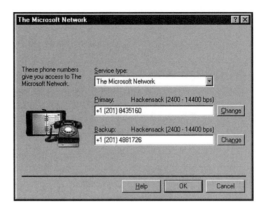

Below the **S**ervice Type drop-down list are separate listings for your **P**rimary and **B**ackup numbers. Each listing shows the complete phone number and also reports the city or town dialed by that number and the range of modem speeds supported (2,400 to 14,400 bps or 2,400 to 28,800 bps).

To change either access number, click the **C**hange button next to the number you want to change. A screen appears like the one in Figure 2.3. This screen lists access numbers only for the Country and State/Region listed. First make sure that the country and state for which you want an access number are shown and then select a new number from the **A**ccess Numbers list. Click OK when finished.

*Tip*

> If you use a 28,800 bps modem, be sure to choose access numbers that support 2,400 to 28,800 bps access. If you choose an access number that supports only 2,400 to 14,400 bps, you can still use MSN, but you do so at 14,400 bps—half the performance your modem is capable of.

**FIGURE 2.3.**

*Changing access numbers.*

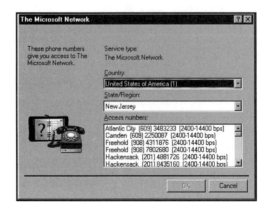

# Dialing Properties

Click the **D**ialing Properties button on the Connection Settings dialog box to display the screen shown in Figure 2.4. The information shown in this Dialing Properties dialog box was collected when you installed and configured your modem in Windows.

Windows 95 uses this information to decide how to dial a modem call. For example, because the Default Location option shows the area code and country in which your PC is located, Windows knows it must add a country code to international calls, and it knows it needn't dial the area code or the 1 that precedes long-distance calls if the number to be dialed is in the same area code. (You can force Windows to dial a number within your area code as a long-distance call—including the 1 and the area code—by checking the Dial as a **L**ong Distance Call checkbox at the bottom of the Dialing Properties dialog box.)

**FIGURE 2.4.**

*Changing dialing properties.*

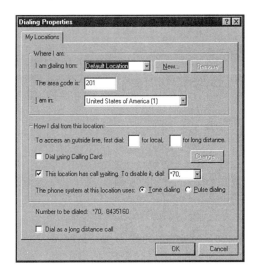

In Figure 2.4, take note of the Number To Be Dialed line near the bottom of the dialog box. This number shows how Windows dials your primary access number when connecting to MSN. In my case, my primary access number (1-201-843-5160) is a local call, so my Number To Be Dialed omits the area code and long-distance 1.

Use the selections in the How I Dial From This Location group to add any special dialing instructions. For example, if you use MSN from an office, you may need an extra number to access an outside line. If a brief pause is required after you dial the number for the outside line, follow that number with a comma (,). When finished, click OK. The new version of the Number To Be Dialed appears next to the Dialing Properties button on the Connection Settings dialog box.

*Tip*

In Figure 2.4, notice that I used the settings in the How I Dial From This Location group to instruct Windows to dial *70 before dialing the access number. (I followed the *70 with a comma, which inserts a brief pause after the computer dials *70 and before it dials the rest of the number.)

The *70 is the code my telephone company requires for disabling *call waiting*, the optional phone service that beeps you when you have an incoming call and lets you pick up the call by flashing the switch hook. I do this because I have only one phone line—and I have voice mail on my phone line in addition to call waiting. When I use MSN, callers are automatically transferred to my voice mail box instead of beeping me with call waiting.

If you have call waiting—even if you don't have voice mail—it's a good idea to disable call waiting by using options on the Dialing Properties dialog box. Disabling call waiting achieves two things:

◆ It prevents your modem from receiving the *beep* signal from incoming calls. Although most modems are designed to recover from the momentary interruption the beep causes, it is possible for the beep to disrupt communications sufficiently to disconnect you from MSN or cause communications errors.

◆ When call waiting is disabled, your callers receive a busy signal (unless you have voice mail) instead of an unanswered ring. The busy signal lets callers know you're home. If they know you well, they may surmise you're on MSN and may send you an e-mail message asking you to call when you're through.

# Changing Your Password

To change your MSN password, you must be connected to MSN. While connected, choose **T**ools, **P**assword from any menu bar. A screen like the one in Figure 2.5 appears.

**FIGURE 2.5.**

*Changing your password.*

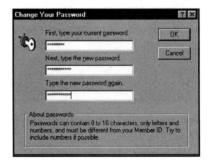

> So a snoop can't learn your password while you perform this task, all entries you make in the dialog box shown in Figure 2.5 appear as asterisks when you type them. You must type carefully, making sure that you type exactly what you want, because you can't read your entries to verify that they're correct.

To change your password, enter your current password in the top box (this step ensures that it's you changing the password). Then enter your choice for a new password in the second box. Be sure to follow the rules and guidelines for composing a password, summarized on the Change Your Password dialog box and detailed in Chapter 1, "Signing Up, Signing In, and Signing Out."

Finally, type your new password again in the third box. (Because you can't see what you're typing, Windows makes you type your new password twice to make absolutely sure that you type what you want.) Click OK to change your password.

# Changing MSN Options

To change your MSN options, you must be connected to MSN. The Options dialog box for MSN appears when you select **V**iew, **O**ptions from any menu bar in MSN. The Options dialog box contains a variety of options for changing the way MSN looks and behaves. You reveal and work with each set of options by clicking the appropriate tab, as described in the following pages.

> In the Options dialog box, only the Folder and General tabs have options for general-purpose MSN maintenance. The File Types tab contains the file-types registry (you can edit this registry to control which applications Windows 95 runs automatically to open certain types of files; see Chapter 11, "Advanced Configuration Options"). The View tab contains no relevant options for MSN.

## The Folder Tab

In the Options dialog box, click the Folder tab to change the Browsing Options—the way new windows are handled. Below each of the two options on the Folder tab (shown in Figure 2.6), an example shows how the option affects the behavior of windows. By default, MSN is configured for the second option, Browse MSN Folders By Using a Si**n**gle Window…. If you change MSN's browsing option to the first choice, Browse MSN Folders By Using a **S**eparate Window…, each time you open a new folder, the previous folders remain open in windows behind the current folder.

**FIGURE 2.6.**

*Choosing a browsing option.*

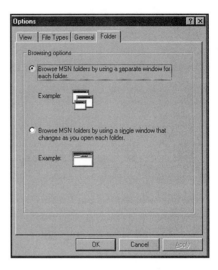

The first browsing option enables you to easily navigate backward through folders you've opened in MSN, or even jump among them, simply by clicking on the window or by choosing its button in the taskbar to bring it to the top of the pile.

If you use this option, however, you may discover that your desktop is quickly clogged with open windows. You can close the windows one by one or you can clear your desktop by right-clicking the taskbar and selecting **M**inimize All Windows.

## General Tab

In the Options dialog box, click the General tab to change the way MSN handles auto-disconnect, languages, and auto-display of MSN Today (see Figure 2.7).

**FIGURE 2.7.**

*Choosing General options.*

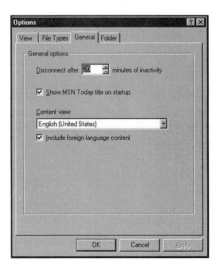

## Setting an Auto-Disconnect Time

The auto-disconnect option controls the number of minutes of "inactivity" MSN waits before automatically disconnecting you. This feature saves you from accidentally piling up connect charges on MSN and tying up your phone line if you leave your PC for a time or switch to another Windows application and forget to sign out from MSN.

By default, auto-disconnect is set to 20 minutes; if you do not perform any activity in MSN for 20 minutes, MSN signs you out and disconnects you automatically. In the General tab, in the box following **D**isconnect After, you can specify any number of minutes from 1 minute to 59 minutes. You cannot set auto-disconnect to wait longer than 59 minutes.

> It's important to understand that the auto-disconnect feature defines *inactivity* differently than screen savers, power-management systems, and other programs that initiate an action after a specified inactive period. With these other programs, the computer is considered inactive (or *idle*) if you do not press a key or move the mouse.
>
> But to MSN's auto-disconnect feature, *inactivity* is when you do nothing in MSN itself. Although you may perform other tasks in other programs on your PC, MSN considers you inactive and automatically disconnects you after the specified period.

## Preventing MSN Today from Appearing Automatically

By default, MSN displays the MSN Today page automatically when you sign in. On one hand, MSN Today is a great way to keep abreast of fun or important events and developments online. On the other hand, once you've found the MSN services you use regularly, you may want to get straight to them in most sessions and not be interrupted by MSN Today. Not only does MSN Today require an extra step from you (closing or minimizing it to reveal MSN Central), it also takes a long time to appear—and once MSN Today starts to appear, MSN won't let you close it until it appears completely.

If you're not typically interested in the day's special MSN events, you may not want MSN Today to appear automatically. After all, you can display MSN Today anytime by choosing it from the home page or by choosing **E**dit, **G**o To, **O**ther Location and then typing `MSN Today` from anywhere in MSN.

If, like me, you sign onto MSN several times a day, having MSN Today appear automatically is especially annoying. It's doubtful whether I want a list of the day's events once in a day, but I'm *positive* I don't want to see such a list twice!

To prevent MSN Today from appearing automatically at startup, deselect the checkbox next to **S**how MSN Today Title on Startup on the General tab of the Options dialog box.

### Specifying the Content View

The Content View is the language in which material is displayed in MSN. By default, this is set to English with the Include Foreign Language Content checkbox selected to allow foreign language material to be displayed.

For more about working with languages on MSN, see Chapter 11, "Advanced Configuration Options."

# Working with Billing

Using MSN's billing tools, you can review your charges or make changes to your billing information or payment method. You can work with billing information only while connected to MSN.

To begin, choose **Tools**, **Billing** from any menu bar; you see a submenu with three choices, as shown in Figure 2.8. Each choice is covered in the following sections.

**FIGURE 2.8.**

*Options for reviewing and changing your billing information.*

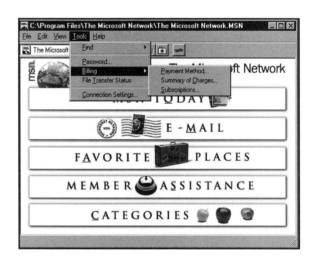

### Billing Information

To review or change your name and address or method of payment on MSN, choose **Payment Method** from the **Tools**, **Billing** submenu. A dialog box like the one in Figure 2.9 appears.

◆ To change your **N**ame and Address information, click the envelope button. A dialog box appears, identical to the Name and Address dialog box you filled in when you signed up for MSN (see Chapter 1, "Signing Up, Signing In, and Signing Out"). Make any necessary changes and click OK to return to the dialog box shown in Figure 2.9.

**FIGURE 2.9.**

*Changing your billing information.*

◆ To change your Payment Method, click the bank check button. A dialog box appears, identical to the Payment Method dialog box you filled in when you signed up for MSN. Make any necessary changes and click OK to return to the dialog box shown in Figure 2.9.

When you've made your desired changes to the name and address and payment method information, click OK to return to MSN.

## Online Statement and Subscriptions

To display your Online Statement, choose Summary of Charges from the Tools, Billing submenu. When you first display it, the Online Statement simply shows your current MSN balance, remaining free time under your current subscription plan, and the end of the current period (as shown in the top lines of Figure 2.10) without itemizing charges. To see an itemized list of your MSN charges for a given period, click **G**et Details and then select a billing period from the Get Details dialog box (also shown in Figure 2.10). When you click OK, an itemized statement appears for the period you selected (see Figure 2.11).

**FIGURE 2.10.**

*Selecting a billing period for which you want to see itemized charges by clicking Get Details.*

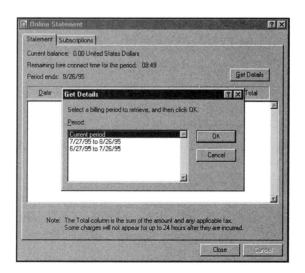

**FIGURE 2.11.**

*An itemized statement. For each charge, the date on which the charge was recorded, a description of the charge, and the amount of the charge are listed.*

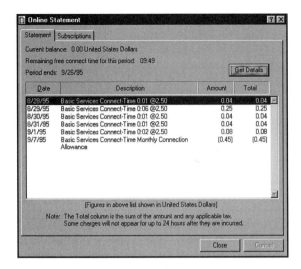

To review or change the MSN pricing plan, or *subscription*, used for your account, click the Subscriptions tab. A screen like the one in Figure 2.12 appears, naming your current subscription and describing it in the lower pane. To change your subscription to a different plan, click **C**hange and select a new plan from the list that appears.

Clicking the Subscriptions tab from the Online Statement has the same effect as choosing **S**ubscriptions from the submenu that appears when you choose **T**ools, **B**illing.

**FIGURE 2.12.**

*Reviewing your subscription information.*

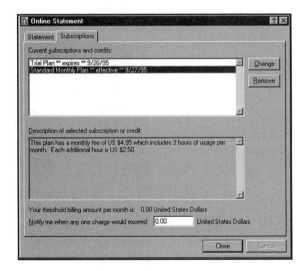

At the bottom of the dialog box in Figure 2.12, notice the **Notify** Me When Any One Charge Would Exceed option. By default, this is set to 0.00 dollars; when you take an action on MSN for which there is an extra charge of any amount, a message pops up to alert you to the charge and give you a chance to cancel the action and avoid the charge.

But if you have deep pockets and would rather not be bothered with warnings about what you consider trifling sums, you can enter a number of dollars and cents here. You are notified only when an action would incur a charge that exceeds the amount you entered.

# Contacting MSN Support

Of course, I hope this book answers your questions so well that you'll never need Microsoft's help. But even if you don't need Microsoft's help, part of what you pay for when you use MSN is support costs, so you might as well ask a question now and then.

## Help

The first place to check for help with MSN is the MSN help file through Windows Help, which you can do offline:

1. Choose **H**elp from the Start menu.
2. Click the Index tab.
3. Type `msn` to automatically scroll to the entry `The Microsoft Network`; click that entry. A list box appears, offering two choices for help on MSN.

If you can't find your answers offline, try MSN's online help, which you can access from any MSN window by choosing Help, Help Topics.

## Member Assistance

When you're online, you can find a number of good sources for answering questions and solving problems:

◆ In the MSN Member Lobby folder (shown in Figure 2.13), you'll find a number of helpful folders, including one called *Member Support*, which contains Member Guidelines (described in Chapter 3, "Member Rules and Etiquette") and a BBS for exchanging questions and answers about the general use of MSN. (To learn how to use a BBS, see Chapter 5, "Reading and Contributing to Bulletin Boards and Newsgroups.")

◆ In any forum, you can open the *kiosk*, an online document you display by double-clicking it (a kiosk icon—the lowercase letter *i* in a dark circle—is shown in

Figure 2.13, labeled *About the Lobby*). Not only does the kiosk describe the general operation of the forum, it also contains the member ID of the *forum manager*, the person responsible for the overall operation of the forum. You can use that member ID to send e-mail to the forum manager and ask any forum-related question.

◆ You can also address e-mail to the member ID sysop (see Chapter 8, "Composing, Sending, and Receiving E-Mail") to ask important questions about the overall operation of MSN. The *sysop* (system operator) ID is shared by a group of people responsible for keeping MSN running. That's a big job, so you probably should not bother the sysop with questions that can be answered through Help, member assistance, or a forum manager.

**FIGURE 2.13.**

*The Member Lobby folder.*

## Telephone Support

When all else fails, you can call somebody on the phone. When online, you can display the current list of MSN telephone support numbers by choosing **H**elp, Member Support **Num**bers, Member Support Phone Numbers.

In case your problem is so serious you can't *get* online, the member support numbers (as of this writing) are listed in Table 2.1. Note that these numbers are only for MSN-related problems and questions, not for questions about Windows 95 or other Microsoft products.

Table 2.1. MSN telephone support.

| *North and South America Customer Service (11 A.M. to 5 P.M. Eastern Time)* | |
| --- | --- |
| English Language Support | 800-386-5550 |
| Spanish Language Support (North America) | 95-800-215-6987 |
| Spanish Language Support (South America) | 813-577-9916 |
| French Canadian Language Support | 800-952-1110 |

| *Europe, Asia, and Africa Customer Service (11 A.M. to 5 P.M. Local Time)* | |
| --- | --- |
| Austria | 0660 5829 |
| Belgium (French) | 0800 13721 |
| Belgium (Dutch) | 080013867 |
| Czech Republic | +32 2 739 8325 |
| Denmark | 80 01 81 61 |
| Finland | 0800 1132 72 |
| France | 0591 7242 |
| Germany | 0130 814479 |
| Hong Kong | 800 5373 |
| Hungary | 00800 12416 |
| Ireland | 1800 709904 |
| Israel | 177 440 3796 |
| Italy | 1678 76720 |
| Japan | 0031 44 4192 |
| Korea | 0078 441 3791 |
| Kuwait | +32 2 739 8327 |
| Malaysia | 44 181 247 9038 |
| Netherlands | 06022 2081 |
| Poland | 32 2 739 8302 |
| Portugal | 32 2 739 8302 |
| Russia | 956 0885 |
| Saudi Arabia | +32 2 739 8327 |
| Singapore | 800 4481045 |
| Spain | 32 2 739 8301 |
| South Africa | 0800 991027 |
| Sweden | 020 795 173 |
| Switzerland (French) | 155 4719 |
| Switzerland (German) | 155 4718 |
| Switzerland (Italian) | 155 3859 |
| Taiwan | 0080 444017 |
| Thailand | 001 800 44 13795 |
| United Kingdom | 0800 750800 |

*continues*

**Table 2.1. continued**

| *Oceana Customer Service* | |
| --- | --- |
| Australia | 02 934 9000 |
| New Zealand | 0800 441901 |
| Other Oceana | +44 181 247 9043 |

# What Now?

Your pre-navigation checklist is nearly complete. All you need now is some indoctrination in the rules and customs observed on MSN. Because even regular MSN accounts provide access to Internet e-mail and newsgroups, you need to know not only how to behave on MSN, but also how to behave on the Internet. In Chapter 3, you learn both.

You also learn important facts about how the MSN culture is managed. Is it censored? Is it kid safe? Well, yes and no. See Chapter 3.

# CHAPTER 3

# MEMBER RULES AND ETIQUETTE

About MSN and "Cybersleaze"

Member Guidelines

Netiquette

Internet Shorthand

Emoticons

What Now?

Before I visited the Dominican Republic, I bought a *Fodor's* travel guide to the Caribbean. Among other things, I learned from that book not to let anyone handle my bags at the airport in Santo Domingo and never to give anyone U.S. currency, even if they asked me—it's against Dominican law.

Aware that I'm sort of stupid about such things, I'm entirely convinced that, had I not read that book, I would have added to my trip a little time at the local police station explaining why I gave that guy a buck, and to this day my shirts would still be in Santo Domingo. But because I read that book, my shirts are in New Jersey, my international police record is clean, and I have wonderful memories of a great country and its beautiful people.

Sure, you can journey onto MSN without knowing anything about the rules. But by doing so, you risk running afoul of local laws and maybe offending somebody. That's hardly a good way to first visit a place to which you intend to return.

This chapter covers the rules and customs you're expected to follow online, both on MSN and on the Internet:

◆ Where MSN stands in the messy balance of online censorship versus online pornography

◆ How to look up MSN's member rules and guidelines online

◆ How to observe "netiquette," the unofficial code of personal conduct for MSN and the Internet

# About MSN and "Cybersleaze"

The interrelated issues of online pornography, censorship, hate speech, pedophilia, and other aspects of so-called "cybersleaze" are unfolding rapidly at this writing and cannot be appropriately analyzed or addressed within the scope of this chapter. Unless you've been under a rock for the past year, you probably already know that:

◆ There are pictures, writings, and video clips available through the Internet and through commercial online services (CompuServe, America Online, Prodigy) that many judge to be obscene.

◆ Minors have discovered (accidentally or deliberately) this unsavory material, even on the online services that have the capability to monitor and censor online content (something that's not done on the Internet, as a whole).

◆ Minors have been lured into running away from home through e-mail-based relationships that began through meetings in online BBSs and chats.

◆ Even adults have been offended by material they've discovered online because of its sexual or political content.

◆ Congress is debating online censorship bills—among others, the Communications Decency Act—which, if passed by both houses and not vetoed by the president, face almost certain constitutional challenges that will drag on for years.

All of this happened before the debut of MSN, the newest online service. So the question naturally arises: Is MSN an absolutely safe, wholesome environment for children, teens, and sensitive adults?

Well, not exactly. Here's the deal....

## How MSN's Content Is (and Is Not) Controlled

Microsoft's approach to online censorship is two pronged. It can best be summarized as "We'll do our best to keep it clean, but dirt is in the eye of the beholder; don't blame us if you see something you don't like."

The MSN Member Agreement and its friendlier analog, the Member Guidelines (see "Member Guidelines," later in this chapter), specifically state that members are not to send "obscene" or "pornographic" material to publicly accessible areas of MSN, such as BBSs, file libraries, and chat sessions. To forum managers and chat hosts falls the general responsibility for making sure that users follow the rules and for removing from MSN any objectionable content (or, in extreme cases, the members responsible for it).

But none of that should be mistaken as a promise that MSN is antiseptic, or is even attempting to be so. In the Member Guidelines, Microsoft specifically states that MSN can and will contain "adult content," and that protecting you or your children from it is your responsibility, not Microsoft's. No one under 18 years old is permitted to sign up for MSN; your kids can't sign up on their own, and if you let them use your account, you assume the responsibility for keeping them out of harm's way. Also, forum managers are not required to check every message posted to bulletin boards and libraries. Even when they do check, they will—being human and all that—exercise varying judgment about what is and is not acceptable, depending not only on their own discretion but also on the topic of the forum.

There are some areas where "adult content" is blocked out, by default, from every MSN account. To see all content in these areas, a user must fill out an online agreement MSN calls an *e-form* (an electronic form) located within the forum where the content is censored. Where they appear, these e-forms are accompanied by an online document that explains them. Members wanting access to adult material must open the e-form, fill it out, and wait for an e-mail confirmation from MSN that they now have access to all material in the forum. But this feature is not widely implemented; where it is used, the mechanisms do not successfully block all potentially offensive material. These attempts at censorship do, however, manage to throw out the baby with the bath water—they block out a great deal of material that wouldn't make your grandmother blush. That's also true of the blocks on Internet newsgroups, in which newsgroups devoted to altogether innocent topics like business are censored along with the "adult" content. (See Chapter 5, "Reading and Contributing to Bulletin Boards and Newsgroups," to learn more about using e-forms and accessing "adult" content.)

Finally, Microsoft respects the privacy of e-mail. In the Member Agreement, Microsoft promises not to intercept or open e-mail unless the sender, receiver, or authorized legal authorities ask it to. Why is that important? It's important because the recent cases in which minors were lured to run away began as apparently innocent meetings in online chats and BBSs (on America Online, perhaps the most carefully censored of the online services) and veered into corruption only when the relationship evolved into private e-mail exchanges, which cannot be censored. Therefore, the only censorship that could have prevented these events would have been to prevent the victims from using an online service at all, or—dare I say it?—parental supervision.

Now that you understand how Microsoft does and does not control online content, what you choose to do is up to you. The important thing to remember is that MSN, in general, is pretty safe. But if you want guarantees, you can't have 'em—from Microsoft or from me.

Keep in mind, however, that there is great stuff for kids on MSN. In particular, there's a For Kids folder in the Home and Family category folder full of great activities for kids (see Figure 3.1). All the language used in For Kids is kept simple, and all the words and letters are displayed in big, colorful fonts to make using them easy and fun for kids.

**FIGURE 3.1.**

*For Kids, an MSN play space for kids.*

Unfortunately, there is no way to restrict your account, even temporarily, to kid-friendly categories and forums. You have to supervise your kids when they use their parts of MSN to be sure that they don't wander where you don't want them to go. One great way to do this is to keep only kid-friendly shortcuts in your Favorite Places folder; teach your kids that they are allowed to use only the services included in Favorite Places.

To keep your MSN account secure, follow these guidelines:

◆ Don't teach your kids your MSN password.

◆ Don't check the Remember My Password checkbox on the Sign-In dialog box (described in Chapter 1, "Signing Up, Signing In, and Signing Out").

◆ For extra security, use a username and password to log on to Windows 95 (see Windows 95 Help).

## My Two Cents' Worth

Having given you the lowdown on MSN censorship, I feel an obligation to offer my opinion—both as a writer about the world online and as a parent—about this issue. I understand completely if you couldn't care less about my opinion—just skip the rest of this sidebar. If you do read on, feel free to disagree.

With deep respect and empathy for those concerned about endangering our children and ourselves, I must make the following observations:

◆ On both MSN and the larger Internet, the amount of potentially objectionable material is but a tiny fraction—perhaps less than one tenth of one percent—of the material available.

◆ Except in extremely rare cases, it's almost impossible to find smutty stuff unless you're looking for it—smut doesn't just pop up by accident in cooking forums. I've heard the stories about parents who left their kids alone with the computer for five minutes and returned to find them viewing photos of bestiality. My experience suggests to me that these stories are scare tactics—or that the parents in question prefer the unlikely story that the porn popped up accidentally to the more likely story that they have curious, mischievous, computer-savvy kids who would, in the absence of a computer, peek at a *Penthouse* down at the convenience store. Their problem isn't the evils online—it's unsupervised, curious kids behaving like kids do sometimes.

◆ The world is a dangerous place for kids, online or off. As a parent, my job is to keep them away from what they're *not* ready for, supervise them during what they *may* be ready for, and turn 'em loose only when I *know* they're ready. That's true whether the activity is crossing the street, making a phone call, taking the bus, talking to strangers, or going online.

◆ The world online is loaded with stuff that can enchant, entertain, educate, and inspire my children. I don't intend to deny them those benefits simply because there are risks. Instead, I'll supervise them and guide them, and I won't let them work online unsupervised until I know they're ready. After all, I wouldn't deny my kids the experience of using the public library just because it may have a few Harold Robbins novels on the high shelves.

◆ Among the folks who want to censor online communication to protect kids are many with honorable passions. However, there are others who would, given the chance, censor everything according to their personal views on pornography, religion, politics, gender issues, and culture. If the price of my freedom of speech and religion is to leave a few dirty pictures on the Internet, I can live with that.

# Member Guidelines

During sign-up, you're required to read the entire MSN Member Agreement and indicate your consent to it. (See Chapter 1, "Signing Up, Signing In, and Signing Out.") If you didn't actually read the agreement during sign-up, or if you read it and now can't remember a single thing it said (don't blame yourself; it's in legalese), you ought to read it more carefully now. The Member Agreement not only spells out your rights and obligations as an MSN member, it also covers such things as the circumstances under which Microsoft has the right to sell information about you to other companies for direct-sales purposes.

To review the MSN Member Agreement, follow these steps:

1. Sign in to MSN.
2. Close (or minimize) MSN Today to reveal MSN Central; then click Member Assistance. The Member Lobby folder opens.
3. Choose Reception Desk and then select Member Guidelines. A screen like the one in Figure 3.2 appears.

**FIGURE 3.2.**

*The Member Guidelines folder, where you find the MSN Member Agreement and Member Guidelines.*

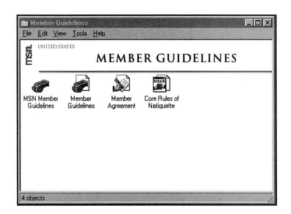

Double-click the icon labeled Member Agreement shown in Figure 3.2. MSN downloads the Member Agreement to your PC and opens WordPad or another word processor on your PC to display the file. Read the file within the word processor. When finished, you can use your word processor's Save or Print feature to save or print the Member Agreement, or you can simply close the word processor to return to MSN.

In Figure 3.2, notice that there are two icons with the label *Member Guidelines*; one uses a whistle over a page icon and the other uses a plain whistle (it's an icon that represents an MSN multimedia "title," a unique way of presenting information online in a dynamic, colorful, easy-to-use way ). MSN Today is another MSN title.

Behind the two Member Guidelines icons is the exact same information; only the method of presentation differs. The "page" version is an online document you can read in exactly the same way you read the Member Agreement. The "title" version displays the Member Guidelines online, one section at a time, through MSN's Online Viewer (see Figure 3.3). On the left side of the screen shown in Figure 3.3 are "links" to each section of the Guidelines. To read any section, click its name; that section of the document appears in the window pane on the right.

**FIGURE 3.3.**

*The Member Guidelines title.*

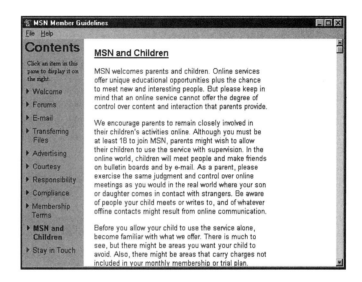

For more about titles and links, see Chapter 9, "Viewing and Operating Titles."

Whichever way you choose to display it, the Member Guidelines document is a great way to learn about how you're expected to behave online. Although most of what it says is also covered in the Member Agreement, the Member Guidelines document is much easier to read and understand.

The next section of this chapter covers "netiquette," the code of personal behavior on MSN and the Internet. You can also learn more about netiquette online, in the Netiquette Center. To get there, follow these steps:

1. Sign in to MSN.

2. Close (or minimize) MSN Today to reveal MSN Central; then click Member Assistance. The Member Lobby folder opens.

3. Choose Reception Desk and then select Netiquette Center. A screen like the one in Figure 3.4 appears.

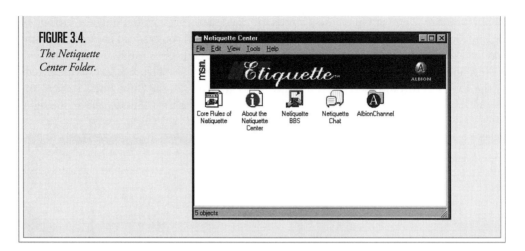

**FIGURE 3.4.**
*The Netiquette Center Folder.*

# Netiquette

Although the MSN Member Agreement and Member Guidelines contain specific rules regarding the posting of obscene material on MSN, most of the rules of conduct in those documents are adaptations of basic "netiquette," the customary code of conduct on the Internet. Because even regular MSN accounts cross paths with the Internet on newsgroups and in e-mail, it's important for all MSN users to be familiar with it.

In general, except for the use of obscene or objectionable material, MSN is likely to be more forgiving of an ignorance of netiquette than are users of Internet newsgroups, Internet Relay Chat, and Internet e-mail. MSN is new and hosts a higher proportion of newcomers to online communication—"newbies," as they're called both fondly and derisively—than the Internet. There is likely to be a broad range of experience levels everywhere on MSN—and a lot of netiquette *faux pas*. On the Internet, however, you encounter a higher level of online experience and a sometimes hostile attitude toward those perceived to be unacquainted with online customs. Also on the Internet, you'll see a much greater application of shorthand, emoticons, and other online abbreviations. Even if you choose not to use these, you should know about them so that you can comprehend what some Internet users write.

*Note*

> There's one way in which MSN can be more strict about etiquette than the Internet: enforcement. If you break customs repeatedly on the Internet, about the worst that can happen to you is that other users send you nasty messages; in rare cases, you can be barred from particular newsgroups—but not from the whole Internet. If you persistently break MSN's policies, however, your MSN account can be terminated at Microsoft's discretion. (See the Member Agreement.)

The tips in the following sections cover the basics of netiquette for messaging activities (BBSs and newsgroups, e-mail, and Chat), all of which are covered in later chapters). Whenever you type, keep these "rules" in mind.

# Watch Your Language

Remember that you're writing, not speaking. Sarcasm, facetiousness, comic hyperbole, and other colorful techniques of spoken expression depend heavily on speech inflection. They often fail to achieve their desired effect when written.

If you try to be clever online, your message may backfire. The most common example occurs when one person writes something silly or exaggerated in fun, and someone else reads it completely seriously—and takes offense. Write what you mean, clearly and directly. Save the color for those with whom you've established a strong rapport.

# Avoid "Capital" Offenses

Some folks like to use ALL CAPITALS for emphasis or to point out that YOUR LAST MESSAGE WAS TOTALLY OFF-BASE, YOU MORON. A few of these folks are holdovers from the old mainframe computing days when all program code was written in uppercase, and so e-mail was also typed in uppercase, from habit. (Some folks left the Caps Lock key on all the time.) Most modern Internet users, however, type in uppercase letters TO SHOW THAT THEY'RE SHOUTING. It annoys readers. Don't do it. Make your point with strong, well-chosen words and persuasive logic, not tall letters.

# Curb Quoting

The Reply features in Exchange, BBSs, and newsgroups automatically "quote" the complete text of the message you're responding to by inserting it beneath your response. Quoting helps you show exactly what you're responding to. (During an argument, haven't you ever wanted the ability to show the other person *exactly* what he or she said?)

Unfortunately, some people use this feature lazily and leave the entire text of the copied message in every reply. In the course of an ongoing e-mail, BBS, or newsgroup exchange, such messages grow like fungi because each new volley carries the entire history of the conversation within it. The mushrooming exchange lays unnecessary storage and transmission burdens on MSN or the Internet, and slows down some activities, such as retrieving e-mail. It also wastes the time of readers who scroll through the old news to make sure that there's no new stuff wedged in. Cut quotes down to what matters; cut them completely when they're unnecessary.

# Be Discreet

BBS and newsgroup postings and Chat comments are public—anybody can read them. E-mail is supposed to be private, but really isn't. MSN e-mail is more secure than Internet e-mail, but any e-mail is vulnerable to computer thieves. Also, your e-mail recipient can copy your message and forward it to others, without your knowledge. The laws regarding electronic communication are evolving, but in general, an e-mail message is the property of its recipient, not its sender. You may have no legal protection against the copying and distribution of what you write to others. Also, if you send offensive or threatening e-mail to someone, he or she can bring it to the attention of MSN, who will report it to the authorities. Finally, under current laws, business owners have the legal right to examine all e-mail stored on company-owned computers, without employees' consent or knowledge. If you use an office PC for MSN, or if your e-mail recipients do, your e-mail is not secure.

The moral? Phrase everything you say on the Internet or MSN as if you were talking to Geraldo Rivera. If you don't want the world to know about it, send a letter by U.S. post, make a phone call, or arrange a meeting in a dark alley—but keep it offline. Don't make the mistake of thinking your BBS and newsgroup postings are read only by strangers around the world. You never know when your boss, co-worker, neighbor, spouse, or personal banker may come across one of your postings. E-mail is safer, but not air-tight. So be careful out there.

## Keep Cool

*Flaming* is the Internet word for sending an irate message. Flames may be appropriate in response to some events, but—as with all violent acts—flames have a way of igniting counterflames and escalating into "flame wars," in which the offense that ignited the first flame is lost in the mêlée and never resolved. Flames also tend to make the writer seem like one of those ranting idiots who write letters to the editor all the time. (Why do they print those?)

The nature of online communications naturally allows people to lose their heads more freely—after all, if you flame at Phil in Tokyo, you don't worry about running into him later at the gas station and getting your face bashed in. Still, hot flashes online rarely accomplish anything. So stay cool. Make your points with reason. If somebody posts something stupid, tell him or her so—calmly. And remember: For all you know, Phil in Tokyo has a meeting with your boss next week.

## Communicate Efficiently

Avoid sending unnecessary words or unnecessary messages. You don't have to truncate your sentences down to telegrams (`Have read yr msg...Think you wrong...will send u 2nd msg to xplain...stop`), but try to be concise. Consider using shorthand (see "Internet Shorthand," later in this chapter), where appropriate, to save space and time.

Internet users expect messages to be polite, but they don't expect entire messages to be sent solely for the sake of politeness. If someone answers your question in a newsgroup or list, don't post (or even e-mail) a thank you unless you can work it into a message that has something else to say. Not posting thanks isn't considered rude; posting messages with no new information is.

## Post No Bills

Advertising of any kind is expressly forbidden on MSN itself—unless, of course, you've paid Microsoft for the privilege. Posting an ad in a BBS or sending out a bunch of ads with e-mail can get you booted from MSN pronto, per the Member Agreement.

On the Internet, commercial activity—including advertising and selling—was once restricted, was recently tolerated, and is now encouraged. Still, such activities should be reserved to appropriate commercial zones, such as the World Wide Web (see Chapter 16, "Browsing the

World Wide Web"). Sending unsolicited e-mail ads, or posting ads on newsgroups, is almost certain to ignite flames.

The exception is private sales among subscribers within a newsgroup. For example, I frequent a video laserdisc newsgroup; folks there often sell or trade their used laserdiscs with other subscribers. Although this is tolerated in newsgroups, be warned that it's still *verboten* in MSN BBSs.

If you're in business, however, and want to sell your product or service on the Net, restrict your selling to Internet tools where it's appropriate. An easy way to find out whether commercial activity is tolerated in a given Internet tool is to hang out there awhile (*lurk* there), watching for any commercial activity and the responses to it. Lurking should tell you not only whether commercial activity is tolerated, but what type of activity is well received.

> One type of commercial activity tolerated nowhere online is chain letters. These are sometimes posted on newsgroups and BBSs or are broadcast with e-mail. Like paper-based chain letters, these are sometimes just games but are often money-making scams. Just say no.

# Internet Shorthand

Over the years, a system of abbreviations has emerged for frequently used phrases. These "shorthand" abbreviations help writers keep messages concise. They're most useful in IRC (or MSN Chat) sessions when it's important to type quickly. But shorthand is also used in other types of messaging. Shorthand isn't netiquette (nobody expects you to use it), but it's there if you need it. At the very least, you should be familiar with shorthand so that you can understand the messages of others who use it.

Following are the basic shorthand abbreviations. Despite the netiquette discouragement of using ALL CAPS, (see "Avoid 'Capital' Offenses," earlier in this chapter), shorthand is always typed in caps, as any letter abbreviation should be.

| Abbreviation | Meaning | Example |
|---|---|---|
| BTW | By the way | BTW, where's a good FTP site for downloading a picture of Burt Reynolds? |
| IMHO | In my humble opinion | Burt Reynolds has the dramatic range of a carrot, IMHO. |
| IMO | In my opinion (without the sarcastic/ humorous tone added by *humble*) | Reynolds has some screen charm, IMO. |

*continues*

| Abbreviation | Meaning | Example |
|---|---|---|
| LOL | Laughing out loud (tags a joke or a statement that's patently ludicrous) | Burt Reynolds is an important film actor (LOL). |
| OTF | On the floor (laughing, presumably; same as LOL, only stronger) | Reynolds has twice deserved, and been denied, an Oscar (OTF). |
| OTOH | On the other hand | OTOH, he was pretty good in *Deliverance* and *The Longest Yard*. |
| ROTFL | Rolling on the floor laughing (same as LOL but much stronger) | Reynolds is a modern-day Cary Grant (ROTFL). |
| YMMV | Your mileage may vary (functions as a disclaimer to evaluations or experiences, telling the reader not to expect the same results you describe) | Actually, I enjoyed Reynolds a lot in *Starting Over* and *The End*,YMMV. |

### Proper Use for Shorthand and Emoticons

Shorthand and emoticons (described next) are considered informal techniques and really aren't appropriate in formal communications such as e-mail business letters. They can also be overused, leading to messages that seem to be written in some bizarre, secret code. Use them selectively and sparingly. Avoid using both in the same message.

More importantly, observe whether they're used by those you correspond with, or by others in the BBSs, newsgroups, or lists you frequent. If they're not used, your readers may not even understand shorthand and emoticons, in which case you'd best stick to words. This is especially true in MSN BBSs and Chat sessions, where the many newbies may be baffled by your abbreviations.

# Emoticons

*Emoticons* are little sideways faces formed out of two or more text characters. (The term derives from "emotion icons.") To see the face, you have to tilt your head to the left or lay your monitor on its right side (head tilting is better). Table 3.1 shows the most common emoticons.

Sometimes also called *smileys* after the most common example, emoticons are used to give the reader a sense of your emotional tone. For example, if you write, *I'll clean your garage for a nickel,* but you're only kidding, you can make your intention clear by following your statement with a smile `:-)` or a wink `;-)`. You may also use emoticons to express an emotion outright—a smiley often follows the word *Thanks!*.

Some emoticons attempt not to express an emotion, but rather to give the reader a sense of the writer's appearance—or rather, the appearance of the writer's online alter-ego. If you get mail from someone using the emoticon for the Pope `+-(:-)` be polite to this person, but keep your confession to yourself.

**Table 3.1. Emoticons (tilt your head left to see the faces).**

| *Emoticon* | *Means You Are...* |
| --- | --- |
| `:-)` | Smiling |
| `:-(` | Frowning |
| `(:-(` | Frowning severely |
| `;-)` | Winking |
| `:-o` | Surprised |
| `8-0` | Shocked |
| `:-S` | Confused |
| `:-\` | Skeptical |
| `:-)'` | Drooling |
| `:-)8` | Well dressed (see the bow tie?) |
| `8-)` | Wearing glasses |
| `*<¦:-)` | Santa Claus (see the hat?) |
| `=:-)=` | Punk rocker with a goatee |

*Tip*

In addition to emoticons and shorthand, you'll see messages annotated and embellished one more way. Some people surround action words with greater-than and less-than signs (< >), and use them in the same way shorthand is used. The words are physical actions, but they're used to describe facial expressions or body language that indicates emotion, tone, or inflection. Examples include these:

```
<grin>
<shrug>
<wink>
<sigh>
```

Sometimes these are boiled down to a letter or two:

&lt;g&gt;    a grin
&lt;l&gt;    a laugh
&lt;s&gt;    a sigh
&lt;jk&gt;   just kidding

Last, and maybe least, comes a shorthand that many readers mistake for a typo:

&lt; &gt;    no comment

# What Now?

That's it for advance preparation. In Part I of this book, you've signed up and signed in, learned how to customize and maintain your account, and boned up on the customs and lingo online. There's nothing left to do except dive into MSN and see where it takes you.

Part II of this book begins with a top-to-bottom primer on making your way around the MSN landscape. Then you learn, a chapter at a time, how to use each of the types of MSN activities you encounter online.

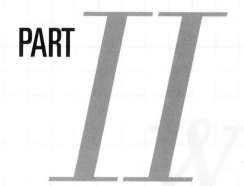

**PART** *II*

# NAVIGATING THE MICROSOFT NETWORK

Basic Navigation Techniques    61

Reading and Contributing to Bulletin Boards and
Newsgroups    81

Hanging Out in Chat Rooms    107

Downloading and Uploading Files    121

Composing, Sending, and Receiving E-Mail    141

Viewing and Operating Titles    157

# CHAPTER 4

# BASIC NAVIGATION TECHNIQUES

Understanding Windows 95 Concepts

Understanding MSN Concepts

Browsing The Microsoft Network

Browsing with Windows Explorer

Making a Beeline for Anything on MSN

Opening Files

What Now?

When I was a schoolteacher, I once visited a kindergarten class. I watched as a five-year-old studiously created some sort of free-form construction-paper collage. When the tot took a quick break, he noticed me, shrugged, and sagely observed, "Cut and paste, cut and paste. Where does it getcha?" Confucius never offered wiser insight.

I sometimes remember that student when I navigate The Microsoft Network. I think to myself, "Point and click, point and click. Where does it getcha?" That's exactly how you may feel after a few MSN browsing sessions. Navigating to anything productive, and from there to anywhere else, often seems to involve an awful lot of clicking around. But it needn't, once you learn how to navigate efficiently.

The trick to productive MSN navigation is to understand the essential difference between browsers and hunters. *Browsers*—cows, sheep, most bears, lawyers—roam around, hoping to come across a meal. *Hunters*—eagles, lions, some bears, lawyers—seek signs, track, stalk, and kill with a minimum of roaming around. When you first venture onto MSN, it's beneficial to browse a little, to explore, to get the lay of the land, so to speak. But soon, once you identify the specific MSN services you'll use regularly, you'll want to hunt these down in each session with a minimum of fuss and overland travel.

In this chapter, you learn how to browse MSN as a way of getting started and so that you can develop an understanding of the order within the MSN universe. After that, you discover techniques for getting straight to an MSN service without wandering around first.

This chapter shows you how to do the following:

♦ Understand how MSN is organized

♦ Browse freely around MSN

♦ Find your way back home from any browsing journey

♦ Find information about MSN services you discover

♦ Use Windows Explorer to navigate MSN

♦ Go straight to any service from anywhere within MSN

♦ Open informational documents on MSN

When you finish this chapter, you'll know how to navigate to, and learn about, anything on MSN. In Chapters 5 through 9, you'll learn how to *use* what you find on MSN.

# Understanding Windows 95 Concepts

By design, MSN makes all of its offerings look like the Windows 95 files, folders, and programs that reside on your PC; MSN makes these offerings behave the way you expect them to. Clicking a folder icon opens the file; double-clicking a program icon starts the program; clicking a document icon displays the document.

Of course, if you're new to Windows 95 (and who isn't?), you need to understand the following Windows 95 concepts to browse MSN effectively:

◆ **Folders** (see Figure 4.1). Files in Windows 95 are stored in folders, which appear on your Windows desktop as icons resembling file folders. Clicking a folder icon anywhere within Windows 95 or MSN opens a window showing the contents of that folder. In addition to files, folders contain other folders, which may themselves contain still more folders, and so on. This "folder within a folder" concept forms Windows 95 and MSN's hierarchical "content tree," described later in this chapter.

◆ **Shortcuts** (see Figure 4.1). Shortcuts are small files that open a file or folder somewhere within Windows or on MSN. They appear as icons on your Windows desktop, within messages and documents, or anywhere within Windows. When you double-click a shortcut icon, the folder or file it represents opens. You can create your own shortcuts to files and folders to make your work in Windows more convenient.

In Chapter 12, "Trimming Time Online," you learn how to create Windows shortcuts to files and services residing in MSN. Double-clicking these shortcuts automatically connects you to MSN (if you're not already connected) and navigates to the folder, document, or MSN service to which the shortcut is attached.

In Chapter 13, "Power E-Mail," and Chapter 14, "Speeding Up MSN," you learn how to insert MSN shortcuts into e-mail messages and documents so that the reader can automatically open an MSN folder or service by clicking the shortcuts you created.

◆ **Long filenames.** In DOS, filenames cannot include spaces and are limited to eight characters. In Windows 95 and on MSN, filenames can contain spaces and can be as long as you want them to be. Instead of filenames like MYDOGDOC.DOC, you see and use filenames like My Dog Document.

◆ **Context menus** (see Figure 4.1). When you point to an icon and click the right mouse button (an activity referred to as a *right-click*), a context menu for that icon appears. The context menu offers a number of selections, of which the most important are these:

| Option | Description |
| --- | --- |
| Open | Opens the icon as if you had double-clicked it. |
| Explore | Opens Windows Explorer, showing the location of the folder, program, or file the icon represents. |
| Properties | Displays the icon's Properties sheet (described in the next entry). |

◆ **Properties sheets** (see Figure 4.1). An icon's Properties sheet provides valuable information about the icon, including the type of file the icon represents (a folder, program, data file, shortcut, and so on). In MSN, you can display the Properties sheet for any icon to learn more about the activity that icon leads to. MSN also has a Properties sheet for each member; you can display a member's Properties sheet to learn more about that member.

◆ **Views** (see Figure 4.1). When you open a folder, a window appears showing the files and folders within the folder. Using the **V**iew menu on the window's menu bar or the View buttons on the toolbar (as described in the next entry), you can choose how the contents should be displayed. You can choose from the following options:

| Option | Description |
| --- | --- |
| Large icons | Shows contents in rows and columns of icons with labels and large icons (32 pixels by 32 pixels). |
| Small icons | Shows contents in rows and columns of icons with labels and small icons (16 pixels by 16 pixels, half the size of large icons). |
| List | Shows contents as a list of icons. In Figure 4.1, the open window in the upper-left corner is in List view. |
| Details | Shows contents as a one-column list of icons and descriptions, plus other information about each icon, including the type of file it represents and the date it was created. In Figure 4.1, the open window in the lower-right corner is in Details view. |

◆ **Toolbars** (see Figure 4.1). Every window has a toolbar, which you can display by choosing **V**iew, **T**oolbar from the window's menu bar. The toolbar contains handy buttons for performing the most commonly used activities.

*Tip*

> To find out what any toolbar button represents, rest the mouse pointer on the toolbar button for a few seconds; a short description of the button appears in a yellow box.

# Understanding MSN Concepts

Although most of the standard Windows 95 concepts are at work in MSN, MSN introduces a few new concepts of its own. Understanding what follows can help you make more sense of what you see in your first sessions online (each of these concepts is covered in greater detail later in this book).

**FIGURE 4.1.**

*A Windows 95 desktop, showing many of the new concepts in Windows 95. All these concepts are incorporated into MSN.*

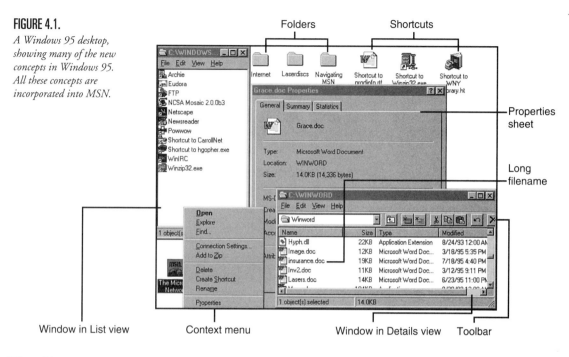

## New Terms

The following are some of the new terms MSN adds to the Windows 95 lexicon:

◆ **Category.** A category is a type of folder within MSN. It contains all the *forums* (described in the next entry) covering a certain general subject area (Arts, Sports, and so on) or other category folders that themselves contain forums. Category folders may also contain *kiosks* (described later in this list) and may contain any other type of MSN icon as well—a *BBS, chat room,* and so on.

◆ **Forum.** A forum in MSN is a folder containing a BBS, chat room, documents, or files related to particular topic. A forum is the final destination of most journeys into MSN. Each forum is overseen by a forum manager, whose member ID you can learn from the forum's *kiosk.*

◆ **Kiosk.** Kiosks contain documents that provide useful information about the folder or forum they're in. To read the kiosk, double-click the kiosk icon.

◆ **BBS.** A BBS (short for *bulletin board service*) is a place where MSN members with a common interest can post news, questions, and comments related to the forum topic. Members can also read and respond to news, questions, and comments posted by others. Members can attach files to the messages they post in BBSs and download to their PCs the files posted by others. (For more about BBSs, see Chapter 5, "Reading and Contributing to Bulletin Boards and Newsgroups.")

◆ **Library.** A library is simply a BBS in which every message has an attached file. Libraries are set up in forums as repositories for files forum visitors might be interested in—programs, graphics, video clips, and so on.

◆ **Chat room.** A chat room is where *chats* on a particular topic are held. Chat is an MSN facility that allows multiple members to engage in a live, online conference. (See Chapter 6, "Hanging Out in Chat Rooms.")

◆ **Online documents.** You'll see document files scattered throughout MSN, usually offering information that may be especially useful to visitors of the category folder or forum where the document icon is located. When you double-click an online document, MSN copies the document to your PC and opens a word processing program on your PC (usually WordPad) to display the document. A kiosk is one type of online document. Most online documents feature a date in their icon label, showing when the file was created or last updated.

◆ **Title** (see Figure 4.2). MSN can display multimedia *titles* through its Online Viewer. Titles use elaborately formatted screens, graphics, and *links* (described in the next entry) to fill the role of a textbook, manual, or a guidebook to a special event. MSN Today is an example of an MSN title. (For more about titles, see Chapter 9, "Viewing and Operating Titles.")

◆ **Link** (see Figure 4.2). A link is an icon, picture, or highlighted text that starts an activity or takes you somewhere in MSN when you click it. When the mouse pointer is near enough to a link to activate it, the pointer changes from the regular "arrow" pointer to a pointing finger to show that you are on a link. (Links are the main means of navigating the Internet's World Wide Web; see Chapter 16, "Browsing the World Wide Web.")

**FIGURE 4.2.**

*An MSN title about the America's Cup sailing race. When the arrow pointer changes into a pointing finger, this indicates that the pointer is over a link, which is activated when the left mouse button is clicked.*

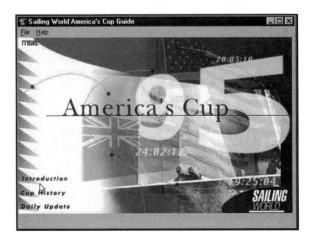

*Tip*

In Windows 95, one folder icon looks like all other folder icons. But in MSN, folder icons—and most other types of icons, including BBS icons and titles—may be customized with a flourish or decoration of some kind sitting on top of (but not completely obscuring) the standard icon.

For example, the following are all folder icons:

Arts and          Computers and      Special Events    People and        The MSN
Entertainment     Software                             Communities       Member Lobby

You can always tell what the icon represents by what lies behind the decoration. However, when in doubt, you can find out exactly what any icon represents—category, BBS, title, and so on—in one of two ways:

◆ Choose **V**iew, **D**etails from the menu bar to switch to Details view. In this view, the Type column (see Figure 4.3) shows a description of what each icon represents.

◆ Display the icon's Properties sheet (right-click the icon and then choose **P**roperties from the context menu) and click the General tab, which contains a description of the icon's contents.

**FIGURE 4.3.**

*An MSN category folder, shown in Details view.*

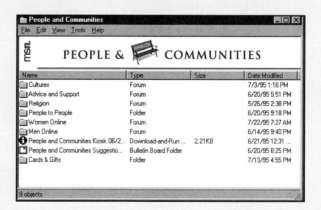

# The "Content Tree"

In an effort to make MSN's organization simpler through metaphor, Microsoft describes MSN's organization as a "content tree." The only problem with the metaphor is that the tree is upside down.

The folders and files on MSN are organized *hierarchically*, just as the folders and files are on your PC. Each folder contains files and other folders; each of the folders within a folder contains still other files and folders, and so on. On MSN, you'll see folders containing other folders, which themselves contain other folders, which then contain forums or still more folders.

You can see the hierarchical organization of the folders and files on your PC by opening Windows 95's Explorer (choose **P**rograms from the Start menu and then choose Windows Explorer). On the left side of your Explorer screen is a list of folders. Folders containing other folders have a plus sign (+) next to them; click these folders to display an indented list of folders within the folder. Some of the folders in the indented list may themselves have plus signs, which means that they contain still more folders. In Explorer, you can click your Windows folder to see how folders reside within a folder (see Figure 4.4).

**FIGURE 4.4.**

*The hierarchical organization of files and folders in Windows 95, displayed through Windows Explorer.*

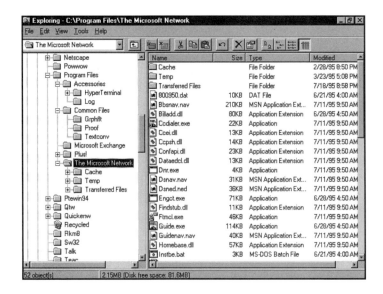

The hierarchical organization of Windows 95 folders can be visualized as an upside-down tree. From a single base, various branches split off; from each of these branches, further branches may split off, and from each of them still more branches may split off. Unfortunately, it's customary to describe the base from which everything begins as the "top" of the tree, even though, in a real tree, the base is at the bottom. As you move out through the levels of branches in the MSN content tree, you're said to be moving "down" the tree, not up it, as you would in a real tree.

Internet newsgroups, available to any MSN user (even those without Internet access), are organized hierarchically on MSN. To access a specific newsgroup, you must navigate your way down through a fairly complex hierarchy, sometimes navigating through four or five newsgroup folders before you reach an actual newsgroup. That's yet another reason why an understanding of hierarchical organization is a must for effective MSN navigation. (For more about Internet newsgroups, see Chapter 5, "Reading and Contributing to Bulletin Boards and Newsgroups.")

As shown in Figure 4.5, the top of the MSN content tree is the MSN home page (also called MSN Central), the starting point for all MSN activities. From the home page, you move down the content tree to all other MSN folders and services.

It's important to remember, in MSN terms, which way is up. The File menu in any open MSN folder contains the choice Up One Level, which, when selected, takes you "up" to the folder containing the one from which you chose the Up item—that is, you move one level closer to MSN Central, the home page.

If, from a spot somewhere out on the MSN tree, you keep choosing Up from every folder, you eventually return to the top, the home page, from which there is no more Up.

# Browsing The Microsoft Network

Once you understand that MSN is organized hierarchically, you know all you need to know to dive in and browse MSN. Sign in to MSN and display the MSN home page, also known as MSN Central (described in Chapter 1, "Signing Up, Signing In, and Signing Out"). Then choose **C**ategories, the general starting point for journeys down the content tree.

The Categories folder (see Figure 4.6) contains all the category folders that lead down the content tree—the main branches of the tree, in effect. (Member Assistance may also lead through a few levels of special-purpose folders, but it's a low shoot, not a main portion of the tree.) Until you develop your own set of Favorite Places shortcuts (described later in this chapter), begin your browsing sessions by clicking **C**ategories and then choosing any of the categories within that folder.

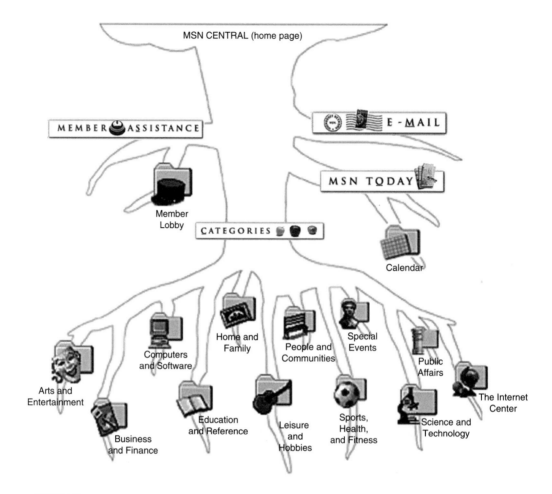

## FIGURE 4.5.

*The Microsoft Network is organized as an upside-down "content tree," whose "top" is MSN Central, the MSN home page. Navigate down the tree from the home page to other MSN folders and services; navigate up the tree to return to the home page.*

**FIGURE 4.6.**

*The contents of the Categories folder.*

# Climbing Down the Content Tree

Except for MSN Today and the small group of special documents and services accessible from Member Assistance, the whole universe of MSN is accessible through the Categories folder.

To help you browse, Microsoft has organized most MSN activities by subject. In Figure 4.6, observe that most category folders have names that describe general topics: Arts and Entertainment, Sports, and so on. Within each of these category folders are other folders that break the topic down into more specific categories or forums pertaining to a specific topic.

For example, when you click the Arts and Entertainment folder, you open a new window like the one in Figure 4.7.

**FIGURE 4.7.**

*The contents of the Arts and Entertainment folder, which was opened from the Categories folder.*

Among the category folders appearing in the Arts folder shown in Figure 4.7 is one for Books and Writing. Double-click that icon to arrive at the screen shown in Figure 4.8.

**FIGURE 4.8.**

*The contents of the Books and Writing folder, which was opened from the Arts and Entertainment folder, which was opened from the Categories folder.*

Among the folders appearing in the in the Books and Writing folder shown in Figure 4.8 is a Reading folder. When you double-click it, you arrive at the Reading forum, shown in Figure 4.9. Note that no further folders appear among the icons in Figure 4.9. Note also that a fancy forum title appears at the top of the window. You have come to the end of this particular branch of the content tree. From here, you can go no further down the tree, but you *can* venture back up the tree to choose another route.

**FIGURE 4.9.**

*The Reading Forum.*

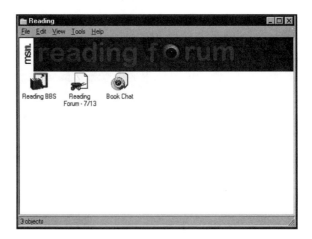

In the Reading forum, icons appear for the following topics:

◆ A BBS for exchanging comments, questions and answers, and files about books.

◆ A document file containing recent news, instructions, and other information from the forum manager. Unlike the information you find in the BBS, what you read here is supplied only by the forum manager and pertains not so much to the topic of the forum as to the use of the forum itself.

◆ A chat room for chatting about books.

You'll almost always find at least these three items—a BBS, a document (often a kiosk), and a chat room—in every forum. In some forums, however, you may find several BBSs, a library BBS, several chat rooms, a number of documents, and more. Every forum is a little different.

## Climbing Up the Content Tree

After navigating down through the content tree, you'll undoubtedly reach a point from which you want to navigate back up the tree to broader subject areas or to explore another branch of the tree.

To exit the current forum or folder and move back up the tree one level, choose **File**, **U**p One Level from the menu bar (see Figure 4.10). You can accomplish the same thing by clicking the Up One Level button on the toolbar (a folder with a crooked up-arrow on it). You arrive at the folder containing the one from which you chose **U**p One Level. You can then branch off in a different direction from that folder by choosing a folder or other icon, or select **File**, **U**p One Level again to move up one more level through the tree, towards the home page.

**FIGURE 4.10.**

*Moving up the content tree.*

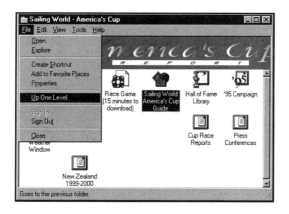

If you choose **U**p One Level enough times, you eventually return to MSN Central, the home page. Of course, if home is your goal, there's an easier way to get there, as described in the next section.

Like any window in Windows 95, MSN can be configured to use either of two browsing options, shown in Figure 4.11. To reach the page shown in Figure 4.11, choose **V**iew, **O**ptions from anywhere in MSN to display the Options dialog box; then click the Folders tab.

**FIGURE 4.11.**
*Changing the browsing option.*

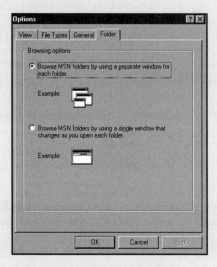

The default choice for MSN is the second option, Browse MSN Folders By Using a Single Window.... When you select this option, every time you open a new window in MSN, it replaces the existing window. No matter how many folders and activities you move through in a session, no more than one MSN window appears on your desktop.

If you change MSN's browsing option to the first choice, Browse MSN Folders By Using a **S**eparate Window..., each time you open a new folder, all previously opened folders remain open in windows behind the current folder. You can navigate up the content tree, jump to any of the open folders, or even go home (to MSN Central) simply by switching windows.

In Windows 95, you switch to any open window in one of four ways:

◆ Click any area of the window you want.

◆ Click the desired window's button in the taskbar.

◆ Press Alt+Esc until the desired window appears.

◆ Press Alt+Tab until the desired window appears.

When all the open windows start to look cluttered, you can straighten them up by right-clicking an empty area of the taskbar and then choosing **C**ascade, Tile **H**orizontally or **C**ascade, Tile **V**ertically.

## Getting Back Home (MSN Central)

To return to MSN Central (the MSN home page) from any folder, forum, or other activity, do one of the following:

◆ Click the MSN Central button (the little house) on any toolbar.

◆ Choose **E**dit, **G**o To, **M**SN Central from any window in MSN.

# Browsing with Windows Explorer

As you probably realize by now, navigating up and down the content tree through folder and menu selections is a great way to explore MSN and visit new and different places. However, this method is a somewhat laborious way to get to a given spot when you already know exactly where you want to go. More importantly, when you browse this way, it's difficult to get a sense of the whole of MSN, to understand where every branch and leaf fits on the content tree.

If you're an experienced Windows 95 user, you recognize that the browsing methods covered so far follow the My Computer model for browsing the contents of your own PC. If you open the My Computer icon on your Windows 95 desktop, you can browse through your PC's contents by opening folder after folder, exactly the same way you've been browsing MSN so far in this chapter.

Windows Explorer allows you to view the organization of your PC's contents—and work with those contents—in a more efficient, comprehensive way than My Computer. Windows Explorer can do the same for The Microsoft Network. Explorer can show you the entire content tree and present you with the information and tools to locate and use any MSN service quickly and conveniently.

To open the Explorer view of MSN, right-click any folder or BBS icon in MSN and choose **E**xplore from the context menu that appears (see Figure 4.12). You can also open Explorer by choosing **F**ile, **E**xplore from any folder or BBS menu bar.

**FIGURE 4.12.**

*Opening Windows Explorer through a context menu.*

Explorer opens, showing the content tree on the left; on the right are the contents of the selected folder or BBS (see Figure 4.13). From here, you can navigate freely among the whole MSN content tree, regardless of your starting point.

For information about using Windows Explorer for advanced MSN techniques, see Chapter 12, "Trimming Time Online."

**FIGURE 4.13.**

*MSN, as seen through Explorer.*

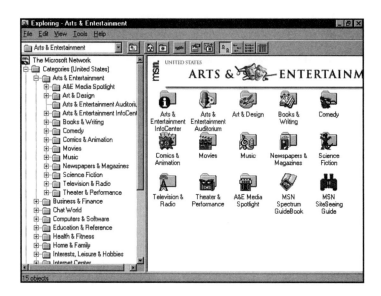

# Making a Beeline for Anything on MSN

Whichever way you choose to browse MSN—clicking through the content tree or locating and opening resources from Explorer—you're still browsing, scouting for services. Once you've identified a resource you want to visit again, wouldn't it be great to be able to jump right to it, without any browsing or multiple navigation steps?

MSN offers two ways to jump straight to anything from anywhere on MSN: Favorite Places and Go.

## Your Favorite Places Folder

When you identify an MSN icon you think you'll use regularly, create a Favorite Places shortcut for it. After you create the shortcut, you can open the icon quickly and easily from anywhere in MSN. Note that a shortcut can be created for any icon in MSN—a folder, a BBS, a chat session, a document, a file, and so on.

To create a shortcut, navigate to the icon you want a shortcut for. Right-click the icon and choose Add to Favorite Places from the icon's context menu, as shown in Figure 4.14. Alternatively, highlight the icon by single-clicking it and then click the Add to Favorite Places button (a combination of a page, a folder, and a plus sign) on the toolbar, or select File, Add to Favorite Places.

The new shortcut is stored in your Favorite Places folder. You can open your Favorite Places folder from MSN Central, but you can also access it from anywhere in MSN by choosing Edit, Go To, Favorite Places.

Once you open your Favorite Places folder, double-click any shortcut to jump to where the shortcut was built to go.

**FIGURE 4.14.**

*Creating a new Favorite Places shortcut.*

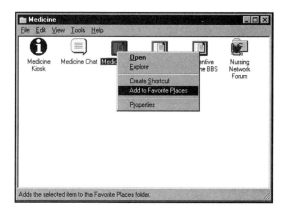

In addition to Favorite Places, you can use MSN shortcuts in other ways. You can insert shortcuts in documents and messages and even put them on your Windows 95 desktop. You learn about other ways to use shortcuts in several chapters in Part III of this book, "Taking Control of MSN."

*Tip*

# Go

Most icons in MSN (but not all) have their own, unique "Go word." An icon's Go word is the word you type in the Go dialog box to jump directly to that icon from anywhere in MSN. Go is a great way to jump quickly to a resource when you don't already have a shortcut for it.

To learn the Go word for an icon, display its Properties sheet by right-clicking the icon and then choosing **P**roperties from the icon's context menu. Click the General tab to see a screen like the one in Figure 4.15. The **G**o word, if there is one, is identified beneath the **N**ame. (You may also find useful Go words for the icons within a category or forum listed in kiosks.)

**FIGURE 4.15.**

*The Properties sheet for the For Kids front page, showing its Go word.*

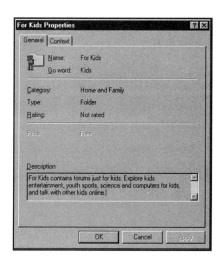

To use Go, follow these steps:

1. From anywhere in MSN, choose **E**dit, **G**o To. A submenu like the one in Figure 4.16 appears.

2. Click **O**ther Location to display the Go To Service dialog box (see Figure 4.17). Type the Go word and press Enter.

**FIGURE 4.16.**
*Displaying the Go submenu.*

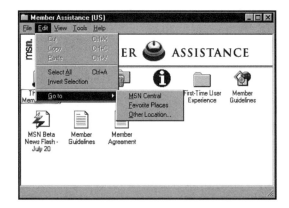

**FIGURE 4.17.**
*Entering a Go word in the Go To Service dialog box.*

When typing a Go word in the Go dialog box, don't worry about capitalization. The Go word Books takes you to the Books and Writing category whether you type **Books**, **books**, **BOOKS**, or **bOOkS**. Appendix A, "Go Word Directory," offers a list of all the Go words you can use to reach the major MSN categories and the top-level folders and forums within them.

# Opening Files

Most of the time in Windows 95, when you double-click a data file (a document, a text file, a picture file, a sound clip, and so on), Windows automatically opens an application capable of displaying or editing that file and then opens the file within the application. Windows can do this because of a File Types registry that associates any file using a given file extension with a particular application. The File Types registry tells Windows which program to run to open a particular type of file.

Many programs update this registry when you install them. For example, Windows 95 opens Microsoft Word documents in WordPad by default. If you install Word for Windows, however, the registry is updated so that double-clicking a Word document opens Word instead of WordPad. You can also modify the File Types registry yourself by choosing **V**iew, **O**ptions from any window and then choosing the File Types tab (see Figure 4.18).

**FIGURE 4.18.**
*Registering file types.*

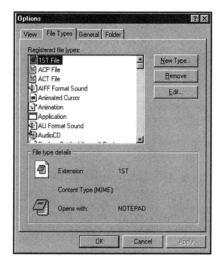

To change the programs MSN uses to open files, you have to change your registry. There are good reasons for doing this: you may have a program on your PC that opens more quickly than the one MSN is using. You learn about changing the File Types registry in Chapter 11, "Advanced Configuration Options."

MSN counts on the File Types registry to tell Windows which program to run to open documents you choose online. Nearly all documents on MSN are in Rich Text Format (RTF). In their Properties sheets and in the Details view in MSN, these documents are described as *Download and Run files* because of what happens when you double-click them: They transfer to your PC and run an application that can display them.

When you double-click a document icon, MSN downloads the file to your PC and instructs Windows to open the file using the program registered for opening RTF files. On a PC with no other word processor installed, RTF documents are opened with WordPad. If you've installed a word processor that can open RTF documents, your registry has probably been updated to open your word processor instead.

When you finish viewing a document, you can close the viewing program and return to your work in MSN. However, if you expect to open other documents during the current session, it's better to minimize the viewing program rather than closing it. That way, when you open another online document, Windows needn't load and open your viewing program all over again.

MSN downloads document files to your PC so that you can read them, but the files are not automatically retained on your PC—they're deleted as soon as you end your MSN session. To save a document on your hard disk so that it is not deleted by MSN, choose **F**ile, **S**ave from the viewing program while you are viewing the document.

## What Now?

By now, you've got your compass and maps all ready to go. You have all the skills and information you need to reach any corner of MSN—and make it back alive. However, you don't yet know how to work the MSN activities you find at the end of every navigation. You know *how* to get somewhere on MSN, but not *what* to do when you arrive.

In the remaining chapters of Part II, you learn how to exchange messages in BBSs and newsgroups, chat in chat rooms, download and upload files, exchange e-mail, and control MSN's multimedia titles. Once you know all that, you're an MSN virtuoso. All that's left is the Internet, covered in Part IV.

# CHAPTER 5

# READING AND CONTRIBUTING TO BULLETIN BOARDS AND NEWSGROUPS

Finding and Opening a BBS

Reading Messages

Writing Messages

Finding and Opening a Newsgroup

What Now?

I remember real bulletin boards. They were made of cork and wood and were punctured with thumbtacks and staples. Nobody much uses bulletin boards anymore. People scribble dry-erase marker messages on plastic whiteboards, or scrawl messages on Post-It notes and stick 'em on the wall. (Pardon the annoying nostalgic ramble… My brain was co-opted by Andy Rooney.)

But in the rugged, pioneering days of online services, the term *bulletin board service* (or *bulletin board system*) was coined to metaphorically describe the public information exchange enabled by online systems. Soon abbreviated to *BBS* (as all things must be, per standing orders from IBM), online bulletin boards enabled their subscribers to post public messages on the system so that any other user could read them. Readers of the BBS posted new messages responding to what they read there, and inevitably, the art of online conversation—carried out through posted messages and replies to those messages—evolved.

*Tip*

In addition to BBSs, there is another way to have a multiuser, topic-centered discussion on MSN: a *chat*. The important difference is that chats are "live" exchanges (like telephone conference calls); BBS and newsgroup conversations are carried out more slowly, through a day-to-day message exchange of posted messages. Using a BBS or newsgroup is more like engaging in an ongoing exchange of e-mail messages, except that the messages are public and the participants many.

For more about chats, see Chapter 6, "Hanging Out in Chat Rooms."

Although BBS traffic originated in a thousand small, local online systems, the concept was quickly refined and offered through the first widely used international online services: GEnie and CompuServe. Because the big services had far too many subscribers to carry on a meaningful conversation on a single BBS, each service offered multiple, separate BBSs, each dedicated to a specific topic. Devotees of the topic at hand—*Star Trek*, anatomy, current affairs, and so on—could exchange news, advice, opinions, and counter-opinions with similarly inclined users from all over the world.

By the early '90s, the main BBS activity on the Internet had been standardized and consolidated into Internet *newsgroups*, topic-centered bulletin boards now accessible not only through the Internet, but also from MSN and other online services (CompuServe, America Online, and Prodigy) through their Internet gateways. (Note that Internet newsgroups do not require an MSN Internet account; they are available to all MSN members.)

For MSN's online bulletin boards, Microsoft borrowed the traditional BBS handle and fronted its BBSs with icons meant to represent tiny bulletin boards but that more accurately resemble little slices of melba toast. (I get hungry every time I see one.) Topic-centered and spread all over MSN, all MSN BBSs work the same way and require the same skills—each simply covers a different topic. You'll discover at least one BBS in each forum, providing a place for news, opinions, questions, and answers—plus attached files containing documents, graphics, or program files related to the forum's topic. (You can easily download attached files from BBSs and use them on your PC.) In addition to the traditional forum BBSs, you can find other BBSs peppered here and there for other types of public message exchanges; for example, in the Member

Support folder (located in the Member Lobby) you can find BBSs for communicating with MSN Customer Service. By handling support questions through a BBS, Microsoft makes the questions and answers visible to everyone so that members can see how other members solved their problems.

Reaching an Internet newsgroup on MSN, in most cases, requires a different navigation path than reaching a BBS. But once you reach a newsgroup, you find that using it is virtually the same as using a BBS. In effect, from the viewpoint of MSN members, Microsoft has transformed every Internet newsgroup into an MSN BBS so that members need learn only one set of message reading/writing skills to use either type of "bulletin board" offered on MSN. Although that approach may help MSN users who are new to the Internet, experienced newsgroup users may find MSN's approach to newsgroups confusing and limiting because it deviates from the approach used in most *newsreaders*, the software used by regular Internet users for working with newsgroups, and is hampered by additional limitations, as described later in this chapter.

In this chapter, you learn how to do the following:

◆ Find BBSs and newsgroups on MSN

◆ Read, post, and reply to messages

◆ Send messages in special ways, such as by e-mail

◆ Save messages in files

◆ Create Favorite Places shortcuts to messages

◆ Undo (or leave in place) Microsoft's censorship of controversial newsgroups

In BBSs and newsgroups, you'll find files attached to messages. These files may contain programs, documents, graphics, or sound or video clips—if it can be put in a computer file, it can be attached to a message. In a BBS message, an attached file is represented by a shortcut icon that appears in the body of the message itself. In a newsgroup, files are not so much attached as they are included in the message itself, in a special code. Although BBSs and newsgroups are similar in most other respects, files are handled very differently on the two bulletin boards.

You can copy files from BBSs and newsgroups to your PC and use them there. You can also insert files from your PC into the BBS messages you post (you cannot do the same in newsgroups, however).

To learn about copying files to and from MSN, see Chapter 7, "Downloading and Uploading Files."

# Finding and Opening a BBS

Anytime you see the BBS icon (the melba toast), a BBS lurks beneath it. In most cases, you get to a BBS by navigating down the content tree to a forum that interests you and then opening the BBS in that forum by double-clicking its icon. When you double-click any BBS icon, a list of current messages appears, from which you can select any message to read (see "Reading Messages," later in this chapter).

Note, however, that not all BBSs serve the same function. Although the primary use of a BBS is to provide topical information exchange within a forum, many BBSs can be found outside of forums. For example, you may find a BBS or two in a category folder. These BBSs provide a place for a more broad-based discussion than do BBSs in forums. You will often see a Suggestion Box like the one shown in Figure 5.1. The Suggestion Box BBS within a category folder is for an exchange of suggestions about the operation or content of the category as a whole, including all forums within it.

**FIGURE 5.1.**

*The Sports category folder features a BBS Suggestion Box for comments on the category and its forums.*

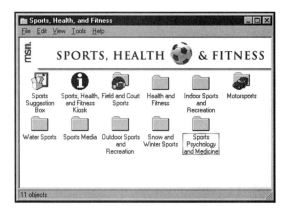

*Tip*

Although all BBSs use the BBS icon, not all icons are labeled *BBS*. As a rule, the traditional BBSs in forums include *BBS* in their icon description; special-purpose BBSs, such as Suggestion Boxes, leave out the *BBS* term. However, you use all BBSs in the same way, regardless of how they're labeled.

You can also find multiple BBS icons in other places, such as Microsoft's forum (see Figure 5.2).

**FIGURE 5.2.**

*At this writing, the Microsoft forum has two BBSs.*

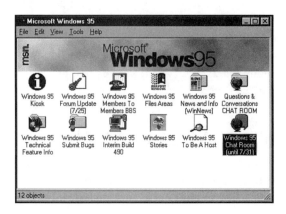

BBSs can pop up anywhere to handle potential questions and problems. For example, at this writing, a BBS appears in the Newsgroups folder (see Figure 5.3) to answer questions and solve problems related to the Full Access EForm, the form you must fill out to undo Microsoft's newsgroup censorship (see "Undoing Newsgroup Censorship," later in this chapter).

**FIGURE 5.3.**

*The Newsgroups folder includes a BBS for discussing problems related to Microsoft's newsgroup censorship approach.*

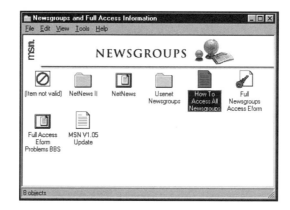

Once you locate a BBS you know you'll want to visit often, add it to your Favorite Places folder. Select the BBS icon by single-clicking it, then choose **F**ile, Add to Favorite Places; alternatively, click the Add to Favorite Places button on the toolbar.

The next time you want to navigate to the BBS, open your Favorite Places folder by choosing Favorite Places from the home page or by choosing **E**dit, **G**o To, **F**avorite Places from any menu in MSN. Then double-click the BBS shortcut icon you created.

*Tip*

Finally, many forums—particularly those covering especially popular or wide-ranging topics—include more than one BBS. For example, the Indoor Sports forum, shown in Figure 5.4, features several BBSs, each with a different purpose.

**FIGURE 5.4.**

*The Indoor Sports forum features multiple BBSs.*

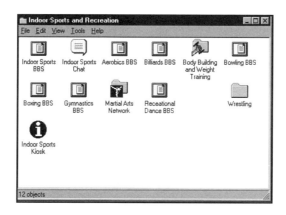

You can learn more about a particular BBS in two ways:

◆ Open and read the kiosk that appears in the same folder or forum as the BBS. The kiosk may contain descriptive information about the BBS and any special instructions.

◆ Right-click the BBS icon and then choose **P**roperties. (You can also highlight the icon with a single click and then choose **F**ile, **P**roperties.) A Properties sheet like the one shown in Figure 5.5 appears. Click the General tab to see a description of the BBS.

**FIGURE 5.5.**

*The Properties sheet for the Recreational Dance BBS.*

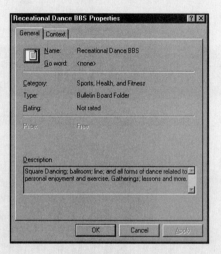

# Reading Messages

Once you navigate to a bulletin board (as described earlier in this chapter), double-click the BBS icon to display a list of current messages, sometimes also called *articles*. The list appears in a window called the *BBS window*, which features a scrollbar for scrolling through the list if it is longer than the window (which it usually is).

*Note*

Although navigating to an Internet newsgroup is different from navigating to a BBS, using either type of bulletin board is essentially the same once you arrive (except for working with files, which is covered in the next chapter). This section about reading messages applies to both BBSs and newsgroups; any exceptions are noted as they come up.

To learn more about newsgroups and how to navigate to them, see "Finding and Opening a Newsgroup," later in this chapter.

In Figure 5.6, note that the first two listings are folders. These contain other messages, grouped together and set off from the rest by the forum manager. (You can open a folder to see the list of messages it contains and read any message.) The rest of the listings are messages. Those preceded by a plus sign (+) are messages for which there are *replies*, other messages that are replies to the first message. Those preceded by page icons have no replies.

**FIGURE 5.6.**

*The BBS window: a list of current messages in the Work-At-Home Dads BBS.*

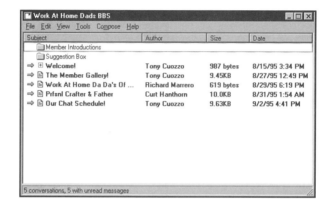

The column headings above the items in the list indicate what the parts of each message listing represent. Each listing begins with the *subject*, a descriptive line written by the message's author to note what the message is about. Subject lines are important because they help other MSN members decide whether to read a particular message. The remaining columns of each message listing indicate the author's full name (not member ID), the size (in bytes) of the message, and the date the message was created and sent to the BBS.

> The size indicated for a *BBS message* includes only the text within the message body; it does not include the size of any attached file.
>
> The size indicated for a *newsgroup message* includes the entire contents of the message, files and all.

## Organizing Messages in Views

Using the choices on the BBS window's **V**iew menu or the toolbar, you can change the way the list of BBS articles is presented in the BBS window. The view you choose is important because, when viewing a message, you can use menu options or toolbar buttons to jump directly to the "next" message or the "previous" message in the list. Exactly which message qualifies as "next" or "previous" is determined by how you organized the list.

## Conversation View

Conversation view (shown in Figure 5.7) groups replies to a message underneath the original message (the parent message), in much the same way that Windows Explorer groups files and folders within a folder underneath the folder to which they belong. The replies themselves are listed in ascending chronological order (oldest down to newest). In this way, Conversation view arranges messages so that you can follow the actual flow of the conversation; the parent message appears first, directly followed by all replies to it. A parent message has a plus sign (+) in front of it. Clicking that message displays its replies beneath it, which are indented to show that they're replies.

**FIGURE 5.7.**

*A list of current messages in the Antiques BBS, in Conversation view, with all conversations expanded.*

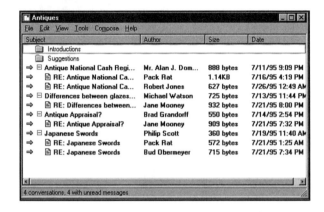

In a BBS, a reply may have a different subject line than its parent message. In a newsgroup, a reply always has the same subject line as the message to which it is a reply. The letters RE: (regarding) are added to the subject line in BBS replies.

In a conversation, there are naturally a number of replies to the original message. But there may also be replies to the replies. These are also grouped together in Conversation view. Each new level of replies is indented under its parent, which may itself be a reply to a parent of its own. All replies in the same level are arranged in ascending chronological order (oldest to newest).

When you first view a list of messages in Conversation view, the messages appear as a simple list like the one in Figure 5.6 (shown earlier). The parent messages have plus signs next to them, but the replies themselves do not appear in the original list. This is done to make it easier for you to skip past conversations that don't interest you. To see replies, you must "expand" the conversation by clicking a parent, or by choosing **V**iew, **E**xpand All Conversations. When you expand the Conversation view, you see all messages and their replies, organized into conversations (as shown in Figure 5.7).

On the Internet, the grouping of a message and its replies—called a *conversation* on MSN—is more commonly known as a *thread*, a term that derives from the sense of following the thread of a conversation. Threads are presented in the same way conversations are. Only the terminology differs.

## List View

By default, List view lists all messages in ascending chronological order; or rather, the order in which they were sent to the bulletin board. Because this order rarely matches the order in which replies to messages are posted, there's no gathering together of messages with their replies (a reply to a message may show up in the list 50 messages away from the original message; the next reply may be another 50 messages away). However, using the **A**rrange Messages item on the **V**iew menu, you can sort the list alphabetically by author or subject. List view can be useful when you want to review all the messages by a given author or about a certain subject.

Figure 5.8 shows the same current message list as Figure 5.7, sorted by date in List view.

**FIGURE 5.8.**

*The list of messages in the Antiques BBS, in List view and sorted by date.*

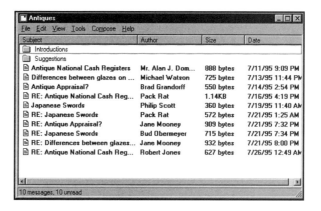

Messages are frequently updated in MSN BBSs. If you've been working in a particular BBS for an hour or so, you may want to click the Refresh button on the toolbar (or choose **V**iew, **R**efresh) to retrieve the most current message list. The new list may contain new messages received since you opened the BBS.

Because newsgroups are updated much less often than BBSs (newsgroups are typically updated once a day), refreshing newsgroup listings is unnecessary.

## File View

File view displays only those messages that have files attached to them; this view is useful when you're file-hunting and don't want to slog through messages that don't contain files. Messages with attached files are indicated by a paperclip icon in the BBS window.

MSN *libraries* (see Chapter 7, "Downloading and Uploading Files") are BBSs configured to use File view only. Using the **A**rrange Messages item on the **V**iew menu, you can sort the list alphabetically by author or subject. Figure 5.9 shows the Political Reference Library in File view.

**FIGURE 5.9.**

*A list of messages with attached files, shown in File view.*

| Political Reference File Library | | | |
|---|---|---|---|
| File Edit View Tools Compose Help | | | |
| Subject | Author | Size | Date |
| JPG-President Bill Clinton | Bill Safsel | 1.84KB | 7/19. |
| JPG-Member of Congress Seal | Bill Safsel | 1.83KB | 7/19. |
| JPG-Bob Dole | Bill Safsel | 1.81KB | 7/19. |
| JPG-Newt Gingrich | Bill Safsel | 1.83KB | 7/19. |
| JPG-US Senate | Bill Safsel | 1.82KB | 7/19. |
| The US Constitution | Bill Safsel | 1.86KB | 7/24. |
| The Declaration Of Independence | Bill Safsel | 1.99KB | 7/24. |
| The Gettysburg Address | Bill Safsel | 1.94KB | 7/24. |
| The GOP "Contract With Amer... | Bill Safsel | 2.14KB | 7/24. |
| Martin Luther King Jr.'s "I Hav... | Bill Safsel | 1.95KB | 7/24. |
| The Emancipation Proclamation | Bill Safsel | 2.86KB | 7/24. |
| Flat Tax Plan...Armey/Shelby | Bill Safsel | 1.90KB | 7/24. |
| What is the Libertarian Party? | Bill Safsel | 1.93KB | 7/24. |
| Phone/Fax #'s of the US memb... | Bill Safsel | 2.00KB | 7/24. |
| 23 messages, 23 unread | | | |

> **Note**
>
> In newsgroups, files are not attached as they are in BBSs; files are inserted into the message as text. As a result, File view does not recognize the "attached" files in newsgroup messages. If you display a newsgroup message list in File view, it always appears to be an empty list, even though messages in the group may indeed contain files.

## Reading a Message

Regardless of what view you're in, when you see a message that interests you, you open it by double-clicking it. A window like the one in Figure 5.10 appears, showing the message. If the message is longer than the window, a scroll bar appears so that you can scroll through the complete message.

**FIGURE 5.10.**

*A BBS message opened and ready to read.*

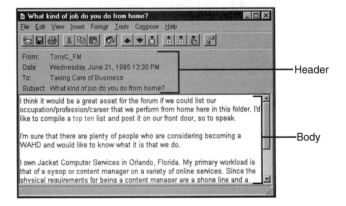

In Figure 5.10, observe the lines below the toolbar. This information makes up the *header* of the message; the actual message text below the header is known as the message *body*. The header always tells you who wrote the message, when, and what the message is about. (E-mail messages also use headers for the same purpose.)

In the header, you'll find this information:

- ◆ From: (the member ID of the author of the message)
- ◆ Date: (the date and time the message was sent to MSN)
- ◆ To: (the name of the BBS to which the message was sent)
- ◆ Subject: (the subject of the message, as entered by the author)

When you finish reading a message, you can do any of the following:

- ◆ Close it and return to the message list by choosing **F**ile, **C**lose.
- ◆ Move directly to another message by choosing **V**iew from the menu bar and then selecting one of the navigation choices offered there (see Figure 5.11).

**FIGURE 5.11.**

*Navigation choices (beginning with Previous Message) available on the View menu while reading a message.*

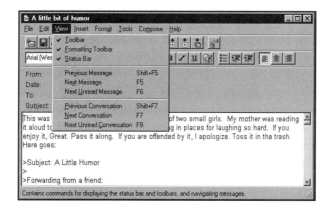

- ◆ Reply to or forward the message, as described later in this chapter.
- ◆ Print the message on your local Windows printer by choosing **F**ile, **P**rint.
- ◆ Save the message in a file on your PC by choosing **F**ile, **S**ave. By default, messages are saved in Rich Text Format (RTF), which preserves the fonts, colors, and other formatting in messages. However, you can choose **F**ile, Save **A**s and save the file as a normal text (TXT) file.

> If you see a file icon within the BBS message, you can select the icon and choose **F**ile, **S**ave to download the file to your PC. If the file icon is *not* selected and you choose **F**ile, **S**ave, you simply save the message itself in an RTF file on your PC.
>
> See Chapter 7, "Downloading and Uploading Files."

When you finish with a message and return to the message list, notice that the entry for the message you've just read looks different from the rest: it appears in normal type, while all other messages appear in **bold** type (see Figure 5.12). This is MSN's way of showing you which messages you've read.

**FIGURE 5.12.**

*Messages in bold are those you haven't read yet.*

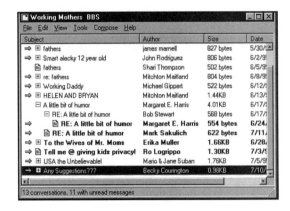

You can mark messages as "read" without actually reading them and you can unmark messages you have already read. In this way, you can make messages you want to be sure to read later easier to see because they'll stand out in bold type. From the message list, select a message or a group of messages and then choose **T**ools.

The **T**ools menu lists a number of ways to treat the messages you've selected. You can mark them as **R**ead or as **U**nread. You can also use two Mark Conversation choices to mark all the messages in a conversation as read or unread, even if the conversation is not expanded in the message list.

Finally, you can select **M**ark All Messages As Read. Use this option when nothing in the present list interests you but you want to be able to instantly see which messages are new the next time you open the BBS. If you mark all messages as read and exit the BBS, the next time you return, only the new messages appear in **bold** type.

## Learning More About the Author

No, not me…the author of a BBS message. While viewing a message, choose **T**ools, Member Properties. A Member Properties sheet like the one in Figure 5.13 appears.

You can edit and expand the member properties information for your own ID. See Chapter 11, "Advanced Configuration Options."

You cannot display member information for the authors of messages in newsgroups. These messages come from the Internet, which doesn't maintain a database of information about its users, as MSN does about its members.

**FIGURE 5.13.**

*Learning more about a member through Member Properties.*

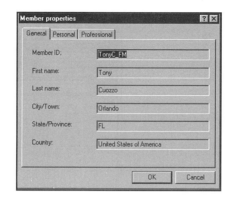

# Writing Messages

Writing messages and posting them on bulletin boards is a complete no-brainer—it's even easier than e-mail. The real power of writing messages, however, is learning to exploit the options, especially the Replay and Forward features built into MSN.

> Although navigating to an Internet newsgroup is different from navigating to a BBS, using either type of bulletin board is essentially the same once you arrive (except for working with files, which is covered in the next chapter). This section about writing messages applies to both BBSs and newsgroups; any exceptions are noted as they come up.
>
> To learn more about newsgroups and how to navigate to them, see "Finding and Opening a Newsgroup," later in this chapter.

***Before you begin, however*...** If you have not yet read Chapter 3, "Member Rules and Etiquette," do so before posting any messages on a BBS or, more importantly, on a newsgroup. Nowhere is observing the courtesies of netiquette and the rules of MSN more important.

## Composing and Posting a New Message

To compose a new message (not a reply) and post it in a BBS, follow these steps:

1. Open the BBS so that the BBS window appears.
2. Choose Compose, New Message. A window like the one in Figure 5.14 appears. Observe that the To: line of the header has been filled in with the BBS name. The rest of the header is filled in automatically, behind the scenes, except for the Subject line.
3. Click in the Subject text box and type a subject. Be brief, but describe your subject carefully and accurately so that other members can judge by your subject line whether to read your message.

**FIGURE 5.14.**

*Composing a new message to send to a BBS.*

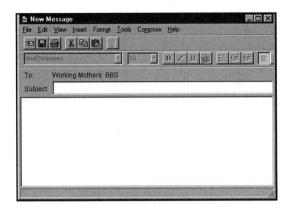

4. Click the message area and type your message. Using the choices in the Format menu, you can format your message with different fonts, character styles, and colors, just as you can with any word processing document in Windows. You can also choose View, Formatting Toolbar to display a formatting toolbar from which you can choose fonts and colors and create bulleted lists within your message. Note that formatting is just for fun—it's not required.

5. When you finish composing your message, choose File, Post Message; alternatively, click the Post Message button on the toolbar. Within a few minutes, your message appears in the BBS. (Unless you exit the BBS and return, you must choose View, Refresh to see your message and any other messages posted since you opened the BBS.)

---

### Newsgroup Exceptions

You cannot apply fonts or colors to newsgroup messages. Newsgroups allow only plain text.

Although your BBS message will be available to all MSN users within a few minutes after you send it, a newsgroup message typically takes from several hours to a day or more to appear in the message lists of Internet and MSN users because of the way newsgroups are stored and distributed. (See "About Newsgroups," later in this chapter.)

---

## Posting a Reply

To compose and send a reply to a message you're reading, follow these steps:

1. Open the message to which you want to reply.

2. Choose Compose, Reply to BBS. A window like the one in Figure 5.15 appears. Observe that the header has been filled in automatically with the name of the current BBS and the subject of the message to which you're replying.

Note that in a BBS reply, you can change the subject line from that of the parent message, although there's no reason to do so. Your reply will still appear as a reply in Conversation view. However, newsgroups depend on subject lines to indicate replies. Do not change the subject line of a reply to a newsgroup message.

**FIGURE 5.15.**

*Composing a reply.*

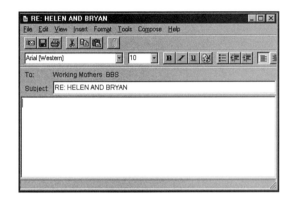

3. Click the message area and type your message. Using the choices in the Form**a**t menu, you can format your message with different fonts, character styles, and colors, just as you can with any word processing document in Windows. (See "Composing and Posting a New Message," earlier in this chapter, for additional information on formatting and newsgroup exceptions.)

4. When you finish composing your message, choose **F**ile, Post Message; alternatively, click the Post Message button on the toolbar.

> By default, the entire text of the message to which you're replying appears as a quote at the bottom of your reply. A dashed line separates your new text from the quote. Although including the quote may help the reader understand what you're replying to, a quote may not always be necessary. When replying, edit the quote (or cut it altogether) as necessary, to avoid sending messages that are unnecessarily lengthy.

*Tip*

## Replying and Forwarding by Mail

The normal way to reply to a message is to reply back to the BBS or newsgroup. After all, these are supposed to be public exchanges and others may be interested in your response.

However, there are circumstances under which your reply should be sent as an e-mail message directly to the member who wrote the message you're responding to, instead of to the BBS where everyone can read it.

For example, sometimes a message mentions or alludes to something that veers off the topic of the BBS. Per netiquette (see Chapter 3, "Member Rules and Etiquette"), your messages should stick to the subject the BBS or newsgroup is designed to address. If you post a reply to an off-topic comment, you contribute to the deviation from the subject. But if you really want to make a comment to the author of the original message, send your reply with e-mail so that only he or she can see it.

There may be many other reasons for posting a replay with e-mail, and only you can decide when it's appropriate. Just ask yourself before replying, "Will what I'm about to say be interesting to others in the BBS, and is its subject and content appropriate for the BBS?" If the answer is no, reply with e-mail.

To reply with e-mail to a message you've read on a BBS or newsgroup, follow these steps:

1. Open the message to which you want to reply.

2. Choose Co**m**pose, **R**eply by E-Mail. Exchange (your MSN e-mail program) opens and displays a New Message window preaddressed to the person who wrote the message you opened in the BBS.

3. Click in the message area and type your message.

4. When finished, choose **F**ile, **S**end; alternatively, click the Send button on the toolbar. You can then close Exchange to return to the BBS.

> When sending a reply by e-mail, you have at your disposal all the special sending and formatting features of Exchange. For example, you can automatically send copies of the message to anyone you choose. To learn more about sending e-mail with Exchange, see Chapter 8, "Composing, Sending, and Receiving E-Mail."
>
> You can make newsgroup replies by e-mail exactly as you make BBS replies by e-mail. Exchange addresses the reply to be sent by Internet mail.

If you see a message you think may be of interest to someone who does not frequent the BBS, or even to someone who is not a user of MSN, you can *forward* a copy of the message to that person, through e-mail.

To forward a BBS message by e-mail, follow these steps:

1. Open the message you want to forward.

2. Choose Co**m**pose, **F**orward by E-Mail. Exchange opens and displays a New Message window (see Figure 5.16). The complete text of the BBS message appears in the message area, including its header. Above the message appears a dashed line—the *reply separator*.

3. Click the To: area of the header and type the recipient's MSN member ID or other e-mail address, such as an Internet address or CompuServe ID (see Chapter 8 for more information on these types of IDs). If you want, you can click the message area above the reply separator and add your own comments to the message.

4. When finished, choose **F**ile, **S**end; alternatively, click the Send button on the toolbar. You can then close Exchange to return to the BBS.

**FIGURE 5.16.**

*Forwarding a message from a BBS.*

Reply separator

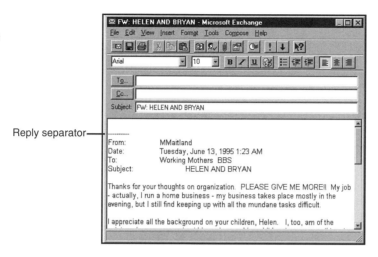

## BBSs Versus Newsgroups: Comparing Apples and . . . Bigger Apples

Other than the steps required to navigate there, the ways files are handled, and a few options, what's the difference between an MSN BBS and an Internet newsgroup? Apart from underlying technical differences, the practical differences are the size and scope of the audience and the speed of posting.

All the messages you read on MSN BBSs are written by other MSN members (except for a very small number that may be sent to the BBS with e-mail from somewhere beyond MSN). When you post a message on a BBS, only other MSN members can read it. Perhaps more importantly, because all MSN members use Windows 95, you can rest assured that almost any file attached to an MSN message can be used within Windows 95. What you read in Internet newsgroups, on the other hand, comes from millions of Internet users, plus subscribers to CompuServe, America Online, Prodigy, and of course, MSN. Anything you post on a newsgroup may be read by anyone in this huge group as well. And because there are all types of computers on the Internet, not all attached files are made for Windows. Although many files you find through newsgroups are Windows compatible, many are for Macintosh, UNIX systems, and other types of computers and operating systems.

Your postings to an MSN BBS can be read by other MSN users within minutes. A posting to a newsgroup, on the other hand, may not show up on Internet users' screens for hours, or even a day, because of the way newsgroups are distributed (see "About Newsgroups," later in this chapter).

The bottom line: BBSs are a quicker, more dynamic way to interact with a relatively small audience. Newsgroups are a slower way to reach a potentially larger audience. Of course, even though there are 25 million Internet users, there's no way to know how many of them actually frequent any given newsgroup. Despite MSN's smaller membership, it's actually possible for a given BBS to be more richly populated than a newsgroup covering the same topic.

# Finding and Opening a Newsgroup

Usenet
Newsgroups

As MSN evolves, Microsoft is attempting to make Internet newsgroups more accessible by hooking them into forums. You may notice Usenet Newsgroups icons in various forums and categories. Clicking these icons opens a folder containing the newsgroups related to the forum topic. As MSN matures, you'll see more of these folders. The folders are handy because, at this writing, there are over 13,000 Internet newsgroups. In the absence of a forum folder, finding the newsgroup you want may demand a little exploring.

However, for now, the principle way to navigate to most newsgroups is through MSN's Internet Central:

1. Choose **C**ategories from MSN Central (the home page).

2. Choose The Internet Center icon.

3. Choose Internet Newsgroups. A screen like the one in Figure 5.17 appears.

**FIGURE 5.17.**

*The Newsgroups folder.*

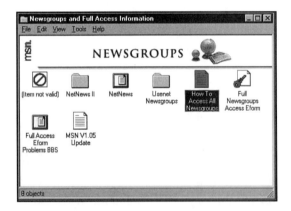

From the Newsgroups folder, getting to a particular newsgroup demands a little more digging. Before beginning to work with newsgroups, however, you can benefit from learning where newsgroups come from and how they're organized. This background can help you navigate among the newsgroups and learn how Microsoft has divided and censored the groups.

*Note*

> By default, your MSN account does not provide access to all Internet newsgroups. It provides access only to what are called *Usenet newsgroups* (described later) and leaves out many others in a not-altogether-successful attempt to screen out "adult" content.
>
> You can easily request access to all newsgroups, regardless of content. See "Getting Access to All Newsgroups," later in this chapter.

# About Newsgroups

From the user's perspective, all newsgroups and their messages appear to be in the same place: on MSN. In a way, that's true; the newsgroups you access from MSN are all stored on Microsoft's *news server*. But they don't start out there.

The original databases containing all current articles for a given newsgroup are stored on different news servers all across the Internet. On a regular schedule, each news server receives copies of the group databases stored on the other news servers. That's why a message posted to a newsgroup may take a day or more to show up in the article list; it doesn't go on the list until the servers have been updated. Most servers are updated daily; some are updated more frequently.

# Usenet Newsgroups

Most newsgroups are known as *Usenet newsgroups* because they are distributed through the services of a software program originally developed to enable newsgroups. The group of computers that uses the software is known as *Usenet*, but despite the implications of the name, they are linked only in that they use Usenet software for creating, managing, and distributing newsgroups. The Usenet computers have no other affiliations and do not fall under any kind of centralized management or administration. The one exception is that, through mutual agreement, all the news servers observe a set procedure for the establishment of new newsgroups. All proposals for new Usenet newsgroups must be made through a procedure than involves announcing the proposal and getting feedback from the network community. Only if a proposed new group is determined to be necessary or popular is it allowed to join the Usenet team.

Usenet newsgroups are named using a hierarchical system of categories and subcategories. (MSN uses this naming system to create a hierarchical system of folders for newsgroups on MSN, as you discover later in this chapter.) A newsgroup name is made up of a series of words or abbreviations separated by periods. The first word indicates the broad subject area of the newsgroup; each word to the right more specifically defines the topic. Consider the names of these groups:

```
misc.forsale.computers.pc-specific.motherboards
misc.forsale.computers.pc-specific.portables
misc.forsale.computers.pc-specific.software
misc.forsale.computers.pc-specific.systems
```

All these groups fall under the same main category (`misc`) and three levels of subcategories (`forsale.computers.pc-specific`); each defines its specific topic in the final word.

All Usenet groups fall under one of the major headings. Sometimes, these headings indicate the subject area; other times, they indicate the type or style of information to be found there. Note that, for some topics, two groups have been set up; one is for the posting of news, the other is for discussion.

The following list shows newsgroup names you can find in each of several categories.

### comp—Computer Subjects (Both Recreational and Professional)

```
comp.edu.languages.natural
comp.internet.net-happenings
comp.sys.ibm.pc.games.marketplace
```

### sci—Science Topics

```
sci.aeronautics
sci.agriculture
sci.anthropology
sci.bio.ecology
sci.cryonics
sci.life-extension
sci.med.nutrition
sci.space.shuttle
```

### soc—Social Issues: Culture, Politics, Environmentalism, and So On

```
soc.couples.intercultural
soc.culture.caribbean
soc.feminism
soc.genealogy.surnames
soc.history.war.vietnam
soc.religion.christian.youth-work
soc.singles
```

### talk—Groups on Any Subject but Especially Devoted to Online Debate

```
talk.abortion
talk.environment
talk.philosophy.humanism
talk.politics.guns
talk.religion.buddhism
```

### news—Information About Usenet and Newsgroups in General

```
news.announce.newgroups
news.answers
news.groups.questions
```

### rec—Recreational Subjects: Hobbies, Sports, the Arts, and So On

```
rec.antiques.marketplace
rec.arts.books.tolkien
rec.arts.comics.marvel.universe
rec.arts.erotica
rec.arts.startrek.fandom
rec.boats.racing
rec.food.recipes
rec.games.backgammon
rec.music.beatles
rec.sport.boxing
```

### misc—Subjects Difficult to Categorize (*Potpourri* as They Say on Jeopardy)

```
misc.activism.progressive
misc.education.home-school.misc
misc.fitness
misc.invest.funds
misc.jobs.offered
misc.kids.pregnancy
```

# Non-Usenet Newsgroups

Usenet's software accepts feeds from other sources—as long as the other sources observe the basic Usenet conventions for message headers and formatting. Once those feeds are accepted by a Usenet server, their articles can be distributed along with all other newsgroups.

Many of these newsgroups are groups whose potential audience is so small, so trivial, or so weird that the group would probably not survive the formal Usenet acceptance procedure. For example, there are newsgroups designed primarily for local interest; I can access several groups about things to do here in New Jersey. You may find a huge listing of groups, all beginning with *ba*, about happenings and issues in greater San Francisco (a.k.a. the *Bay Area*).

Other non-Usenet (but certainly not trivial or weird) groups you can find cover events and issues in other countries. There are entire sets of groups devoted to Israel, Germany, China, and other countries. These newsgroups are frequented by residents of those countries, citizens of those countries residing elsewhere (and wanting news from home), and others interested in foreign lands. Note that many of the articles in these groups are written in the official language of the country covered.

Some such groups are distributed only locally; others find their way into the whole Usenet distribution chain. (The people who create a non-Usenet newsgroup can control the breadth of its distribution, from locally to regionally to universally.) Even when these groups are distributed everywhere, the system administrators of specific news servers can "filter out" specified newsgroups so that local-interest newsgroups are often not seen beyond their local borders.

The other major type of non-Usenet newsgroup is the alternative newsgroup, designed to support more off-the-wall topics and a loose, freeform style of exchange. The names of many of these groups begin with `alt`, though some `alt` newsgroups are legitimate Usenet groups.

Actually, although they have a reputation for raunchiness, the many `alt` groups are interesting, thoughtful groups that cover books, politics, and much more. The `alt` groups are also the principle carriers of porno writing and binary sex photos, nutball conspiracy theories, and hate-mongering. Virtually all `alt` groups are *unmoderated* (see the sidebar, "Newsgroups in Moderation," later in this section), which means that anything goes. Here are some examples of `alt` newsgroups:

```
alt.acme.exploding.newsgroup
alt.airline.class.action.lawsuit
alt.books.beatgeneration
alt.fan.bob-dole
alt.fan.fabio
alt.food.waffle-house
alt.internet.talk.bizarre
alt.personals.aliens
alt.pets.hamsters
alt.sports.baseball.bos-redsox
alt.support.househusbands
alt.tv.twilight.zone
```

Plumbing the depths of alternative newsgroups has its risks; it is not for the squeamish or easily offended. But if you're selective about which `alt` newsgroups you check out, you may find a gem among the rubble.

---

### Newsgroups in Moderation

*Moderated* newsgroups are patrolled by one or more *moderators*, gatekeepers of sorts who read every article before it is posted, judging the message on its relevance, appropriateness, newsworthiness, or other criteria. Articles deemed inappropriate (or, in some groups, profane) are not posted. Moderated groups are relatively uncommon; even so, most of the moderating is not zealous—a message often has to be *way* off base to be rejected. However, most of the moderated groups are part of Usenet; nearly all non-Usenet newsgroups are unmoderated. That's part of Microsoft's reasoning in censoring non-Usenet groups.

Moderated groups have advantages and disadvantages. Visit an `alt` group someday—virtually all of which are unmoderated—and you'll see what I mean. Mixed in with the useful information and reasonable questions and answers are discussions veering completely out of the jurisdiction of the group. These tangents usually begin as appropriate discussions, but when folks get sidetracked, there's no one to put a stop to it. In unmoderated newsgroups, you find much more repetition, petty squabbling, profanity, shouting, and flaming than you do in moderated newsgroups.

On the other hand, some newsgroup users fear that moderation is equivalent to censorship. It's unlikely that any moderator sets out to be a censor, but when cast as a judge, anyone can subconsciously base choices on personal bias. Advocates of unmoderated newsgroups believe it's better to post everything and let users decide whether or not it's appropriate.

Newsgroup users themselves can effectively keep the discussion on track by bringing peer pressure to bear—in the form of instructive and corrective messages—on users who post inappropriate material. Of course, that approach favors mob rule over censorship, which does not necessarily result in a more open flow of information (the biases of the moderator are simply replaced by the biases of the majority).

Such issues remind us that the Internet is, in effect, a global community. The culture will evolve, but there will always be controversy and disagreement—which is just as it should be.

---

## How MSN Organizes Newsgroups

In the Newsgroups folder (shown in Figure 5.17, earlier in this chapter), MSN offers two icons that both contain the same newsgroups, organized differently.

*Note*

> The description of newsgroup organization in this section pertains to MSN accounts that have not yet requested access to all newsgroups (as explained later in this chapter). This section describes the way newsgroups appear to you the first time you visit them.

The folder icon labeled Usenet Newsgroups contains a small group of bulletin board icons, as shown in Figure 5.18.

The BBS icon labeled NetNews organizes newsgroups in a long, scrolling list of folders (see Figure 5.19). Each folder's name is the first portion of a newsgroup name; open the folder, and you'll find more folders for newsgroups whose names begin with those characters.

Usenet
Newsgroups

NetNews

**FIGURE 5.18.**

*Newsgroups in the Usenet folder.*

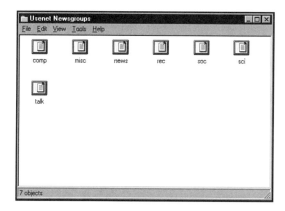

**FIGURE 5.19.**

*Newsgroups in the NetNews folder.*

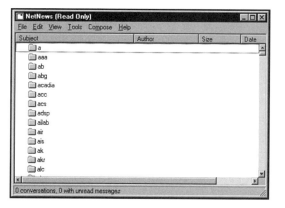

# Getting Access to All Newsgroups

Microsoft's approach to censoring newsgroups is hardly effective. What's censored is all non-Usenet newsgroups (including all the `alt` newsgroups) plus those newsgroups fed into the newsgroup system from another network, the Bitnet (`bit`) groups. The apparent philosophy underlying the censorship is that Usenet newsgroups, having had to qualify for Usenet, can be expected to be generally populated with serious, proper conversation. In addition, many Usenet groups are moderated (although most aren't). In contrast, most of the so-called "adult" activity is in the `alt` groups, none of which are moderated. The other censored newsgroups—including regional and international newsgroups—feature extremely variable levels of content and taste.

Lacking an effective mechanism for locking out newsgroups on a newsgroup-by-newsgroup—or even message-by-message—basis, Microsoft has opted to offer everyone access to the safest overall group of groups (Usenet) and deny access to all other groups. The problem with this approach is twofold:

◆ There's really little to prevent "adult" content from being posted in Usenet newsgroups. It's less common there, but it does appear.

◆ The overwhelming majority of the content of the censored newsgroups is harmless. Sure, there are groups like `alt.sex` or `alt.pictures.erotica`. But censored along with these are `alt` groups covering sports, music, literature, and a host of other valuable, wholesome topics; there are also non-Usenet groups like those in Bionet, a set of groups dedicated to the study of biology.

Whether you want access to all newsgroups is up to you. If you want access to all newsgroups, follow this procedure:

1. In the Newsgroups folder (shown earlier in Figure 5.17), double-click the Full Newsgroups Access EForm icon. After a few moments, you see a screen like the one in Figure 5.20.

2. Select the checkbox next to **I** Am Over the Age of 18 and Agree with the Following. Then click Send.

**FIGURE 5.20.**

*Requesting access to all newsgroups.*

*Tip*

Note that the dialog box shown in Figure 5.20 has a second tab: Remove Access. If you decide later that you don't want full newsgroup access, you can use that tab to reapply MSN's newsgroup censorship.

Within 24 hours, you'll receive an e-mail message confirming that your full newsgroup access has been approved. When you next navigate to the Newsgroup folder, you'll see the screen shown in Figure 5.21 (compare this screen to the one in Figure 5.17).

**FIGURE 5.21.**

*The Newsgroups folder in an account with full access.*

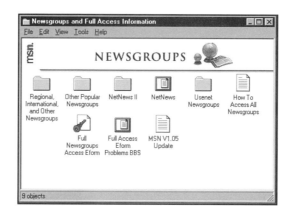

In the Newsgroups folder, two new icons appear: One containing regional and international groups, and the other containing Other Popular Newsgroups, including the `alt` groups.

The contents of the Usenet folder remain the same, but the NetNews folder now includes all the newsgroups also found separately under the Regional, Other, and Usenet icons. These other newsgroup icons serve as your starting point when you have an idea of the type of newsgroup you want; the NetNews icon serves as your master list to everything you have access to.

# What Now?

BBSs and newsgroups both contain files you can download from MSN to your PC. These files can contain programs, pictures, books, video clips, and much, much more. In Chapter 7, you learn how to reach out and grab 'em. You also learn how to send your own files to MSN so that others can download them.

But first, it's time for a conversation. In Chapter 6, you learn all about Chat, MSN's facility for live, group conferencing.

CHAPTER

6

# HANGING OUT IN CHAT ROOMS

Finding and Entering a Chat Room

Understanding How Chats Are Run

Participating in a Chat

Advanced Chatting

Learning More About Chat

What Now?

What's Chat? Chat is *now*. Chat is *interactive*. Chat is *live*.

On MSN, a *chat* is like a telephone conference call except that the participants type their statements instead of speaking them. A group of two or more MSN members discuss a given topic, through typed messages, in *real-time*—as each participant enters his or her comments, questions, or answers, they appear on the screens of everyone participating in the chat in a scrolling screen full of statements, more or less following the flow of the conversation. In the scrolling list of statements, called the *chat history*, Chat tags each participant's statements with his or her member ID so that everyone can tell who's talking. Figure 6.1 shows what a Chat session looks like.

**FIGURE 6.1.**

*An active Chat session (in this case, a live tarot card reading in the New Age Chat Room).*

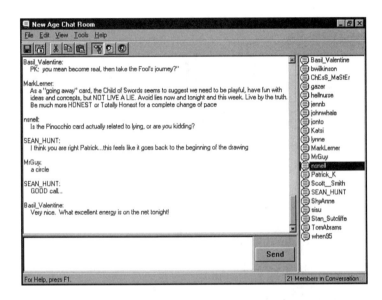

If you're an experienced Internet user, you may notice that using Chat is nearly identical to using a good Windows-based Internet Relay Chat (IRC) client for an IRC session on the Internet. Note, however, that Chat is not IRC—these Chat sessions are exclusive to MSN; only MSN members can watch or participate.

If you have an MSN Internet account, you can participate not only in chats, but also in IRC sessions, which are like chats but are populated by participants from all over the Internet. To learn more about IRC, see Chapter 19, "Advanced Internet Techniques."

Chats are underway all the time on MSN, mainly in the many topic-centered forums, each of which may have several different chat rooms. A *chat room* is a way of imagining the space within which a particular chat takes place. Each chat icon on MSN can be seen as a doorway to a single chat room. In forums, each chat room is dedicated to a particular topic; only conversation related to that topic is permitted there. However, some chat rooms are deliberately set up as free-for-alls and the topic of discussion is wide ranging and ever changing. There are also scheduled, special-event chats featuring important (and sometimes nearly famous) guests.

The chat rooms in forums are open 24 hours a day. You can drop in any time to see who's chatting and join in—although it's not uncommon to enter a room and find yourself alone. A better bet are the regularly scheduled chats and special-event chats. You can learn about both by checking out MSN Today and the Calendar of Events.

You'll find that joining and participating in a chat is simple to master and fun. But by learning a few special skills, you can make your Chat session even more fun and more productive.

In this chapter, you learn the following:

◆ How to find chat rooms

◆ How to join in a chat

◆ How to contribute your own comments, questions, and answers to the chat

◆ How to save a chat history in a file

◆ How to chat only with selected members in the room

# Finding and Entering a Chat Room

As with bulletin boards, the most common way to find a chat is to navigate to a category or forum covering a topic that interests you. Whether they're labeled Chat or not, chats can always be identified by their icon: a "word bubble" like the ones that hold cartoon characters' quips in the funny papers. (Except for *Doonesbury*, which sometimes forgoes bubbles for a simple line connecting a character to the words. This cartooning *faux pas* is why many papers put *Doonesbury* on the editorial page.)

Each day, you can usually find at least one Chat session listed as a special event on the MSN Today page (see Figure 6.2). Regularly scheduled chats can be found in the Calendar of Events (see Figure 6.3). Don't forget that all times shown are Pacific Time; to display times for other time zones, single-click the time shown. Chats listed in MSN Today (and in the Calendar of Events) do not show their chat icons, but clicking on the graphic that describes the chat takes you there.

*Tip*

Once you find a chat room you're interested in, display its Properties sheet to learn more about it. Right-click the chat room's icon and then choose **P**roperties from the context menu.

You can enter any chat announced in MSN Today or the Calendar of Events by double-clicking the chat room's name, which appears in cyan (pale blue) in the announcement. Of course, don't bother entering the room until the scheduled time for the chat approaches.

**FIGURE 6.2.**

*MSN Today always announces a special chat or two (notice the link to a chat about the Beijing Women's Conference and another about MS Publisher) and has a link to the Calendar of Events.*

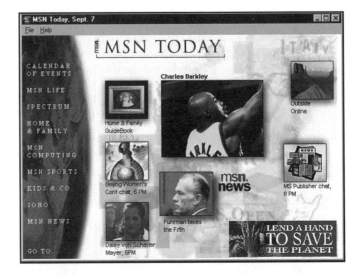

**FIGURE 6.3.**

*The Calendar of Events lists regularly scheduled chats of general interest.*

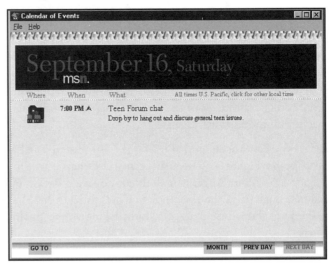

To enter a chat room, click its icon. Your MSN software takes a few moments to load the Chat program (a message appears, begging your patience during loading). After loading, the Chat window appears, as shown in Figure 6.4.

**FIGURE 6.4.**
*A Chat window.*

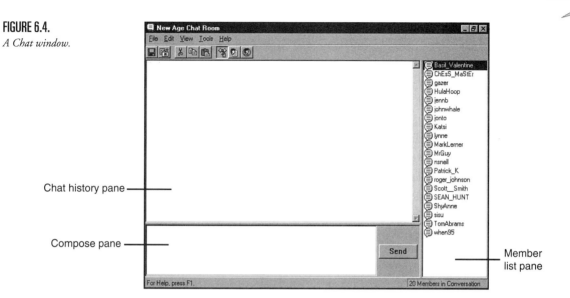

Chat history pane ——————

Compose pane ——————

Member list pane

The Chat window has three *panes*:

◆ The largest pane is the *chat history* pane. That's where all the statements made by everyone in the chat, including you, appear. Each statement in the chat history is labeled with the member ID of the person who made it. The chat history doesn't begin to appear until after you arrive, so when you first enter a chat room, the pane is empty like the one in Figure 6.4. (If, after 30 seconds or so, the chat history pane remains empty, it's *very* quiet in there.) Using the scrollbar in the chat history pane, you can scroll backward through the chat history, up to the first statement made after you entered the room (you cannot see statements made before you entered). In addition to statements made by others in the chat, you may see messages from MSN in the chat history pane, telling you when anyone enters or leaves the chat. Such messages from MSN always appear <u>underlined</u>.

◆ The long pane on the bottom is the *compose* pane, in which you type any statements you want to contribute to the chat.

◆ The tall pane on the right is the *member list* pane. When you enter a chat room, you see your member ID listed in the member list pane, along with the member IDs of others currently in the chat room. Note that your member ID appears in everyone else's member list pane, as well.

---

If, when arriving in a chat room, you see only your own member ID in the member list pane, you're alone. You can hang around and see whether somebody else shows up or exit to try a different room or try the same chat room later.

From the moment you enter the room until you leave, everything contributed to the chat by any of the participants, including you, appears in the chat history pane. You won't see anything in the window the moment you enter; it takes a few moments for the first statements made after you joined to reach your screen. When they appear, they statements appear like those shown earlier in Figure 6.1.

*Note*

> The order of statements appearing in the chat history generally follows the order in which statements were issued. You know how it goes:
>
> 1. Member A asks question 1.
>
> 2. Member B answers question 1.
>
> 3. Member A makes statement 1.
>
> 4. Member C argues with statement 1.
>
> 5. Member B agrees with member C's argument with statement 1.
>
> 6. Member A explains that member C misunderstood statement 1.
>
> However, some people type more slowly than others, some type longer or shorter statements than others, and the statements of some members may take longer to reach MSN's server than others'. That means the statements can get jumbled a little:
>
> 1. Member A asks question 1.
>
> 2. Member A makes statement 1.
>
> 3. Member C argues with statement 1.
>
> 4. Member B answers question 1.
>
> 5. Member A explains that member C misunderstood statement 1.
>
> 6. Member B agrees with member C's argument with statement 1.
>
> Although the chat history can be a little confusing at first, after a little practice, most people adjust to the flow and have no trouble following the conversation. However, you can make discussions easier to track by suppressing the display of all statements by members not involved in the part of the conversation you're following. See "Chatting Only with Certain Members," later in this chapter.

# Understanding How Chats Are Run

You'll encounter three types of people in a chat room. You can tell which type each is by the icon that appears next to the member ID in the member list pane:

◆ **The Host.** The host moderates the chat, making sure that participants behave civilly and courteously and stick to the subject (see Chapter 3, "Member Rules and Etiquette"). The host, and only the host, has the power to designate any other member in the chat as a *participant* or *spectator*. There can be more than one host.

Also, particularly in forum chat rooms, there may be no host—just participants. When there is a host in a forum chat room, it is usually the forum manager.

◆ **Participants.** Participants can view all activity in the chat history pane and they can contribute to the conversation by entering their statements in the compose pane. In general, when you enter a chat in a forum, you are automatically designated as a participant.

◆ **Spectators.** A spectator can view the chat history but can't make any contributions to the chat. In special-event chats, typically attended by dozens of members, it isn't practical to let everybody participate. The host designates most attendees as spectators, sometimes changing them to participants near a chat's end to open the floor to questions.

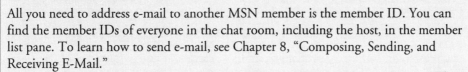

> Got a question or comment about a chat session? Send e-mail to the host. Want to communicate outside the chat room with somebody you met in the chat room? Send that member e-mail.
>
> All you need to address e-mail to another MSN member is the member ID. You can find the member IDs of everyone in the chat room, including the host, in the member list pane. To learn how to send e-mail, see Chapter 8, "Composing, Sending, and Receiving E-Mail."

# Participating in a Chat

Before opening your mouth—uh, fingers—in a chat, it's important to do three things:

1. Review MSN's Member Guidelines and netiquette (see Chapter 3, "Member Rules and Etiquette") so that you can chat efficiently and politely.

2. Read any kiosk file that appears in the same folder as the chat icon you intend to open. The kiosk may contain guidelines, pointers, or other instructions for the chat(s) in the forum and may report the times for the forum's scheduled chats.

3. Enter the chat room and lurk. To *lurk* is to listen, to see what participants are expressing and how they're expressing it, and to see how other participants and the host are reacting to the statements. True, conformity is the hobgoblin of small minds. But much of the time, when you first attend a chat, you are entering a room other participants have already attended many times; they have already set a tone for that room. As a newbie, you're expected to make mistakes; after gaining some experience, you may try to steer the room in a direction of your choosing. But at first, you're a guest (sort of). It's polite to observe local customs until you've established yourself.

**Tip**

In addition to observing basic netiquette and lurking, try to be on time for scheduled chats by entering the chat room a few minutes before the scheduled starting time. Folks who join chats late invariably ask questions that have already been asked and answered, annoying other participants. Obviously, such redundant questions are unavoidable in nonscheduled chats, so members are patient about them.

While lurking, pay attention to these items:

◆ **The Topic.** What is the topic? What is the general level of the discussion—does it appear to be a discussion among experts, novices, or members with a range of expertise?

◆ **Length of Statements.** Does the apparent "rhythm" of the discussion seem to lean toward volleys of brief questions and comments or to longer, more considered statements?

◆ **Style.** What is the tone of the conversation? Scholarly? Humorous? Friendly? Wild? Are statements heavily Net-literate (packed with shorthand abbreviations and smileys) or not?

**Tip**

If you see a lot of Internet shorthand or smileys used in a chat (see Chapter 3, "Member Rules and Etiquette"), you don't have to use them yourself. Everyone will understand you fine without them. Anyway, it's risky to attempt a conversation in a language you're not fluent in.

On the other hand, if you don't see shorthand or smileys used, avoid using them yourself. MSN hosts a broad range of experience levels; if you don't see Net-speak used, the members in the chat may not understand you if you use it.

Once you've properly indoctrinated yourself in online etiquette and the particular style and substance of the chat at hand, you can contribute to the conversation (provided that you have participant privileges).

To contribute to a chat, follow these steps:

1. Click in the compose pane.
2. Type your statement (as shown in Figure 6.5).
3. Press Enter or click Send.

**FIGURE 6.5.**

*Contributing to a chat. I'm asking about a comment the tarot reader, MarkLerner, made earlier, implying that the Pinocchio card represented lying.*

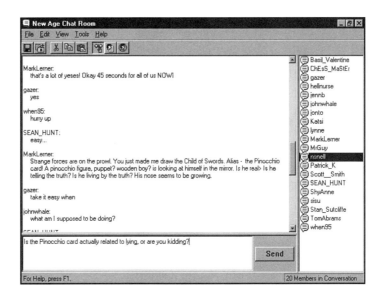

To see as much of the chat history as possible (which may help you follow the conversation more easily), you can do one of the following:

◆ Maximize the chat window.

◆ Choose **T**ools, **O**ptions and make sure that the Insert Blank Line Between Messages checkbox is not selected.

◆ Cut down the size of the compose pane to make more room for the chat history pane. Move the pointer to the horizontal line between the chat history and the compose panes until the pointer becomes a two-headed arrow. Then click and hold the left mouse button, drag the line down until the compose pane is only one-line high, and release the mouse button.

When typing statements in the compose pane, you have a few editing options. As a rule, your contributions to chats are short, simple statements, so you may not use either of these options. But for what it's worth...

◆ To start a new line in the compose pane, press Ctrl+Enter.

◆ To indent a line, press Ctrl+Tab.

You can cut and paste text from any Windows application into the compose pane (when you know in advance what you plan to say, I suppose). Select the text in the other application, choose **E**dit, **C**opy, switch to the Chat window, click in the compose pane, and choose **E**dit, **P**aste (or click the Paste button in the toolbar).

# Advanced Chatting

Chatting is a pretty straightforward activity, once you know your way around the Chat window. There are, however, a few techniques some members find handy for controlling the chat and the way it is presented, or for working with the chat history.

## Saving and Clearing the Chat History

At any time during a Chat session, you can save the current chat history in a file. Choose **F**ile, **S**ave History or click the Save button on the toolbar. By default, chat histories are saved as RTF files, like all other MSN documents, to preserve the exact formatting used in the chat. However, you can save the chat history as a plain text (TXT) file by choosing **F**ile, Save History **A**s and saving the history as a text file. After you save the file, you can open it later (even offline) in WordPad or your word processor to print it.

You can also clear the chat history. When you clear the chat history, the complete contents of the chat history pane (including any material you can scroll to) is deleted. To clear the chat history, choose **E**dit, Clear **H**istory.

By default, the chat history is cleared automatically when it reaches its limit. If you want to be sure you have the chance to save the chat history before it is cleared, use the Save Chat History options (see "Chat Options," later in this chapter).

## Hiding Spectators

By default, everyone in the chat room appears in the member list pane. If you prefer to see only the host(s) and participants and do not want to include spectators in the list, choose **V**iew, **S**how Spectators to add a checkmark next to the **S**how Spectators item; alternatively, click the Show Spectators button. To see spectators in the member list pane, choose **V**iew, **S**how Spectators again to remove the checkmark.

## Chat Options

The Chat program offers several options for controlling the way Chat sessions behave. Once you set these options, they remain in effect for all future chats (even in different chat rooms) until you change them again.

From the Chat window, choose **T**ools, **O**ptions. A dialog box like the one in Figure 6.6 appears.

The first two checkboxes in Figure 6.6 control whether MSN notifies you when members enter or exit the chat room. The notifications appear in the chat history pane as underlined statements.

- ◆ **J**oin the Chat: Check this box to instruct Chat to report the name of any member who joins the chat.
- ◆ **L**eave the Chat: Check this box to instruct Chat to report the name of any member who leaves the chat.

**FIGURE 6.6.**

*The Chat Options dialog box.*

The third checkbox in Figure 6.6 automatically saves the chat history to a file before you exit a chat and before the chat history is cleared (both automatically and when you specifically clear the chat history pane).

The final checkbox, which is selected by default, automatically inserts a blank line between each message appearing in the chat history. Leave this checkbox selected to make individual messages easier to see. Deselect it to see more messages on the screen at once.

## Chatting Only with Certain Members

In heavily populated chat rooms in which tens of members may be chatting, there's a natural tendency for smaller groups to form; two, three, or four members carry on their own little dialog within the chat, more or less ignoring the rest of the traffic in the chat history. When such "subchats" emerge, you can actually prevent the display of any statements from selected users, to restrict the chat history to statements from members with which you are conversing. Preventing the display of statements from selected members is called *ignoring* them. Note that you cannot ignore yourself or the host(s).

To ignore selected members, follow these steps:

1. In the member list pane, select the members you want to ignore.
2. Choose **V**iew, **I**gnore Members. In the dialog box that appears, choose Ignore Messages From **S**elected Members and click OK. Chat puts a line through the names of members you are ignoring (see Figure 6.7).

You can also ignore a member by right-clicking that member's ID in the member list pane to display the context menu and then clicking Ignore.

If you want to chat with only a few members in a conversation that has many members, there's a quick way to ignore everyone whose comments you don't want to see:

1. In the member list pane, select the members you *do* want to chat with (see Figure 6.8).
2. Choose **T**ools, **S**elect Members, **I**nvert Selection to select everyone except those you selected in step 1.
3. Choose **V**iew, **I**gnore Members. In the dialog box that appears, choose Ignore Messages From **S**elected Members and click OK. Chat puts a line through the names of members you are ignoring (see Figure 6.9).

**FIGURE 6.7.**

*Ignoring members. (By the way, note in the chat history pane that the tarot reader has answered my query about the Pinocchio card, which I asked in Figure 6.5.)*

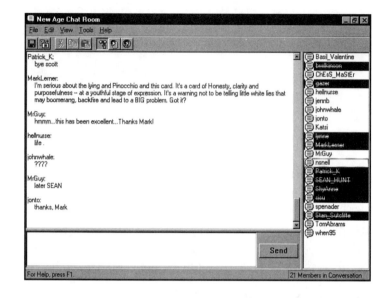

**FIGURE 6.8.**

*Selecting members with whom you want to chat.*

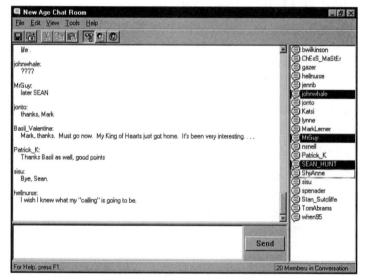

**FIGURE 6.9.**

*The selection in Figure 6.8 was inverted and those members ignored, so that only statements made by the few, not-crossed-out members appear.*

## Learning More About a Participant

To learn more about any member in the chat room, display the member's Properties sheet (see Figure 6.10) in any of three ways:

◆ Double-click the member's ID in the member list pane.

◆ Select the member's ID and choose **V**iew, **M**ember Properties.

◆ Right-click the member ID in the member list pane and choose Properties from the context menu.

**FIGURE 6.10.**

*The Member Properties sheet for a participant in the current chat.*

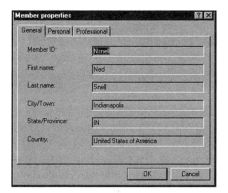

# Learning More About Chat

MSN now features a category called Chat World, dedicated to free-form, nontopical chatter. The category also includes a variety of helpful resources, including BBSes for exchanging chatting tips and even a Lobby Photo and Audio Gallery (see Figure 6.11) from which you can download pictures and voice clips from friends you meet in Chat World.

**FIGURE 6.11.**

*The Chat World folder.*

# What Now?

In this chapter, you've discovered live chats, one of the most stimulating ways to spend your time online. You'll find chats fun, informative, and rewarding. You may also find them addictive—something that's raised concerns on the Internet. There have been legitimate cases of addiction to Internet chatting (called IRC). But hopefully, Microsoft's connect-time charges will provide a built-in antidote to chat addiction.

Next on your tour of MSN services is a return to familiar territory: BBSes and newsgroups, which you discovered in Chapter 5. In Chapter 7, however, you won't be reading and writing messages. Instead, you'll be uploading and downloading files containing programs, pictures, movie clips, and more.

# CHAPTER 7

# DOWNLOADING AND UPLOADING FILES

First Files to Download

Downloading a File from a BBS or Library

Uploading a File to a BBS

Downloading a File from a Newsgroup

What Now?

I've given it a great deal of thought, and I've concluded that there's a conspiracy afoot. It's not *that* conspiracy—the plot wherein Microsoft and Disney are engaged in a secret contest to see who can take over the world first, after which the two will merge into the world's sole corporation, government, and cultural bureau, "MickeySoft" (or "GatesLand," depending on who wins). No, it's the conspiracy between hard disk manufacturers and online services.

You see, from the very beginning, online services have been a source of files—shareware and freeware applications, utilities, pictures, video clips, sound clips, books, and much more. By the time it came online, MSN already boasted an impressive repository of files for downloading, most of them uploaded to MSN by the thousands of prelaunch MSN "beta testers" all over the world. Add to MSN's own stores the hundreds of thousands of files available through the Internet, and you have a library from which you can extract almost anything that can be stored in a computer file.

That library has caused computer users to load up their hard disks with more megabytes of crap than they could ever possibly purchase. In the absence of online services, freeware, and shareware, most of us could get by on 200M hard drives. But because files can easily be copied—*downloaded*—from cyberspace to a user's computer, folks buy hard drives that can store the complete database of the Pentagon. I figure a system of kickbacks between the disk makers and the online services (and maybe the Pentagon) is behind it all. I'm ready to blow the whistle, but Morley Safer won't return my calls.

*Note*

> In MSN's Help, you may see file downloading referred to as *copying files from MSN.* That's an accurate description of what happens: a copy of a file stored on an MSN server is transmitted to your PC and stored there. The universally accepted term for this procedure is the less friendly *downloading*, and that term is used in this chapter because it is better understood by those who have any experience with other online systems. But in your MSN and Internet travels, you'll see *downloading* variously described as *copying from* or *transferring from*; *uploading* is described as *copying to* or *transferring to.*

Your role isn't to expose the conspiracy. Your role is to exploit and enjoy its fruits until the truth comes out and somebody pulls the plug. In the meantime, you can easily download from MSN's bulletin board systems (BBSs) and libraries files that serve both practical purposes (programs, utilities, drivers) and impractical purposes (games, movie clips, sounds, photos). And if you can't find what you want in MSN BBSs and libraries, you may find it in an Internet newsgroup, from which you can also download files (although with much more difficulty than downloading files from MSN).

In this chapter, you learn the following:

◆ About programs you may want to download because they are required for working with certain types of files you may download from MSN

◆ How to download files from libraries, BBSs, and Internet newsgroups

◆ How to upload files to BBSs

◆ How to perform the required post-download processing of files acquired from newsgroups

◆ How to customize the way MSN handles file transfers

In addition to the methods described in this chapter, there are several other ways to pick up files through MSN. On the Internet, files are available through the World Wide Web, Gopher, and FTP (see Part IV of this book, "Navigating the Internet Through MSN").

You can search for files available through MSN using any of these methods:

◆ To find any file on an MSN BBS or library, use MSN's Find utility (see Chapter 10, "Finding Anything on MSN").

◆ To find downloadable Internet files, use Web searching techniques (see Chapter 16, "Browsing the World Wide Web") or a tool called Archie (see Chapter 18, "Downloading Files with FTP").

# First Files to Download

The store of files available in MSN BBSs and libraries is not nearly as extensive as what is available on the Internet or even on CompuServe. But that's deceptive. Nearly all the programs and files available on MSN are for Windows; much of what's available elsewhere is not. That makes finding and downloading the best and latest freeware, shareware, drivers, and other Windows files easier on MSN than anywhere else (see Figure 7.1, later in this chapter).

Check out the CD-ROM that accompanies this book to find some of the files described in this section; other files on the disc may serve the same purpose as those described here. Note that, although the programs on the disc are useful, you'll ultimately benefit from knowing how to download your own set of MSN support files like the ones on the disc so that you can obtain updated versions when they debut or pick up another program you may prefer to one on the disc.

Any DOS or Windows application or utility program (whether for Windows 3.1, Windows NT, or Windows 95) found online should run on any MSN-capable PC, as long as the PC has sufficient memory to run the given program.

The one type of Windows program Windows 95 is not pre-equipped to run is a program written in Microsoft's Visual Basic programming language. Visual Basic programs are not common on MSN or elsewhere, but when you run across one, you'll need Visual Basic's runtime extensions, a set of files whose names begin with *VBRUN*, to run them. The extensions are available many places on MSN; you can find them by using MSN's Find utility to search on the word VBRUN* (see Chapter 10, "Finding Anything on MSN").

However, Windows 95 does ***not*** come pre-equipped to do the following:

◆ Display all the types of picture files available online

◆ Play all the types of multimedia files (sound, video, and animation) found online

◆ Decompress files stored in compressed format

◆ Decode files found in newsgroups, which, unlike files found on MSN BBSs, require special decoding steps before they can be used

The next several pages describe programs you can download to round out your system's capabilities. With these programs and Windows 95's built-in capabilities, you'll be equipped to decompress, display, and play just about everything on MSN—and nearly every Windows-compatible file on the Internet to boot.

All the programs described are currently available on MSN—most in more than one place on MSN. Unfortunately, over time, files move around, so this book cannot give you definitive directions to their locations. Instead, I suggest you use MSN's Find utility (see Chapter 10, "Finding Anything on MSN"), and enter the program's name as your search term. This simple technique quickly reveals every BBS and library from which a given program can be downloaded. Alternatively, you can search for descriptions (as described in Chapter 10) using the file type to be played (for example, MPEG) as your search term.

You can also browse for these programs or for alternatives to them. A good place to start program hunting is the MSN Shareware Forum, shown in Figure 7.1. You can reach this special forum by using the Go word SharewareForum (choose **E**dit, **G**o To, **O**ther Location and then enter **SharewareForum**).

*Tip*

You can manually open files in any of the programs about to be described by choosing File, **O**pen from the program's menu bar or by dragging a file icon and dropping it on the program's icon. However, for the most flexible use of these programs, associate each program with a specific file type in theWindows File Types registry. When a program is registered to a given file type, the following are possible:

◆ Double-clicking a file icon of that type automatically opens the program and the file within it.

◆ MSN's download and open capability can automatically open the program to run a file you have just downloaded (see "Downloading a File from a BBS or Library," later in this chapter).

Often, when you run an automated Install or Setup routine for a program, the routine automatically updates the File Types registry. However, if you install a program and the registry isn't automatically updated, you must register the program manually. To learn how to register file types and programs, see Chapter 11, "Advanced Configuration Options."

**FIGURE 7.1.**
*The MSN Shareware Forum screen.*

## Viewers and Players

If you're interested in downloading multimedia files containing pictures, video, and sound clips, you need programs to play those files on your PC—the MSN client software has no built-in play or display capabilities for such files.

### Audio

Most audio files on MSN are of these types:

AU—basic audio
WAV—Windows sound clip
MID—MIDI music sequence

Windows 95's Media Player applet plays WAV and MID files, so you're all set for those. However, you need a player for AU files, which are found on MSN and are the most common type of sound file on the Internet. Download and install a program called Wham, in the file WHAM133.ZIP.

### Video

Most video files on MSN are of these types:

AVI—Video for Windows
MOV—QuickTime movie clip
MPEG—MPEG movie clip

Windows 95's Media Player applet plays AVI files, but you also need players for MOV and MPEG files. Surprisingly, there are at least as many MOV and MPEG files on MSN as there are AVI files, so players are essential if you want to be able to download and play any video file found on MSN.

To play MPEG movies, you need an MPEG player, such as the freeware player MPEGplay. To play QuickTime files, you need Apple's QuickTime for Windows extensions and a player application that uses QuickTime for Windows to play MOV files. QuickTime for Windows includes a basic player. You can also use a freeware player called Enjoy, shown in Figure 7.2.

**FIGURE 7.2.**

*A QuickTime movie (a short publicity trailer for Disney's* Pocahontas*) playing in Enjoy.*

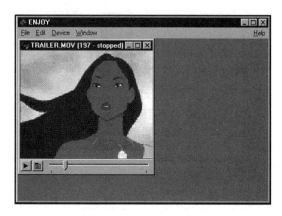

*Note*

Windows 95's Media Player can be configured with QuickTime extensions so that it can play QuickTime (MOV) video files. But because Media Player can be unreliable playing downloaded QuickTime files, a third-party player remains the best option.

*Tip*

Although Windows 95 and MSN require only 4M of RAM on your PC, playing MOV or MPEG files, regardless of the player you use, typically requires a minimum of 8M. Also, MOV and MPEG files generally look better when played in 16-bit "high-color" (16,000+ colors) mode. Because MSN may perform better in 256-color mode, it's a good idea to play video files offline, switching first to high-color mode by using Windows 95's Display Properties settings.

## Pictures

Most graphics files on MSN are of these types:

    PCX—Publisher's Paintbrush bitmap
    BMP—Windows bitmap file
    JPG—JPEG high-resolution image
    GIF—GIF high-resolution image

Windows 95's Paint applet opens PCX and BMP files, but you need a viewer for JPG and GIF files. A freeware application called Lview can display both.

Microsoft's Internet Explorer browsing software for the World Wide Web (see Chapter 16, "Browsing the World Wide Web") automatically displays GIF and JPG images and plays AU audio files without the need for external viewers or players. In fact, when you install Explorer, the Windows File Types registry is automatically updated so that, when you open a GIF, JPG, or AU file, Explorer opens automatically to display/play it—online or off.

However, Explorer is a sizable application that demands a great deal of memory and may open rather slowly. Even if you have Explorer, you may find it more convenient to pick up viewers for GIF, JPG, and AU files because these viewers open and close more quickly and do not drag overall system performance to the extent that Explorer can.

## Compression/Decompression

A *compressed file* is one that has been processed by a compression program to make it smaller—so that it can be uploaded or downloaded more quickly and so that it takes up less disk space. Compressed programs must be restored to their original, full-size state—*decompressed*—before they can be used.

Although there are many different compression/decompression programs out there, the online world (including the Internet, MSN, and other online services) has embraced a shareware program called PKZIP. You can recognize files that have been compressed by PKZIP because they use the extension ZIP. A ZIP file may contain a single compressed file or a group of files, compressed and stored together in a ZIP *archive*. Nearly all compressed files on MSN and on the Internet are ZIP files. (Some compressed files are stored in *self-extracting* archives with EXE extensions. When you double-click the file icon for a self-extracting archive, the file decompresses itself automatically without the need for a decompression program.)

To decompress ZIP files and separate the files in a ZIP archive, you need a program called PKUNZIP (or another program, called WinZip, which is included on the CD-ROM that accompanies this book). If PKUNZIP is installed on your PC is and registered in the File Types registry as described in Chapter 11, "Advanced Configuration Options," MSN can automatically run PKUNZIP or WinZip to decompress files the moment you download them. (If you plan to upload large files, you may want to compress them first using PKZIP to save uploading time.)

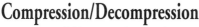

The examples used later in this chapter to explain file downloading show how to download the self-extracting PKZIP archive, PKZ204g.EXE. This archive contains the decompression program PKUNZIP.EXE (for decompressing files after downloading them), the compression program PKZIP.EXE (for compressing files before uploading them), and associated README and instructional text files.

## Decoding Newsgroup Files

As you learn later in this chapter, downloading a file from a newsgroup is an entirely different procedure from downloading a BBS or library file. On newsgroups, *binary* files—programs, pictures, and multimedia files—are *encoded*, translated from binary form into text so that they can travel the newsgroup network (which supports text only). Before you can use these files, you must decode them back into their original binary form. Large files are not only encoded, they are also broken into a series of several separate messages. These must be recombined into a single file and then decoded.

Newsreader client programs for accessing Internet newsgroups can automatically decode files, but because MSN does not permit the use of newsreader software, you must acquire your own decoding program. A good choice is a freeware decoder called WinCode. The examples shown later in this chapter for decoding newsgroup files show how to use WinCode.

# Downloading a File from a BBS or Library

On MSN, files available for downloading appear as icons within messages posted in BBSs and libraries (libraries are simply read-only BBSs designated for the distribution of files rather than for discussion). When a message contains a file or files, a paperclip icon appears next to the file's entry in the BBS message list. When you open such a message, an icon representing the file appears in the message body (see Figure 7.3). A description of the file and any special instructions or requirements for using it may also appear in the message body, above or below the file icon.

To learn how to navigate to, open, and read BBS and library messages, see Chapter 5, "Reading and Contributing to Bulletin Boards and Newsgroups."

To learn how to locate a specific file anywhere on MSN, see Chapter 10, "Finding Anything on MSN."

**FIGURE 7.3.**

*A file icon in a BBS message.*

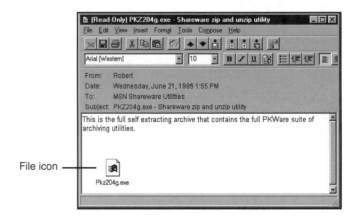

File icon

# Basic Downloading

To download the file whose icon appears in a message, follow these steps:

1. Double-click the file icon. A Properties dialog box like the one in Figure 7.4 appears. The Properties dialog box shows how long the file will take to transfer to your PC and the charge for this file, if any. (Charges shown apply only to any special charges associated with a file, not to the connect-time charges that accrue as the file is downloading.)

**FIGURE 7.4.**

*The Properties dialog box for an attached file.*

When you begin to download a file that carries an additional charge (beyond regular connect-time charges), MSN displays a note reporting the charge and giving you a chance to cancel the download and avoid the charge.

You can configure MSN so that this message appears only when a charge exceeds a certain dollar amount. See Chapter 2, "Maintaining Your MSN Account."

2. To download the file, click **D**ownload File. A File Transfer Status window like the one in Figure 7.5 appears. The File Transfer Status window lists all files currently downloading (or waiting to be downloaded) and shows the Destination path on your PC where each file will be stored. The status line at the bottom of the window reports the status of the file being transferred, telling you the percentage of the file that has been downloaded so far and reporting the download time remaining. When the entire file has been downloaded, you can close the window. To abort a download, close the window during the download.

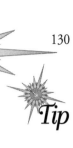

> By default, files are downloaded to the folder C:\Program Files\The Microsoft
> Network\Transferred Files. You can select a different default download folder or specify
> a different directory at the time you download. See "Downloading Options," later in
> this chapter.

**FIGURE 7.5.**

*The File Transfer Status window.*

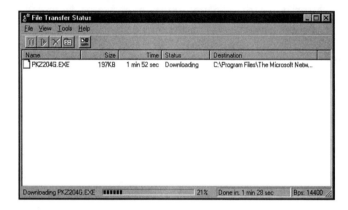

By design, the MSN client software is a multitasking system. That means you needn't
wait through an entire file transfer before going on to other tasks. During downloading,
you can minimize the File Transfer Status window—or open other windows on top of
it—to continue your work in MSN as the file transfer proceeds in the background. You
can even choose more files to download; any additional files are added to the list in the
File Transfer Status window and are automatically downloaded, one at a time, in the
order you selected them, until the list is empty.

Be warned, however, that although MSN responds slowly under normal conditions, it
is *achingly* slow when you attempt to perform other MSN activities while downloading
a file or files. In part, this is because MSN assumes that a fast file transfer is more
important than system responsiveness in your other work, and gives the file transfer first
dibs on system resources. Although you *can* do other work while files transfer, you may
not *want to*, given the time you wait for MSN windows to open and close.

At 14,400 bps, only very large files (such as video clips) take more than a few minutes
to transfer. So I don't multitask during transfers. I take a break—play with my son, load
the dishwasher, have some rice pudding—and resume my work when the transfers are
complete.

For more about MSN performance, see Chapter 14, "Speeding Up MSN."

# Downloading Options

The simple downloading procedure given in the preceding section does the job: it copies a file from MSN to your PC, where you can do whatever you want with it. However, you have several options for changing the way the download is conducted.

## Other Ways to Initiate the Download

In addition to double-clicking a file icon, you can initiate the download procedure in two other ways. Open the message containing the file icon and then do either of the following to download the file:

◆ Right-click the file icon to display the context menu (see Figure 7.6), then choose File **O**bject. From the File Object submenu, you can do any of the following:

 ◆ Choose **D**ownload to download the file without first viewing the Properties sheet.

 ◆ Choose **P**roperties to display the Properties dialog box (shown earlier in Figure 7.4).

 ◆ Choose **O**pen to download the file and open it as described later in this chapter.

◆ Choose **F**ile, Save **A**s. Click the **A**ttachments radio button and choose a save path, as described in "Choosing the Save Path," later in this chapter.

**FIGURE 7.6.**

*Choosing downloading options from a context menu.*

# File Transfer Options

Regardless of how you initiate the transfer, downloading (or uploading) a file always involves the File Transfer Status window (shown earlier in Figure 7.5). From this window, you can control the way files are downloaded by choosing **T**ools, **O**ptions. The File Transfer Options window shown in Figure 7.7 appears. The choices you make in this window remain in effect for all file transfers and all MSN sessions until you change them.

◆ **P**ause Files as They Are Queued. Select this checkbox to instruct MSN to pause between files when you are downloading more than one file. A prompt appears between files, giving you the option to download the next file in the queue or to cancel it and move on to the file that follows that one.

◆ **D**elete Compressed File after Decompressing. Select this checkbox to instruct MSN to delete the downloaded, compressed ZIP file from your hard disk after it is  decompressed. Decompressing the ZIP file restores the file or files it contains to their original, uncompressed state and stores them on your hard disk so that you no longer need the compressed file. MSN can automatically delete the ZIP file from your disk to save disk space. This option is available only if the next checkbox, **A**utomatically Decompress Files, is selected.

◆ **A**utomatically Decompress Files. Select this checkbox to instruct MSN to automatically run PKUNZIP to decompress compressed ZIP files after downloading. This option works only if the program PKUNZIP.EXE is installed on your PC and registered to ZIP files in the File Types registry (see "Compression/Decompression," earlier in this chapter).

◆ **D**efault Download Folder. In this box, you can enter a different disk or path to store downloaded files in (you can also browse for one by clicking the **B**rowse button). The default folder is C:\Program Files\The Microsoft Network\Transferred Files. Alternatively, you can specify at download time the folder in which you want to store a file (see "Choosing the Save Path," later in this chapter).

**FIGURE 7.7.**

*The File Transfer Options dialog box.*

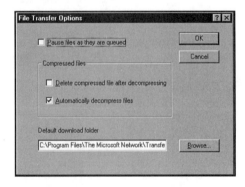

## Transfer and Disconnect

To automatically sign off from MSN as soon as all files in the File Transfer Status window have finished downloading, choose **F**ile, **T**ransfer and Disconnect, or click the Transfer and Disconnect button on the toolbar.

For more about making file transfers quickly, see Chapter 12, "Trimming Time Online."

# Download and Open

After downloading a file, MSN can automatically open it in Windows. You enable this option by doing one of the following:

◆ Clicking Download and **O**pen from the file icon's Properties dialog box (refer back to Figure 7.4).

◆ Choosing File **O**bject, **O**pen from the file icon's context menu (refer back to Figure 7.6).

In general practice, opening a file after downloading is not a particularly useful option for the following reasons:

◆ To save connect-time charges, it's better to sign out of MSN before working with files you've downloaded.

◆ The MSN client software makes such heavy demands on your PC's resources that files and programs tend to open and respond very slowly when MSN is running; large programs and files may not open at all.

If you choose to use Download and Open, observe the following conditions if you want the process to work properly:

◆ If the file to be downloaded is compressed, you must use the **A**utomatically Decompress Files option (see "File Transfer Options," earlier in this chapter) when downloading the file.

◆ If the file to be downloaded is of any type other than a program (EXE) file, the program must be of a type Windows can open automatically; alternatively, a program capable of opening the file must be installed on your PC and must be registered in the File Types registry.

# Choosing the Save Path

To select the folder on your PC into which a specific file will be downloaded, initiate the download procedure by opening the message containing the file icon and then choosing **F**ile, Save **A**s. A dialog box like the one in Figure 7.8 appears. Then follow these steps:

1. In the Save box, click the radio button next to **A**ttachments. The file appears in the Save box and in the File**n**ame box. (If the message contains more than one file icon, select the file or files to download from the Save box.)

2. Use the **F**olders and Dri**v**es lists to select the folder in which you want to save the downloaded file.

3. Click OK to begin downloading.

**FIGURE 7.8.**

*Choosing the save path.*

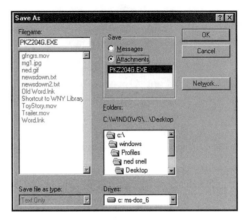

# Uploading a File to a BBS

To upload a file, you must follow the steps for creating and posting a message on a BBS (see Chapter 5, "Reading and Contributing to Bulletin Boards and Newsgroups"). As a rule, note that libraries are "read-only." They permit you to download a file, but not to upload one.

To insert a file icon in the body of your message, follow these steps:

1.  Compose your message; click in the message body at the spot where you want the file icon to appear. Choose **I**nsert, **F**ile (see Figure 7.9). A dialog box like the one in Figure 7.10 appears.

**FIGURE 7.9.**

*Composing a message into which a file will be inserted.*

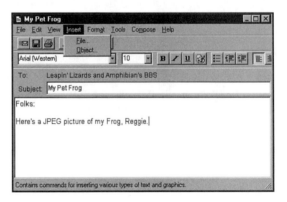

2.  In the Insert As box, click the radio button next to An **A**ttachment. Select the file to be inserted and click OK. The file icon appears in the message body (see Figure 7.11).
3.  Choose **F**ile, **Po**st Message, or click the Post Message button on the toolbar.

**FIGURE 7.10.**

*Choosing the file to insert.*

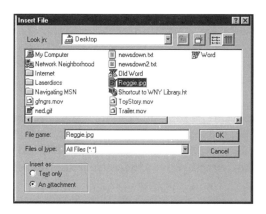

**FIGURE 7.11.**

*A file inserted in a BBS message, ready for uploading.*

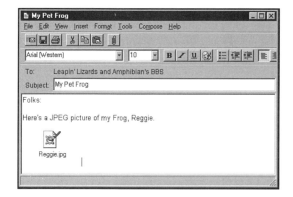

## What You Can and Cannot Upload

Microsoft enforces specific rules about what you can and cannot upload to MSN. These rules are spelled out in the MSN Member Agreement and Member Guidelines (see Chapter 3, "Member Rules and Etiquette").

In general, you're forbidden from uploading the following:

◆ Anything obscene

◆ Anything that defames another person

◆ Anything you do not have the free right to distribute (for example, copyrighted software, photos, or other such materials)

◆ Advertising

These rules are, of course, open to interpretation (the Supreme Court can't even decide what *obscene* means and also has a little trouble figuring out what *defamatory* means on an online service). On MSN, the interpreters of the law are the forum managers, who have sole, inviolate, and final authority on which uploads to permit—no jury, no appeal. The forum managers not only reject files for violating MSN rules, they may also reject files deemed inappropriate for the particular forum or BBS—in fact, some managers are more diligent about trashing off-topic material than material that breaks MSN policy. Any MSN member who repeatedly and knowingly uploads inappropriate material can have his or her MSN membership revoked. So there.

When a file has been reviewed and approved by the forum manager, the words Approved by the forum manager appear on the file's Properties sheet.

It's a good idea to spend plenty of time on a BBS before uploading anything to it. You should have a feel for the BBS population and its needs before you can assess whether a certain file will be useful and relevant to the group. And of course, unless you created the file yourself, check first to see whether someone else has already posted it.

# Downloading a File from a Newsgroup

The network news transfer protocol (NNTP) is a close relative of the Internet's e-mail protocol. NNTP is used to exchange messages between Internet (and MSN) users and newsgroup servers. NNTP cannot carry binary data; it can carry only text (which is why you cannot apply any special fonts or character formatting to newsgroup messages).

*Note*

To learn how to navigate to, open, and read newsgroup messages, see Chapter 5, "Reading and Contributing to Bulletin Boards and Newsgroups."

Note that newsgroups contain many files designed for computers and operating systems other than PCs and Windows. Read any descriptive information supplied with a newsgroup message before downloading it to make sure that the file will run in Windows 95.

However, there *are* files in newsgroup messages. The files are *encoded*—that is, translated from binary form into text characters that can travel across the newsgroup network. When you open a newsgroup message that contains a file, you see a nonsensical garble of characters beneath the message header (see Figure 7.12). This garble must be *decoded*—translated back into binary form—on your PC before you can use the file. Getting a file from a newsgroup is a matter of downloading the message to your PC and then decoding it, as described later in this section.

**FIGURE 7.12.**

*An encoded file in a newsgroup message.*

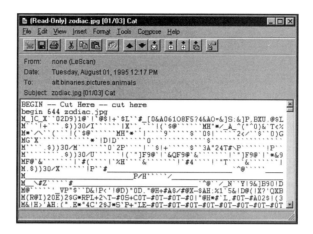

> Because files are part of the text of a newsgroup message (they are not attachments, as files are in BBS messages), they are not recognized as files by MSN. MSN doesn't place paper-clip icons next to newsgroup messages that contain files. If you change to Files view while viewing a list of newsgroup messages, the list appears to be empty because MSN believes none of the messages contain files, even though many may.

*Note*

Typically, messages containing files are much longer—100 lines or more—than ordinary messages (which average fewer than a dozen lines of text). Because of the extra length, opening a message that contains a file may take a few moments longer than opening a regular message.

Large files, such as video clips or JPEG images, are often broken into a series of messages. These *multipart* files appear as multiple messages in the list (see Figure 7.13). At the end of the subject line, numbers appear to help you make sure that you retrieve all the messages containing the file. The first message's subject line, for example, may end in (1/5) or (1 of 5), informing you that there are five messages you must retrieve to download the entire file. A message numbered zero (for example, 0/5), may also appear. This message contains information about the file or any special instructions about using the file.

**FIGURE 7.13.**

*A multipart file (an image of a cat named Zodiac) embedded in newsgroup messages.*

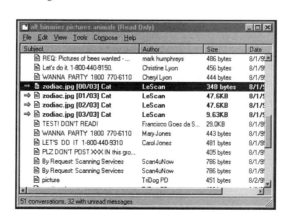

Finally, in addition to (or instead of) being broken into separate messages, files in newsgroups are often compressed into ZIP files. The several files that make up one application are typically compressed into a single ZIP archive and then encoded and posted on the newsgroup as one or more messages. To acquire the application, you must download the message or messages containing the ZIP file, decode the file (and combine multipart messages into a single file), and then decompress the result. Although that sounds like a lot of trouble, it's really not all that difficult; and believe it or not, it actually works.

## Saving the Message File

To retrieve a newsgroup message containing a file, follow these steps:

1. Open the message by double-clicking it in the BBS window.

2. Choose Save **A**s to display the Save As dialog box shown in Figure 7.14. Save the file using any filename and the extension UUE. This extension is required by many decoding programs to recognize the message as an encoded file. Note that the particular name you give the file is not especially important; after decoding, the file uses its original, intended filename.

**FIGURE 7.14.**

*Saving a newsgroup message containing an encoded file.*

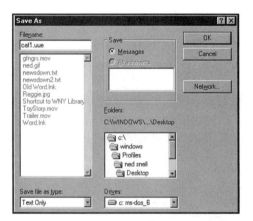

To save multipart files, open and save each message using the two-step process just described. Make sure that you save the complete set of messages. Although it's a good idea to give the messages sequential filenames (for example, FILE1.UUE, FILE2.UUE), some decoding programs can reassemble the multipart file regardless of the filenames you assign. The file numbered 0, if one is included, is not actually part of the file. You don't have to download or decode it, although you may want to save it as a text file if it contains useful information about the multipart file.

After saving the message(s), decode the file as described in the next section. You do not have to be connected to MSN to decode the file.

# Decoding the File

To decode a file downloaded from a newsgroup, you need a decoding program compatible with the UUENCODE/UUDECODE encoding method used by most newsreaders. An example is WinCode (mentioned earlier in this chapter and provided on the CD-ROM that accompanies this book).

To use WinCode to decode files you saved from a newsgroup, follow these steps:

1. Open WinCode (you can be either online or offline to perform these steps).
2. Choose **F**ile, **D**ecode. A dialog box like the one in Figure 7.15 appears.

**FIGURE 7.15.**

*Choosing a message file to decode.*

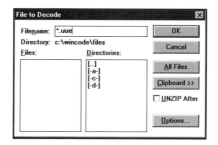

3. Enter the path and name of the file you want to decode; alternatively, click through the **D**irectories list to locate the file.

   To decode a multipart file, navigate to the directory in which the separate files are stored; hold the Ctrl key as you click each file until all parts of the multipart file are selected (see Figure 7.16).

**FIGURE 7.16.**

*Selecting all the parts of a multipart file to decode and reassemble into a single file.*

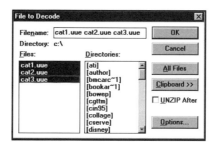

If PKUNZIP is installed on your PC and registered in the File Types registry (see "Compression/Decompression," earlier in this chapter), you can select the **U**NZIP After checkbox in the File to Decode dialog box. This option automatically decompresses files after they're decoded. This is necessary only if the original file was a ZIPped before it was posted.

3. Click OK to begin decoding. After decoding, the file is stored on your hard disk using its original (pre-encoding) filename and extension. If its extension is ZIP, you must decompress it before using it. Otherwise, you can run the file (if it is a program) or open it in a program. Figure 7.17 shows the JPEG image of the widdle putty tat that was downloaded and decoded in the preceding procedure. *Awwwwwwwwwwwwwwwww.* (It's so lifelike I feel my allergies tingling.)

**FIGURE 7.17.**

*A JPEG image of a cat, retrieved from multiple encoded newsgroup messages and restored to a single, decoded JPEG file by WinCode. Displayed by the Lview viewer for JPEG and GIF image files.*

# What Now?

MSN is a terrific source for programs, pictures, sounds, and video. Obtaining these items is simple, and in most cases, they cost nothing but the connect time to download them. But there are thousands more files out on the Internet. Many files are available in newsgroups, and this chapter told you how to get files from that resource. But many more are available through the World Wide Web, Gopher, and FTP. See Part IV of this book, "Navigating the Internet Through MSN," to learn how to find and acquire files from the Internet.

Or move on to Chapter 8, where you'll discover the most important, the most popular, and—remarkably—the simplest of activities online: e-mail.

# CHAPTER 8

# COMPOSING, SENDING, AND RECEIVING E-MAIL

About E-Mail

Have You Received E-Mail?

Receiving E-Mail

Using Embedded Links and Shortcuts

Composing and Sending a New Message

Formatting Messages

Replying and Forwarding

Addressing Mail Beyond MSN

What Now?

A warning: The title of this chapter is misleading. It implies that you learn about e-mail in the following order: composing it, sending it, and *then* receiving it. In reality, this chapter shows first how to *receive* e-mail and then how to compose and send it. That's because you'll likely receive some e-mail before you send any, so you'll need to know how to deal with incoming mail before outgoing mail. Also, it's easier to understand how to create an e-mail message when you've already seen an example.

So why didn't I just call this chapter "Receiving, Composing, and Sending E-Mail"? Well, it just didn't sound right. Sue me. I guess I could have called it "Using Microsoft Exchange," since Windows 95's Exchange program is the tool you use for MSN e-mail. But Exchange can be used for purposes other than MSN e-mail, and I don't cover its use beyond MSN.

*Note*

Why will you probably receive e-mail the first time you sign in? Two reasons:

◆ MSN publishes a Monthly Letter, sent through e-mail to all MSN subscribers. The letter keeps you abreast of any new developments or important changes in the evolution of MSN. When you first sign in, you'll probably find the current month's letter waiting for you.

◆ Microsoft allows its business partners to e-mail you "important announcements" about new products and services; in other words, you'll be getting electronic junk mail.

If you can forgive me the title and read on, you'll discover that day-to-day e-mail operation is very easy—which explains why so many people use it. The reason e-mail seems complicated at times is that it's so versatile.

You can send e-mail to multiple recipients, send "carbon copies" and "blind copies," forward to others messages you've received, send faxes with e-mail, format text in messages, attach files to messages, insert multimedia *objects*—such as sound clips, video clips, and pictures—into e-mail messages, play multimedia objects embedded in messages you receive, and send and receive messages to and from the Internet, CompuServe, Prodigy, America Online, and more. None of these optional capabilities is difficult to master, but put together, they take a lot of explaining. Day-to-day, uncomplicated sending and receiving of MSN e-mail is quick and easy.

Just as there is basic e-mail and power e-mail, there are basic e-mail users who simply want to be able to send and receive messages, and there are power e-mail users who want to exploit every bell and whistle e-mail has. With this schism in mind, this book includes two e-mail chapters. The one you're reading offers an introduction to the basics of e-mail. Many MSN members will find there's nothing they want from e-mail that's not covered here. For those who want to make MSN e-mail do handstands, there's Chapter 13, "Power E-Mail."

In this chapter, you learn the following:

◆ About the different parts of an e-mail message and what they mean

◆ How to retrieve, read, and organize messages you receive on MSN

◆ How to reply to messages you've received and how to forward messages to others

◆ How to use the shortcuts and files in messages you receive

◆ How to compose and send e-mail to other MSN members, plus others on the Internet, CompuServe, and elsewhere on the information superhighway

◆ How to send the same e-mail message to more than one person

In case you were wondering, the advanced techniques in Chapter 13 include these:

◆ Sending a fax through MSN

◆ Attaching files to, and inserting files and objects in, messages you send

◆ Sending messages to a personal distribution list

◆ Composing and sending e-mail directly from Windows applications

◆ Managing information about your e-mail partners in your Exchange "Personal Address Book"

◆ Using special options in Exchange to customize the way messages are sent and the way Exchange behaves

In Chapter 12, "Trimming Time Online," you learn about ways to retrieve your e-mail quickly so that you can get offline sooner. You also learn how to compose messages offline and send them later.

Finally, in Chapter 10, "Finding Anything on MSN," you learn how to look up another MSN member's ID.

# About E-Mail

Most e-mail systems, including MSN and the Internet, operate according to a principle called "store and forward," which means that the file containing the message is stored temporarily on one or more computers along its journey and then forwarded to its destination.

When an MSN member sends e-mail to another MSN member, the scenario is quite simple: Member A composes a message on his or her PC, addresses it to Member B, and sends it according to the steps described later in this chapter. The message is transmitted to the MSN data center in Washington state, where it is stored. When Member B retrieves his or her e-mail, the message is transferred from the MSN data center to Member B's PC, and the delivery is complete.

On the Internet, this same principle is used, but the delivery is much more complicated. A message may pass through, and be temporarily stored on, several computers before reaching its destination. When you send e-mail to the Internet or to other online services such as CompuServe, the message is first stored in the MSN data center, then forwarded to the Internet or online service.

# The Anatomy of an E-Mail Message

All e-mail, like all paper mail, requires only two basic parts: the name and address of the recipient and the message itself. In an e-mail message, all the name and address information is contained in a block of lines called a *header;* the message itself is called the *body*, as shown in Figure 8.1. (An optional block of lines can be added to the bottom of the message to further identify the sender; such lines are called a *signature*.)

**FIGURE 8.1.**

*The parts of an e-mail message.*

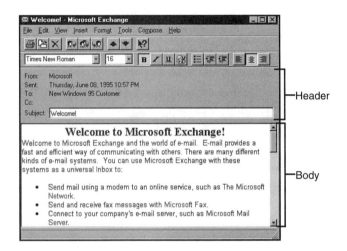

# The Header

The *header* is made up of several lines, each containing one piece of information about the message:

◆ From: The sender's MSN member ID or full name (or Internet address or online service ID, if the message is being sent from outside of MSN).

◆ Sent: The date and time at which the message was sent.

◆ To: The receiver's MSN member ID or full name (or Internet address or online service ID, if the message is being sent outside of MSN). You can put more than one ID in the To: line, to send the same message to more than one person.

◆ Subject: The subject of the message. This line is optional.

There may be other lines in a header as well, depending on how the message was sent. For example, the Cc: line contains the IDs of recipients who received the message as a carbon copy (see "Cc: and Bcc:," later in this chapter.)

When sending a message, you never have to deal with every line in a header because some are filled in automatically by Exchange and others may be optional, depending on what you're doing. The Sent: line, for example, is generated automatically, as is the From: line—it's filled in automatically with your member ID.

Typically, you only have to fill in the `To:` line to fully address a message. The `Subject:` line is optional, but courteous users always supply one. Your `Subject:` line appears in the list of messages your recipients see when they retrieve their e-mail. If you enter no subject, your recipients have to open and read your message to know what it's about. Nobody likes that. Worse, some busy e-mail users routinely delete messages that lack a subject line, assuming that such messages are unimportant.

Because headers on messages received from the Internet sometimes report extra information (such as a listing of all the machines the message passed through on its way to you), headers can be intimidating. You really needn't pay much attention to them, however; most of the time, all you really need to know is who you're sending a message to or who a message is from. Consider the rest an electronic postmark.

## Cc: and Bcc:

To send the same message to several people, you put all their IDs in the `To:` line of the message header. But as with paper mail (especially business correspondence), you may want to e-mail copies of a message to people who are not the message's primary recipients but who you think need to see the message anyway. This is where two optional lines of the header, `Cc:` and `Bcc:`, come in:

◆ `Cc:` The `Cc:` (carbon copy) line duplicates the effect of Cc: copies of letters and memos. For example, when addressing a complaint to a mail-order company, you can Cc: your attorney, just to keep him informed. When you use the Cc: option, the addresses of the Cc: recipients appear in the message header (in a line labeled `Cc:`) so that all recipients can easily see who else received the same message.

◆ `Bcc:` The `Bcc:` line works the same as the `Cc:` line except that the names of the recipients are not added to the header. When you send a Bcc: copy, the other recipients—those in the `To:` and `Cc:` lines—do not know that a Bcc: copy was sent, or to whom. Bcc: copies are useful when you want to keep a third party abreast of an exchange without the knowledge of the other person. If you want your lawyer to know about your communications with the mail-order company, but you don't want the mail-order company to know your lawyer is involved yet, use the Bcc: option.

## The Body

The *body* of an e-mail message is the meat of the message itself. Using MSN's formatting tools, you can spice up your message body with various fonts and colors; create bulleted lists; and use left, center, and right text alignment. You'll see such formatting in messages you receive from others. You can also attach files and shortcuts to messages, and retrieve files and run shortcuts created by others.

## Signature

A *signature* is a block of text at the bottom of the message body used to close a message. It can be as simple as a traditional letter signature (*Hugs & kisses, Ned*). On the Internet, however, people like to use a few lines of text that tell the reader something about them or their personality. Businesspeople may use the signature like a letterhead or logo, listing the company's voice and fax numbers, regular mail address, slogan, and lines of business. Others use their favorite quote, joke, or slogan. It's all very personal.

The only e-mail program you can use to send MSN e-mail, Microsoft Exchange, does not provide an automatic way to add a signature to all messages as most full-featured e-mail programs do. So you'll see few signatures on messages from other MSN members. However, you *will* see signatures on the e-mail you receive from outside MSN, particularly on messages from the Internet. Of course, if you really want to use a signature in your MSN mail, you can write one, store it in a simple text file, and insert that file in each message you send, as described in Chapter 13, "Power E-Mail."

## About Exchange

Microsoft Exchange is Windows 95's built-in e-mail program, which is installed on your PC automatically when you install Microsoft Mail, Microsoft Fax, or The Microsoft Network. Microsoft calls Exchange a "universal messaging client" because it not only sends and receives e-mail from MSN, it also sends and receives e-mail to and from other e-mail systems and manages the activity of Microsoft Fax.

*Note*

> Exchange can be configured for sending and receiving Internet mail, but MSN members do not need this feature. Exchange's Internet Mail facility is used for sending and receiving e-mail from a regular Internet account, *separate* from MSN. Unless you have a separate Internet account in addition to your MSN account, you do not need Exchange's Internet Mail. All your Internet mail is handled automatically through regular MSN e-mail.

Exchange not only enables you to send and receive MSN mail, it also serves as an application for managing your incoming and outgoing messages. Exchange organizes your messages much as Explorer organizes your files and folders. Each message on your PC is automatically stored in one of four folders:

◆ **Inbox.** Open the Inbox folder to display the list of messages you have received. Figure 8.2 shows Exchange with the Inbox folder open.

◆ **Outbox.** Open the Outbox folder to see messages waiting to be sent. After a message has been sent, it moves from the Outbox to the Sent Items folder.

◆ **Sent Items.** Open the Sent Items folder to see a list of messages you have sent.

◆ **Deleted Items.** Open the Deleted Items folder to see a list of messages you have deleted from other folders. The Deleted Items folder functions much like Windows 95's Recycle Bin; that is, it's a safety net. When you delete a message from your Inbox, Outbox, or Sent Items folder, that message appears in the Deleted Items folder. When you delete it from there, the message is gone for good.

**FIGURE 8.2.**

*Exchange's Inbox folder.*

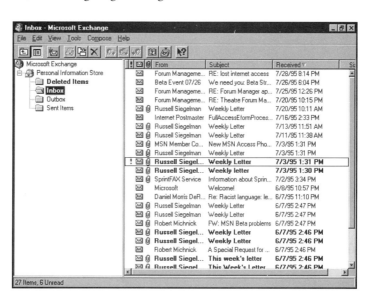

In Figure 8.2, observe the column headings in the list of messages. The From and Subject portions of each message listed are taken directly from the From and Subject portions of the message headers. (A RE: in the subject line indicates that a message is a reply to another message.) The Received column indicates the date and time you retrieved the message (not the time it was sent, which appears in the Sent: line of the header). In the list, any messages you have not yet read appear in **bold** type.

Just as you can with BBS and newsgroup message lists (described in Chapter 5, "Reading and Contributing to Bulletin Boards and Newsgroups"), you can manually mark messages as unread (**bold**) or read (not bold), whether you've actually read them or not. You may want to mark a messages you've already opened once as unread, in case you didn't finish reading it or want to be sure to read it again. Also, if you can tell from the subject line that you're not interested in reading a message, but just can't quite bring yourself to delete it yet, you can mark it as read so that it stops **shout**ing at you from the message list.

To mark messages as read or unread, select the messages to be marked and choose **E**dit, Mark as **R**ead or **E**dit, Mark as **U**nread.

While viewing any folder in Exchange, you can sort the message list. By clicking a column heading, you can re-sort the list by the contents of that column; for example, click Subject to sort messages by subject. For more advanced ways to sort messages, choose **V**iew, **S**ort. A dialog box like the one in Figure 8.3 appears. The **S**ort Items By drop-down list offers many ways to sort; the radio buttons offer a choice of **A**scending order (lowest to highest) or **D**escending order (highest to lowest).

**FIGURE 8.3.**

*Options for sorting the message list in Exchange.*

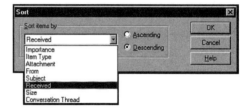

## Have You Received E-Mail?

If you have any mail waiting for you, MSN automatically notifies you when you sign in. At some point during the time when the MSN home page and MSN Today are forming on your screen, a box like the one in Figure 8.4 appears.

**FIGURE 8.4.**

*A new mail notification.*

Click **Y**es to open Exchange and automatically open the Inbox folder. Alternatively, you can click **N**o, work in MSN, and navigate to the Inbox later (even in another session) by clicking **E-M**ail on MSN Central (the home page) or by simply opening Exchange (when you are still online) from your Programs menu or from the Inbox icon on your desktop.

Tip

Chapter 12, "Trimming Time Online," shows how you can sign in to MSN, collect your new e-mail, and sign off quickly to read it—offline—at your leisure.

## Receiving E-Mail

Once Exchange opens, you retrieve your waiting e-mail by choosing **T**ools, **D**eliver Now. A box appears, informing you that MSN is Checking for new messages.

Exchange is a "universal messaging client" capable of retrieving messages from a variety of messaging "services," including MSN, CompuServe, Microsoft Mail, and others. If the only service configured in Exchange is MSN, you select **Tools**, **D**eliver Now to retrieve e-mail. If you have other services installed in addition to MSN, choose **Tools**, **D**eliver Now Using to display a submenu listing your installed services; then choose the messaging service (MSN, CompuServe, or whatever) from which you want to retrieve messages. If you use multiple services, you'll see an **A**ll Services choice on the Deliver Now Using submenu. Choose All Services to connect to the listed messaging services, one at a time, and retrieve any waiting messages from each.

After a few moments, the box disappears, and any new messages appear in your Inbox folder, at the top of the list of messages. Like all unread messages, they appear in **bold**. To read any message, double-click it; alternatively, select it and choose **F**ile, **O**pen. The message opens in a message window like the one in Figure 8.5.

**FIGURE 8.5.**

*Reading a message.*

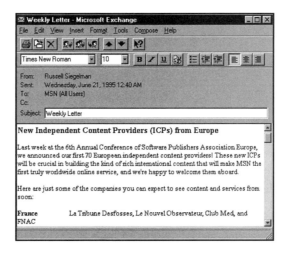

While viewing the message, you can choose **F**ile, **P**rint (or click the Print button on the toolbar) to print the message. When finished reading the message, choose **F**ile, **C**lose (or click the × close button) to close the message window and return to the Inbox folder. The message now appears in the Inbox in regular type (not **bold**) to show that you have read it. The message remains in your Inbox until you delete it. You can open the message again at any time (even offline) to review it.

While a message is open, you can do the following:

◆ Reply to the message—conveniently compose and send a message back to the sender of the open message.

◆ Forward the message—send a copy of the message to another MSN user.

Both of these techniques are covered later in this chapter.

# Using Embedded Links and Shortcuts

Many messages include attached files and shortcuts in the message body. These are represented by icons, as shown in Figure 8.6. (Shortcut icons take you somewhere in MSN; you can copy to your PC the files represented by the file icons.) Note that messages containing attached files have a paperclip icon next to them in Exchange's message list.

**FIGURE 8.6.**

*Icons in the message body represent attached files or shortcuts.*

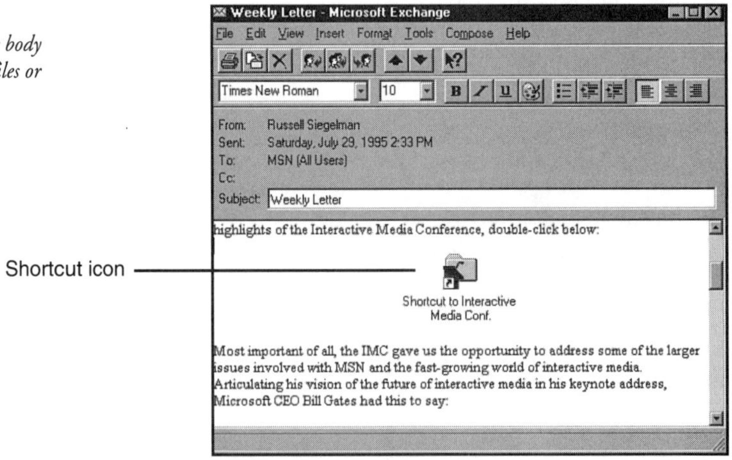

Shortcut icon ——————

◆ To retrieve an attached file, select the icon and choose **F**ile, **S**ave. The file is transferred to your PC in exactly the same way a file is transferred from a BBS or library (see Chapter 7, "Downloading and Uploading Files," for more about transfer options and using files once you retrieve them).

◆ To use a shortcut, double-click it. You navigate directly to where the shortcut points.

*Tip*

If you read an e-mail message offline and click a shortcut icon, the icon opens the MSN Sign In dialog box. After you sign in, the shortcut takes you to where it points.

# Composing and Sending a New Message

To compose and send an e-mail message, follow these steps:

1. Connect to MSN, click E-**M**ail on the home page (MSN Central) to open Exchange, and choose Co**m**pose, **N**ew Message. The New Message window appears, as shown in Figure 8.7.

**FIGURE 8.7.**

*Composing a new message.*

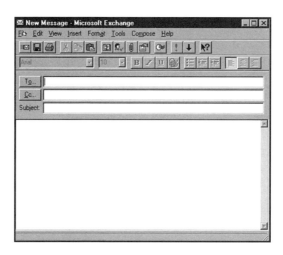

2. In the To: line, type the MSN member ID of the person to whom you want the mail sent. To send the message to multiple recipients, type as many member IDs in the To: line as you want. Separate the names with semicolons (;) and no spaces.

   There are several ways you can fill in the To:, Cc:, and Bcc: lines, including using the recipient's full name or a nickname you make up (see Chapter 13, "Power E-Mail"). If you don't know the recipient's member ID, you can look it up online (see Chapter 10, "Finding Anything on MSN"). To learn how to enter the addresses of people who are on the Internet or another online service, see "Addressing Mail Beyond MSN," later in this chapter.

3. If you don't want to Cc: this message to anyone, leave the Cc: line blank and move on to step 4. To Cc: the message, enter the member IDs of one or more Cc: recipients in the Cc: line, separating names with semicolons (;). To send a Bcc: copy, select View, Bcc Box: and enter one or more recipients in the Bcc: line, separating names with semicolons (;).

4. Enter a subject in the Subject line. Although you can leave the Subject line blank, it's impolite to do so.

5. Click in the body area of the message window and type your message. Note that the Tools menu has a spelling checker option you can run when you finish entering your message. (Your recipients will thank you if you spell-check your messages.) Also become familiar with a few options you can choose from the toolbar or menus:

   ◆ Insert, File/Message/Object or the Insert File toolbar button (the paperclip). Use either of these options to embed files containing graphics, video clips, or sound into your e-mail messages (see Chapter 13, "Power E-Mail").

   ◆ Format, Font/Paragraph. This option controls fonts and character attributes (bold, italic, underline, colors) and enables you to format your message with bulleted lists and left-aligned, centered, or right-aligned paragraphs. See "Formatting Messages," later in this chapter.

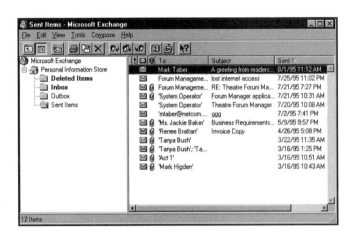

6. When you finish entering your message, do one of the following:

◆ To send the message, click the Send button (the envelope) on the toolbar or select **F**ile, Se**n**d.

◆ To save the message for later editing, choose **F**ile, **S**ave. You can open the message later (choose **F**ile, **O**pen) to make changes and then send it as just described. The file type for messages is MSG; by default, Exchange assigns your message a name using the message's subject line as the filename and MSG as the extension.

After you send the message, it appears in your Sent Items folder, as shown in Figure 8.8. Its listing in the folder shows the time it was sent; the To: column shows the member's full name, which MSN looks up from the member ID you used to address the message. You can open a message in the Sent Items folder at any time to review it.

**FIGURE 8.8.**

*The sent message now appears in the Sent Items folder in Exchange.*

# Formatting Messages

When creating your message, you can dress it up with fonts, colors, and paragraph formatting. The formatting tools appear in the Form**a**t menu on the New Message window, and also on the Formatting toolbar (which you display by choosing **V**iew, **F**ormatting Toolbar). Figure 8.7 (shown earlier) shows the new message window with the Formatting toolbar displayed.

Choosing Form**a**t, **F**ont brings up the Font dialog box (see Figure 8.9). From this dialog box, you can change the font, attributes (bold, italic, underline), and color of any text in your message. These same functions are available from the first six items on the toolbar: two drop-down lists for font and font size; buttons for bold, italic, and underline; and a palette button for color.

Choosing Form**a**t, **P**aragraph brings up the Paragraph dialog box (see Figure 8.10). From this dialog box, you can set the text alignment to **L**eft, **R**ight, or **C**enter; you can also create a bulleted list by selecting the **B**ullet checkbox. These same functions are available on the Formatting toolbar, as are two more items: one for indenting to the right, and another for decreasing the indent.

**FIGURE 8.9.**
*Formatting characters with the Font dialog box.*

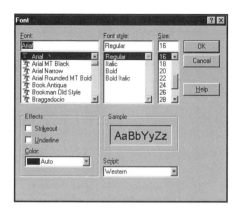

**FIGURE 8.10.**
*Formatting paragraphs with the Paragraph dialog box.*

Fonts, colors, and paragraph formatting appear when your recipient reads your message only if one of the following is true:

◆ Your recipient is an MSN member.

◆ Your non-MSN recipient uses a Windows-based, MIME-compliant e-mail program such as Exchange. (For more about MIME, see Chapter 13, "Power E-Mail.")

Otherwise, your message appears to the recipient as plain, left-aligned text. As a rule, don't bother formatting unless your recipient is an MSN member.

# Replying and Forwarding

While viewing a message you have received, you can choose either of two reply options from the toolbar or the Compose menu. Both options open the New Message window with the To: and Subject: lines filled in and the original message quoted (including its header) in the message box. The Subject: line is automatically filled in with the subject of the message you're responding to, with RE: inserted at the beginning to show that your message is a reply.

Above the quote of original message is a dashed line, a *reply separator* (see Figure 8.11). This line is meant to separate your comments from the original message you're responding to. Also notice that the quote is indented to help distinguish it from your comments. You enter your reply above the separator, as shown in the figure.

**FIGURE 8.11.**

*Replying to a message received. Note the dashed line (the reply separator), and that the quote of the original message includes the header.*

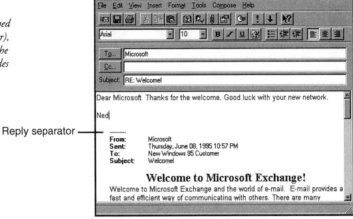

Reply separator ———

Exchange offers several different ways to reply:

◆ The **R**eply to Sender option addresses the reply to only the name listed in the message header as the sender—the From: address.

◆ The Reply to **A**ll option addresses the reply to everyone whose name appears in the header: the sender, all Cc: recipients, and anyone who forwarded the message.

> Watch out when using the Reply to All option. You don't want to flood mailboxes with unnecessary messages. Always check the header to make sure that everyone listed really needs to see the message before selecting the Reply to All option.

A **F**orward option also appears on the toolbar and in the Co**m**pose menu. This option opens a New Message window, quotes the original message, and leaves the To: line blank for the address. The header of the forwarded message shows that you were the original recipient and that you forwarded the message. You can add your comments above the reply separator.

# Addressing Mail Beyond MSN

Just because your aunt Shirley isn't on MSN doesn't mean you can't send her e-mail. You can send mail through MSN to the Internet and to users of any of the major commercial online services, including America Online, CompuServe, Prodigy, and others. Users of these services can send you e-mail from the services, as well. The exact steps and costs involved vary by service.

All the steps for sending e-mail from the Internet or to an online service are the same as for an MSN message; the only thing that changes is what you enter to name recipients in the To:, Cc:, or Bcc: lines. Each service requires a slightly different approach. Note that the Reply and Forward options also work with other mail services; if you reply to a message that originated on CompuServe, it is automatically addressed to go back to CompuServe.

> You can use the address formats that follow anywhere you use an MSN member ID: in the To:, Cc:, and Bcc: lines. You can also send the same message to both MSN and non-MSN users. For example, you can enter an MSN member ID in the To: line, and an Internet address in the Cc: line.
>
> In case you were wondering, you can also mix addresses from different e-mail systems in the same list of addresses, separating each address with a semicolon. For example, in the To: line, you can enter an MSN member ID, a semicolon, an Internet address, a semicolon, and a CompuServe address. The message is delivered to all three recipients. You can do the same in the Cc: and Bcc: lines.

**The Internet:** Enter the recipient's exact Internet address. Internet e-mail addresses are made up of three parts: a username, the "at" symbol (@), and a *domain*, which identifies to the Internet the specific computer the user is on. Domains are typically made up of several words, each separated by a period. To send e-mail from MSN to an Internet user whose address is mtaber@samsnet.mcp.com, enter the following in the To: line:

mtaber@samsnet.mcp.com

> To send you e-mail, Internet users must address the mail to your member ID with the characters @msn.com added to the end. For example, to send me (member ID nsnell) e-mail, Internet users must address Internet e-mail to me in this way:
>
> nsnell@msn.com
>
> If you send your Internet friends and associates e-mail, they will have no trouble finding out how to send e-mail to you. On your messages, Internet users see your complete Internet e-mail address—including the @msn.com—in the From: line of the message header.

**America Online:** Add the letters @aol.com to the end of the user's America Online username. For example, if the username is fredo, address e-mail like this:

fredo@aol.com

**CompuServe:** Add the letters @compuserve.com to the end of the user's CompuServe ID number, and change the comma that appears in the middle of every CompuServe address into a period. For example, if the user's ID number is 72727,3322, address e-mail this way:

72727.3322@compuserve.com

**Prodigy:** Add the letters @prodigy.com to the end of the user's Prodigy username. For example, if the username number is TFKH12A, address e-mail as follows:

TFKH12A@prodigy.com

# What Now?

Having discovered e-mail, you've acquired the key to the whole online world. E-mail reaches everywhere, and makes you accessible to the world.

A single stop remains on your tour of MSN activities—and unlike e-mail, this one's unique to MSN. See Chapter 9 to learn about MSN's online "titles," multipage, *hypermedia* presentations that serve as terrific reference works, guidebooks, online tutorials, and picture books.

# CHAPTER 9

# VIEWING AND OPERATING TITLES

Identifying Titles

Title Types

Using Titles

What Now?

MSN "titles" are weird li'l pups. Unlike BBSs, chat rooms, and other basic MSN entities, titles have variable icons. In many cases, you know a title *is* a title only if you open it or read its Properties sheet. Even the term *title* varies. Some are called *multimedia titles;* others are called *MSN titles, Media Viewer titles,* or *Microsoft Network titles.* You should realize that a title is a title is a title....

Using a title has much in common with using a *page*, or document, on the World Wide Web (see Chapter 16, "Browsing the World Wide Web"). However, don't confuse titles with Web pages (Web pages are far more powerful and sophisticated than titles). A *title* is a discrete document on MSN that contains words, pictures, links to other places within itself, and shortcuts that lead to other MSN resources. Web pages are distributed across the Internet and can contain words, pictures, video, sounds, animation, and links to places within itself, elsewhere on the Web, and elsewhere on the Internet. Of course, today there are millions of Web pages, and only a handful of MSN titles.

So what the heck are titles for? Well, it seems their simplicity is their purpose. The main applications for MSN titles are instructional manuals, magazines, and glossy, graphical picture books (which are often thinly disguised online advertising). When one is trying to teach or sell, one doesn't want the student or buyer to struggle with operating the medium. One wants the presentation medium to be so simple and so intuitive that the reader experiences only the message, not the medium. If achieving that simplicity requires a medium that's limited in scope, so be it. That's titles in a nutshell. Heck, they're so scaled down, they don't even offer a Print menu item.

MSN titles aren't for serious fact-digging or for splashy, state-of-the-art multimedia presentations (both of which are the province of the Web). Titles are for short, colorful, simple manuals and presentations. They offer a friendly, painless way to learn just a little. Think of them as instructional pamphlets or ad brochures—nothing more, nothing less. That doesn't mean they can't be informative, or even fun—they're always one or the other, and occasionally both. But *comprehensive* and *exciting* are not adjectives you apply to MSN titles. That might compromise a title's purpose: simplicity.

*Note*

> Although titles are an important part of MSN now, they're a temporary technology, a stop-gap measure that provides for document presentation on MSN until Microsoft completes work on a new, far more sophisticated multimedia presentation system called *Blackbird.* Ultimately, titles will be replaced with splashier Blackbird documents that will offer greater multimedia capabilities than titles can support.
>
> The techniques you'll need to operate a Blackbird title, however, are likely to be nearly identical to those used for titles.

In this chapter, you learn the following:

◆ How to locate and identify a title

◆ The ways titles are applied on MSN

◆ How to operate a title presented as a guidebook

◆ How to operate a title presented as a magazine or special-event brochure

> If you've been on MSN, you've already seen at least one title. MSN Today, which appears when you sign in to inform you of events online, is an MSN title. The Calendar of Events, which appears when you click a link on the MSN Today screen, is also a title.

*Note*

# Identifying Titles

Titles are found all over MSN, but at this writing, they're concentrated in two places: the Special Events category and the various folders within Member Assistance. As more Independent Content Providers (ICPs) begin pitching their products and services online, you'll begin to see more titles, many built to sell.

In some cases, you can recognize a title by the standard title icon, a collage made up of a globe, picture frame, CD-ROM, and book. The icon is meant to suggest the title's multimedia capabilities, but it overstates: Titles contain just words and pictures (not too impressive, considering that current multimedia often incorporates animation, video, and sound).

However, many titles have different icons that bear no resemblance to the standard icon. Typically, these titles do not even use the word *title* in their icon labels. The following icons all represent MSN titles:

How To Chat

Finding Places
Fast

United Nations
- Interactive
Title

Tips for New
Users

Core Rules of
Netiquette

If you open the Properties sheet for any of these icons (right-click the icon and choose Properties) and look at the General tab, you see the words `MSN Title` or `Media Viewer Title` (or some other name that includes the word *title*) listed as the Type.

So, how do you recognize a title?

◆ If it uses the title icon (the collage), it's a title.

◆ If it does not use a title icon, and does not use a folder, BBS, chat, document, or library icon, it's probably a title. (Sorry, that's the best I can do. I doesn't design the stuff, I just writes about it.)

When in doubt, check the icon's Properties sheet. Better yet, just open the silly thing (double-click the icon) and see what happens. What can it hurt?

---

### Trolling for Titles

To find a title related to a given subject, navigate to a folder or forum dedicated to that subject to see whether any titles are offered there. You can also use MSN's Find utility (see Chapter 10, "Finding Anything on MSN") to find titles. Enter a word for the subject in the **C**ontaining field and choose Multimedia Titles from the **O**f Type drop-down list.

To produce a list of all the titles on MSN, leave the **C**ontaining field blank and choose Multimedia Titles from the **O**f Type drop-down list. After you click Find Now, the Find utility generates a list of titles like the one shown in Figure 9.1.

**FIGURE 9.1.**
*Searching for titles.*

---

# Title Types

Technically, a title can be any type of presentation that incorporates text, graphics, links, and shortcuts. Many different styles and types of titles are evolving. However, today, most titles fall into one of two basic types:

◆ **Guidebook.** Guidebooks (see Figure 9.2) are textbook-style titles designed to teach you about a given subject (usually how to operate something on MSN).

◆ **Magazines.** Flashy and highly graphical, magazine-style titles (see Figure 9.3) are designed to mimic a magazine or to showcase a product or special event (special-event titles mimic a brochure or program for an event). Magazines typically contain many graphics that may also serve as links; they also have many shortcuts to related online resources. Like real magazines, they're updated from time to time. Figure 9.3 shows a typical "special event" magazine; Figure 9.4 shows *MSN Life*, a monthly online magazine published by Microsoft, covering happenings on MSN.

**FIGURE 9.2.**

*An MSN title of the guidebook type.*

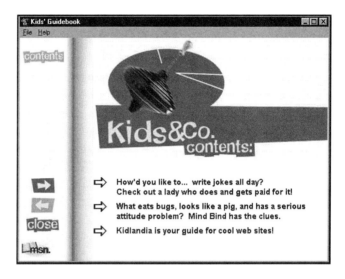

**FIGURE 9.3.**

*An MSN title of the magazine type.*

**FIGURE 9.4.**

*MSN Life, a monthly online magazine.*

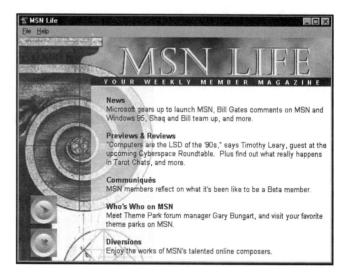

# Using Titles

When you open a title icon (double-click it or select it and choose **File**, **O**pen), MSN opens a program called the Online Viewer to present it. As the title opens, the viewer automatically resizes the window to accommodate the title's particular size and shape (the window size and shape of titles vary). MSN closes the Online Viewer when you close the title (choose **File**, **E**xit or click the × button in the upper-right corner).

When your pointer is on a *link*, it changes from Windows 95's default arrow pointer (or whatever you changed the arrow pointer to, if you customized Windows 95) to a pointing finger. If you click the left mouse button while the pointer is a finger, the link closest to the pointer is activated. Links always take you to another page of the same title. After executing a link, you can press F2 or choose **File**, **B**ack to return to the previous page (the one from which you executed the link).

*Note*

> In a title, the function of the F2 function key and **File**, **B**ack is different from **File**, **U**p One Level. F2 and Back always return you to the page you last displayed (which may or may not be one that's "up"—higher on the table of contents or in the hierarchy of pages from the current page).

MSN *shortcuts* also appear in titles. There are two types of shortcuts:

◆ Some shortcuts appear like regular MSN shortcuts, using the same icons as the MSN resources they lead to. Double-click a shortcut icon to jump to the resource—a BBS, a chat room, another title, and so on.

◆ "Star" shortcuts appear in text as little star icons (see Figure 9.5, in the following section). These shortcuts can lead anywhere regular shortcuts lead; they're used instead of regular shortcuts for aesthetic reasons. You activate a star shortcut with a single click. You cannot display a Properties sheet for a star shortcut.

> If you have any experience using a graphical browser on the World Wide Web, it's important to understand the differences in the behavior of links and shortcuts on titles and Web pages:
>
> ◆ On a Web page, a link can take you to another spot in the same document, to another Web page, or even to another Internet resource (such as a file to be downloaded). In a title, links lead only to other pages in the same title; shortcuts (both types) lead out of the title to other MSN resources.
>
> ◆ When you click a link on a Web page, regardless of where it takes you, you can return to the previous Web page using your browser's Back function. Similarly, you can use the title's Back function to go back after executing a link—but not after executing a shortcut. To return to the title after executing a shortcut, you must navigate back to the title using basic MSN navigation techniques.

*Note*

## Using a Guidebook

The opening page of a guidebook shows a table of contents along the left side of the screen (see Figure 9.5). Each entry in the table of contents is a link; click one to go to the page that entry describes. The link for the page you're viewing always appears in **heavy** type (see `Meet other members` in Figure 9.5). If you click the link `Use a bulletin board` in the table of contents, the page shown in Figure 9.6 appears. In Figure 9.6, note that the new current page, `Use a bulletin board`, now appears in heavy type.

From the screen shown in Figure 9.6, you can do any of the following:

**FIGURE 9.5.**

*The top page of Getting Started, an introduction to MSN.*

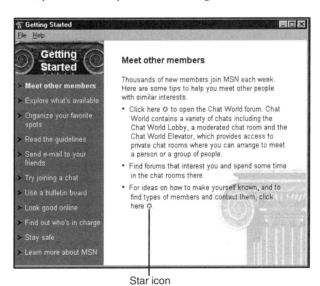

Star icon

**FIGURE 9.6.**

*The page that appears when I click a link in Figure 9.5.*

◆ Click the star shortcut (in the sentence just above the bold word *Tips*) to navigate to a practice BBS.

◆ Press F2 (or choose **F**ile, **B**ack) to return to the page shown in Figure 9.5.

◆ Choose **F**ile, Create **S**hortcut to create an MSN shortcut to this specific page of this title (see Chapter 12, "Trimming Time Online" to learn more about creating short-cuts).

# Using a Magazine-Style Title

Depending on your system configuration and modem speed, you may find that titles take a long time to open. In particular, magazines take a long time to appear because of the huge amount of graphical data MSN must transmit to your PC.

Pictures in titles appear through a scheme called *progressive rendering*, a technique that is also used by many Web browsers. The data making up the pictures is written to your screen a little at a time, so that a fuzzy image first appears, then a sharper one, and finally the recognizable image. Text may appear before the graphics finish sharpening up on your screen. As soon as you can recognize a link, you can use it to proceed. You need not wait until the pictures have completely finished rendering before you use them.

In a magazine, words *and* pictures serve as links. Often, there's no way to tell what's a link and what isn't—except by moving the pointer around the screen to see where it changes into a pointing finger. With experience, you'll learn to make educated guesses about where the links lie.

Examine the golf tournament screen in Figure 9.7. (Where better to explore "links"?) On this screen, I'd guess that each of the golfer photos is a link to information about that golfer. And you know what? I'd be wrong! There's only one link on this page; the text in the center that says Click here to continue. When I do as I'm told, the screen shown in Figure 9.8 appears.

In Figure 9.8, I find the type of links I expect to find in a magazine title. Clicking any of the three photos along the top of the screen opens a new page with information about the subject indicated by the pictures. After I read that information, I can press F2 (or choose **F**ile, **B**ack) to return to the page shown in Figure 9.8.

**FIGURE 9.7.**

*The opening page of a brochure for the 1995 U.S. Open golf tournament.*

**FIGURE 9.8.**

*The page that appears when I click the text in the center of the screen in Figure 9.7.*

Clicking either of the golfer photos to the left displays information about that golfer. (I had the right instinct before, just the wrong page.) The scrollbar on the right side of the page allows me to read all the text on this page.

Finally, clicking on the *Golf Digest* magazine on the left side of the page displays information about that veteran duffer's rag, the real sponsor behind this page. This is an excellent example of how companies use titles on MSN, mixing useful, interesting information with a little friendly sales pitch, all in an easy-to-swallow, pretty package. It's perfect for your cyber-coffee table.

# What Now?

Having acquired all the skills necessary to operate the skill-proof MSN titles, your MSN abilities are complete. You know all you need to know to operate all the basic services that make up MSN—and to make the most of them.

Indeed, you are powerful—but you are not a Jedi yet. Part III of this book, "Taking Control of MSN," offers advanced techniques for finding anything on MSN, tweaking your configuration, saving online minutes (hence dollars), embedding MSN content in documents as OLE objects, and much more. None of what Part III offers is mandatory, but the techniques described there endow you with more precise control over MSN.

*Power-shmower* you say—I wanna get on the Internet! Okay by me. Skip to Part IV, "Navigating the Internet through MSN."

PART *III*

# TAKING CONTROL
# OF MSN

Finding Anything on MSN    169

Advanced Configuration Options    181

Trimming Time Online    191

Power E-Mail    199

Speeding Up MSN    219

# 10

# FINDING ANYTHING ON MSN

Finding Services

Finding People

Finding It on the Internet

What Now?

MSN is organized by subject (more or less). That makes it possible to browse for MSN resources related to a given topic—*possible*, yes, but not always efficient.

Subjects overlap, and valuable information about a given subject can wind up in an unrelated MSN category or forum. In addition, MSN is growing rapidly; as the number of forums and resources expands, finding anything specific will become more difficult and time consuming. *Point-and-click* is a search method for folks who have lots of free time and no immediate needs. Those who need something specific, and need it now, require a more targeted search method.

Fortunately, MSN has a companion Find utility that looks up any MSN resource quickly: a file, a title, a document, a BBS message, or any other MSN content that matches a search term you supply. The Find utility works much like the Windows 95 Find program for locating anything on your PC or local network, but the MSN Find utility is actually easier to use.

When you're hunting for a person rather than a resource, MSN has an answer for that, too. Although many MSN members don't even know it's there, MSN offers a member Address Book you can search to find a specific MSN member, or even a list of members, matching a specific profile: name, profession, place of residence, and so on.

In this chapter, you learn the following:

◆   How to find MSN resources matching a search term you supply

◆   How to find MSN members by name or personal profile

◆   About the Internet search tools covered in detail in Part IV of this book, "Navigating the Internet through MSN"

---

*Note*

As Microsoft continues to integrate Internet resources into the MSN interface, many people may begin to think of MSN and the Internet as a single, cohesive environment. But it's important to understand that, as far as the Find utility is concerned, MSN and the Internet are separate worlds. (Although Find may locate MSN shortcuts to Internet resources, these shortcuts point to only a tiny fraction of the full Internet.) The same holds true for the MSN Address Book; it lists and searches for only MSN members, not the universe of Internet users.

MSN Find searches for information located only in MSN resources—folders and forums, BBSes and libraries, chats, titles, and kiosks. In a limited way, MSN Find can also search Internet newsgroups (it searches only the newsgroup name, not the newsgroup's contents). Find does not find anything on the World Wide Web, FTP sites, or other regions of the Internet.

To learn about searching the Internet, see "Finding It on the Internet," later in this chapter.

# Finding Services

After you set up The Microsoft Network on your PC, a new item is added to the Find submenu of every Windows 95 window and to the Find item on the Start menu. Online or off, if you choose **T**ools, **F**ind from any window in Windows 95 or MSN, or you choose Find from the Start menu, you see these three choices:

| Option | Description |
| --- | --- |
| **F**iles or Folders... | Searches the contents of your PC for files or folders |
| **C**omputer... | Searches for a computer on your local network (if you are connected to a local network) |
| On The **M**icrosoft Network... | Searches for resources on MSN |

If you choose On The **M**icrosoft Network from a Find submenu while connected to MSN, the screen shown in Figure 10.1 appears. (If you choose this item while offline, the MSN Sign-In dialog box appears. After you sign in, the screen shown in Figure 10.1 appears.)

**FIGURE 10.1.**
*The MSN Find utility.*

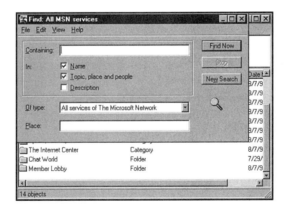

When online, you can also open the Find utility by right-clicking the MSN icon in the taskbar to display its context menu. Then choose **F**ind.

*Tip*

---

### A Basic Search (for the Impatient)

The Find utility is as simple, or as complicated, as you make it. You can easily phrase a basic, simple search, or use the upcoming information in this chapter to tailor your search.

To perform a basic search, follow these steps:

1. Enter a word in the **C**ontaining box that you think may be contained in information about the resource you're looking for. For example, to find resources related to boating, enter **boat** in the **C**ontaining field.

2. Select all the checkboxes.

3. Leave the default entry (All Services...) in the **O**f Type box.

4. Leave the **P**lace field blank.

5. Click **F**ind Now.

After searching, Find opens a pane at the bottom of the dialog box and lists any likely matches there. Jump to the resource described by any listing by double-clicking the entry.

---

Recall from Chapter 4, "Basic Navigation Techniques," that everything on MSN has its own Properties sheet. The Find utility searches through the information contained in Properties sheets to identify MSN resources that match your search criteria.

> Internet newsgroups do not have Properties sheets. The Find utility looks for your search term (the word in the **C**ontaining field) in the newsgroup name.

At the top of the Find dialog box in Figure 10.1 is the **C**ontaining text box. In this field, you enter a word or part of a word (a *substring*) you believe may be contained in the Properties sheet of the service you're looking for. (Although it's not labeled so here, the word or substring you enter is generally described as a *search term*.)

In the remaining areas of the Find dialog box, you customize the search by telling Find which parts of Properties sheets to consider in the search (in one case, you specify what to look for there). Table 10.1 lists the areas of interest in the Find dialog box.

**Table 10.1 Options of interest in the Find dialog box.**

| Option | Description |
|---|---|
| **N**ame | The name of the service (see the Properties sheet in Figure 10.2). If this box is selected, Find searches the Name fields in Properties sheets to find matches for the search string. |
| **T**opic, Place, and People | If this box is checked, Find searches the Topics, Place, and People fields (three separate fields) in the Properties sheets to find matches for the search string (see Figure 10.3). The Topics field is just that: the topic of the item. The Place field specifies the geographical region in which MSN users have access to the item—usually The world. The People field specifies the group of MSN users who has access to the item—usually Everyone. |
| **D**escription | If this box is checked, Find searches the Description field in the Properties sheets to find matches for the search string (see Figure 10.2). The Description field contains descriptive text for this item. |
| **O**f Type | In this drop-down list, you can leave the default (All Services...) if you want to search through the Properties sheets of all types of items on MSN. Alternatively, you can choose a specific type of resource from the drop-down list, which includes entries for folders and forums, BBSs and libraries, chat rooms, titles, kiosks and other documents, and Internet newsgroups. Find searches only the Properties sheets whose Type field (see Figure 10.2) matches the selection you make here. |
| **P**lace | You can leave this text box empty to search all Properties sheets without regard to the entry in the Place field. Alternatively, you can type a place name in the box. In searching for matches for your search term, Find searches only the Properties sheets whose Place field matches the entry you make here. As you can for the **C**ontaining box, you can type a full place name or a substring. For example, if you enter **New** in the **P**lace box, Find searches Properties sheets containing the places New York, New Jersey, and New Hampshire. |

**FIGURE 10.2.**

*The General page of a Properties sheet, which Find searches for matches to Name, Description, and Type entries.*

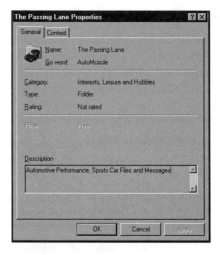

**FIGURE 10.3.**

*The Context page of a Properties sheet, which Find searches for matches to Topic, People, and Place entries.*

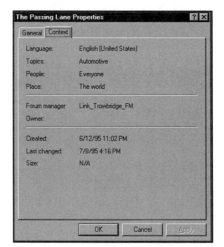

# Phrasing Search Terms

The two text boxes in the Find dialog box, **C**ontaining and **P**lace, allow you to enter a word, words, or *substrings* (partial words with wildcard characters) to fine-tune your search. In either box, you have a number of powerful options for tailoring your search.

*Tip*

Find is not case sensitive. Entering the search term New York, new york, or NEW YORK produces the same results.

## Matching Multiple Words

You can search for matches to multiple words in three ways. To explain, I'll use various terms and abbreviations for the Internet's World Wide Web (which is variously abbreviated as *Web*, *WWW*, or *W3*). I can enter these terms to search MSN for information or programs related to the Web.

**And.** Separate words with and to match only those Properties sheets that contain *all* the words in the search term. Consider these examples:

| Search Term | What It Finds |
| --- | --- |
| web and internet | Matches only services whose sheets contain both web and internet. |
| web and internet and browser | Matches only services whose sheets contain all three words. |

**Or.** Separate words with a comma (,) to match only those Properties sheets that contain any one or more of the words in the search term. The "or" approach casts a wider net than the "and" approach: It picks up all the entries the same term would if phrased with "and" *plus* other entries containing only one of the words. Consider these examples:

| Search Term | What It Finds |
| --- | --- |
| web,www | Matches all services whose sheets contain either web or www. Also matches services whose sheets contain both terms. |
| web,www,w3 | Matches all services whose sheets contain one, two, or all three words in the search term. |

**Exact.** Surround words with quotation marks (" ") to match only those Properties sheets that contain the exact sequence of words entered. Consider these examples:

| Search Term | What It Finds |
| --- | --- |
| "world wide web" | Matches only Properties sheets that contain the exact phrase world wide web. |
| "web browser" | Matches only Properties sheets that contain the exact phrase web browser. |

> If you place words together, do not separate them with a comma, and do not place them in quotation marks, Find assumes you mean "and." For example, entering **gates microsoft** is the same as entering **gates and microsoft**.

*Tip*

## Matching Partial Words (Substrings)

To match a partial word, use the wildcard characters ? and * at the end of, or in the middle of, a word or partial word. (You cannot use a wildcard at the beginning of a word.)

**Asterisk (*).** An asterisk stands in for one or more characters. Consider these examples:

| Search Term | What It Finds |
|---|---|
| brows* | Matches browse, browsing, browser, and browsed. |
| b*ball | Matches baseball and basketball. |
| net* | Matches nets, network, networks, Netware, netting, and Netscape. |

**Question Mark (?).** A question mark stands in for a single character. You may use more than one question mark to stand in for a specific number of characters. Consider these examples:

| Search Term | What It Finds |
|---|---|
| brows? | Matches browse but *not* browsing, browser, or browsed. |
| b???ball | Matches baseball but *not* basketball. |
| net???? | Matches network, Netware, and netting but *not* nets, networks, or Netscape. |

You can also use both wildcards together. For example, "w?? brows*" matches the exact phrases web browsing, web browser, web browsers, www browsing, www browser, and www browsers.

# Finding People

As a matter of habit, you should make note of any interesting MSN members you meet in your travels and add them to your Personal Address Book (see Chapter 13, "Power E-Mail"). On BBSs and in chat rooms, you meet people with whom you share interests; you should keep track of their member IDs so that you can contact them again to ask a question, share information, and so on.

But you can also look up other MSN users by their names, place of residence, or even personal information about them (such as their occupation). The first step is to open the MSN Member Directory in Exchange's Address Book facility:

1. While connected to MSN, choose E-**M**ail from the home page, MSN Central (or double-click the Inbox icon on your desktop).

2. When Exchange opens, click the Address Book icon on the toolbar (or choose **T**ools, **A**ddress Book). The Address Book window appears.

3. On the right side of the Address Book window is a drop-down list with the label **S**how Names From The. Select Microsoft Network from the list. The MSN member directory appears, as shown in Figure 10.4.

**FIGURE 10.4.**

*The MSN member directory.*

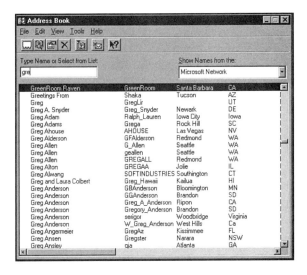

The directory is sorted alphabetically, by member name (not member ID, which appears in the second column). To locate a member by name, use the scrollbar, or type the first few letters of the name in the Type Name or Select From List box, as shown in Figure 10.4.

When you find the member you're looking for, you can do any of the following:

◆ Select the entry and then click the Add to Personal Address Book button (the open book with a down arrow above it) on the toolbar to add this user to your Personal Address Book (see Chapter 13, "Power E-Mail.")

◆ Double-click the entry to display the Member Properties sheet for the member. The Member Properties sheet shows the member's full name, member ID, city and town, plus any optional personal or professional information the user has disclosed (see Chapter 13 to learn how to enter information about yourself in your own Member Properties sheet).

When you don't know the member's name, you'll have to search. With the member directory open, choose Tools, Find. A blank Properties sheet appears like the one in Figure 10.5.

**FIGURE 10.5.**

*A Properties sheet for finding an MSN member.*

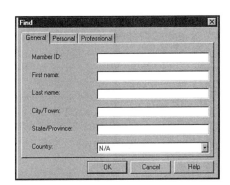

The Properties sheet shown in Figure 10.5 is a blank version of the sheet available for every MSN member. To search for a member, enter as much information as you know about the member; use any of the tabs. Click OK. Don't enter too much information; if you enter any incorrect information, your target member will be rejected by the search. Simply enter what you know.

For example, if you know the member's last name is *Welke* and he lives in Needham, MA, enter only this much information and click OK. The Find utility displays its results in the Address Book window. If it turns out that there's more than one MSN member named Welke living in Needham, MSN displays a list of the answers. Read each entry, or display each entry's Properties sheet, to determine which Welke is your Welke.

In Figure 10.6, I know the member's full name is *Mark Taber*, but I don't know where he lives. I fill in just the First Name and Last Name fields and click OK; I discover that there are two Mark Tabers on MSN—one in Indiana and one in England (see Figure 10.7). I'm pretty sure my Taber's domestic, so I've found him—even though I started with nothing but a name and never bothered to fill in a country for my search.

**FIGURE 10.6.**

*Searching for all MSN members named Mark Taber.*

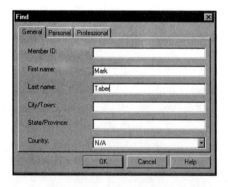

**FIGURE 10.7.**

*The search results: the only two Mark Tabers on MSN.*

For every MSN member, the General tab of the Member Properties sheet—which contains the member ID, name, city/town, state, and country—is always completely filled in. Any entry you make in the General tab of the Find dialog box is a reliable way to find MSN members.

However, all the information on the other tabs is optional; it is not supplied unless the member has filled it in. (You learn how to fill in your own Member Properties sheet in Chapter 13, "Power E-Mail.") Beyond the General tab, members are free to disclose as much—or as little—about themselves as they choose. A great many members never bother filling in this information—or aren't aware that they can. That's why you cannot rely on entries in the Personal or Professional tabs of the Find dialog box to locate a specific MSN member (although you can try it when more reliable methods fail to deliver).

However, you can perform searches using entries in the Personal and Professional tabs to locate lists of members who share any of the following personal/professional criteria with you:

◆ Date of birth

◆ Language

◆ Job description

◆ Employer

Of course, you can also use the City/Town entry in the General tab to find MSN members who *live* in the same town; you can use the City/Town entry in the Professional tab to find MSN members who *work* in the same town. Such member lists may be useful for meeting new people or for professional networking.

Just keep in mind that the results will not show *all* MSN members who may match the criteria. The results show only members who have disclosed that information.

Once you locate your member, highlight the member's listing and do one of the following:

◆ Click the Add to Personal Address Book button in the toolbar to add that member to your Personal Address Book so that you don't have to search for him or her again.

◆ Click the Compose New Message button (the envelope) in the toolbar to compose an e-mail message addressed to that member.

# Finding It on the Internet

Everything on MSN proper is in one place: the MSN data center. That makes searching through MSN a fairly simple operation. The Internet, however, is not nearly so centralized; as a result, there's no such thing as a truly comprehensive Internet search method. And there probably never will be.

However, there are a number of very effective Internet search tools. Although they can't search the whole Internet, that doesn't mean they can't turn up what you're looking for. These tools are operated from within Internet client software (see Chapter 15, "Understanding the Internet"), not from within the MSN client software.

- ◆ **Web Searches.** Web search tools are perhaps the most useful search tools. They are a variety of search engines and directories on the World Wide Web that match your search term not only to Web pages, but to other Internet resources such as files for downloading. See Chapter 16, "Browsing the World Wide Web."

- ◆ **Archie Searches.** When you're looking for a particular file or program on the Internet, and you know its exact name, Archie is the quickest and most powerful way to find it. See Chapter 18, "Downloading Files with FTP."

- ◆ **Veronica Searches.** A system of menus called Gophers makes navigating to and using many Internet resources as simple as clicking through menu items. Veronica is a search engine that can find any menu or menu item among the many thousands that make up Gopherspace. See Chapter 17, "Browsing Gophers."

# What Now?

In addition to turning up the MSN resources and members you're looking for, the search tools described in this chapter provide another valuable service: they save *time*. After all, how long would you have to browse for a given resource if there were no Find utility? Because all MSN pricing plans charge a per-hour rate when you exceed a fairly low monthly minimum, on MSN, time is literally money. And time saved is money earned.

Chapter 12, "Trimming Time Online," is devoted to that principle. It offers tips and techniques for getting online, getting your business done, and getting offline again in the minimum time—and dollars—necessary.

# CHAPTER 11

# ADVANCED CONFIGURATION OPTIONS

Registering File Types

Changing Language

Filling in Your Own Member Properties

Setting Up Multiple Accounts

What Now?

Like any Windows program, MSN does a pretty good job of making default configuration selections. Most people will undoubtedly accept the defaults and work happily within them. Don't allow the defaults, however, to mislead you into thinking that you do not control the behavior of MSN.

To supplement the modifications you can make with the techniques described in Chapter 2, "Maintaining Your MSN Account," this chapter describes some powerful ways you can modify your MSN or Windows 95 configuration to make important changes to MSN's appearance and behavior. Not many users will bother with these changes, but the few who need them will appreciate MSN's flexibility in these areas.

In this chapter, you learn how to do the following:

◆ Choose which programs MSN runs to display documents and open downloaded files

◆ Change the language used in MSN, or adapt MSN to display material in languages other than English

◆ Enter information about yourself in your MSN Properties sheet so that other MSN members can learn more about you

◆ Set up more than one MSN account on the same PC

# Registering File Types

MSN relies on Windows 95's File Types registry to open applications to display or play files copied to your PC. For example, whenever you open an MSN document icon, such as a kiosk, MSN copies the document file to your PC and then displays the file by opening it in the program your File Types registry designates for opening Rich Text Format (RTF) files. When you download a document, sound, picture, video, or other data file from a BBS with the Download and Run options (see Chapter 7, "Downloading and Uploading Files"), the file is opened on your PC using the application the File Types registry associates with the extension used by the file you downloaded.

*Tip*

> Unlike other Web browsers, Internet Explorer relies on the Windows 95 File Types registry when displaying or playing some types of files located on the Web. (Most Web browsers use their own internal configuration screens for defining viewers.) In Internet Explorer, you can change the programs Internet Explorer uses by editing the File Types registry as described in this chapter.

The File Types registry is used not only by MSN, but throughout Windows 95 to open applications. When you double-click a data file's icon in Windows Explorer, My Computer, or on the desktop, Windows can automatically open the application required for editing or playing the file. For example, double-clicking the icon for a WAV sound clip automatically opens Windows 95's Media Player to play the sound because Media Player is registered to WAV files by default. Also by default, small text files automatically open Notepad and larger text files open WordPad.

After some experience with MSN, you may find that you want to change the File Types registry. For example, installing Word for Windows changes the default program used to open DOC files from WordPad to Word. But Word is a large application that takes a long time to open; WordPad is comparatively smaller and quicker.

---

### Registering for Actions Other than Open

The most common use of registering files is to open the application to display or play the selected file. You can, however, use registrations to perform any action on the file—as long as that action is supported by a command line. For example, you may be able to print a file, play a clip, or dial a modem connection. You can use these capabilities to automatically print any document you find on MSN. (See "Editing a Registered Action," later in this chapter.)

---

All the procedures given in this chapter for working with file types can be performed offline—and *should* be done offline (unless you don't care how high your MSN bill gets).

## Registering a File Type

To change registrations for file types (or to create new registrations with actions other than opening the file), choose **V**iew, **O**ptions from any menu in My Computer, Windows Explorer, Internet Explorer, or MSN. Click the File Types tab. A screen appears, showing a list of registered file types, including their descriptions and file type icons (see Figure 11.1). When you select a file type, the File Type Details area shows the extension and the file used to open the file type.

**FIGURE 11.1.**

*The current File Types registry.*

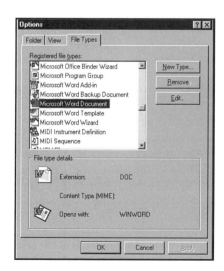

To edit an existing registration, select a file type and click **Edit**. You see a screen like the one shown in Figure 11.2; Figure 11.2 shows a description of a current registration for Word documents (DOC files).

**FIGURE 11.2.**

*Changing an entry for the File Types registry.*

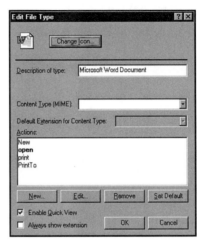

> Note the two checkboxes at the bottom of the screen shown in Figure 11.2:
>
> ◆ Select the first checkbox to add a Quick View item to the context menu so that the files can be viewed through Quick View. (Quick View is an optional Windows 95 feature for viewing files without opening them.)
>
> ◆ Select the second checkbox to prevent Windows Explorer from hiding the file's extension, which it does by default for all registered file types.

Each of the actions in the **Actions** list box appears in the context menu for a file of that type. The action shown in bold (**open**, in Figure 11.2) is the default; that's the action taken automatically when you double-click a file of this type. The other actions are usually selected from the context menu. The Print action can be selected from the context menu or executed by dropping the file on a printer icon.

## Editing a Registered Action

Behind the scenes, each action listed is performed by a command line, typically an application start-up command. (You may use any command supported under Windows, including application command-line switches. If you're unfamiliar with command structures, see Windows 95's Help, your Windows documentation, or a good general-purpose Windows 95 book, such as *Windows 95 Unleashed*, published by Sams.) To see the command, select an action and click **Edit**. For this example, click the **open** action and then click **Edit** to see a screen like the one in Figure 11.3.

**FIGURE 11.3.**
*Editing a registered action.*

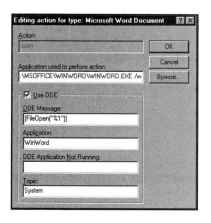

Note that the command shown is the command to open Word. You can create any action for which a command line is available to work on the particular file format selected.

◆ To edit the command line for an action, enter a new path and program in the Application Used To Perform Action text box (or click the **B**rowse button to browse for one) and click OK to close the dialog box.

◆ To create a new action for this file type, click the **N**ew button on the Edit File Type screen (shown earlier in Figure 11.2). Enter a name for the action, preceded by an ampersand (for example, &Print). Then enter a command line (and switch, if necessary). After you finish, your new action appears in the context menu for all files of that type.

◆ To make an action the default (the action taken when you double-click an icon for that file type), select the action from the Edit File Type screen (shown earlier in Figure 11.2) and click **S**et Default.

# Changing Languages

Because you're reading this, it's reasonable to assume that you read English, a language I use here and there throughout this book. That's just as well, because—despite the fact that it is an international service—the overwhelming majority of MSN content is in English, supplied by English speakers in the United States and abroad.

However, speakers of other languages do contribute to MSN, and MSN itself can be configured to display only the submissions in certain languages (at this writing, English, French, and German are supported, but more will be added). Note that nothing is translated on MSN. When you switch languages, you don't see the same documents and BBS messages in another language. You see MSN content ordinarily filtered from U.S. members' screens.

Language settings affect only the MSN client interface. They have no effect on the language used in, or the content displayed by, your Internet client software.

To edit your language options, connect to MSN and choose **V**iew, **O**ptions. On the Properties sheet that appears, click the General tab. A screen appears like the one shown in Figure 11.4.

**FIGURE 11.4.**

*Changing the language settings for MSN.*

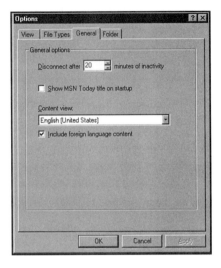

To change the language for which you want to see MSN content, select a language from the **C**ontent View list. MSN displays a message confirming that you have changed your content view and informing you that the change will take effect the next time you sign in. Figure 11.5 shows MSN's German content view.

**FIGURE 11.5.**

*MSN in German.*

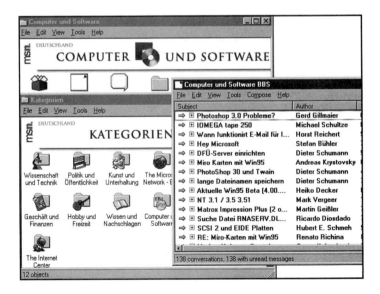

By default, the checkbox next to **I**nclude Foreign Language Content is not selected, meaning that MSN filters out BBS messages and other content submitted to MSN in languages other than the one selected in **C**ontent View. (Whether those languages are "foreign," as Microsoft labels them, of course, depends on who you are and where you live.) To instruct MSN to give you access to all content, regardless of language, select this checkbox.

There's another way to get a look at non-English content on MSN. After checking the **I**nclude Foreign Language Content checkbox (and signing out/signing in again so that the change can take effect), open the drop-down list shown on the toolbar of all category windows. Choose Worldwide Categories from this list. You can also switch MSN to Explorer view (as described in Chapter 4, "Basic Navigation Techniques") and choose Worldwide Categories from the drop-down list in Explorer's toolbar, as shown in Figure 11.6. From the folders on the right, you can navigate down to forums in French (Catégories) and German (Kategorien).

**FIGURE 11.6.**
*Navigating to*
*Worldwide Categories.*

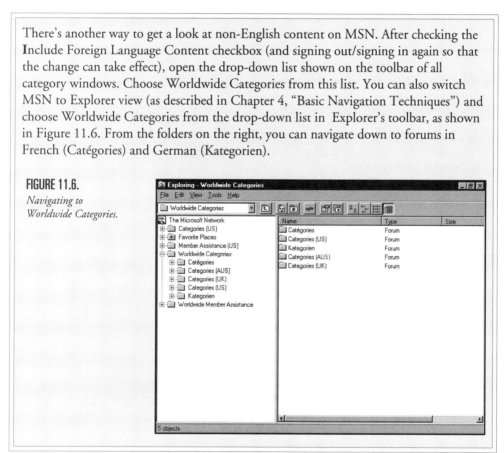

# Filling in Your Own Member Properties

Every MSN member has a Properties sheet that can be displayed by any other MSN member in a variety of ways. For example, you can open a BBS message from a particular member and choose **T**ools, **M**ember Properties or right-click a member's ID in a chat window and select Properties from the context menu.

The General tab of every member's Properties sheet is filled in automatically by MSN. The General tab shows a member's member ID, first and last names, city/town, state/province, and country. But there are two other tabs—Personal and Professional—in which a member can choose to disclose his or her date of birth, marital status, language spoken, job, company, and other personal or professional information.

To add information about yourself to your Member Properties sheet, follow these steps:

1. Sign on to MSN and select E-**M**ail from MSN Central.
2. Choose **T**ools, **A**ddress Book. Your Personal Address Book appears (see Chapter 13, "Power E-Mail").
3. In the Show Names In drop-down list, change Personal Address Book to Microsoft Network to open the MSN Member Directory.
4. In the Type Name… text box, type your full name. Exchange scrolls to your name in the member directory. Double-click your directory listing to open your own Properties sheet (see Figure 11.7).
5. Make any changes to any of the three tabs and then click OK.

**FIGURE 11.7.**

*Filling in your Member Properties sheet.*

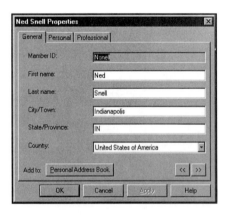

You are not required to supply any information in your Properties sheet other than what's automatically supplied in the General tab. Please consider that anything you enter in your Properties sheet can be accessed by thousands of other people you do not know. MSN members have the power to search for lists of members whose Properties sheets contain certain information (see Chapter 10, "Finding Anything on MSN").

Adding information to your Properties sheet invites the possibility (however unlikely) that you may be contacted not only by those with similar birthdays or professions, but by pests, scam artists, or those who want to sell you something. Do not disclose on your sheet anything you consider personal, or anything that exposes you to contacts you may not desire.

To put it another way, if you wouldn't disclose something in an ad in *USA Today* or tell it to a telemarketer, don't put it in your Properties sheet.

# Setting Up Multiple Accounts

Although you cannot (as yet) set up more than one member ID on the same MSN account, you can set up separate accounts on the same PC. This allows people who share a PC to each use a unique ID, to send and receive e-mail under that ID, and to be billed separately from any other users on the same PC.

Multiple accounts on the same PC are completely separate, with separate member IDs and billing information. (Although the accounts must use separate IDs, they can use identical billing information, as might be the case for separate accounts within a family.) However, all accounts on the same PC must share the same Favorite Places folder. The MSN software does not know how to create or access multiple Favorite Places folders on the same PC.

To create a second (or third or fourth) account on a PC on which an MSM account has already been installed, follow these steps:

1. Locate the Sign Up program, SIGNUP.EXE, in the folder C:\Program Files\The Microsoft Network.

2. Begin the sign-up procedure by double-clicking the Sign Up program icon. A screen like the one in Figure 11.8 appears.

**FIGURE 11.8.**

*Installing a second MSN account.*

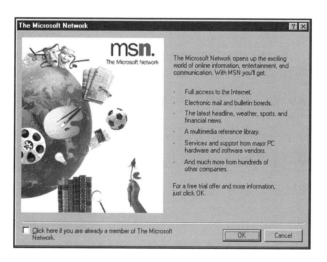

3. Make sure that the I Am Already a Member checkbox is not selected and proceed with installation as described in Chapter 1, "Setting Up, Signing In, and Signing Out."

During installation, the member ID you choose must be different from any other member ID on the PC (or from any other member ID on MSN, for that matter). All other information, including name and address, billing, and other information, can be the same or different. For example, you can choose not to give an account Internet access, even if other accounts on the same PC have Internet access.

# What Now?

When first learning about MSN, many folks think of it as a place to "hang out"—to browse, to explore, to spend time—and that's fine. But others can't work long on MSN without thinking about the charges that accrue for every online minute.

In some MSN sessions, those folks have no interest in exploring. They want to get online, do a job, and get off as quickly—and cheaply—as possible. Chapter 12 shows how to do just that.

# CHAPTER 12

# TRIMMING TIME ONLINE

Creating and Using Shortcuts

Linking and Embedding MSN Content

Using MSN Help Offline

Saving E-Mail Minutes

What Now?

"Time is money" is the principle upon which America functions. (Or is it "Money Talks"? I can never keep those straight.) Having discovered that simple truth, Microsoft chose to make some of its money based on the amount of time people spend on MSN (see Chapter 1, "Signing Up, Signing In, and Signing Out"). Now our time is Microsoft's money.

If you consider either your time or your money (or both) precious, you'll be happy to learn about ways to complete certain MSN tasks in the absolute minimum minutes online. These techniques are also useful when somebody else needs the phone line, when the house is on fire, or when you're in a hurry for any reason. Along the way, you'll pick up useful techniques that don't require a hurry.

In this chapter, you learn the following things:

◆ How to create shortcuts to MSN services

◆ How to create OLE links to MSN content

◆ How to consult MSN's Help file offline

◆ How to compose and read e-mail offline

◆ How to send and receive e-mail quickly

*Tip*

> If you're seriously interested in saving online time and money, consider applying the techniques described in Chapter 14, "Speeding Up MSN." After all, you're paying for the time you spend waiting for windows and programs to open. Make things happen faster, and you can get more done for less dough.

# Creating and Using Shortcuts

You can create a desktop shortcut to any icon in MSN. Note that you cannot create a shortcut to a specific BBS message or file within a BBS or library. But you can create a shortcut to the BBS or library itself, or to any folder, MSN title, chat room, newsgroup, document, or other MSN content represented by an icon.

## Creating an MSN Shortcut

To create a shortcut to an icon, right-click the icon to display its context menu and then choose Create Shortcut. (You can also select the icon and choose File, Create Shortcut.) A shortcut to the icon appears on your Windows desktop. You can leave it on your desktop, move it to any folder on your PC, or add it to your Start menu as you would any shortcut or program. (Right-click the taskbar, choose Properties, click the Start Menu tab, and choose Add.)

You cannot add shortcuts you create this way to your MSN Favorite Places folder. Only shortcuts created by selecting Add to Favorite Places appear in the Favorite Places folder.

## Using MSN Shortcuts

MSN shortcuts are like any Windows 95 shortcuts, with one important difference. They are smart enough to know whether you're online or not. If you are online, double-clicking an MSN shortcut takes you to the resource the shortcut points to. If you're offline, double-clicking an MSN shortcut opens the Sign In dialog box. After you sign in to MSN, the shortcut automatically takes you to the resource it points to.

You can insert MSN shortcuts in documents: follow the same steps you use to insert any file in a document. You can insert shortcuts in e-mail messages and BBS messages you compose; you can also insert shortcuts in document files you send to other MSN members. (Note that you cannot insert MSN shortcuts in newsgroup messages.) As long as the reader of a document has an MSN account, he or she can double-click the shortcut icon in your message to navigate to the MSN service.

While connected to MSN, you can insert a shortcut in an e-mail message or BBS message by opening the message, moving the pointer to the icon for which you want to create a shortcut, dragging the icon, and dropping it in the message.

While disconnected from MSN, you can insert a previously created MSN shortcut in an e-mail message, BBS message, or document you're composing offline by opening the message, moving the pointer to the shortcut on your Windows desktop, dragging the icon, and dropping it in the message.

A good example of how this technique may be applied is to invite others to join you in a chat room (see Chapter 6, "Hanging Out in Chat Rooms") at a prearranged time. To each person you want to chat with, send an e-mail message containing a shortcut to the chat room (see Figure 12.1). At the appointed time, each invitee can open the e-mail message in Exchange, double-click the shortcut, and go directly to the chat room. Alternatively, you can insert the shortcut in a document file and send the document file to each member. At the appointed time, each member can open the document on his or her PC and execute the shortcut.

If you regularly send e-mail messages to a group of people, create a personal distribution list for that group, as described in Chapter 13, "Power E-Mail."

**FIGURE 12.1.**

*An MSN shortcut in an e-mail message.*

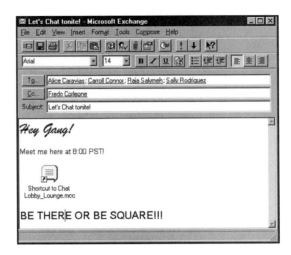

# Linking and Embedding MSN Content

MSN supports Windows 95's Object Linking and Embedding (OLE) features so that you can embed or link MSN content within documents on your PC. The application used to create the document in which you embed or link content must be OLE compliant (as most major Windows word processors and other document-producing applications are). In a non-OLE compliant application, you can only copy MSN content into a document; you cannot embed or link it.

How are linking and embedding different from copying? First, OLE objects carry with them program code from the application that created them. This code allows you to edit an object within the application you inserted it in—using the editing tools from the application that created the object. When you link or embed an object, you also have a greater ability to preserve formatting of text; copying often discards text formatting and copies only the text.

Here's a breakdown of the differences between linking and embedding:

◆ A *linked object* remains tied to the source from which you copied it. When the original MSN content changes, you can update the linked content to match it by choosing a menu item, as described later in this section.

◆ An *embedded object* is separated from the source and cannot be automatically updated to match the source if the source changes.

To link or embed MSN content in a document on your PC, follow these steps:

1. Open the document into which you want to insert the MSN content.

2. Connect to MSN and navigate to the content you want to insert in the document.

3. Select the content and choose **Edit**, **Copy**.

4. Switch to the document; choose **Edit** and then choose one of the following options:

| Option | To Do... |
|---|---|
| **P**aste | Embed the object. |
| Paste **S**pecial Link | Link the object. A screen like the one in Figure 12.2 appears. |

**FIGURE 12.2.**

*Creating a link to MSN content.*

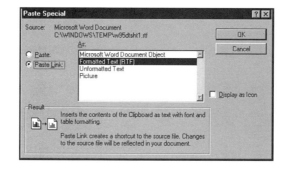

To finish creating a link using the screen shown in Figure 12.2, click the Paste Link radio button and then choose from the **A**s list the way you want the information treated in the document (the choices in this list differ depending on the content you select). Click OK when finished.

To update a link to MSN content once the link has been created, follow these steps:

1. Connect to MSN.
2. Open the document containing the link; choose **E**dit, **L**inks.
3. Select the MSN link from the list that appears and then choose **U**pdate Link.

To learn more about OLE, see Windows 95 Help.

# Using MSN Help Offline

Under most circumstances, you'll want to open Help when you're online to answer a specific question and then jump back to MSN to use what you've learned. But there may be circumstances under which you want to consult MSN Help at your own pace, offline, to learn new techniques or to solve complex questions.

To use MSN Help offline, follow these steps:

1. Choose Run from the Start menu.
2. Enter `winhelp msn`.

# Saving E-Mail Minutes

When you compose and read e-mail while connected to MSN, you burn money. There's no reason not to read and compose your e-mail offline, at your own pace, for free.

---

### Composing BBS and Newsgroup Messages Offline

You can compose the body copy of BBS and newsgroup messages offline, as well:

1. Compose a message in your favorite word processor or text editor and leave the file open on your desktop.
2. Sign on to MSN and navigate to the BBS or newsgroup to which you want to post the message.
3. Choose Co**m**pose, **N**ew Message to open a New Message window.
4. Switch to the open document on your desktop, highlight the text of your precomposed message, and choose **E**dit, **C**opy.
5. Click in the body of the New Message window and choose **E**dit, **P**aste.

---

## Composing Mail Offline

To compose e-mail offline, follow these steps:

1. Open Exchange but do not connect to MSN.
2. Choose Co**m**pose, **N**ew Message. Compose and address your new message.
3. When finished, click the Send button or choose **F**ile, **S**end. The message is stored in Exchange's Outbox folder, where it remains until you connect to MSN, open Exchange, and choose **T**ools, **D**eliver Mail Now (as described in Chapter 8, "Composing, Sending, and Receiving E-Mail").

*Tip*

Addressing MSN e-mail offline is more convenient if you have created a Personal Address Book, which allows you to choose a name from a list instead of typing an address. See Chapter 13, "Power E-Mail."

## Reading Mail Offline

To read mail offline, connect to MSN, open Exchange, and choose **T**ools, **D**eliver Mail Now. When the message Checking for New Messages disappears, all new e-mail has been copied to your PC. You can sign out and read your mail at your leisure.

To retrieve mail in the shortest time possible, follow these steps:

1. While offline, open Exchange.
2. Choose **T**ools, **D**eliver Mail Now (as described in Chapter 8, "Composing, Sending, and Receiving E-Mail").

Exchange opens the MSN Sign In dialog box. After you sign in, Exchange checks for new messages, copies any waiting e-mail to your PC, and then immediately disconnects from MSN.

# What Now?

The techniques described in this chapter allow you to do whatever you want to do on MSN, but to do it quickly so that you save time and money.

Chapter 13, "Power E-Mail," offers techniques for making the most of MSN's electronic mail facilities.

CHAPTER

# 13

# POWER E-MAIL

E-Mail Options

Using Your Personal Address Book

Creating and Using a Personal Distribution List

Attaching Files to E-Mail Messages

Sending MSN E-Mail from Windows Applications

Combining MSN E-Mail with Other Services

Sending Faxes Through MSN

What Now?

Ninety-five percent of the people on this planet who communicate with e-mail do so in only the most low-rent way. They type somebody's e-mail address (from memory, usually), type a short message in flat, unformatted text, and send the message on its way. And quaint as that seems, it gets the job done. A working 72 Volkswagen may not have all the features of a 96 Lexus, but it gets you to K-Mart all the same. What more do you *really* need?

None of the advanced e-mail techniques described in this chapter is an essential part of e-mailing (in fact, many MSN members will never do any of this stuff). But should you choose to discover the tips and techniques offered here, you'll acquire skills that make your e-mailing more convenient and more powerful. You can use e-mail not simply as a way to send a batch of words across a wire, but as a medium for files and pictures. And you can better organize and manage information about the people with whom you exchange messages online.

In this chapter, you learn how to do the following:

◆ Customize Exchange

◆ Create and use a Personal Address Book

◆ Create and use a Personal Distribution List

◆ Attach files to e-mail messages

◆ Send MSN e-mail directly from Windows applications

The material in this chapter assumes you understand the principles and techniques covered in Chapter 8, "Composing, Sending, and Receiving E-Mail."

Also, Chapter 12, "Trimming Time Online," describes ways you can save money by trimming the online time required for e-mail activities.

# E-Mail Options

Choose **T**ools, **O**ptions to display the Exchange Options dialog box, which allows you to customize the way Exchange behaves. The next several pages describe the Exchange options that are especially useful or relevant in MSN. (Remember, Exchange can be used for other e-mail systems, and for faxing, as well.) In several instances, the Options dialog box merely sets defaults for options you can also set for individual messages when you compose them.

## The Read Tab

The Read tab (shown in Figure 13.1) controls what happens when you delete or move an open message, and whether and how the text of an original message is to be quoted when you reply to that message or forward it.

In the After Moving or Deleting an Open Item area at the top of the Read tab, select one of the three radio buttons to control what happens when you move or delete an open message. You

can instruct Exchange to automatically open the message (item) above the moved or deleted message, open the message below it, or close the message window and return to the message list.

In the When Replying to or Forwarding an Item area of the Read tab, you can select from these options:

◆ Select the **I**nclude the Original Text When Replying checkbox to automatically quote the text of the message to which you are replying, separated from your message by a reply separator.

◆ Select the Indent the **O**riginal Text When Replying checkbox to indent the quoted message to help distinguish it from your message.

◆ Select the **C**lose the Original Item checkbox to close the original message after you begin to compose your reply.

◆ Click the **F**ont button to select a unique font for the reply text to further distinguish it from the quoted portion of the message.

**FIGURE 13.1.**

*The Read tab of Exchange's Options dialog box.*

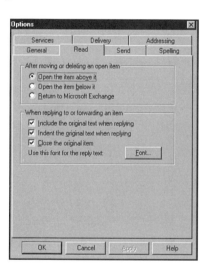

## The Spelling Tab

The Spelling tab of the Options dialog box (see Figure 13.2) offers options for controlling how spell checking is handled.

◆ Select the Always **S**uggest Replacements for Misspelled Words checkbox to instruct the spell checker to suggest replacements for any misspelled words it finds. Although this option is handy, note that it slows down spell checking considerably.

◆ Select the Always **C**heck Spelling Before Sending checkbox to instruct Exchange to run the spell checker automatically whenever you click Send.

◆ Select the Words in **UPPERCASE**, Words with **N**umbers, or The **O**riginal Text in a Reply or Forward checkbox to instruct Exchange to ignore these items when spell checking.

**FIGURE 13.2.**

*The Spelling tab of Exchange's Options dialog box.*

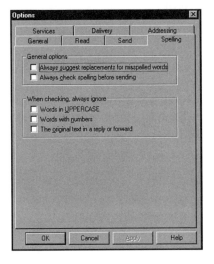

## The Send Tab

The Send tab of the Options dialog box (see Figure 13.3) offers options for controlling how messages are sent.

◆ Click **F**ont to select a default font for message text. You can also change the font selectively for any message by choosing Form**a**t, **F**onts while you are composing a message.

◆ Select The Item Has Been **R**ead checkbox to request that the recipient's e-mail program send to you a receipt message when your message has been read by your recipient.

◆ Select The Item Has Been **D**elivered checkbox to request that the recipient's e-mail program send to you a receipt message when your message has been delivered to the recipient, but not necessarily read.

*Note*

Receipt options require that your recipient use an e-mail program that understands them and can respond with an appropriate receipt message. Because all MSN users use Exchange for e-mail, both of these receipt options always work in messages to other MSN members. Either or both receipt options may not work in messages to the Internet, CompuServe, or other systems outside of MSN, depending on the e-mail program used by the recipient. In general, the receipt when delivered option is more reliable than the receipt when read option.

**FIGURE 13.3.**

*The Send tab of Exchange's Options dialog box.*

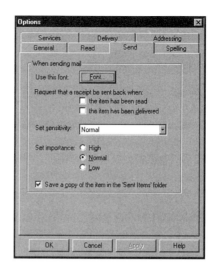

The Set **S**ensitivity options can add or remove a `Sensitivity` line in the headers of messages you send. This line helps define the type of content the message contains, and in one case can restrict the receiver's reply and forward capabilities. Here are the available sensitivity choices:

◆ **Normal.** No sensitivity line appears in the message header.

◆ **Personal.** Adds a sensitivity line to the header, which reads `Sensitivity: Personal`.

◆ **Private.** Adds a sensitivity line to the header, which reads `Sensitivity: Private`. This option also prevents the recipient from making any changes to the quote of your message when replying to it or forwarding it.

◆ **Confidential.** Adds a sensitivity line to the header, which reads `Sensitivity: Confidential`. This option simply *informs* the reader that you intend the message as confidential. It does not provide any special protection against the message being forwarded or blabbed around. You have to rely on the integrity of the recipient.

The Set Importance options can add or remove an `Importance` line in the headers of messages you send. In some recipient's e-mail packages (including Exchange), this header line is used to add an icon next to the message's entry in the message list. In Exchange, an exclamation point (!) appears next to messages sent as Hi**g**h Importance; a down arrow (↓) appears next to messages of **L**ow Importance; no icon appears next to messages of **N**ormal Importance.

The Set Importance options change only the default importance selection. You can select the High or Low Importance button from the toolbar while composing a message to override the default setting (the toolbar button for High Importance is the exclamation point; the toolbar button for Low Importance is a down arrow). Alternatively, you can deselect both options to send your message with Normal Importance.

*Note*

> Don't be misled by the importance options. The "importance" of a message has absolutely no effect on the speed or priority at which it is delivered. The Importance options simply tag the message as more or less important to help the recipient decide how quickly to read it.
>
> Of course, there's nothing to prevent a recipient from completely ignoring a message tagged as High Importance—which is just as well. What's terribly important to the sender may not be so important to the recipient. I have received several advertisements through MSN e-mail, all tagged as High Importance by their senders, and all completely unimportant to me.

The final checkbox on the Send tab, Save a **C**opy of the Item in the 'Sent Items' Folder, automatically saves a copy of any message you send in Exchange's Sent Items folder after you send the message. Until you delete a message from the Sent Items folder, you can open it there to review what you have sent. After deleting it from the Sent Items folder, you can review it in the Deleted Items folder. After you delete it from the Deleted Items folder, the messages is gone.

### The Addressing Tab

From the **S**how This Address List First drop-down list on the Addressing tab, you select the default Address Book that appears when you choose **T**ools, **A**ddress Book or click the Address Book button in the toolbar. If you create a Personal Address Book as described later in this chapter, choose Personal Address Book from this drop-down list. Otherwise, choose Microsoft Network to display MSN's Member Directory when you open the Address Book.

## Using Your Personal Address Book

Your Personal Address Book holds name and address information for all the folks you reach through Exchange, including MSN members and others you reach through MSN (Internet users, CompuServe users, and so on). You can also use your Personal Address Book to reach people through Microsoft Fax, Microsoft Mail, and any other non-MSN services Exchange is equipped to use. Your Personal Address Book enables you to do the following:

- ◆ Quickly look up addresses for those with whom you correspond often
- ◆ Conveniently copy addresses to the To:, Cc:, and Bcc: lines in message headers to address a message
- ◆ Manage other information about your contacts including voice and fax numbers, addresses, and notes

You open the Address Book window by clicking the Address Book button (the open book) on the toolbar almost anywhere in Exchange. Alternatively, choose **T**ools, **A**ddress Book. When you do, you see a list of names for those people currently in your Personal Address Book, as shown in Figure 13.4.

**FIGURE 13.4.**

*The list of names currently defined in a Personal Address Book.*

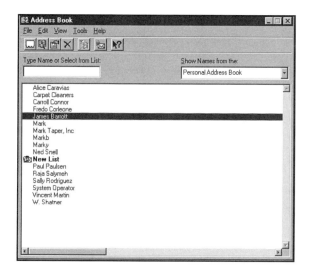

The address information for each name is listed in a Properties sheet for that name. Display the Properties sheet by double-clicking the name. The Properties sheet looks like the one in Figure 13.5.

**FIGURE 13.5.**

*The Properties sheet for an MSN entry in a Personal Address Book.*

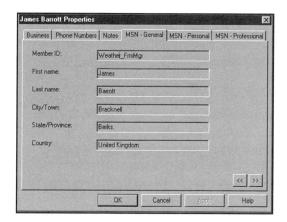

The MSN-General tab (the one in the middle of the Properties sheet) contains the only required information for the entry. The other tabs allow you to enter optional information about the entry.

To add an MSN member to your Personal Address Book, open Exchange and click the Address Book icon on the toolbar (the open book). The Address Book window shown in Figure 13.4 opens. You can then add entries in either of two ways:

◆ Add MSN members or non-members offline by filling in their information from memory or from notes.

◆ Add MSN members online by looking them up in the MSN Member Directory and then copying their Properties information to your address book.

Both methods are described in the next several pages.

## Adding an MSN Member or Non-Member Offline

You can use the procedures in this section to add the addresses of anyone you reach through MSN mail—including non-MSN members you reach through MSN's support of Internet mail, CompuServe, America Online, and so on.

 With the Address Book window open, click the New Entry button on the toolbar (the Rolodex card). A dialog box appears, prompting you to select the Exchange service through which this person will be contacted. Under The Microsoft Network, choose The Microsoft Network Member. (Another choice that appears under The Microsoft Network, Internet Over The Microsoft Network, is superfluous; see following note.)

It is not necessary to use the Internet Over The Microsoft Network choice for Internet addresses; you can create entries for Internet addresses using the regular The Microsoft Network Member dialog box shown in Figure 13.6. (If you choose to use the Internet Over The Microsoft Network choice, it is described later in this section.)When adding a non-MSN member by using the dialog box in Figure 13.6, be sure that you format the e-mail address correctly for the non-MSN service when you fill in the address as described next. To learn how to properly address MSN e-mail to non-MSN members, see Chapter 8, "Composing, Sending, and Receiving E-Mail."

If you choose The Microsoft Network Member, a New The Microsoft Network Member Properties dialog box appears (see Figure 13.6). Fill in the MSN-MSN Member tab with the member's member ID (or Internet address, or other non-MSN e-mail address, such as a CompuServe address) and full name. Note that you can use a nickname instead of a full name in the Name field to make addressing mail more convenient. You enter whatever is in the Name field—whether it's a full name or nickname—on a To: or Cc: line to address a message to this person.

When adding an entry to your address book, you are required to fill in only the MSN-MSN Member tab. The other three tabs are optional but they allow you to keep expanded information about important business or personal contacts.

◆ On the Phone Numbers tab, you can record up to eight different telephone numbers (business, fax, pager, and so on) for this person. Offline, you can click the Dial button next to one of these numbers to instruct your modem to dial that number for you.

◆ On the Business tab, you can record information about the addressee's workplace and position.

◆ On the Notes tab, you can enter any special information about this addressee.

**FIGURE 13.6.**

*Creating a new MSN entry in your Personal Address Book.*

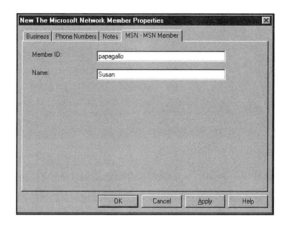

If you choose Internet Over The Microsoft Network, a dialog box like the one in Figure 13.7 appears. Only the MSNINET-Internet Address tab is required; the others are optional. To enter the Internet address in the MSNINET-Internet tab, you must break the address into its parts. All Internet e-mail addresses are made up of three parts strung together: a username, the "at" sign (@), and a *domain name* that locates and identifies the computer system the addressee uses. To complete the MSNINET tab, you enter the username in the E-Mail Address field, forget about the @, and enter the domain name in the Domain Name field. Fill in the addressee's full name in the Name field; the name you enter there is what you enter in a To: line to address mail to this person (it's also the name that appears in your Personal Address Book). You may use a nickname in the Name field. Figure 13.7 shows the MSNINET tab filled out for the Internet address mtaper@netcom.com (Mark Taper).

## Adding an MSN Member from the Member Directory

You can use the procedure described in this section to add only MSN members to your Address Book. To add the addresses of non-MSN members (Internet addresses, CompuServe addresses, and so on), see the preceding section, "Adding an MSN Member or Non-Member Offline."

**FIGURE 13.7.**

*Creating a new Internet entry in your Personal Address Book.*

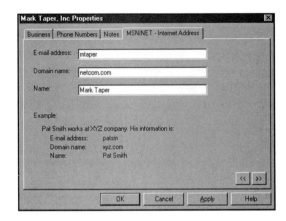

While online or offline, open the Address Book and change the entry in the Show Names From The drop-down list box to Microsoft Network. This displays the complete MSN Member Directory (see Figure 13.8). If you make this change while offline, the MSN Sign In dialog box appears. After you sign in, the Member Directory appears in the Address Book window. Display the list entry for the member you want to add to your Personal Address Book in any of the following ways:

◆ Scroll to the name of the MSN member.

◆ Type the first letters of the MSN member's first name (not ID); keep typing through the full name until the list scrolls to the correct entry.

◆ Use Find by choosing **T**ools, **F**ind (see Chapter 10, "Finding Anything on MSN").

**FIGURE 13.8.**

*The MSN Member Directory.*

Once the member's directory entry appears in the Address Book window, add that member to your Personal Address Book in either of two ways:

◆ Highlight the entry and click the Add to Personal Address Book button on the toolbar.

◆ Double-click the entry to open the member's MSN Properties sheet; click the Add to Personal Address Book button that appears on the Address Book toolbar.

When you add an MSN member to your Personal Address Book with this method, the member's Properties sheet contains the three tabs in every MSN member's Properties sheet: General, Professional, and Personal (see Chapter 11, "Advanced Configuration Options"). In addition, the Properties sheet contains the Phone Numbers, Notes, and Business tabs described earlier in this chapter. To fill in the new tabs, double-click the member's entry in your Personal Address Book.

## Addressing E-Mail from Your Personal Address Book

When addressing a message, click the To: or Cc: button to display a listing from your Personal Address Book like the one shown in Figure 13.9.

**FIGURE 13.9.**

*Using your Personal Address Book to address MSN e-mail.*

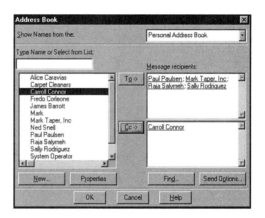

To add names to your list of message recipients, select the names from the list in the left pane and click To-> to copy the names from the left pane to the Message Recipients box on the right. Select the names from the list in the left pane and click Cc-> to copy the names to the box on the right. When finished selecting names, click OK. The names you selected appear in the message's header. If you selected multiple addressees for either the To: or Cc: line, the addresses appear in header lines, separated by semicolons (;).

You can mix MSN members and non-MSN members in the address lines of the e-mail header. MSN routes each copy of the message to its proper destination.

You can manually enter any name shown in the Personal Address Book in the To: or Cc: line to address mail. This may seem like the "old-fashioned" way to enter an address, but if you use just first names or short nicknames—or even initials—for the names you enter when creating Address Book entries, you may find it quicker and more convenient to type these short names in To: and Cc: boxes than to locate them in the address book.

# Creating and Using a Personal Distribution List

A *Personal Distribution List* is a predefined list of names to whom you sometimes send the same message. For example, while hanging out in chat rooms or on bulletin boards, you may develop a list of MSN members with whom you share certain interests; you may want to send them all a weekly message about your shared interest. Or perhaps you have a set of business associates on MSN you want to keep apprised of your latest news and activities. You can create as many different lists as you want, giving each a different name.

To create a Personal Distribution List, follow these steps:

1. Open your Personal Address Book as described earlier in this chapter.

2. Choose **F**ile, **N**ew Entry or click the New Entry toolbar button (the Rolodex card). The New Entry dialog box appears, prompting you to select a service. Instead of selecting The Microsoft Network (as you do to create a new entry for an MSN member), choose Personal Distribution List. A Properties sheet like the one in Figure 13.10 opens.

**FIGURE 13.10.**
*Creating a Personal Distribution List.*

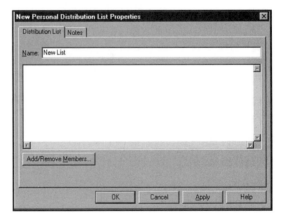

3. On the Distribution List tab, enter a name for this distribution list. On the optional Notes tab, enter any descriptive information about this list.

4. From the Distribution List tab, click Add/Remove **M**embers. A dialog box like the one in Figure 13.11 appears.

**FIGURE 13.11.**

*Adding names to a Personal Distribution List.*

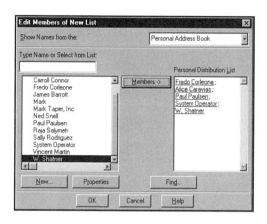

5. Add names to your Personal Distribution List in any of three ways:

   ◆ To add names from your Personal Address Book, select them from the left pane and click the **M**embers-> button to copy them to the Personal Distribution List pane on the right.

   ◆ To add names from the MSN Member Directory, change the selection in **S**how Names From The drop-down list box to The Microsoft Network. This action displays in the left pane the complete MSN Member Directory. (If you make this change while offline, the MSN Sign In dialog box appears. After you sign in, the Member Directory appears in the left pane.) To add MSN members to your Personal Distribution List, follow the steps described earlier in this chapter (in "Adding an MSN Member from the Member Directory") for finding addresses in the Member Directory. When you have selected a member to add, click the **M**embers-> button to copy the member to your Personal Distribution List.

   ◆ To create a new entry for a non-MSN member or for an MSN member (without the help of the Member Directory), click **N**ew. Fill in the address information by following the instructions for adding a new member (given in "Adding an MSN Member or Non-Member Offline," earlier in this chapter) and then click the **M**embers button.

When your Personal Distribution List is complete, click OK. The Properties sheet for the list reappears, showing the names in your list in the bottom pane of the Distribution List tab. Click OK.

A new entry appears in your Personal Address Book; the new entry has the name you assigned to your Personal Distribution List. The name appears in **bold**, and an icon representing a group of people appears next to the entry, showing that it is a distribution list (see Figure 13.12).

To send e-mail to your distribution list, click the To: or Cc: buttons when composing a message; select the name of the list from your Personal Address Book just as you would select the name of an individual person.

**FIGURE 13.12.**

*A Personal Distribution List entry (with the little "group" icon) in a Personal Address Book.*

# Attaching Files to E-Mail Messages

Binary files such as programs, graphics, and any other computer files can be "attached" to MSN e-mail messages and sent along to the recipient.

---

### I BINHEXed

Because Internet e-mail is technically capable of carrying only text, when you send a file to an Internet user, the file must be converted into a text-character format by the sending e-mail program and converted back into its original form by the receiving program. The principle way this is accomplished today is using a method called BINHEX. BINHEX converts binary data to and from *hexadecimal*, a format that uses only text characters that can travel through e-mail. Unfortunately, Exchange does not support BINHEX files.

Like a growing number of e-mail programs, Exchange uses Multipurpose Internet Mail Extensions (MIME), a more sophisticated method of adding binary information to e-mail messages. When you attach a file using MIME, the file's recipient must also have a MIME-compliant e-mail program to decode the file back to its binary form. MIME also supports text formatting, fonts, graphics, and other enhancements to e-mail messages—as long as both the sender and the recipient use MIME-compliant programs.

---

Using Exchange's **I**nsert menu, you can send binary files through MSN in two ways: as regular MIME attachments or as embedded OLE objects. You can send any type of file as a regular attachment; you can send as objects only the files Windows recognizes as objects. Still, sending objects has some great advantages—such as the ability to display a graphic within your message or play a video clip.

# Inserting a File

When composing the body of a new e-mail message, insert a file in the message by following these steps:

1. Position the edit cursor at the point in the message at which you want the file icon to appear.

2. Choose **I**nsert, **Fi**le or click the Insert File toolbar button (the paperclip); the Insert File window shown in Figure 13.13 appears.

   In the Insert As box at the bottom of Figure 13.13, notice the two radio buttons:

   ◆ Te**x**t Only converts the file to a text file and displays it in the body of the message. Use this option to insert documents or text files as all or part of the body of your message (see Chapter 12, "Trimming Time Online").

   ◆ An **A**ttachment attaches the file as a binary attachment and inserts an icon in the body of the message to represent the file.

**FIGURE 13.13.**

*Inserting a binary file in an e-mail message.*

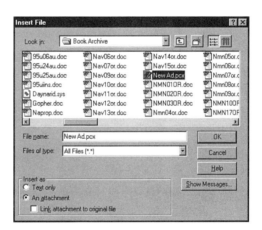

> Select the Lin**k** Attachment to Original File checkbox to prevent the selected file from traveling along with the e-mail message. Instead, this option adds a link to the message that, when selected by the recipient, opens the file in its original location. The original file must be stored in a place accessible by the recipient.
>
> This feature is designed for use on a local area network in which all users have access to shared files. It's essentially useless for MSN mail transactions.

3. To attach a binary file, select it from the Insert File dialog box, click the An **A**ttachment radio button, and click OK. An icon appears at the insertion point (see Figure 13.14) in the body of your message; the attached file travels with the message when you send it.

**FIGURE 13.14.**

*An icon in the message body, representing an attached binary file.*

---

When you send a file as an attachment, your recipient must have the necessary application to open the file if he or she is to make use of the file. And to open the file conveniently from within Exchange, your recipient must know the file type of the file you send and register that file type to the appropriate program on his or her PC (see Chapter 11, "Advanced Configuration Options"). If no file-type registration has been configured on the recipient's computer for the type of file you send, the recipient can still open the file manually, outside the e-mail message, using any compatible application.

---

It's a good idea to compress (ZIP) files before you send them. Doing so shortens the time it takes you to transmit the files to MSN; it also shortens the time your recipient requires to retrieve them. To learn more about ZIP files, see Chapter 7, "Downloading and Uploading Files."

---

## Inserting an Object

In addition to inserting files as described in the preceding section, you can embed objects using Windows 95's OLE (object linking and embedding) 2.0 facilities.

Unlike simple file attachments, an object insertion sends an OLE object to your recipient. An *object* contains not only the binary file, but also any program code required to play that file (in Windows, of course). For example, a video-clip object includes not only the video-clip file but also portions of the Windows Media Player utility necessary to play the clip. To play an object in one of your messages, the recipient need only click the object's icon. When you embed a picture or a text object, the picture or text can appear in the message itself, automatically, instead of an icon.

The advantage of objects over attachments is that, with objects, you never have to worry about whether the recipient has the right program to play the file, or whether the recipient's File Types registry is properly configured to play the file. The file is played by the program code that travels with it, not by a program on the recipient's PC. Of course, there are a few disadvantages, as well:

◆ Obviously, your recipient must have Windows to play your object. That's not a problem when you send an object to another MSN user, but it can be if you send an object to a non-MSN user, such as an Internet user. Some types of files, including several types of video clips and pictures—can be played on both Macintoshes and Windows PCs—the two most common personal computer varieties on the Internet and the online services. If you send such files as attachments, both Mac and PC users can run them (provided both have MIME-compliant e-mail packages). If you send these files as objects, only Windows (3.1, NT, or 95) users can run them.

◆ The added program code used in objects makes them larger than attached files, which means they take longer to send to MSN and longer to retrieve by the recipient.

◆ Not all types of files are recognized as objects by Windows.

> When sending to other MSN users a file that is opened or played by default within Windows 95 (for example, an AVI file or DOC file), it is usually more convenient to send the file as an attachment rather than an object. All MSN users have Windows 95 and can easily open such files; sending the extra object functionality is unnecessary.

To insert an object while working in the message body, choose **I**nsert, **O**bject. A dialog box like the one in Figure 13.15 appears.

**FIGURE 13.15.**
*Inserting an OLE object in a message.*

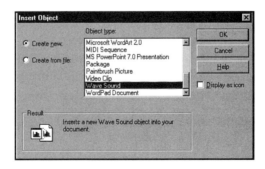

Click the Create **N**ew radio button to display a list of object types. Select an object type to open the application required to create a new object of that type. For example, choose Wave Sound to open Windows's Sound Recorder, which works with the recording features of your sound card to record new sounds. After you create a new sound and save it, the sound icon (a little speaker) appears in your message at the insertion point (see Figure 13.16). When your recipient clicks this icon, the sound plays.

**FIGURE 13.16.**

*A sound object inserted in a message.*

By default, any object that can be displayed normally within a message—such as a bitmap graphic image—is displayed. Objects that must be played are represented in the message by icons. This feature allows you to insert picture or text objects and have them actually appear within the body of the message.

To force an object to appear as an icon anyway, select the **D**isplay as Icon checkbox shown in Figure 13.15.

Click the Create from **F**ile radio button in the Insert Object dialog box to enter (or browse for) an object file already stored on your hard disk. After you select a file, the object's picture or icon appears in your message.

Using the OLE features supported by Exchange, you can use e-mail as voice mail. Using a recording sound card, record your own voice saying whatever you like. Then embed the sound clip (or clips) in an e-mail message to a MIME-compliant recipient who can play your voice files.

# Sending MSN E-Mail from Windows Applications

You don't have to go straight to Exchange to compose and send e-mail. Windows applications compatible with the Windows MAPI (Messaging API) standard have a **S**end item added to their **F**ile menus when Exchange is installed. MAPI-enabled applications include Microsoft Word versions 6.0 and later and Microsoft Excel.

To use Send, compose a document in the MAPI-enabled application. Save the document (but leave it open) and choose **F**ile, **S**end. Send opens an Exchange New Message window with the document file inserted in it (see Figure 13.17). Treat this file as you would any other insertion (see "Attaching Files to E-Mail Messages" earlier in this chapter). Address the message in the To: line provided and send it as you would any other message. (Click the To: button to select an address from your Personal Address Book.)

**FIGURE 13.17.**

*Sending a document straight from Word.*

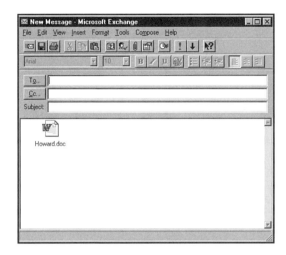

# Combining MSN E-Mail with Other Services

Exchange, as you know by now, is not simply MSN's e-mail program. It is what Microsoft calls a "universal messaging client," which means it can send and receive messages to and from virtually any "messaging service" for which a MAPI driver exists. Windows 95 includes MAPI drivers for MSN, Microsoft Mail, Microsoft Fax, and CompuServe mail. The Internet Jumpstart Kit (available in the Microsoft Plus! package and on the CD-ROM that accompanies this book) also includes a MAPI driver for Internet Mail, but it's important that MSN users not be confused by this. Exchange's Internet Mail driver is for using Exchange to send and receive mail to and from a regular Internet account, not for Internet mail through MSN. New MAPI drivers will certainly become available for nearly all commercial e-mail systems.

When you install MSN, Exchange is automatically set up on your PC and the MSN driver is installed in it as a "service." To add other services, you must open the Control Panel and then open Mail and Fax. A dialog box appears, listing the currently installed services (see Figure 13.18). Click Add to open a dialog box from which you can select a service from the list of what's already on your PC; click Have Disk to install MAPI drivers not included with Windows 95.

When you add new entries to your Personal Address Book as described earlier in this chapter, you're given an opportunity to select the service through which that addressee will be reached. After you complete the entry, you need only address messages to that person using the Address Book entry. Exchange automatically uses the service necessary to reach that person.

**FIGURE 13.18.**

*Installing new services in Exchange.*

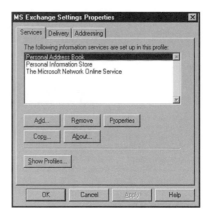

You can mix addressees from multiple services in the To:, Cc:, and Bcc: lines of the message header to send the same message across more than one messaging service; you can also mix services in a Personal Distribution List for the same purpose. For example, you can compose a single message and address it to an MSN member, an Internet user (through MSN), a fax recipient, and a Microsoft Mail recipient.

# Sending Faxes Through MSN

Commercial faxing services are setting up shop on MSN. Today, there's one—but there undoubtedly will be more. These services allow you to upload a file to MSN that the fax service delivers for you as a fax to anyone, anywhere.

If you're like most people, the modem you use to reach MSN is also a fax board, so you may question the utility (and the economics) of using an MSN fax service. You pay a fee for such services (on top of what you pay for the connect time to upload your document file to MSN). But these services do have some advantages. For example, you needn't dial and redial when a fax machine is difficult to reach. Just send your document to the fax service and let them worry about getting through.

Whether it's cheaper to use a fax service or not depends on many factors. You must compare the long-distance charges you would pay to send a long-distance fax yourself to the fax service's fee plus the MSN connect-time charges you incur while uploading your document to the fax service.

To learn which fax services are available, run Find (see Chapter 10, "Finding Anything on MSN") and enter **fax** as your search term.

# What Now?

In this chapter, you discovered how powerful and flexible something as seemingly simple as e-mail can be. In Chapter 14, you'll apply some of the skills you picked up here, and some from other chapters, to embed links to MSN content in documents, e-mail messages, and BBS messages.

# 14

# SPEEDING UP MSN

Tuning MSN

Tuning Windows 95 Performance

What Now?

There's no getting around it: If there's one thing about MSN that disappoints, it's performance. It's true, MSN is slow. But that's not MSN's fault; it's ours.

Let me explain. Almost everything you can do on MSN has been done in one form or another with online services from the beginning. But until around 1993, very little online activity was graphical. Online services—and the Internet, for that matter—were text-only activities. Until the early '90s, a 2,400 bps modem provided pretty reasonable performance; a 9,600 bps modem was lightning fast. Moving text across a wire and displaying it on a PC screen is a pretty simple activity that demands little effort from the modem, the PC's processor, or the display processor.

By 1993, Windows 3.1 had been out for two years, and users were beginning to frown on anything that wasn't splashed with boxes, borders, buttons, and icons. The last holdout, online communication, was beginning to slip into Windows. Prodigy (although not originally a Windows-based service) had in the preceding few years picked up an impressive subscriber base largely because it included a graphical environment. In 1993, America Online—a fully graphical environment—debuted to strong early success, as did Mosaic, the first graphical browser for the Internet's World Wide Web. In the years since, the tremendous upswing in the popularity of going online has been caused largely by the sexy, graphical coat of paint online communication got from Prodigy, AOL, Web browsers, and the competitors that followed suit.

Unfortunately, the move to graphical communication dramatically increases the amount of data that must be transferred for even basic tasks. Graphics also increase the extent to which the PC's processor, display processor, and hard disk must participate in putting the online service on your screen. Despite faster systems and faster modems, all graphical online communication is slow. MSN is really no worse and no better than its competitors. And all online communications are going graphical because you and I—by investing in Windows—have sent the market-makers the message that we won't tolerate anything that's not Windows-like. We did this to ourselves. We wanted color and pictures, and we got 'em—at the price of our time.

So *now* what do we do? Well, there's not really anything you can do to speed up the MSN client software itself. But you may be able to improve the speed of MSN by improving the overall performance of Windows 95. You can also speed things up by observing performance-oriented work habits, and—obviously—by upgrading your hardware (although hardware upgrades are not always an effective solution).

In this chapter, you learn the following:

◆ How to adopt performance-improving online work habits

◆ Which hardware upgrades have the greatest impact on MSN performance

◆ How to tune up and maintain your Windows 95 system for maximum MSN (and overall) performance

---

### My Definition of Performance

Before proceeding, it's important that you understand how I define *performance*. I don't define it as MIPS, Winstones, Nielsen households, or whatever other machine-measurable benchmark the magazines offer. I'm not interested in what a test program thinks—programs don't use Windows, people do. So I measure performance in people terms, according to two criteria:

◆ Apparent responsiveness—When you click a button or icon, how long do you seem to wait before you get results?

◆ Productivity—How quickly can you move through the steps of an activity or from one activity to another?

It is these two aspects of "performance" the techniques described in this chapter are designed to improve.

---

# Tuning MSN

Believe it or not, there's an actual rationale to the order in which performance advice is presented in this section. Except where noted, this section goes through performance tips from most effective to least effective. In other words, you have to decide whether to try each tip. But bear in mind that, in general, the earlier a tip is covered, the greater its potential impact on your MSN performance.

## Hardware Choices

In Chapter 1, "Signing Up, Signing In, and Signing Out," you learned that Microsoft's official "minimum configuration" for MSN is hardly an adequate minimum for performance purposes. The MSN client application is an extremely memory-hungry, 32-bit, multithreaded, multitasking Windows 95 application, as is Exchange. Although that means these applications multitask smoothly and reliably in Windows 95, it also means they demand a well-equipped system.

Although it's common to think of modem speed as the hardware criteria that most affects the performance of an online system, don't underestimate the importance of overall system performance in the responsiveness of an online system like MSN. True, some of the time you spend waiting can be attributed to communications lag. But much of the time you spend waiting for MSN, you're waiting for programs such as the Online Viewer and Exchange to load and unload, or you're waiting for memory pages to be swapped to and from the disk. None of this time is attributable to modem speed, and isn't helped by a faster modem.

You have to attack your system first where it is weakest. For example, a system with a 14,400 bps modem and only 4M of RAM will show greater overall MSN performance improvement by upgrading RAM than by updating the modem.

The following list ranks system upgrades in the general order in which they're likely to impact MSN performance, from most effective to least effective. Of course, if your particular system is unusually strong or weak in a given area, your priorities may differ.

1. **Memory.** Most computers in the field today running Windows 95 (especially when you factor in notebooks) have 14,400 bps modems, but only 4M of RAM. Because of the memory demands of Exchange and the MSN client software, upgrading RAM to 8M will do more for overall MSN responsiveness than updating the modem. Upgrading to 16M of RAM is even better, especially if you plan to do much multitasking of MSN with Internet client software or other applications.

*Tip*

> Most 32-bit Web browsers, including Internet Explorer (see Chapter 16, "Browsing the World Wide Web"), require a minimum of 8M of RAM.

2. **Modem.** A 14,400 bps modem is the practical minimum for MSN and for Web browsing. The next step up is twice as fast: 28,800 bps—and today, about twice as expensive (although prices are dropping). However, if you upgrade, don't expect to double your performance. Many slow tasks in MSN, such as opening and closing certain programs, are unrelated to modem speed. More importantly, as of now, every local MSN access number provides at least 14,400 bps access, but not all support 28,800 bps access. Unless a local access number in your area supports 28,800 bps access, you'll have to run that snappy modem at half-speed through a local 14,400 bps access number or access MSN at a nonlocal 28,800 bps access number—a toll call. Provided that your PC has at least 8M of RAM and you have a local 28,800 bps access number, a 28,800 bps modem is your next-best bet for speeding up MSN.

3. **Processor.** In real terms, a processor upgrade still means a PC upgrade. Chip-only upgrades are rarely practical; although they may speed up processing operations, they leave intact other limiting aspects of the original system, including bus type and speed. In most cases, if you need a faster PC, you need a new PC.

   If you've got 8M or more memory, a 28,800 bps modem, an accelerated display card, anything less than a 75 MHz processor (Pentium or 486DX4), and what you still feel is unsatisfactory MSN performance, your next alternative is a system upgrade. But be warned about hair-splitting when it comes to speed. Magazines like to print test benchmarks to show the relative speeds of differing systems. The use of a test benchmark usually means that a real human won't notice the difference.

   As a rule, all other system aspects being equal, only upgrades in both the class *and* clock speed of the processor are meaningful. For example, if your current processor is a 66 MHz 486DX2, you need to move up to at least a 90 MHz Pentium or a 100 MHz 486DX4 to notice an appreciable difference in system responsiveness; a move to a 75 MHz chip, even a Pentium, will probably impress only a benchmark test, not your eyes.

4. **Graphics adapter.** Windows 95 performs best with an accelerated graphics adapter with at least 1M of display memory. Accelerated adapters take some of the display-processing burden off your PC's processor. If you lack an accelerated adapter, it's next on the upgrade list. Bear in mind, though, that an accelerated adapter does little to speed up the display of on-screen pictures in MSN titles or in Web pages—which is probably the single slowest activity you'll encounter. The bottleneck in those cases is the time it takes the image to travel to your PC, not your PC's graphics-rendering speed.

5. **Hard disk.** As you can tell if you watch your disk light or listen carefully while online, MSN leans hard on your hard disk. Much of the disk activity is a result of *paging*, swapping data from disk to memory and back again as needed. Paging, and thus MSN's reliance on your disk, can be minimized by adding RAM. But MSN will still access the disk often to load programs (such as the Online Viewer and Exchange) and to load portions of the MSN client software itself. If you have a hard disk with an access time that exceeds 40 ms, you may be able to improve MSN's speed during paging and program loading by upgrading to a faster disk—one with an access speed below 15 ms. If your slow disk uses a 16-bit interface, upgrading your PC to one with a 32-bit PCI bus will speed up disk operations considerably.

---

If Windows 95 does not have a compatible 32-bit driver for your hard disk, Windows will use the drive's old 16-bit DOS driver through its "compatibility mode." Compatibility mode seriously degrades not only disk responsiveness but overall Windows responsiveness as well. To achieve better response, install a Windows 95 driver for your disk (see "Disk Tuning," later in this chapter) or upgrade to a disk that is fully compatible with Windows 95.

*Tip*

---

## Work Habits

Once you've made all the hardware improvements you (or your bank account) can stand, it's important to recognize that your online work habits have a huge impact on the apparent responsiveness of MSN. The following tips can make MSN seem a more sprightly place on any system.

1. **Curb multitasking.** True, Windows 95 is a bona fide multitasking system. And Windows 95 is much less prone to the multitasking-produced crashes and lockups Windows 3.1 experienced, thanks to greatly expanded resource handling in the new architecture. None of that, however, means that you can run as many programs as you want with no impact on system performance. In particular, don't multitask MSN with 16-bit (Windows 3.1) applications, which have a detrimental effect on performance.

Whenever possible, run only the MSN client software when you're online. When accessing the Internet through client applications, minimize the MSN client, open one

Internet client at a time, and close it when you're finished. Open Exchange only to send or receive e-mail (read and compose e-mail offline, as described in Chapter 12, "Trimming Time Online"), and close Exchange as soon as you're done with it.

2. **Eschew Plus! themes.** If you purchase the Microsoft Plus! companion package for Windows 95, you'll get a family of way-cool desktop "themes" that paste some slick wallpaper on your desktop, dress up your icons and screen fonts, and add related WAV sounds to system events. Themes are great fun, but they're deadly for system performance. You must choose between a responsive MSN environment or a cool desktop. You can't have both.

*Tip*

> Using the Passwords icon in the Control Panel (see your Windows 95 documentation), you can set up your PC with multiple *user profiles*. For each user profile, you can have a completely different desktop configuration, username, and password.
>
> You can create two user profiles on your PC—one that uses themes or other MSN-slowing programs, and another pared down for MSN sessions. Whenever you intend to use MSN, log in to the pared-down account for better performance.

3. **Use 32-bit, smaller helper applications.** Evaluate the "helper applications" run by MSN and your Web browser to open and play the files you download. Consider whether each is a 32-bit program (which Windows 95 tends to multitask more effectively and run more quickly than 16-bit applications). Also consider whether the application may be too much program for the job at hand. For example, because Word for Windows is installed on my PC, MSN opens Word to display documents, such as kiosks, that are in RTF format. But WordPad also opens RTF documents and is a quicker, smaller application than Word—and WordPad opens much more quickly than Word. I edited my File Types registry (see Chapter 11, "Advanced Configuration Options") so that WordPad, not Word, is automatically used to open RTF files. Similarly, when you install Internet Explorer, it updates your File Types registry so that Explorer opens to play several types of multimedia files. Although Explorer is a 32-bit program, it is a much larger program than many quick, small utilities you can acquire to play multimedia files.

4. **Navigate efficiently.** When you browse through MSN, MSN and your PC spend a lot of time and effort opening and closing folders and displaying their contents. To the extent that you exploit navigation techniques that take you directly to a given service—desktop shortcuts, Favorite Places, Go words—without opening a lot of folders to get there, you save time, and your PC and MSN save effort.

5. **Work offline.** Use the tips in Chapter 12, "Trimming Time Online," to perform offline anything that *can* be done offline. Not only do these techniques save you connect-time charges, in many cases, they also improve MSN's performance when you are online. For example, printing a document while in MSN means that you multitask the MSN client software with Windows's print engine, itself a pretty memory-hungry

application. Your MSN performance slows to a crawl while the document prints. It's better simply to save documents to your hard disk and print them later, offline.

6. **Save file downloading for the end of a session.** Although you can download files in the background while performing other tasks, doing so is very slow. Instead, queue files for downloading, but don't begin the transfer until you complete all your other work for the current MSN session. After starting the transfer, click the Transfer and Disconnect button on the toolbar.

7. **Turn off auto-display of MSN Today.** If you sign in only once a day, you may want to display MSN Today automatically at the beginning of each session to keep abreast of new MSN developments. However, if you sign in several times a day, as I do, you'll spend a lot of time waiting for MSN Today to appear, just so that you can close it again. See the instructions in Chapter 2, "Maintaining Your MSN Account," to learn how to disable the automatic display of MSN Today.

# Tuning Windows 95 Performance

Many of the tuning procedures discussed in the following sections begin on the Windows System Properties sheet. To reach it, open the Control Panel, open System, and then click the Performance tab. (You can also right-click My Computer and choose Properties from the context menu and then click the Performance tab of the Properties sheet.) You see a screen like the one shown in Figure 14.1.

**FIGURE 14.1.**
*The Performance tab of the System Properties dialog box.*

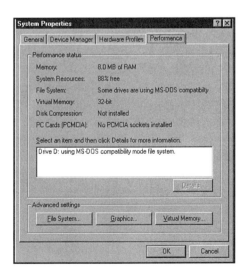

All the performance-tuning techniques described in the following sections can—and should—be performed offline.

## Memory Management

Your PC's memory is Windows's workspace. If you give it a large, uncluttered area to work in, Windows can fly. If you give it a small, messy room, it sits there feeling sorry for itself. The next few pages show you how to provide Windows 95 with a memory space that lets it soar.

### Freeing RAM

As mentioned earlier in this chapter, to run Windows well, there is no substitute for equipping your PC with sufficient memory—8M or more. If you must run Windows 95 and MSN with only the minimum of 4M, however, the tips that follow can help you live more comfortably in that space by reducing the size of the Windows 95 *working set*, the program code that Windows keeps active in memory at all times. If you have 8M of RAM but run into heavy paging on MSN or when multitasking certain applications, you can try the following suggestions to free RAM and reduce the need for swapfile paging.

◆ Run only one network client and no more network protocols and services than you absolutely require. If possible, disable any local network clients you use before signing into MSN. Each client and each protocol takes up some memory, even when you're not logged on to the network.

◆ Don't put any programs in your Startup folder. Run programs when you need them and close them when you're done.

◆ When uploading or downloading files, minimize the File Transfer Status window until the operation is complete. Minimized programs use less memory than windowed or maximized ones because they save the memory required to report their progress to you.

### Virtual Memory Management

By default, Windows 95 manages the virtual memory swapfile dynamically, expanding it and contracting it as the demand for memory rises and falls. This sounds suspiciously like Windows 3.1's default "temporary" swapfile, which was a major performance inhibitor. Performance-minded 3.1 users always switched to a permanent swapfile as the first step in boosting performance.

It's natural if your first temptation is to distrust Windows's defaults and start monkeying with the swapfile—but restrain yourself. New high-performance algorithms make the dynamic swapfile the best performance choice for almost all users. There are only a few instances when an adjustment to the swapfile results in improved performance—and these really come into play only in machines with more than one hard disk drive.

By default, Windows 95 sets up the swapfile on the same disk on which Windows is stored. If another drive in your system is any of the following, you can speed up your system by relocating the swapfile to the other drive:

◆ Faster

◆ Less full

◆ Uncompressed (and the drive containing Windows is compressed)

You can also move the swapfile to or from a compressed disk on the same physical drive.

To change your virtual memory settings, open the System Properties dialog box to the Performance tab and click the **V**irtual Memory button. You see a screen like the one shown in Figure 14.2.

**FIGURE 14.2.**

*Changing virtual memory settings.*

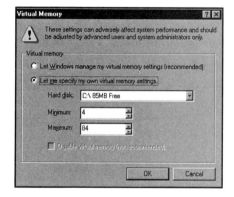

To change the location of the swapfile, click the radio button next to Let **M**e Specify My Own Virtual Memory Settings; then select the disk from the Hard **D**isk drop-down list. Note that the list indicates the amount of free space on each disk.

After you select a disk, notice that the Mi**n**imum allowable cache size remains at 0M (4M if you have Microsoft Plus! installed) but the value for Ma**x**imum is the entire amount of free space on the disk, expressed in megabytes. There's no real reason to change either of these settings. The Mi**n**imum of 0 (for those not using Plus!, which requires virtual memory at all times) allows your system to run free of any swapfile when none is required (which is often the case if your system has a healthy amount of RAM and you tend to use only one application at a time). The default Ma**x**imum expressed in the dialog box isn't really valid; what it should say is *all the free space on the drive*, because this value dynamically grows and shrinks as the actual amount of free space on the drive changes. If you change the Ma**x**imum value manually, the size of the swapfile can never exceed the value you enter *or* the amount of free space, whichever is smaller.

Never select the checkbox at the bottom of the Virtual Memory sheet. This checkbox reads Di**s**able Virtual Memory and then adds, correctly, *not recommended*. This box is provided so that you can shut off virtual memory at the request of a Microsoft technical support person who is trying to isolate a problem. If you select it on your own, your performance will certainly suffer and your system may not even restart. There is no circumstance under which disabling virtual memory can improve performance. What was a useful option in Windows 3.1 is an integral, essential part of the operating system in Windows 95.

When finished with the Virtual Memory dialog box, click OK.

## Disk Tuning

Beyond choosing a fast disk in the first place, you can do the following to ensure that your disk performs as quickly and reliably as possible under Windows 95:

◆ Make sure that 32-bit disk access is enabled

◆ Remove unnecessary files

◆ Optimize graphics display

◆ Maintain top performance

### Avoid DOS Disk Utilities

When Setup installs Windows 95, a number of your old DOS external-command executables are deleted from the disk. Do the same with old versions of Norton Utilities, PC Tools, and the like. Windows 95's new Installable File System is backwardly compatible with previous versions of DOS, but utilities that delete, sort, defragment, or in some way alter the structure of your hard disk were created *before* Windows 95 and know nothing of the new VFAT file system and its support for long filenames.

Using old DOS utilities can be hazardous to the health of your data because they can corrupt your disk's structures.

## Enable 32-Bit Disk Access

When Windows can't use its 32-bit drivers to access a disk, performance suffers tremendously. Windows has to access the disk in 16-bit real mode, called *compatibility mode* in the Windows 95 lexicon. Not only is the 16-bit access inherently slower, but Windows must switch into compatibility mode every time it accesses the disk and switch back to 32-bit protected mode afterwards—an operation that wastes resources and further degrades performance.

Windows 95 automatically enables compatibility mode when the Setup Wizard determines that the disk requires a real-mode disk driver for which Windows has no compatible 32-bit replacement. Disks compressed with older versions of Stacker or another disk-compression utility may use such drivers, as may disks protected by some security or encryption software and older FAT disks partitioned with unusual third-party utilities.

To find out whether your hard disk is afflicted, open the System Properties dialog box to the Performance tab (see Figure 14.3).

**FIGURE 14.3.**
*Checking 32-bit disk access.*

Note that, on my system, drive D is listed in the **S**elect an Item… box. Anything listed in this box is something for which Windows had to forego its default performance settings to accommodate hardware with compatibility problems. Any reference to *compatibility mode* in the **S**elect an Item box means that Windows could not replace an existing real-mode driver with a compatible protected-mode driver, and must therefore access the hardware in compatibility mode. Note also that, above the box in Figure 14.3, the File System item indicates that a drive is running in MS-DOS compatibility mode.

In my case, it's my CD-ROM drive (drive D) that uses a DOS-based real-mode driver for which Windows 95 has no replacement. (I have to acquire a Windows 95 driver from the manufacturer. However, because I never use my CD-ROM drive while I'm connected to MSN, this particular problem has no effect on MSN performance.) Fortunately, my hard disk (drive C) isn't listed here, which means that Windows is using 32-bit access for it. Further proof of that appears above the box; because the Virtual Memory line in the dialog box reports that my computer is using 32-bit virtual memory, that means I must have 32-bit disk access.

If your hard disk turns out to be using a real-mode driver, you must locate and install a new driver compatible with Windows 95.

◆ If the driver was bundled with your hard disk or PC, contact your hard disk or PC manufacturer and request an updated driver. Alternatively, try the Microsoft Forum on MSN (use **Microsoft** as the Go word), from which you can download updated drivers. After you acquire a new driver, install it by opening the Control Panel and then opening Add New Hardware. The Add New Hardware Wizard leads you through the addition of the driver.

◆ If the driver is part of a compression or security software package, you have several options: You can contact the software manufacturer to find out whether you can upgrade to a newer, Windows 95-compatible version. Alternatively, you may be able to remove the compression or encryption (follow the software manufacturer's instructions), and then use Add New Hardware in Control Panel to reinstall the disk using Windows 95 drivers.

---

### Forget Cache Tuning

Like tuning virtual memory, another tuning favorite in Windows 3.1 was SmartDrive, the disk cache that boosted system performance by caching disk data in RAM to allow Windows to access the hard disk less frequently. Users with plenty of RAM and modest application requirements found that they could increase the size of the cache from the defaults and boost performance.

Windows 95 has a new disk caching system, VCACHE (virtual cache), which dynamically configures itself according to system demand, just like the swapfile does. In fact, the swapfile and the cache work together to balance memory demand with system performance.

VCACHE is not user configurable except in one sense. You can choose from among three basic profiles to select the algorithms Windows applies in managing the cache. Each tunes the cache to the most effective settings for the usage patterns of the PC. During setup, Windows selects the proper setting, so no cache tuning is really possible, or necessary.

---

## Free Storage Space

Tuning and maintaining your hard disk go hand in hand. Fast 32-bit access and the correct cache settings are of little value if your disk is overcrowded, badly fragmented, or infected with accumulated errors and defective sectors.

Regular disk maintenance is a three-step process. Note that the order of the steps is important:

1. As you know, you should make regular backups of your hard disk. Don't perform the other steps listed here until you have a recent and complete backup set so that any mistakes made during disk maintenance can be corrected. The most common error is accidentally deleting an important file; although the Recycle Bin provides some safety from that, the Bin is not permanent and not foolproof. Regular backups are your only guarantee.

2. With a complete backup set available, you should regularly "clean out" your hard disk, deleting (or archiving to floppy disk or tape and then deleting) old, unwanted data files and applications. Opening Explorer from the Programs menu is an excellent way to accomplish this; you can hunt through your entire folder/directory structure to

delete files and even entire directories. Cleaning out the hard disk maximizes free space on the disk, which can improve your disk's performance. More free space also offers the swapfile more room to provide more multitasking capability.

3. Check your disk regularly for fragmentation and defragment the disk any time Windows recommends that you do so. (To defragment your disk, choose System Tools from the Accessories menu and then choose Disk Defragmenter.) Over time, the files on a disk are broken up and spread in pieces around the disk; the free space on the disk is broken up, as well. This fragmentation isn't technically a flaw; your computer can still use the files and free space. As a disk becomes more fragmented, however, disk operations start to slow down because of the extra seek-and-retrieval time caused by the fragmentation. Fragmented files and free space make the disk work harder, which may eventually cause data errors and premature disk failure. Because Windows 95 can use fragmented free space for the swapfile, paging is slowed by fragmentation as well. Always defragment *after* you clean out the disk, not before; if you delete files after you defragment the disk, you give the disk a head start on becoming fragmented again.

Before running the Disk Defragmenter, always run ScanDisk (found in the System Tools folder of your Accessories menu) to check for, and repair, disk errors.

4. If and when you find you're running low on disk space, you can use the Windows 95 built-in disk-compression utility, DriveSpace. DriveSpace expands the amount of space available on a disk. (Choose System Tools from your Accessories menu and then choose DriveSpace.) Unlike some early disk-compression tools, DriveSpace tends not to degrade disk or system performance significantly, although a minor performance decrease is likely. If your disk is severely overloaded, the improvement in system performance you achieve by making more disk space available to Windows more than offsets any potential performance lag caused by DriveSpace.

## Optimize Graphics Display

If you have an accelerated display adapter, Windows 95 can typically exploit all its acceleration features to squeeze out top performance. If you experience certain types of display-related problems, however, you can selectively "turn off" some acceleration functions, trading some performance for better reliability.

If you encounter display problems or want to check whether Windows is exploiting your graphics hardware, click the **G**raphics button on the Performance sheet of the System Properties dialog box. The Advanced Graphics Settings dialog box appears (see Figure 14.4).

**FIGURE 14.4.**
*The Advanced Graphics
Settings dialog box.*

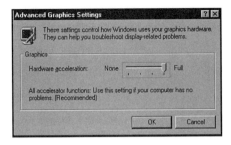

On the Hardware **A**cceleration slide control, the recommended setting is Full (Windows uses all the graphics acceleration features of your hardware). If necessary, change the setting:

◆ **To the 2/3 mark:** Most accelerator functions are enabled, but those that may cause mouse-pointer problems are disabled.

◆ **To the 1/3 mark:** Some basic accelerator functions are enabled, but those that may cause other errors, including program errors, are disabled.

◆ **None:** All accelerator functions are disabled. Graphics hardware functions properly but at greatly decreased performance.

## Maintain Top Performance

After you tune up your system, stay on top of it. Your PC's snappy performance can deteriorate over time without regular tune ups. Here are a few final tips:

◆ Back up, clean out, and defragment your hard disk regularly. This is your best hedge against sluggish disk access and the poor overall performance that results from it.

◆ Recheck the settings on the Performance tab in the System Properties dialog box any time you install new hardware or software. Some setup routines can alter your carefully selected settings or reset them to defaults.

◆ When you upgrade hardware, choose what's best for Windows (see "Hardware Choices," earlier in this chapter). Consider devices compatible with Windows's Plug-and-Play features, not simply because they're easier to install but also because Windows automatically tunes them, when possible, for best performance in your system.

# What Now?

The techniques described in this chapter make MSN a more dynamic, responsive place to be. You needn't apply all of the tips, but even a well-chosen few may lower your impatience meter while online.

That's it for Part III, "Taking Control of MSN." Now move on to Part IV, "Navigating the Internet Through MSN," to dive into the most important, exciting, and misunderstood aspect of MSN: Internet access.

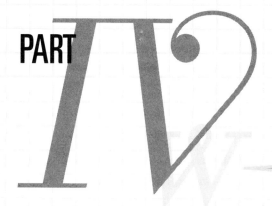

# PART IV

# NAVIGATING THE INTERNET THROUGH MSN

Understanding the Internet    235

Browsing the World Wide Web    249

Browsing Gophers    281

Downloading Files with FTP    297

Advanced Internet Techniques    313

# 15

# UNDERSTANDING THE INTERNET

What "Internet Access" Really Means on MSN

How to Sign Up for Internet Access

About Internet Access

How to Choose Client Software for Internet Services

More About the Internet

What Now?

In early announcements about its MSN plans, Microsoft said it would offer Internet access along with MSN accounts—at an extra charge.

Quicker than you can say *NASDAQ*, Microsoft's competitors announced plans to offer their subscribers a few hours of *free* Internet access every month. By the time of MSN's debut, Microsoft had shifted to an "Internet for everybody" approach to MSN. At this writing, the company is considering "unbundling" Internet access, allowing customers to optionally sign up for Internet access only (no MSN content) or for MSN content only. Clearly, Microsoft has yet to fully define how it wants MSN and the Internet to interrelate.

***Translation:*** What you read here is subject to change. For the moment, at least, what you read here represents the nuts and bolts of how MSN provides Internet access, how you sign up for it, and what you can and cannot do. This chapter also provides important Internet basics, such as addressing conventions, that help you understand the chapters that follow.

In this chapter, you learn the following:

◆ How MSN provides Internet access

◆ How to sign up for Internet access through the regular MSN sign-up procedure

◆ How to add Internet access after signing up for MSN

◆ How to sign up for MSN and Internet access through the Internet Jumpstart Kit in the Microsoft Plus! add-on kit (and on the CD-ROM that accompanies this book)

◆ About Internet addresses

◆ About the types of Internet resources

◆ About Internet client software

# What "Internet Access" Really Means on MSN

In essence, the Internet access provided by MSN is what's known as a *dial-up PPP* account. Because it's the most powerful way you can access the Internet through a modem, PPP accounts are offered by most major independent Internet access providers.

The MSN Internet account runs Windows 95's TCP/IP (Transmission Control Protocol/ Internet Protocol) communications protocol on your PC, plus PPP (Point-to-Point Protocol). TCP/IP is the fundamental "glue" of the Internet, the program that makes the eclectic assortment of hardware on the Net all work together. The PPP protocol is an accessory to TCP/IP that enables a TCP/IP connection to run through phone lines.

Computers that don't run TCP/IP can gain limited access to the Internet through another computer running TCP/IP. But true TCP/IP connections, such as MSN's, are the most powerful, allowing you to run your own selection of Internet client software (see "Choosing Client Software," later in this chapter) and supporting the use of graphical browsers on the World Wide Web.

To use the Internet, the servers your PC connects through must also have TCP/IP connections to the Internet. Some MSN access numbers are for connecting to MSN without Internet access and don't run TCP/IP. As a result, accessing the Internet may change the MSN access numbers you use to connect.

The MSN Internet account is unlike regular Internet PPP accounts in one important respect. Regular PPP accounts allow you to access all Internet resources through your choice of client software. Unlike most Internet providers, Microsoft does not permit PPP access to its news server (for newsgroups) or SMTP/POP3 server (for e-mail). Because of this, even though your MSN Internet account is a true PPP account, you cannot access newsgroups or e-mail through your own choice of client software. You must use e-mail and newsgroups through the MSN client software. If you have access to a news server or e-mail server other than Microsoft's (as you would if you had an Internet account other than MSN), you can use your own client software to access these servers through MSN's Internet access.

> When your PC is connected to the Internet through MSN, it is truly on the Internet—which means that your files and folders can be accessed by other skilled Internet users (although doing so is not easy). This is especially dangerous if your PC is connected to a local area network because the Internet may give outsiders access to network resources through your PC.
>
> To help secure your PC if you have file and printer sharing enabled, MSN issues a prompt when you sign in. The prompt asks whether you want file and printer sharing turned off and gives you the option to do so by clicking Yes. If you choose Yes, sharing is disabled for the Internet connection; it remains enabled for any other network to which you are connected.

# How to Sign Up for Internet Access

You can sign up for Internet access during regular MSN setup or using the Internet Jumpstart Kit included in Microsoft Plus! (and on the CD-ROM that accompanies this book). You can also easily add Internet access after setting up a non-Internet account. All three procedures are described in the following sections.

## Using the MSN Sign-Up Program

During the regular MSN sign-up routine (see Chapter 1, "Setting Up, Signing In, and Signing Out"), a dialog box like the one in Figure 15.1 asks you, Do you want full Internet Access? Click the radio button next to **Y**es and proceed with set-up. The remainder of the set-up procedure is unchanged, except that the access numbers selected are ones that offer Internet and MSN support.

**FIGURE 15.1.**

*Choosing Internet access during the MSN sign-up procedure.*

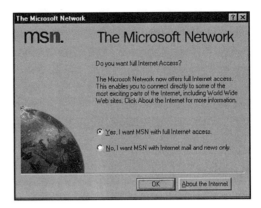

## Adding Internet Access After Sign-Up

The Microsoft Network

If you sign up for a non-Internet MSN account and later decide to add Internet access, you need only change your MSN access numbers to ones that support Internet accounts. Right-click the MSN icon on your desktop and choose Connection Settings from the context menu to display the Connections Setting dialog box. Click **A**ccess Numbers to display the dialog box shown in Figure 15.2; select Internet and The Microsoft Network from the **S**ervice Type drop-down list.

For more about access numbers, see Chapter 2, "Maintaining Your MSN Account."

**FIGURE 15.2.**

*Adding Internet access to an existing MSN account.*

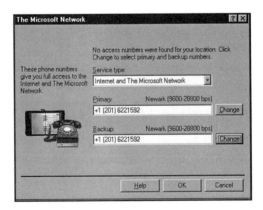

## Using the Internet Wizard

Among other handy and cool add-ins, the Microsoft Plus! kit for Windows 95 features a Setup Wizard for configuring both MSN Internet accounts and PPP accounts with independent Internet providers.

> Microsoft Plus! requires a 486-based PC, 8M of memory, and a 256-color display adapter (a 16-bit, "high-color" adapter capable of displaying over 16,000 colors is strongly recommended). Although these are reasonable requirements for any Windows 95-based PC (especially one used for MSN), they exceed the official minimums required for Windows 95 (386, 4M, 16-color adapter); some Windows 95 users may not be able to run Microsoft Plus!.

In addition to setting up your MSN Internet account, the Setup Wizard enhances your account in several ways. It deposits a nifty Internet icon on your desktop and links your Internet setup to a handy configuration-management program, the Internet Control Panel (described later in this chapter). Finally, the Internet Setup Wizard configures your Internet connection to open the Microsoft Web browser, Internet Explorer, when you connect to the Internet through MSN.

## Signing Up with the Wizard

The procedure described in this section can be used to set up a new MSN Internet account or to add Internet support or the Wizard's Internet enhancements to an existing MSN account.

Begin by installing Microsoft Plus!. When the Plus! installation is almost complete, the Internet Setup Wizard starts automatically. You can set up the Internet right away or click Cancel and restart the Wizard at a later time. (To restart the Wizard later, open Accessories, select Internet Tools, and choose Internet Setup Wizard.) When the Wizard starts up, you see a Welcome screen. From there, follow these steps to use the Wizard to configure your computer for Internet access:

1. From the Welcome screen, click Next to continue. A second screen appears, asking how you want to connect to the Internet: through the Microsoft Network or through your own PPP account.

2. Choose **U**se The Microsoft Network. A screen like the one in Figure 15.3 appears.

3. If you do not already have an MSN Internet account, choose **N**o. (If you're running the Wizard to enhance an existing MSN account, choose **Y**es.) The Wizard opens the MSN sign-up routine, which you complete exactly as described in Chapter 1, "Signing Up, Signing In, and Signing Out."

When the sign-up procedure is complete, you'll find a few changes in Windows 95:

The Internet

◆ A little globe icon with the label *The Internet* appears on your desktop. This icon opens Internet Explorer and then opens the MSN Sign In dialog box (if you're not already connected to MSN) to connect you to the Internet.

**FIGURE 15.3.**

*Using the Internet Setup Wizard.*

◆ In the Control Panel, a new Internet item appears. Use this item to change some of your configuration settings, as described in "Managing Your Configuration Through the Internet Control Panel," later in this chapter.

## Connecting to the Internet

To connect to the Internet, do one of the following:

The Internet

◆ Connect to MSN as usual (double-click the MSN icon). Then open any Internet client software you choose to access Internet resources.

◆ If you used the Internet Wizard, double-click the Internet globe icon. The icon opens Internet Explorer and then opens the MSN Sign In dialog box. After you sign in, you see MSN's Internet home page in Explorer (the page is called *Explore the Internet*; see Chapter 16, "Browsing the World Wide Web"). MSN Central (the MSN home page, as opposed to the MSN *Internet* home page displayed by Explorer) does not appear, but you are connected to MSN. You can double-click the MSN icon on your desktop to open the MSN home page and navigate to MSN Content, or browse the Internet with Explorer, or open and use any other Internet client software.

## Managing Your Configuration Through the Internet Control Panel

The Internet Setup Wizard creates a new Control Panel entry for the Internet. You can reach it through the Control Panel (choose **S**ettings from the Start menu and then choose **C**ontrol Panel) or by right-clicking the Internet icon on the desktop and choosing Properties. The Internet Properties dialog box appears (see Figure 15.4).

On the AutoDial tab, select the **U**se AutoDial checkbox to allow Internet Explorer to automatically dial the Internet when necessary. When AutoDial is on, some Internet client software—including Explorer—can be opened and used offline. The client software dials the Internet automatically as soon as you initiate an action that requires a live connection.

**FIGURE 15.4.**

*The Internet Control Panel Properties dialog box.*

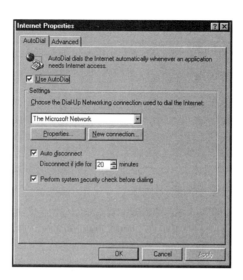

Select the Auto **D**isconnect checkbox and specify a number of minutes if you want Windows to automatically sign you off the Internet if you are inactive for a time—a handy and economical feature, considering MSN's time-based subscription plans. Note that, when using the autodisconnect feature, you are considered "inactive" during any time you do not perform any activity on MSN or the Internet—when you switch to other Windows tasks and work there, autodisconnect considers you "inactive" and will sign you out after the specified number of minutes.

You can also set an auto-disconnect time with the Options dialog box, as described in Chapter 2, "Maintaining Your MSN Account." If both the Internet Control Panel auto-disconnect and the Options auto-disconnect features are enabled, MSN uses whichever shows the lower number of minutes.

The Advanced tab in the Internet Properties dialog box allows you to enter the address of a proxy server. On a local area network (LAN), a *proxy server* is a computer connected to the Internet through which other computers on the LAN can access the Internet. Proxy servers are not supported in MSN connections.

# About Internet Access

If you're new to the Internet, the next several pages can help you ground yourself in basic Internet concepts before you push ahead to your first Internet session.

# Understanding Internet Addresses

Each and every computer on the Internet has a unique *IP address*, expressed in four sets of numbers separated by periods. A typical IP address looks like this:

```
192.48.101.87
```

This address allows any computer on the Net to find any other so that the two can communicate. Whenever you are on the Internet, you have your own IP address as well. On MSN, that address is different each time you sign in. MSN uses a system called Dynamic Host Configuration Protocol (DHCP) to automatically assign each user's computer a new IP address each time the user signs in.

Fortunately, you have another address made out of words, not numbers. That address, sometimes called your *e-mail address* or *Internet address*, never changes. That's why e-mail addressed to you can always find you, even though you have a different IP address each time you sign in.

All Internet e-mail addresses are made up of three parts:

◆ A username

◆ The "at" symbol (@)

◆ A domain name, which identifies the computer through which the user is connected to the Net

As an MSN user, your Internet username is your MSN member ID, and the domain is `msn.com`. My MSN member ID is `nsnell`, so I am known on the Internet as follows:

```
nsnell@msn.com
```

The Internet at large can't really work with these word-based Internet addresses—it needs the numerical IP addresses to locate computers. A program called a *name server* automatically translates word-based Internet addresses into numerical IP addresses and vice-versa. That's why you have one and only one e-mail address, even though your IP address changes.

Domain names are a system unto themselves for identifying computers. They can be as simple as the two-word `msn.com` or they can be much longer. The words in a domain name are separated by periods. Keep an eye on the rightmost word; it often identifies the type of institution or the country the computer is in. This rightmost word is called the *top-level domain*. Top-level domains for computers in the United States use three-letter abbreviations that identify the type of institution:

| Top-Level Domain | Institution Type |
| --- | --- |
| `.com` | A *com*mercial enterprise or business |
| `.edu` | An *edu*cational institution |
| `.gov` | A non-military *gov*ernment office, department, or agency |
| `.mil` | A *mil*itary government office, department, or agency |

| Top-Level Domain | Institution Type |
|---|---|
| .net | A *net*work, typically made up of different types of institutions |
| .org | An institution that doesn't fit any of the preceding categories, usually a non-profit outfit |

For computers residing outside the United States, you may see a two-letter abbreviation identifying the country:

| Domain Abbreviation | Country |
|---|---|
| .au | Australia |
| .at | Austria |
| .ca | Canada |
| .dk | Denmark |
| .fr | France |
| .de | Germany (*De*utschland) |
| .it | Italy |
| .jp | Japan |
| .no | Norway |

On MSN, you use full Internet addresses (*name@domain*) to address e-mail and to identify yourself to others on the Internet.

When using some types of Internet resources, such as FTP, Telnet, and Gopher (see the following section, "About Internet Tools"), you're not accessing a person but a computer. To use these resources, you have to know the domain name of the computer that holds the resource you want. When you use the Web, you enter a special variation of an Internet address, called a URL, that includes the domain of the server on which the resource is located, information about the type of resource, and sometimes the name and directory location of a specific resource on the server.

## About Internet Tools

The Internet is a grab bag of different "tools" (for lack of a better word), each of which is used to retrieve and use a different type of resource. They're all part of the Internet in that they are accessed through the Net and they observe some standard policies such as domain/name conventions for Internet addresses. Beyond that, however, they're all very different, and you must learn to use each as a separate entity.

◆ **World Wide Web (the Web).** You can browse among sites on the World Wide Web, which is a subset of Internet sites that support the use of *hypertext*, (highlighted words that, when selected, branch off to other sites and subjects). To use the Web, you must have a program called a *Web browser*. Web browsing also supports multimedia; full-color graphics, video, and sound can be incorporated into what you see and do on the Web. Although the Web does not encompass the entire Internet, it does make using the Internet more intuitive, flexible, and fun. See Chapter 16, "Browsing the World Wide Web."

◆ **Gopher.** You can navigate among remote sites and visit remote computers through a simple, standardized menu system called Gopher. See Chapter 17, "Browsing Gophers."

◆ **FTP.** You can transfer files to and from remote computers set up as FTP servers. Using FTP, you can download files from remote FTP servers that store software programs, updated drivers, articles, books, photos, sound and video clips—you name it. See Chapter 18, "Downloading Files with FTP."

◆ **Internet Relay Chat (IRC) and MUDs.** You can have fun with these two methods of online, interactive discussion. Chat enables group discussions; MUDs and other interactive discussion games use the basic IRC facility to enable Internet users to join in elaborate online role-playing games. See Chapter 19, "Advanced Internet Techniques."

◆ **Telnet.** When you use Telnet, you log in to a remote computer at a university, research firm, corporation, government, or other organization and use that computer as if you were a local user. Telnet requires the simplest software to get hooked up, but requires some experience to use because every Telnet site has a different system of menus or commands. See Chapter 19.

◆ **Mailing lists.** Using e-mail, you subscribe to a mailing list designed to provide news or discussion about a given topic. After you subscribe, you receive regular batches of e-mail contributed by the other subscribers, all covering the specific topic. You can send in your own messages, too, to be shared with the list. See Chapter 19.

# How to Choose Client Software for Internet Services

By itself, MSN gets you *onto* the Internet, but not around on it. To work the full range of Internet resources, you have to pick up your own Internet software tools. Fortunately, a wide variety of public domain, shareware, and commercial options is available.

Like MSN, most Internet resources are accessed through a mechanism called *client/server processing*. Although a networking expert would beat me up for oversimplifying the definition, client/server processing is a way of controlling the exchange of information between two computers. One computer, called the *client*, sends commands requesting an action (called a *query*) to the server. The server does what it's told and returns the results to the client computer. To make this work, the client must issue commands the server understands.

One of the beauties of Internet client software is that you can mix and match different programs to suit your tastes. Although there are "all-in-one" packages that supply all client functions in some sort of unified interface, you can pick separate clients for each Internet resource. That allows you to select the individual client programs that best fit your needs. It also allows you to use Windows 95's built-in facilities for some functions and third-party programs for others. For example, you can use Windows 95's Telnet program for accessing remote computers, but use shareware clients for FTP, Gopher, and Web access.

This mix-and-match approach is made possible by an application program interface (API) called Windows Sockets (its nickname is WinSock). WinSock is contained in a file called WINSOCK.DLL in your Windows/System folder. WinSock acts as a sort of universal translator between TCP/IP and the client programs. The *sockets* part of the name is meant to convey the notion that programs use WinSock to "plug into" the TCP/IP program, which is just what they do.

WinSock is not quite universal—both the client program and the TCP/IP stack must be written to conform to the WinSock standard for the two to connect. But all popular Windows client programs are written to the standard. Now that Windows 95 has arrived, 32-bit applications written specifically for the new operating system are beginning to emerge.

Like any software, Internet software is available in four basic forms:

◆ **Commercial.** Software you buy, like Windows. Much of the commercial software available today is packaged as complete Internet suites. These "all-in-one" packages include TCP/IP and PPP/SLIP support plus a full set of client programs. Examples include Internet in a Box, Internet Made Simple, Atlantis Internet, and others.

◆ **Demo.** Demo software is a special version of a commercial software product that's crippled in some way (for example, it may be unable to save files) or designed to "expire" after you use it for a while. Demos are designed to demonstrate a commercial product so that you'll pay to get the full-featured version or one that doesn't expire. Note that some people use demos that don't expire for years, putting up with their functional inadequacies as the price of the software.

◆ **Shareware.** Shareware is distributed free, on the honor system. You can try it for free, but if you intend to actually use it beyond the trial period, you are expected to send a nominal license fee (typically $10 to $50) to the programmer. It's widely known that many people—the majority, in fact—who use shareware never pay for it. But apparently, enough people do pay to encourage programmers to continue writing the stuff. (Programmers also write shareware not in the hope of making money from users, but in the hope that a commercial software company will buy the rights—which sometimes happens.) Be that as it may, shareware is produced by professional programmers who deserve to be paid for their efforts. Incidentally, by producing good, inexpensive software, these programmers have greatly contributed to the lowering of prices for commercial software. So support 'em—pay for your shareware.

◆ **Public domain.** Sometimes also known as *freeware*, public domain software is distributed free of charge, out of the goodness of the programmer's heart. Technically, *freeware* is copyrighted software to which the owner grants licenses for free; *public domain software* is uncopyrighted, free software.

All these types of software can be acquired online. Shareware, demo, and public domain software can be downloaded from MSN and from FTP sites; commercial software can be ordered online from software vendors in online shops found on MSN and the World Wide Web.

**Tip**

> The CD-ROM packaged with this book contains a selection of Internet clients and other software and utilities.

In general, for the Windows 95 user, shareware and public domain programs offer the greatest value. Acquiring and managing your own suite of Internet client software is not too difficult; and doing so puts you in complete control. Once you assemble your own Internet tool kit, you have the expertise to upgrade or replace any piece of it as your needs change or as new, exciting programs hit the wires.

# More About the Internet

The next several chapters offer a thorough introduction to the Internet. However, if you want even more detail, the following Internet titles offer excellent expansion on what you've learned here:

*Navigating the Internet with Windows 95*

Author: Me
Pages: 432
A complete rundown on using the Internet with special emphasis on how Windows 95 supports that journey.

*The Internet Unleashed,* Second Edition

Authors: Internet experts
Pages: 1,440
A best-selling encyclopedia (now in its second edition) of the Internet and everything that's on it, geared not only to Windows users but to Mac and UNIX users as well.

*The World Wide Web Unleashed,* Second Edition

Authors: John December and Neil Randall
Pages: 1,350
A compendium of all that is the Web, including advanced navigation tips and instructions for creating Web pages and sites.

*Your Internet Consultant*

Author: Kevin M. Savetz

Pages: 550

A handy Internet reference guide organized in a useful question-and-answer format.

*Teach Yourself the Internet: Around the World in 21 Days*

Author: Neil Randall

Pages: 675

A thorough, all-purpose Internet guide featuring scenarios for applying the Internet in business, education, and scientific tasks.

*The Internet Business Guide,* Second Edition

Authors: Rosalind Resnick and Dave Taylor

Pages: 450

A detailed guide to setting up shop on the Net. Sample business scenarios include creating an online customer service center.

*Education on the Internet*

Author: Jill H. Ellsworth

Pages: 591

Insightful, complete information on the many educational applications of the Internet for teachers, professors, and students.

# What Now?

Now that your Internet feet are wet, it's time to dive in. Chapter 16, "Browsing the World Wide Web," explores the most important, most exciting part of the Internet: the World Wide Web. Once you visit, you may never leave.

And don't forget Appendix B, "Web Highlights," which directs you to many of the slickest sites the Net has to offer.

# CHAPTER
# 16

# BROWSING THE WORLD WIDE WEB

About the World Wide Web

Navigating the Web

Using Popular Web Browsers

Finding It on the Web

What Now?

When Microsoft put together MSN titles, described in Chapter 9, "Viewing and Operating Titles," it had inspiration: the World Wide Web. You use Web pages much as you use a title: by clicking on-screen links to navigate pages. The Web, however, is much more powerful and versatile; it is populated by thousands of times more pages than those in MSN's titles. Put another way, the Web is to titles as the Library of Congress is to the *World Almanac*.

When seen through a software client called a *graphical browser,* the Web is as close as you can get to making the Internet easy to use, good looking, and fun (see Figure 16.1). It's no coincidence that the explosion in mass-media interest in the Internet began with the appearance of Mosaic, the first graphical Web browser. Web-heavy reporting about the Internet has, in fact, led many to believe that the Web *is* the Internet (which it certainly is not). The appeal of Web browsers has also been the major factor in the rise of individual Internet accounts, and probably explains to some extent Microsoft's belief that Internet support was a "must-have" selling feature for Windows 95 and MSN.

**FIGURE 16.1.**

*A page on the World Wide Web.*

In other words, the Internet is fascinating, but the Web is *cool*. In mass-market America, *cool* gets you farther than *fascinating*.

In this chapter, you learn about the following:

◆ Where the Web came from and how it works

◆ How non-Web resources, such as FTP files and Gopher menus, can be accessed through the Web

◆ About using the important features of Windows-based Web browsing software

◆ The ways in which MSN's Web access is restricted compared to regular Internet accounts

◆ How to search for—and find!—anything on the Web

> Microsoft offers its own Web browser, Internet Explorer, which is on the CD-ROM that accompanies this book; Internet Explorer is also featured in the Microsoft Plus! add-on pack for Windows 95 and is on MSN for downloading. Explorer is a perfectly capable browser that is especially well suited to Windows 95 and to MSN Internet accounts, as you discover later in this chapter. But you are not required to use Internet Explorer on MSN; you can use any of the commercial, shareware, and public domain browsers available for Windows, two of which are described later in this chapter.
>
> Because many MSN users will choose Internet Explorer, most figures in this chapter show how Web pages look through Explorer. However, don't let that mislead you into believing you cannot use a different Web browser such as Netscape Navigator or Mosaic. Although the menus, toolbars, and other paraphernalia surrounding a Web page differ from browser to browser, the page itself appears essentially the same, browser to browser, and is used in the same manner.

# About the World Wide Web

The Web was invented in 1990 at CERN, the European Particle Physics Laboratory in Switzerland. Today, an independent organization (of which CERN remains a part—as do M.I.T. and others), the World Wide Web Consortium, oversees and nurtures the Web's growth.

The Web Consortium has defined a set of standards and concepts for adding servers to the Web and for constructing the screens of information that appear to Web surfers. These screens, also known as Web *documents* or simply *pages*, are created within a special formatting language, *HyperText Markup Language* (HTML). A Web browser, by the way, is simply a program capable of interpreting the formatting of HTML documents and the navigation instructions they contain. The browser and the server communicate through another published standard, the *HyperText Transfer Protocol* (HTTP).

By publishing the specifications for HTML and HTTP, the Web Consortium has made it possible for anyone on the Internet to easily create Web documents and publish them. Making Web publishing easy and open has encouraged the growth of resources and activities on the Web. The terrific collection of Web documents available today—and the incredible network of links that connect those documents—was created not by any Web-advocacy organization, but by the Internet public.

## Hypertext and Hypermedia

The essential feature of HTML documents is *hypertext*. Hypertext is a method of embedding in one document links to other documents. These links show up in Windows Web browsers as highlighted words within a document, usually displayed in a bright color that's different from the color of the surrounding text. Click a link and a different page appears, containing its own set of highlighted links for going elsewhere. Links are sometimes also called *hotlinks* or *hyperlinks*.

Often, the links within a document lead to expanded information about a subject. Consider the screen in Figure 16.2, from a document on a Web site called Mr. Showbiz. Notice the underlined words and phrases; each of these is a hypertext link to something else or somewhere else. For example, if you click the hypertext phrase `Michael Moriarty`, the screen shown in Figure 16.3 appears to show you expanded information.

**FIGURE 16.2.**

*The home page of Mr. Showbiz, a site about everything in entertainment.*

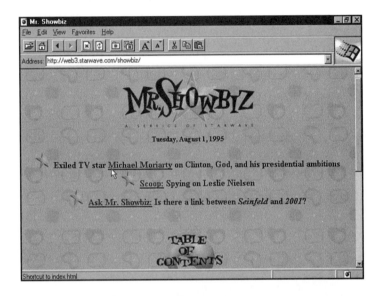

**FIGURE 16.3.**

*The page that appears when a user clicks the link* `Michael Moriarty` *in the Mr. Showbiz page, shown in Figure 16.2.*

> In a Web browser, just as in an MSN title, you can always tell when the mouse pointer is on a link: it changes from the generic pointer used in Windows to something different, usually a pointing finger. To activate a link, move the pointer close enough to the link so that the pointer becomes a finger and then click.

Notice that the screen in Figure 16.3 has links of its own. You can continue browsing through these links or click the Back button in the toolbar to jump back to the document shown in Figure 16.2.

> Your Web browser may show you where you've been by changing the color of links you've used. (Both Internet Explorer and Netscape Navigator do this.) If you use the Back button in the toolbar to jump back from the screen shown in Figure 16.3 to the earlier screen in Figure 16.2, you see that the link Michael Moriarty has changed color. This feature is handy when you're browsing because it prevents you from checking out the same link twice by accident.

The beauty of links is that they can lead to anything on the Web—not just to expanded information about a document but to an entirely different document stored on a different Web server a continent away. Using links, Web document developers create documents with a certain amount of information of their own, peppered with links to other sites and other documents containing related information.

Hypertext is what makes true "browsing" possible. You can navigate to a Web document containing information about a topic you're interested in. Once there, you can use the links to jump around to other documents. This nonlinear, dynamic browsing can result in very productive, exciting research sessions. Machines process information in an orderly fashion; humans jump from idea to idea, the way the Web allows them to. We enjoy free-associating our way around the Web.

Although links appear within the text of documents that also supply some information or descriptive text of their own (as is true in Figure 16.2), some Web documents themselves are just lists of links. These Web "directories" are invaluable resources because they offer a jumping-off point for finding information all over the Web. Figure 16.4 shows a directory for fun stuff on the Web, compiled by Microsoft and offered through Microsoft's MSN Internet home page (described later in this chapter). Every line below the title in this document is a link to somewhere else.

**FIGURE 16.4.**

*A directory of fun stuff,*
*courtesy of Microsoft.*

*Tip*

> Links not only take you to another Web site or document, they can take you to a specific spot within a document. This capability, called *anchoring*, is especially useful for linking to specific, relevant passages in a long document. A link in a long document can even be used to jump to an anchor link somewhere else within the same document. This capability is used to create documents with a table of contents built from links that take you straight to a particular part of the document.

With the advent of graphical Web browsers in 1993, the concept of hypertext was expanded to deal with elements other than text. This enhanced way of working with hypertext, sometimes called *hypermedia*, expands Web browsing in two terrific ways that involve graphics and multimedia. (Technically, what we call *hypermedia* is still accomplished, under the covers, through hypertext. Although experts quibble over the terminology, from the user's point of view, *hypermedia* is an accurate descriptor.)

In the first application of hypermedia, on-screen graphics can themselves be links. Graphical links make browsing intuitive and fun—if you see a picture of something interesting, you can click it to see where it leads. Often, picture links lead to other documents, although they sometimes lead to a larger version of the same graphic. The smaller versions that serve as links are called *thumbnails*.

For example, Figure 16.5 shows a page from an online art gallery, including thumbnail links to artwork. Clicking the thumbnail of *Wild Roses* (by watercolorist Margaret Cornish) activates a link that displays a larger version of the image (see Figure 16.6).

**FIGURE 16.5.**

*An online gallery, with thumbnails of pictures that are also links.*

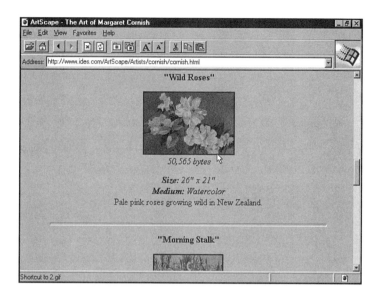

**FIGURE 16.6.**

*The enlarged version of* Wild Roses, *which appears when you click the thumbnail link in the screen shown in Figure 16.5.*

Some text-only Web browsers can access all the same documents as graphical Web browsers but they don't display the pictures.

To be compatible with both graphical and nongraphical browsers, Web pages featuring picture links typically include a set of identical text links somewhere else on the page for the text-only crowd. Of course, even if you use a graphical browser, you can use the text links if you prefer.

In the second application of hypermedia, Web links can open a program and display or play a file within it. For example, a link may be designed to play a sound clip. Double-click the link, and your browser downloads the sound clip file, opens an application that plays sound clips, and plays the clip. Hypermedia on the Web supports full-color graphics, sound, animation, and video.

## File Viewers

It's important to realize that Web browsers themselves don't have the capability to do much more than display text, fonts, and some types of color graphics files. For some other types of multimedia information accessed through the Web, the browser must open on your PC another program capable of displaying or playing the file. These programs are called *viewers*, or sometimes *helper applications*.

Good graphical Web browsers typically include some viewers of their own and may come preconfigured to access Windows programs that can act as viewers as well. For example, a browser may come preconfigured to open Windows 95's Media Player for playing video and sound clips. You can encounter hundreds of types of files on the Web, and you may come across a file type for which your browser has no viewer. When that happens, your browser typically gives you the option to download the file to your PC's hard disk so that you can figure out how to play the file later, offline.

To add support for a file type, you have to locate your browser's viewers dialog box and enter a path and program filename for a program capable of opening the file type. Figure 16.7 shows Internet Explorer's viewers configuration facility, the Options dialog box, which you reach by choosing **V**iew, **O**ptions and then selecting the File Types tab.

**FIGURE 16.7.**

*Configuring viewers in the Internet Explorer with the File Types tab in the Options dialog box.*

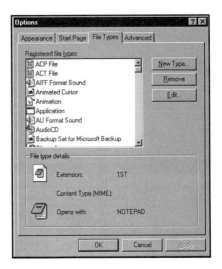

Internet Explorer refers to its viewers configuration as *file types* for consistency with Windows 95's file-association facilities. And in fact, the choices you see on the File Types tab are registered throughout Windows 95 as file associations. Because Explorer automatically creates associations for its built-in viewers, you may find after installing Explorer that Explorer opens automatically when you double-click files of certain types. For example, Explorer has the built-in ability to play basic audio files (those files using the AU extension), which are common on the Internet. If, after installing Explorer, you double-click an AU file anywhere in Windows, Explorer opens automatically to play that file.

For more about registering file types with applications, see Chapter 11, "Advanced Configuration Options."

## Home Pages

An important concept for understanding the Web is *home.* On MSN, *home* means one thing only: the MSN home page, MSN Central. Unfortunately, on the Web, a *home page* can be either of two things:

◆ The top page, or entry point, for all the Web documents and activities within a given Web site is the *home page* for that site.

◆ Your Web browser is configured with a home page, sometimes also called a *startup page*, to which it navigates automatically whenever you start it up. Most browsers come with the browser software company's home page preconfigured as your home page, which isn't such a bad thing. The developers often pack their home pages with a good selection of links to search tools, cool new Web services, and other useful or interesting items—plus, of course, announcements about software updates and other products.

You can use your browser's configuration dialog boxes to designate any page on the Web as your home page.

## Links to Other Resources

Finally, Web browsers can be used as "front ends" to other Internet resources, including the following:

◆ FTP file transfers
◆ Gopher menus
◆ Telnet sessions

---

### What You Can and Can't Do with an MSN Internet Account

As described in Chapter 15, "Understanding the Internet," MSN does not support the same type of flexible Internet access to e-mail and newsgroups that is offered through typical Internet accounts available through Internet access providers. Although you can use any client software you want for the Web, FTP, and other facilities, you can access e-mail only through Exchange; you can access newsgroups only through the MSN client software.

These limitations carry over to Web browsers. Full-featured browsers such as Mosaic and Navigator (described later in this chapter) can double as newsreader clients for accessing newsgroups. These same browsers also allow you to compose and send (but not receive) e-mail directly through the browser software. However, even if your Web browser is capable of accessing newsgroups and sending e-mail, you cannot use it to do either through an MSN Internet account.

The exception to that rule is Microsoft's Internet Explorer, which does not have the ability to access newsgroups or send e-mail when used on a regular, non-MSN Internet account. However, on an MSN Internet account, Explorer does allow you to jump easily from the Web to MSN's newsgroups folders. And Internet Explorer can open Exchange so that you can send e-mail. These capabilities are described later in this chapter.

However, through an MSN Internet account, most Web browsers (including Internet Explorer) can be used to access Telnet, FTP, and Gopher resources.

---

Web navigation is accomplished through Uniform Resource Locators, or URLs (see "Navigating the Web," later in this chapter). URL is pronounced *earl* or *you-are-ell*, depending on whether you believe in acronyms or abbreviations. URLs are a standard way of formatting server addresses and the locations of documents or resources within those locations, regardless of the type of Internet server or resource. URLs can point to Web servers and the HTML documents on them, FTP servers, specific files on FTP servers, Gopher menus, and so on.

You can type URLs yourself to navigate the Web. But the main thing links do is supply URLs to your browser, to tell the browser where to go. Because of the universal nature of URLs, links in Web documents can point to other types of resources. For example, a link may start an FTP session to download a file or display a Gopher menu. This approach is a great way to make resources available through the Web, and it can make certain types of activities—particularly file downloading—much easier.

The downside of this approach is that, to reach a particular resource, a link must be provided to it, or you must know how to phrase a URL correctly to reach what you want. Obviously, the Web has not yet accumulated links to every piece of information on all Internet resources. The Web does not, by itself, make client software for other Internet resources unnecessary.

More importantly, even when a link points to a resource, you can only do there what the link allows you to do. If a link points to an FTP file, you can download that file with a click. But you can't check out other files on the same FTP site or perform other FTP activities there unless Web links are specifically provided for those activities. Finally, most Web links have to be updated manually; even those that are updated automatically do not instantly change when an item changes its location or name. When that happens, an old link is at a loss to find the item even though you may have little trouble finding it with the proper client software.

---

### Where Is the Web?

Nearly all the HTML documents that appear as Web pages are stored on dedicated Web servers. *Web servers* are computers on the Internet especially configured to use the HTTP protocol. HTTP allows browsers and Web servers to communicate with one another and to interpret links. To the extent that Web browsers also reach into FTP servers, news servers, and other Internet computers, it can be said that the Web, in function if not in actuality, reaches into all corners of the Web. But technically, the documents comprising the Web proper are on Web servers; the other stuff is ancillary to the Web, not part of it.

Anyone who wants to create and publish a Web page must set up a Web server or acquire space on someone else's Web server. Some Internet access providers, among others, lease space on their Web servers to anyone who wants to publish a document.

---

# Navigating the Web

Navigating the Web is more than a matter of hyperlinking around. Three basic tools for Web navigation are essential for effective and convenient Web travel: URLs, bookmarks, and toolbar tools.

## URLs

Uniform Resource Locators (URLs) are a way of standardizing the descriptions for Internet resources so that the description always includes the information your browser needs to access a particular item.

---

Look just below the toolbar in any of the screen images shown in this chapter. The URL of the Web page shown appears in a text box there. That spot is also where you can type a different URL to navigate to a particular Web site. When you activate a link, the URL shown in the text box changes to show you the URL where the link takes you.

*Tip*

To navigate across the Internet, your Web browser needs to know the following:

◆ Type of Internet resource (scheme)—Web, FTP, Gopher, Telnet, newsgroup, or send-only e-mail. The schemes permitted on MSN Internet accounts are http (a Web server), ftp (an FTP server), gopher (a Gopher server), and telnet (a Telnet server). In a URL, the scheme is followed by the characters ://  (colon slash slash). Two special schemes—news (for newsgroups) and mailto (for sending e-mail) omit the slashes and are followed only by a colon. Note that the news and mailto schemes are supported on MSN through the Internet Explorer alone; they are not supported under other Web browsers.

◆ Server address (host)—The Internet address, or *domain name*, of the server holding the resource. This is the same information you typically supply to client software.

◆ Port (port)—Sometimes (not always), a port number may be required by some servers for some resources, particularly Telnet resources.

◆ Path (path)—The location (usually a directory/subdirectory path and filename, formatted like a DOS path) of the resource on the server. Like the port, a path isn't always required.

In a URL, this information is formatted in a standard order:

`scheme://host:port/path`

For example, the URL http://www.microsoft.com points to a Web server (http) whose domain is www.microsoft.com. If you enter this URL in your Web browser, you visit Microsoft's Web site. If you enter **ftp://** followed by the address of an FTP site (see Chapter 18, "Downloading Files with FTP"), and the directory location and name of a file, your Web browser downloads that file from the FTP site. If you enter **gopher://** followed by the address of a Gopher server, a Gopher menu appears (see Chapter 17, "Browsing Gophers").

*Note*

> Servers on the Web are case sensitive, which means that you ***must*** enter your URLs in the exact combination of uppercase and lowercase letters required. For example, if you see a reference to the URL ftp://ftp.microsoft.com/Win95/Internet.doc, and you enter it in all lowercase letters (without capitalizing *Win95* and *Internet*), you probably won't get through. Always observe the exact capitalization you are given for any URL you enter.

Although URLs aren't all that tricky, most Web users don't spend much time fooling with them. After all, that's a link's job: to supply your browser with the URL of a Web page or other resource. For any resource you use often, whether you've first used a link to get there or not, you can create a *bookmark* (see "Bookmarks," later in this chapter) so that you can get to that Web page without typing the URL. In general practice, you type URLs only when you have a written reference (not a link) to a resource, like the URLs accompanying descriptions of interesting Web pages in this book.

# Toolbar Tools

On the toolbar of every graphical Web browser (and in their menus, as well), you can find an assortment of useful tools that differs from browser to browser. But you'll always find these four tools somewhere on the toolbar:

◆ Back—A backward-pointing arrow. Click this to jump to the page you were looking at before the one you're on. Clicking Back multiple times takes you back farther, until you ultimately arrive at your home page.

◆ Forward—A forward-pointing arrow. Click this to jump to the page that follows the one you're on. Forward works only after you've used Back. After you've gone back one or more steps, Forward can take you ahead again. If you haven't gone back at all, there's no way for Forward to determine where you want to go—in other words, there is no "forward" until you first go back.

◆ Stop—Usually a stop sign (in Internet Explorer, the Stop button on the toolbar is a page with an X through it). Sometimes, you can click a link or initiate another activity and suddenly realize that's not what you want to do. If it takes a browser a while to locate and transfer the document, you needn't wait until the operation is complete before starting over. Click Stop during any operation to cancel it.

◆ Home—A little house. Home takes you directly to the Web page configured as "home" in your browser. Home is handy when you browse too far into the forest and get lost, cold, or hungry. One click takes you home and reorients you so that you can start off in another direction.

---

### Caching Is Faster

Some Web browsers achieve their Back and Forward capabilities by storing, or *caching*, Web pages on your PC. The number of pages stored varies, but anytime the browser can retrieve a page from memory instead of retransferring it through the Net, the page appears more rapidly. Sometimes, pages are cached in memory and on disk only for the duration of a session; other times, they're saved on disk for rapid retrieval in later sessions (this approach is called *persistent cache*).

It's always better to use the browser's Back, Forward, or Home features to move to a page instead of using a bookmark or reentering the URL—when you have the choice. These toolbar tools typically retrieve cached pages when the pages are available; a bookmark or new URL entry forces the browser to retransfer the document, even if it's already cached.

Microsoft's Internet Explorer takes persistent caching one step further through the autoconnect feature of Windows 95's Internet access (see Chapter 15, "Understanding the Internet"). During a Web session, Explorer stores pages and keeps them on disk even after the session is over. When you open Explorer for another session, Explorer does not connect you to the Internet until you try to access a page it does not already have stored. As long as you work with pages and links you've used recently, you can work offline, using stored pages, until you ask for something new (or choose **V**iew, **R**efresh, which always accesses a page on the Web, even if it's cached, to make sure that it's up to date).

## Bookmarks

On MSN, your Favorite Places shortcuts are markers you create to take you quickly to resources you use often. On the Web, the same thing is accomplished with *bookmarks*—a.k.a. *favorite places* and *hotlists.* Bookmarks contain the URLs of resources you plan to use often. When you're somewhere you like and you want to be able to get back there easily, select your browser's Add Bookmark (or Add to Favorites or Add to Hotlist) feature, which stores the URL of the current page and adds its title to a menu or drop-down list (see Figure 16.8). The next time you want to visit that resource, simply pick it from your bookmark list. The browser reads the URL from your bookmark file and takes you directly to the desired spot.

**FIGURE 16.8.**

*The Favorites menu in my copy of Internet Explorer shows a list of bookmarks to my favorite places.*

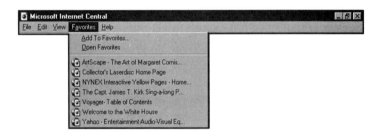

Bookmarks are especially handy if you've had to do a lot of linking and jumping to arrive at a given page and you don't want to repeat that navigation pattern to get there next time. (Yes, I could simply write down the URL but…my kid swiped all my pens.)

During a Web session, most browsers build a "history" list containing the URLs of all the pages you've visited that session. You can access this list from a History menu and select a page to jump back to somewhere you've already been. You can do the same by clicking the Back toolbar button, but if the page you want was visited many links ago, selecting it from the History menu is much faster than clicking Back over and over. Browsers discard the history list at the end of each online session.

# Using Popular Web Browsers

The following pages describe three popular Web browsers: Internet Explorer, Mosaic, and Netscape Navigator. In addition to the three browsers described here, many other Web browsers are available. Because an MSN Internet account allows you to choose any Windows-based Web browser you like, it's a good idea to keep up with magazine reviews of developments in the browser arena. The browser market is very competitive right now; new, exciting browser capabilities debut monthly.

## Internet Explorer

Despite its apparent simplicity, Explorer (featured in the Internet Jumpstart Kit on the CD-ROM that accompanies this book) is a full-featured browser that performs very well for two reasons: First, it's a 32-bit, multithreaded Windows 95 application, a fact that not only boosts performance but also supports simultaneous downloads. Second, it employs "progressive rendering" of graphics. That means that the browser displays all the text before the graphics and then transfers the graphics in stages. Progressive rendering allows you to activate a link and jump to another page without first waiting for the graphics to completely appear. Figure 16.9 shows the default home page that appears when you start up the Internet Explorer.

**FIGURE 16.9.**

*The Internet Explorer at Microsoft's Explorer home page, Explore the Internet (http://www.home. msn.net).*

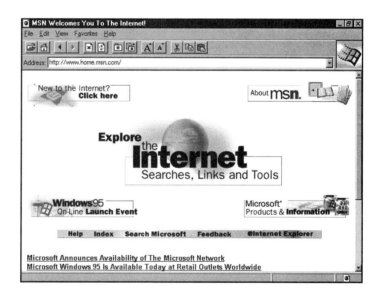

Here are the basics for using Internet Explorer:

◆ **Entering URLs.** You can manually enter and edit URLs in the Address box underneath the toolbar. The Address box is also a drop-down list from which you can select History pages.

◆ **Toolbar tools.** Home, Back, Forward, Bookmarks (Favorites), Cut, Paste, and Stop.

◆ **Home page ("Start Page").** The Explorer's home page is preconfigured to the Explore the Internet page (`http://www.home.msn.net`), but you can change it to any Web page you want by first displaying the page you want to use as a home page and then choosing **V**iew, **O**ptions to display Internet Explorer's Properties sheet. Click the Start tab and then click Use **C**urrent.

◆ **Bookmarks.** Explorer has a F**a**vorites menu you can use to create and jump to bookmarks, which it stores in a Windows 95 folder. To add a bookmark for the current page, choose F**a**vorites, **A**dd to Favorites. To use a bookmark, choose Favorites and then choose the desired bookmark from the Favorites menu.

◆ **History.** Pages or URLs stored as history can be selected from the Address drop-down list or from the bottom of the **F**ile menu. At the bottom of the **F**ile menu is a **M**ore History item that opens a folder containing shortcuts to the last 300 sites you've visited.

◆ **Viewers.** Choose **V**iew, **O**ptions to display a four-tab Options dialog box. The File Types tab sheet is used to create file/program associations and comes preconfigured with Windows 95's default associations. This tab is used in exactly the same way as the File Types dialog box you can reach from any Windows 95 Explorer window by selecting **V**iew, **O**ptions, **F**ile Types.

◆ **FTP and Gopher.** Explorer supports FTP and Gopher protocols so that you can access FTP and Gopher resources two ways: By entering the URL (`ftp://`*address* or `gopher://`*address*) or by activating Web links leading to FTP or Gopher resources.

◆ **Newsgroups:** On MSN Internet accounts, Internet Explorer can take you to MSN's Internet newsgroups folders (see Chapter 5, "Reading and Contributing to Bulletin Boards and Newsgroups") when you activate a Web link leading to a newsgroup or when you enter a URL made up of `news:` followed by a newsgroup name (for example, `news:alt.startrek`). Note that this feature does not allow you to operate newsgroups within the Web browser, as other browsers can on non-MSN Internet accounts. Rather, the feature takes you to newsgroups within the MSN interface.

◆ **E-mail:** On MSN Internet accounts, Internet Explorer can open Exchange to send e-mail anytime you click an e-mail link on a Web page or enter an e-mail URL (`mailto:`*e-mailaddress*). Exchange opens with a Compose New Message window ready to go, with the `To:` line in the header filled in automatically with the desired address.

---

### The Case for Explorer

Like most Web browsers, Internet Explorer is too rich an application to be thoroughly covered in this chapter. However, the following items give you a taste of some of the special features Explorer offers. You probably won't be surprised when you see that Explorer's strong suit is its support of Windows 95's features.

◆ Internet Explorer includes a facility for creating Windows 95 shortcuts to Web pages. When viewing a page, choose **F**ile, Create **S**hortcut. Explorer deposits a shortcut to that page on the Windows desktop. Double-clicking that shortcut icon opens Explorer and displays the page (if it is cached) or causes Explorer to dial the Internet and retrieve the page (if the page is not cached).

◆ Each URL saved in the **F**avorites menu, the **H**istory submenu, or as a desktop shortcut represents a file with the extension URL. You can manipulate these URL files like any others. For example, you can add new folders to the Favorites folder (which is located in your Windows folder) and drop URL files into them. These folders appear as submenus in your **F**avorites menu so that you can organize your favorite places into a series of submenus. You can also drag URL files and drop them into BBS messages (see Chapter 7, "Downloading and Uploading Files") or e-mail messages.

◆ To quickly access anything on the Web through Explorer, you can choose Run from Windows 95's Start menu and then enter the URL. Windows starts Internet Explorer and connects to MSN (if you are not already connected) and navigates directly to the URL you entered.

◆ Internet Explorer is OLE-enabled (see Chapter 12, "Trimming Time Online"), which means you can drag just about anything you see on a Web page and drop it on your Windows desktop or into an OLE enabled application, such as Microsoft Word or Excel. For example, you can click (and hold the mouse button down) on a graphic in a Web page, drag the graphic to a Word document, and drop it there to embed the graphic in your document.

◆ If you hold the Shift key down when you click a link in Internet Explorer, another Internet Explorer window opens. Using this feature, you can multitask the Web. For example, while downloading a file in one Explorer window, you can browse the Web in another. Note, however, that doing so is likely to dramatically slow down any PC with less than 16M of memory.

◆ The various tabs on the Options dialog box (accessed by selecting **V**iew, **O**ptions) include a set of tools for customizing Explorer. You can select the size of the cache and the number of pages to store in persistent cache, choose a new home page (Explorer calls your home page the *start page* but still represents it on the toolbar with a house icon), and customize Explorer in other ways.

# Mosaic 2.0

Mosaic is an important application because, more than anything else, it is responsible for the Internet's recent popularity. Mosaic demonstrated to new users that the Internet can be friendly and fun. Mosaic has always been a "freeware" application, developed and distributed by the

National Center for Supercomputing Applications (NCSA) at the University of Illinois at Urbana-Champaign. (There are licensed commercial versions of Mosaic, as well, of which Internet Explorer is technically one, although it differs substantially from its progenitor.) The NCSA Mosaic home page is shown in Figure 16.10.

**FIGURE 16.10.**

*NCSA Mosaic at the NCSA Windows Mosaic home page.*

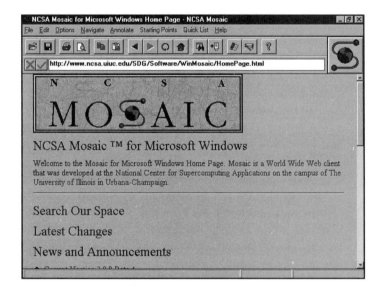

You won't find a more full-featured graphical Web browser. Mosaic is a 32-bit, multithreaded application, so it performs well—as a program—in Windows 95. As a multithreaded application, it can download multiple files, or pages, simultaneously, which also boosts performance.

At this writing, Mosaic does not speed Web browsing by performing progressive rendering of on-screen graphics—something Internet Explorer and Navigator both do. Instead, Mosaic displays little placeholders in place of the graphics as it downloads the graphics in the background. You can go ahead and jump to another page before the graphics appear, but you have no idea what the graphics are going to be until they finish downloading. Progressive rendering displays the graphics in stages, so that you can get an idea of what they'll look like before they actually finish appearing.

Here are the basics for using Mosaic:

◆ **Entering URLs.** You can manually enter and edit URLs in the box under the toolbar, or by choosing **F**ile, **O**pen Document to open a dialog box in which you can type a URL.

◆ **Toolbar tools.** Mosaic's toolbar has Home, Back, Forward, Bookmarks (Add to Hotlist), Cut and Paste, Newsgroups, and E-mail (send only) tools. You stop an activity by clicking the big globe, which spins whenever Mosaic is actively communicating with a server.

◆ **Home page.** Mosaic's home page is preconfigured to NCSA's Mosaic home page (`http://www.ncsa.uiuc.edu/SDG/Software/Mosaic/NCSAMosaicHome.html`) but can be changed through the Preferences dialog box (see "Other useful features," later in this list).

◆ **Bookmarks (Hotlist).** To add a bookmark (a hotlist entry) for the current page, choose **N**avigate, **A**dd Current to Hotlist. You can also click the Add to Hotlist button on the toolbar (the plus sign next to a page on fire).

◆ **History.** Pages or URLs stored as history can be recalled by choosing **N**avigate, **H**istory.

◆ **Viewers.** Choose **O**ptions, **P**references, **V**iewers to configure viewers.

◆ **FTP and Gopher.** FTP and Gopher resources are reached through available Web links. Links to popular Gopher servers appear in Mosaic's Starting Points menu.

◆ **Other useful features.** All Mosaic configuration and customization is performed through the Preferences Properties dialog box (accessed by selecting **O**ptions, **P**references from the menu bar).

In addition to the features mentioned, Mosaic also functions as a newsreader for accessing newsgroups and as a send-only e-mail client. But these features are not supported by MSN Internet accounts. Regardless of the browser you choose, MSN requires you to use Exchange for e-mail and the MSN Client software for newsgroups.

# Netscape

Mosaic was the first graphical browser, but at this writing, Netscape Navigator is the most popular. Navigator's popularity is a result of its simplicity (just the right features, not too many, in big, friendly buttons) and its performance, which has always been sprightly thanks to its use of progressive rendering. The latest version is a 32-bit Windows 95 application—the first Windows 95 Web browser (an older, 16-bit version is also available for Windows 3.1). Figure 16.11 shows the Netscape home page. Navigator is available free of charge to users in educational institutions, or to anyone for a trial period (without tech support or documentation). After the trial period, a $39 registration gets you support and a manual. The trial version can be downloaded from Navigator's home page at `http://home.netscape.com`.

Here are the basics for using Navigator:

◆ **Entering URLs.** You can manually enter and edit URLs in the Netsite box under the toolbar or choose **F**ile, **O**pen Netsite to open a dialog box in which you can type a URL.

◆ **Toolbar tools.** The essentials—Home, Back, Forward, and Stop—are provided in clean, easy-to-see buttons.

**FIGURE 16.11.**

*Netscape Navigator at Netscape's home page.*

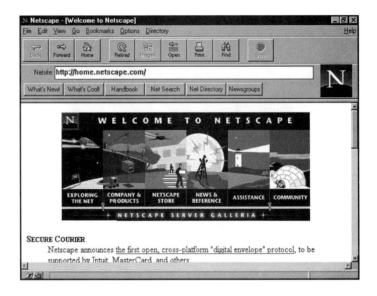

◆ **Home page.** The home page is preconfigured to Netscape's home page (http://home.netscape.com) but can be changed through the Preferences Properties sheet (choose **O**ptions, **P**references, **S**tyles from the menu bar).

◆ **Bookmarks.** To add a bookmark for the current page, choose **B**ookmarks, **A**dd Bookmark.

◆ **History.** Pages or URLs stored as history can be recalled by choosing **G**o, **V**iew History.

◆ **Viewers ("helper applications").** Choose **O**ptions, **P**references, **H**elper Applications to configure viewers.

◆ **FTP and Gopher.** FTP and Gopher resources are reached through available Web links.

◆ **Other useful features.** Netscape features a set of buttons, just below the Netsite URL text box, that activate links to useful pages including search engines (Net Search), helpful Web directories like Yahoo (the Net Directory, described later in this chapter), and the latest fun places to visit (What's New! and What's Cool!). The **D**irectory menu also supplies some helpful starting points.

In addition to the features mentioned, Navigator also functions as a newsreader for accessing newsgroups and as a send-only e-mail client. But these features are not supported by MSN Internet accounts. Regardless of the browser you choose, MSN requires you to use Exchange for e-mail and the MSN Client software for newsgroups.

# Finding It on the Web

When you first surf the Web, it's a free-association blast—point, click, *Wow!*...point, click, *Wow!* Soon, however, the time comes when you want to track down something specific. That's where Web searching comes in.

Web searching can deliver not only the locations of Web resources related to your search term, but also Gopher menus, FTP files, and more. Web searching is powerful because search results are almost always reported as a directory of links: you can easily jump to any resource the search reveals.

## Starting Points

Perhaps the most convenient starting points for Web searching are the default home pages of the Web browsers. Like all savvy Web-based businesses, the browser makers have peppered their home pages with handy links to draw you in—so that you can see their ads. It's a fair deal. Navigator's home page is an especially useful starting place for searches because it contains a link to a set of Net Directories and a link to a set of Net Searches. (If you use Navigator, you can reach these lists any time, whether you're at the home page or not, by clicking the Net Directory or Net Search button.)

---

### The Search/Directory Schism

Web-based search tools are generally separated into two groups:

◆ **Directories** are databases containing index trees of Web document titles, URLs, and descriptive information. In general, directories are created and maintained by people and expanded by contributions from others on the Web who want their favorite sites included. Often, a directory has its own search engine for locating by search term information within the directory database. In some cases, however, you are expected to browse through indexed categories and lists to find what you want.

◆ **Web spiders**, sometimes also called *crawlers*, *worms*, or simply *search engines*, are typically more detailed databases of Web information that include not only titles and URLs, but often keywords from within documents. Of necessity, these databases are created and updated by automated polling programs whose names suggest the way they squiggle around the Web gathering information. Because they contain such a depth of data, these search tools are accompanied by sophisticated search engines for locating information by keyword.

---

For example, selecting Net Search from the Navigator home page (`http://home.netscape.com`) brings up a screen like the one shown in Figure 16.12, which includes links to three keyword-searchable spiders. You can type a search term and initiate an InfoSeek search directly from the home page or you can select one of the other two search engines.

**FIGURE 16.12.**

*Links to search engines are accessed through Netscape's home page (http://home.netscape.com).*

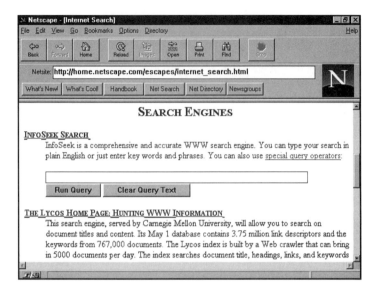

Similarly, Explore the Internet—the default home page for Internet Explorer at http://www.home.msn.net—features links that lead to search engines and directories. From the Explore the Internet page, click Explore the Internet. The page that appears is shown in Figure 16.13; Explore the Internet shows, among other links, a link to an All-in-One Search Page for running three different Web search tools: InfoSeek, Lycos, and Yahoo. You can also reach each of these separately by clicking their names on the page shown in Figure 16.13.

**FIGURE 16.13.**

*Links to searches are accessible through the Explore the Internet link on Explorer's default home page (http://www.home.msn.net).*

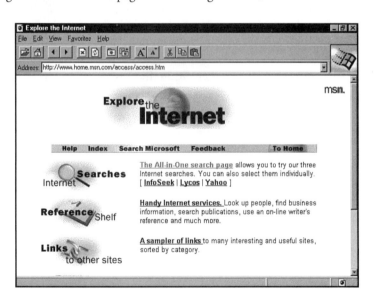

Another great starting point is the Clearinghouse for Subject-Oriented Internet Resource Guides (http://www.lib.umich.edu/chhome.html), a joint effort of the University of Michigan's

University Library and the School of Information and Library Studies. Students find and build links to dozens of searchable Internet directories so that the links can all be accessed from a single point: the Clearinghouse (see Figure 16.14). Some of the guides are just text, but increasingly, the guides are Web pages containing links to other places on the Internet.

**FIGURE 16.14.**

*The Clearinghouse for Subject-Oriented Internet Resource Guides.*

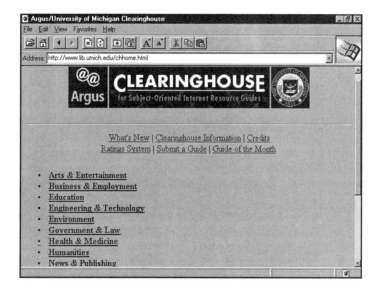

Finally, the World Wide Web Virtual Library (described later in this chapter) includes a page of links to other virtual libraries (see Figure 16.15), which are directories of Web information that can be searched by subject.

**FIGURE 16.15.**

*The Virtual Libraries page of the WWW Virtual Library at http:// www.w3.org/hypertext/ DataSources/bySubject/ Virtual_libraries/ Overview.html.*

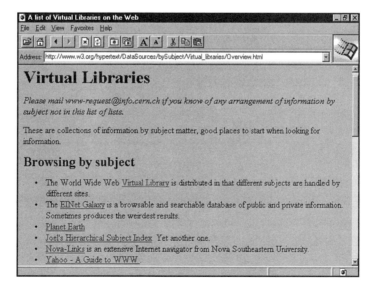

## Web Directories

The next several pages describe useful directories of Web-based information. These directories are databases built by people, usually by accepting submissions from Webmasters who want their pages listed. Directories are organized hierarchically: they first list links representing general categories, each of which leads to more specific subcategories and ultimately to entries describing Web pages, FTP files, and other Web-accessible items. Some directories also have accompanying search tools; other directories don't.

## Yahoo

Yahoo stands for *Yet Another Hierarchical Oracle.* (The developers invite you to fill in whatever you want for the second *O.*) Yahoo is a hierarchical index of the Web. The database is written and maintained by David Filo and Jerry Yang, self-proclaimed yahoos. Anyone else who wants to add to the database is invited to do so; the yahoos themselves verify any additions before making them official.

You can browse Yahoo easily because it's organized hierarchically. As you can probably tell from Figure 16.16, you can click a link named for a subject (Arts, Business and Economy, and so on) to display a further set of links related to that topic. Typically, you navigate down several levels before hitting actual links to Web pages and other resources.

**FIGURE 16.16.**

*Yahoo's home page.*

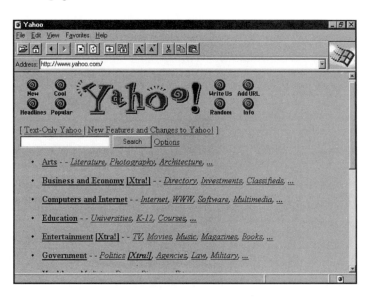

Use the text box in Figure 16.16 to type a search term. To perform a simple search, type a search term and click Search. Or click the Options link (right next to the Search button), to bring up a surprisingly sophisticated search engine (see Figure 16.17). The search engine allows you to specify whether to look for your search term in document titles, URLs, or comments (descriptive text). You can also use case-sensitive matching, string/substring matching, and Boolean phrasing.

Around the title in the page shown in Figure 16.16, notice a number of useful and fun links, including these:

◆ **New:** Displays links to the latest URLs added to the Yahoo database.

◆ **Cool:** Displays links to URLs the yahoos consider fun.

◆ **Popular:** Displays links to the 50 links most frequently accessed from Yahoo.

◆ **Headlines:** A daily news summary.

◆ **Random:** Links you somewhere, completely at random. Close your eyes and see where you end up.

**FIGURE 16.17.**

*Phrasing a Yahoo search.*

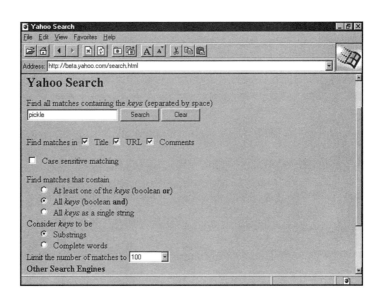

In the example in Figure 16.17, I'm searching for information about *pickle*. I've decided to search all types of information in the database, I've turned off case-sensitivity, and designated my search term as a substring so that *pickles*, *picklepuss*, and *pickler* are all considered matches. At the bottom of Figure 16.17, note that I can specify the maximum number of "hits" (results) to report. I've chosen 100, the default. After phrasing my search, I click Search.

The results of my search appear in Figure 16.18. Each result is a link. Note that my search term is highlighted in each result to show the context in which each hit related to my search term. If I am unhappy with the results, I can click the Back button at the top of the screen to return to the Yahoo search page, from which I can rephrase my search.

**FIGURE 16.18.**

*Results of the Yahoo search phrased in Figure 16.17.*

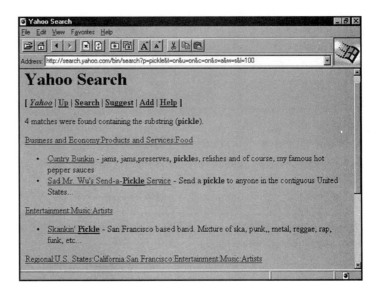

*Tip*

> The creators of Web search tools really want you to find what you're looking for—even if you have to use somebody else's search tool to do it. They are very responsible about supplying on their own pages links to other search engines.
>
> When working within any Web search tool, look near the top and near the bottom of pages for links to other search tools. (***Hint:*** To see the bottom of a Web page, you may have to use the scroll bar to scroll to the very bottom.) For example, if you click Options on the Yahoo search page (http://www.yahoo.com), then scroll to the very bottom, you see links to some other search engines and directories.

## WWW Virtual Library

The WWW Virtual Library (formerly known as the CERN Virtual Library) is maintained by World Wide Web Consortium, the group that oversees the Web as a whole. It is probably the most comprehensive of all Web directories, not just because the Consortium heads it, but because the Consortium relies on others—often leaders in a field—to create and maintain directories of links related to a given subject. The library supplies a link to that directory. Some of the directories covering scientific or social disciplines, for example, are actually managed by university departments in the subject field. The maintainers are in a position to know exactly where the best information can be found—and can supply links to that information.

Figure 16.19 shows the Virtual Library's home page (http://www.w3.org/hypertext/ DataSources/bySubject/Overview.html), which offers general information about the library and links to useful ancillary information. Scroll down past this introductory information to discover the subject headings shown in Figure 16.20.

**FIGURE 16.19.**

*The top of the home page of the WWW Virtual Library.*

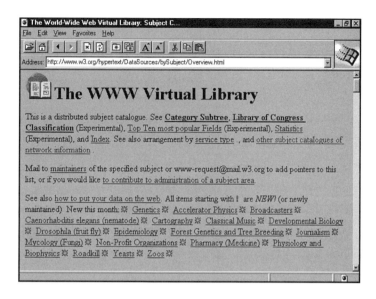

**FIGURE 16.20.**

*Further down on the home page of the WWW Virtual Library, where the subject links live.*

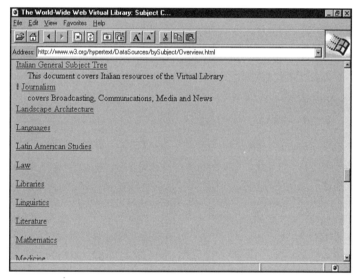

When I select the `Latin American Studies` link in the screen shown in Figure 16.20, I get the directory shown in Figure 16.21. Although it was accessed through the Virtual Library, note that this directory is created and maintained by the Latin American Network Information Center at the University of Texas, a leader in the field of Latin American Studies.

When viewing the subject headings in the WWW Virtual Library, you can choose to see the list in either of two ways. You toggle between the two views by selecting the link following the word *See* in the second sentence at the top of the home page (refer back to Figure 16.19).

**FIGURE 16.21.**

*A directory of links to Latin American Studies information.*

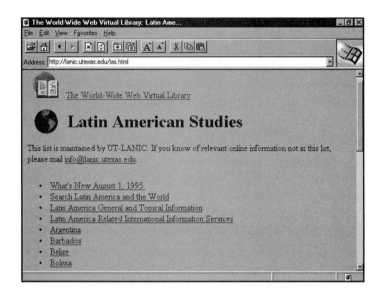

◆ The Overview view shows just the top-level headings. Figure 16.20 shows headings in Overview view.

◆ The Category Subtree view shows the subject headings as well as any subcategories (see Figure 16.22).

**FIGURE 16.22.**

*The WWW Virtual Library in Category Subtree view.*

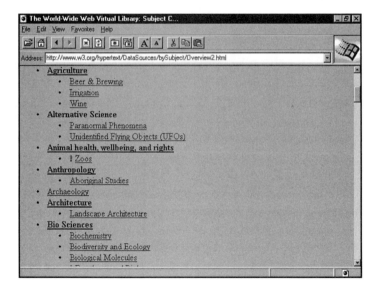

## Whole Internet Catalog

The Whole Internet Catalog is a collection of links to over 1,000 Internet resources, organized by subject and divided into easy-to-surf subject areas. In the screen shown in Figure 16.23, note that the Catalog sells advertising space on its home page.

**FIGURE 16.23.**

*The Whole Internet Catalog at* `http://www.gnn.com/wic/newrescat.toc.html`.

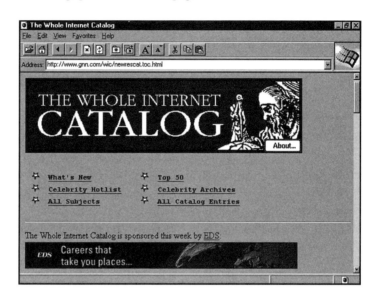

# Web Spiders

The next several pages describe useful "spider"-based searchable databases of Web-based information. Remember from earlier in this chapter that there are two basic types of Web search tools: *directories*, whose databases are largely built by people, and *spiders* (or *crawlers*, or *worms*, or any other crawly name), which use a program that regularly connects to and checks out areas of the Internet to build its database.

## Lycos

Created at Carnegie Mellon University, the Lycos spider employs an unusual approach to crawling around the Web and collecting information. It intelligently exercises preferences about which files to search on a server and what to search for. It accesses a URL and collects simple, basic information from files—titles, headings, the first 20 lines of documents, and any words determined to be important by their placement or frequency. It also makes intelligent choices about which documents to search first, favoring those that show up as links in many other documents (which proves they're used often).

By crawling around this way, Lycos accomplishes two things:

◆ It amasses a particularly effective cross-section of data without having to index every word in every file.

◆ It does its data collection work without causing an unacceptable drain on server resources, which Web spiders can do if they try to analyze many documents in rapid succession.

You can reach the Lycos index in a variety of ways. Links to Lycos appear in most directories of search engines (refer back to Figure 16.12). Lycos has its own home page at `http://lycos.cs.cmu.edu/`. Also, if you click Explore the Internet on Explorer's default home page (`http://www.home.msn.com`), you can access a link to Lycos under Internet Searches (see Figure 16.13, earlier in this chapter). Figure 16.24 shows the basic Lycos search form at `http://lycos.cs.cmu.edu`.

**FIGURE 16.24.**

*A Lycos search form.*

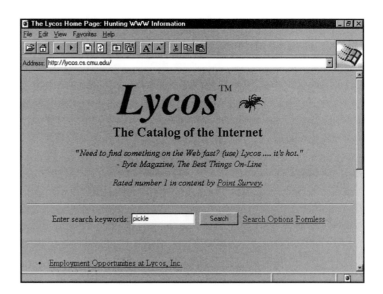

The basic search is made deliberately simple: enter a term and click Search. A few more options are available if you click the `Search Options` link: a screen like the one in Figure 16.25 appears. From this screen, you can control the Terms to Match (which of your search terms to search for, in which Boolean combination), the Number of Results to report, and whether to report complete details of the search or just the basics (Output Level).

**FIGURE 16.25.**

*An advanced Lycos search.*

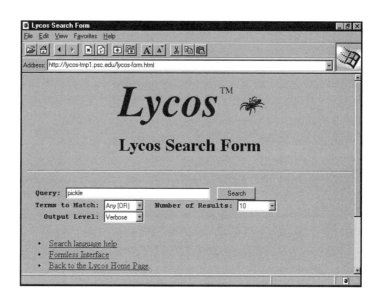

## WebCrawler

When building its database, WebCrawler (`http://webcrawler.com`) not only searches the URLs and links, it also searches the complete contents of Web documents. That makes WebCrawler's database an excellent choice for finding information buried within documents (the kind of information that may not show up in the URL or a title). WebCrawler searches not only Web URLs (those that start with `http://`), it also searches Gophers (`gopher://`), FTP servers (`ftp://`), and other servers off the Web. Its broad search field makes WebCrawler's database a great place to look for things you suspect may not even reside on Web servers. The disadvantage of WebCrawler is that, because it searches so thoroughly, it can't update itself very often.

Searching is simple. A checkbox lets you use the Boolean AND when you type more than one word in the search box; otherwise, the search is assumed to be a Boolean OR search. You can also control the number of results (hits) to report.

## World Wide Web Worm

The World Wide Web Worm—also known as WWWW or just *the Worm*—builds its database by searching the Web for URLs, titles, and links. Its search engine (`http://www.cs.colorado.edu/home/mcbryan/WWWW.html`) allows you to search either URLs alone or all information in the database. The Worm also supports the use of Boolean phrases through a drop-down list. Note that you can also specify the number of matches to report. If you visit the Worm, you'll find several other powerful ways you can tailor your search.

# What Now?

By now, you have the two most important skills for exploiting the Internet: browsing the Web and searching the Web. But to make things simpler, Web browsers have imposed certain compromises on the non-Web resources they access—most importantly, Gopher menus and FTP files.

Chapters 17 and 18 show how to make more of Gopher and FTP resources by tapping them through Gopher and FTP client software, rather than through a browser. Working through these chapters will not only expand your ability to locate and use Gopher and FTP resources, it will also help you understand these resources when you encounter them on the Web. Appendix B, "Web Highlights," offers a selection of great Web sites to visit.

# CHAPTER 17

# BROWSING GOPHERS

Who's the Gopher?

Multimedia Gophers

How to Use a Gopher Client

Cool Gopher Sites for Windows Users

How to Search for Gophers

What Now?

Ah, the menu. Where would we be without it? What could make a computer easier to use than simple on-screen lists of things to do? (Icons, you say? Prove it.)

Before Web links made Internet navigation simpler, Gopher did the same thing with menus. Gopher lays a simple, consistent system of menus on top of a number of Internet sites and activities. Not all the Internet is accessible through Gopher, but everything that is accessible works the same way. Clicking your way through Gopher menus, you can navigate to sites all over the world, read documents, conduct Telnet sessions, and even download files. In certain cases, you can even view images and play multimedia through a Gopher connection. Once you connect to a single Gopher server, you can navigate all over the world without ever typing—or even seeing—an Internet address.

Best of all, once you understand the basics of using Gopher menus, you have acquired a skill that works everywhere in *Gopherspace*, the nickname for all the Internet sites and activities accessible through Gopher menus.

In this chapter, you learn the following:

◆ How to configure a Gopher client to access Gophers and to display and play multi-media files

◆ How to navigate through Gopherspace

◆ How to create bookmarks for rapid access to favorite resources

◆ How to perform powerful searches to find anything in Gopherspace

# Who's the Gopher?

The University of Minnesota is an enormous state university, located across the Mississippi from downtown Minneapolis (for the protection of Minneapolis citizens). Isolated from the bustle of the city, University of Minnesota students have lots of free time. Some ride bikes, some write poetry, many drink beer—a few do all three at once.

A surprising number of students and faculty at Minnesota busy themselves building a better Internet. Over the years, the University of Minnesota has made many significant contributions to the evolution of the Net, but its most significant is the Gopher software. Developed in 1991, the Gopher server software is now used in over 300 nonprofit and commercial sites. The site uses the software to configure one or more *Gopher servers*, computers containing menu text linked to real Internet resources such as files and Telnet and FTP sessions. In concert with the Gopher client software on your PC, the servers present Gopher menus for all activities available through the server. Figure 17.1 shows a typical Gopher menu. (Actually, it's the top menu at University of Minnesota's Gopher, gopher.micro.umn.edu, also known variously as *Gopher Home*, *Mother Gopher*, and even *Mama Gopher* because the University of Minnesota was the original Gopher site.)

**FIGURE 17.1.**
*A Gopher menu.*

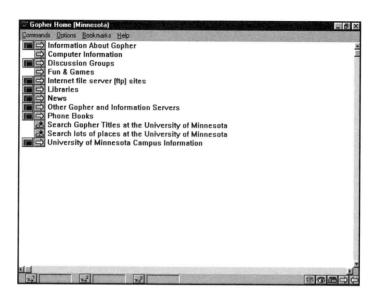

Each Gopher server (sometimes simply called a *Gopher*, to keep things friendly) holds only its own menus and linking details. However, all Gopher servers in the world are linked with one another and share information; when you access any Gopher server, you work as if *everything* was on that server—all the thousands of sites and menus of Gopherspace are at your command.

Through a Windows-based Gopher client, you can literally point-and-click your way around the world, all through a single connection to any Gopher server. Although all you see are simple Gopher menus, you should know that under the fur you're really using Telnet, FTP, and other standard Internet resources. Gopher simply covers up the details and smooths out the inconsistencies to make these resources simpler to use.

Which resources? There are four basic things you can do after you select an item from a typical Gopher menu:

◆ **Navigate.** A menu item may lead to another Gopher menu or submenu, usually containing more specific choices related to the preceding menu item. This is not always the case—a menu item on one Gopher menu may jump to another server, much as Web links jump from site to site.

◆ **Retrieve a document.** Millions of text files are available through Gopher servers. Some are informative, some are fun, and all appear on your screen at the touch of a menu item. You will see an "index" file listed as an item in the top menu of many Gopher servers. Check out that file's contents to save yourself a lot of browsing around.

◆ **Download files.** Binary files (including program files, images, and more) and some text files are available for download through Gopher menus. The transfer is handled by FTP, but you don't have to care; all you do is click a menu item and the file transfers to your PC.

◆ **Conduct Telnet sessions.** A Gopher menu item may start up a Telnet session for you. (See Chapter 19, "Advanced Internet Techniques.") Once the Telnet session has begun, however, you work within it as you do any Telnet session. But using Gopher to start Telnet can make finding the right Telnet site—and getting there—more convenient. Most importantly, a Gopher menu item may report required login instructions—such as the guest username and password—before starting the Telnet session to help you log on.

# Multimedia Gophers

Some Gopher clients and servers are equipped with an enhanced version of Gopher called Gopher+. Gopher+ servers do everything regular Gopher servers do (should we now call them "Gopher-minus" servers?). Regular Gopher servers, however, can display only the text files they receive—anything else gets sent straight to disk for you to work with later. Gopher+ servers, on the other hand, can tell any Gopher+ client the type of file—text, word processing document, image, video, sound, and so on—being transferred. The Gopher+ client uses that information, called the file's *attributes*, to automatically open a viewer program to display or play the file.

The *viewer programs* aren't part of the client software itself. A viewer program is any application capable of playing the file. The client software simply interprets the attribute information to choose which viewer program to open. Some clients have a few built-in viewers, called *internal viewers*, but no client program comes pre-equipped to handle every type of file for which Gopher+ has attributes.

The result is a Gopher that thinks it's the World Wide Web: You click a menu item and an image pops open on your screen, or a sound clip plays, or a movie appears.

Most Web browsers, including all three described in Chapter 16, "Browsing the World Wide Web," function as Gopher+ clients when accessing Gopher+ servers and automatically play Gopher+ files using the same viewers configured for playing Web-based multimedia files.

# How to Use a Gopher Client

You have two choices for a Gopher client:

◆ Use a third-party Windows Gopher client
◆ Use your Web browser as your Gopher front-end

The examples in this chapter use HGopher 2.3c, a popular freeware Gopher+ client included on the CD-ROM that accompanies this book; HGopher 2.3c is also available for downloading through MSN, the Web, or from anonymous FTP. Although minor details differ among true Windows Gopher clients, navigating among Gopher menus is performed the same way in nearly all of them. Put simply, you double-click an item to go wherever that item takes you; you click a back-pointing arrow icon to move backward to the previous menu.

## Setting Up a Gopher Client

As with other client software, your Gopher client needs the address (the IP address or DNS name) of a Gopher server. Any Gopher server will do—they all provide access to all other Gopher servers. Unlike e-mail or newsreader clients, however, Gopher clients often don't give you the luxury of configuring the software to access a single, local server so that you can forget about it. Your access provider probably doesn't run a Gopher server (if your provider *does* have a Gopher server, by all means use it). Also, Gopher servers are notorious for becoming overloaded and refusing new client connections.

To use Gopher successfully, you need the addresses of a small stable of Gopher servers so that you can try each until you find one that works. Fortunately, the following are true:

◆ Most Windows Gopher clients allow you to maintain a Gopher menu of servers so that you can easily jump among them. In Figure 17.1, earlier in this chapter, the menu option Other Gopher and Information Servers leads to a list of servers from which you can choose.

◆ Many Windows clients come preconfigured with a short menu of popular servers to get you started.

Finally, a Gopher client may allow you to specify a "startup" server, which is essentially the same idea as a default home page in your Web browser. Whenever you open the Gopher client, the client attempts to connect to the startup server. A startup server is not required, however; you can simply connect to the Internet, open your Gopher client, and then choose your server.

## Navigating Gopherspace

To navigate Gopherspace, you select menu items until you get what you want. That's it, in an acorn. After connecting to the Internet, you open your Gopher client, which typically displays the top menu of the Gopher server you have selected as your "home" server; alternatively, it displays a list of Gopher servers to which you can connect. The list that appears does not mean you are connected to a Gopher server (unless you have specified a startup server); it's just a list of items. In general, you begin your Gopher session by choosing a Gopher server through which you will access all of Gopherspace. Figure 17.2 shows a typical opening menu listing some bookmarks for Gopher servers and other resources.

**FIGURE 17.2.**

*A starting point: choose a
Gopher server from
available bookmarks.*

---

## Bookmarks Know All

*Bookmarks* are locations in Gopherspace that are recorded in the client software for easy
retrieval. A bookmark can lead to a Gopher server or any menu on that server; bookmarks can also lead to a Telnet or FTP session initiated through a Gopher menu, or to
files and documents located out in Gopherspace or on the local server of the Gopher to
which you are connected. Most Gopher client software comes with a default bookmark
file that contains several Gopher servers and often a bookmark for reaching the software
supplier. Bookmarks are also used by Web browsers in much the same way.

Note that bookmarks work without regard to your starting point. When you select a
bookmark, it takes you to its destination no matter what server you're connected to,
and no matter what menu or other Gopher activity you last performed.

In HGopher, you can create a bookmark for any menu that appears on your screen by
choosing **Bookmarks**, Create Bookmark. With this feature, you create a shortcut for
getting straight back to any Gopher item you find interesting or useful.

In a Web browser, you can use the browser's regular bookmark facilities (called "Favorite Places" in Internet Explorer) to create bookmarks to Gopher resources.

---

Once you connect to a server, you can branch off to any other part of Gopherspace. The top-
level menu at any Gopher server typically includes a range of items leading to local resources
plus one or more choices that lead out into Gopherspace.

If, however, choosing a server bookmark results in a `Too many connections` message, the server
you selected is too busy to accept another client connection. Try another server. With practice,
you'll quickly learn which servers are most accessible and what is the best time of day to use a
given server.

If you want to connect to a server for which you don't already have a bookmark, create a book-mark for that server. In HGopher, you open the set of bookmarks (for example, your default bookmarks) to which you want to add the new bookmark. Then choose **B**ookmarks, Cr**e**ate to display the dialog box shown in Figure 17.3.

**FIGURE 17.3.**

*Creating a new bookmark to connect to a server.*

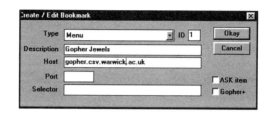

In the Description text box, enter a description for the server (this text will appear as the menu choice you select); type the address of the server in the Host text box. In the figure, the Type box shows Menu, indicating that selecting this bookmark displays another Gopher menu. Other choices for Type indicate that a bookmark leads to a file or a Telnet session.

## All the Gopher Servers in the World

You can retrieve the entire worldwide list of Gopher servers by selecting an item called All the Gopher Servers in the World from the University of Minnesota Gopher (among many other places). Access the University of Minnesota's Gopher at gopher.micro.umn.edu; choose Other Gopher and Information Servers and then choose All the Gopher Servers in the World. You see a list like the one shown in Figure 17.4.

**FIGURE 17.4.**

*The menu for All the Gopher Servers in the World.*

The list of All Servers is itself a Gopher menu; you can double-click any item to check out a particular server. To return from that server to the list, click the back arrow (the one in the lower-right corner of the screen) or choose the Previous Menu selection, as described later in this chapter.

As you discover items that interest you, choose **B**ookmarks, **M**ark Item. When you finish with the list of All Servers, choose **B**ookmarks, **S**ave Bookmarks to save all your marked items in a bookmarks file. This is a quick and easy way to build a list of useful or interesting Gopher starting points.

Remember that, like everything else on the Net, the list of Gopher servers changes constantly. You may want to retrieve the list regularly to get up-to-date addresses. Note that retrieving the list does not update bookmarks; to update your bookmarks created from the list of All Servers (or any other bookmarks, for that matter), you must re-create them.

The eye icon in the lower-right corner of the HGopher screen is used to cycle through Copy modes, which you can also change by selecting **O**ptions, **C**opy Mode.

When the eye appears, you are in View mode—your Gopher client will attempt to display or play any file you retrieve, if a compatible viewer has been configured (see "Configuring a Gopher+ Client," later in this chapter).

When a closed file folder appears instead of the eye, you are in Copy to File mode— files are automatically copied to a file and are not displayed, even if a viewer is available. Copy to File mode is handy when you want to pick up files for later use, but aren't interested in seeing them right away.

When an open file folder appears, you are in Copy to Directory mode—menu links to files are created and added to a Gopher directory, which you name. You can later open that Gopher directory and choose from among the files. Copy to Directory mode is handy when you want to build a list of files, then view or download them selectively.

## Moving Through Menus

Truthfully, all you need to know to browse around through Gopherspace are the following notes:

♦ Double-clicking an item takes you to a submenu, document, file, or FTP or Telnet session.

♦ Clicking once on the back arrow in the lower-right corner of the menu's status bar takes you back one level, to the previous menu. (This back arrow works exactly the way the back arrow in a Web browser works.)

You often see the choice Previous Menu at the very top of a Gopher menu. Choosing this item has the same effect as using the back-arrow button. It may seem redundant to those of us with a button, but the folks with text-only Gopher clients appreciate it!

◆ Clicking the back arrow several times takes you back further, until you eventually arrive at your starting point for the current Gopher session. After you've used the back arrow, the forward arrow becomes available to return you to menus you've previously backed out of. (Back and forward work the same way they do in Web browsers.)

## Configuring a Gopher+ Client

When retrieving image and multimedia files from Gopher+ servers, Gopher+ clients like HGopher can identify the attributes of the files and display or play them. To display or play a given file, however, your PC must be equipped with a program capable of displaying or playing the file, and you must have configured your Gopher client so that it knows which program to use for which file type. Web browsers work the same way; as a rule, you can use the same programs you use for Web browser viewers (or "helper applications") as your Gopher+ viewers. Simply give Gopher the directions to the files, as described in this section.

You configure HGopher to recognize and play files by selecting **O**ptions, **V**iewer Set Up. A dialog box like the one in Figure 17.5 appears.

**FIGURE 17.5.**

*Configuring Gopher+ viewers in HGopher.*

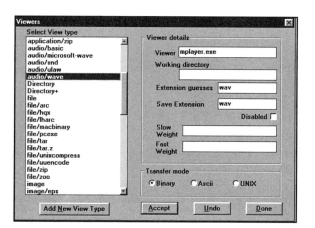

The Select View Type window lists attributes of many different types of files you can retrieve from Gopher+ servers. Your job is to fill in the information in the Viewer Details area for each view type you want your client to be able to display or play. You are required to fill in only the path and filename of your viewing program for that file type. (A path is not required to use standard Windows utilities, such as the Media Player—mplayer.exe.) You may have to select a Transfer type, but Binary is the proper selection for nearly everything but text files; as a rule, you can trust the default settings for Transfer type. The other information in the Viewer details box is optional (see HGopher's Help for more information).

When filling in the viewer's path and program name, you use arguments preceded by percent signs (%) to pass required information from the client to the viewer. For example, placing the characters %f after a program name tells HGopher to pass the filename of the retrieved file to the viewer so that the viewer knows which file to open. The following line tells HGopher to open the Lview graphics viewer and then tells Lview the name of the retrieved file:

```
c:\lview31.exe %f
```

Other arguments you may use include these:

| Argument | Meaning |
| --- | --- |
| %f | The filename |
| %h | The host name of a remote computer |
| %i | The remote host's IP address |
| %p | The remote host's port number |

The last two arguments, %i and %p, are used together when configuring a Telnet viewer for Telnet sessions opened by Gopher (see Chapter 19, "Advanced Internet Techniques"). To use Windows 95 Telnet as your viewer and have HGopher pass to Telnet the host address and port number Telnet requires, enter one of the following lines in the Viewer field:

```
telnet %h %p
telnet %i %p
```

# Cool Gopher Sites for Windows Users

The following chart lists a few interesting starting points for Gophering.

| Address | Description |
| --- | --- |
| gopher.micro.umn.edu | The Mother of all Gophers at the University of Minnesota. A great source for the latest Gopher software and information. |
| gopher.usc.edu | Gopher Jewels, an indispensable subject-sorted guide to the best in Gopherspace. |
| infolib.lib.berkeley.edu | The University of California at Berkeley library. |
| gopher.well.sf.ca.us | The Whole Earth 'Lectronic Library. |
| gopher.eff.org | The Electronic Frontier Foundation, an advocacy group for free speech on the Net. |
| yaleinfo.yale.edu | The Yale library, plus links to many other cool Gophers. |
| gopher.msen.com | A Gopher for looking up the addresses of other Internet users. |
| gopher.unc.edu | Lots and lots of stuff at the University of North Carolina. |

| *Address* | *Description* |
|---|---|
| gopher.tc.umn.edu | A starting point (at the University of Minnesota) for lots of great resources, including a list of news sources (choose News), reference works (choose Libraries and then choose Reference Works). Figure 17.6 shows the News items at this site; Figure 17.7 shows the reference works. |

**FIGURE 17.6.**

*Links to News sources from*
*gopher.tc.umn.edu.*

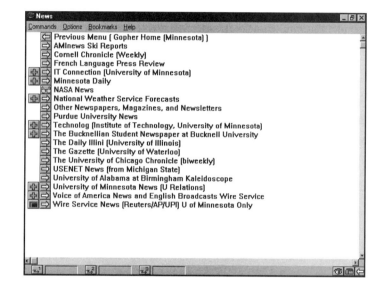

**FIGURE 17.7.**

*Links to Reference works*
*from*
*gopher.tc.umn.edu.*

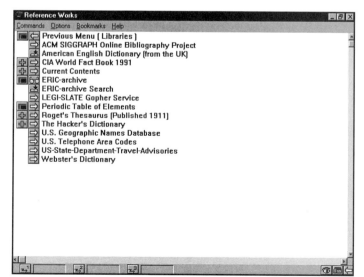

# How to Search for Gophers

Most Web-based search engines and directories (see Chapter 16, "Browsing the World Wide Web") can unearth Gophers as well as Web pages and other Web-accessible resources. However, the most powerful way to search Gopherspace is through Veronica, a search engine that's for finding Gophers and nothing but Gophers. Veronica can be accessed through any Gopher client or through the Gopher features of most Web browsers.

Veronica creates a list of anything in Gopher that contains a search term you supply. The list created by Veronica is itself a Gopher menu; if you see a menu item that looks promising, you can open it right from the Veronica list. If that item turns out to be a dead end, you can easily navigate back to the Veronica list and make another selection. Veronica is best suited to what I call the "ballpark and browse" method of searching—your Veronica search comes up with a number of choices in the right *ballpark*, and you *browse* those choices to zero in on what you want.

Veronica is actually a program that runs on various servers located around the world. These servers poll all Gopher servers (except the few that request not to be included in Gopherspace) on a regular basis (every two weeks or so) to build a database of menus. When you search with Veronica, you search the database—which may not be absolutely up to date. Note also that different Veronica servers may deliver different results because they update their databases on different schedules.

Veronica works *through* Gopher, so you use it from within your Gopher client or Web browser. To begin, use your Gopher client or Web browser to access the main Veronica server at the University of Nevada at the address gopher.unr.edu.

*Note*

> Although the University of Nevada's Gopher is used here as an example, there are many routes through which you may arrive at a Veronica server. Your local server may feature a menu that points to a Veronica. You can also go through the Mother Gopher at the University of Minnesota (gopher.micro.umn.edu), choose Other Gopher and Information Servers, then choose Search Titles in Gopherspace Using Veronica.
>
> Finally, you can access Veronica servers directly. The main servers in the United States are listed here. Note that the Gopher Port setting for each of these is 2347.
>
> ```
> empire.nysernet.org
> info.psi.net
> veronica.sunet.se
> ```

After you navigate to a Veronica server, a screen showing a variety of items appears; one of those items is Search ALL of Gopherspace. Select that item; a screen like the one shown in Figure 17.8 appears.

**FIGURE 17.8.**

*The choices under the Search ALL of Gopherspace option on the main Veronica server (gopher.unr.edu).*

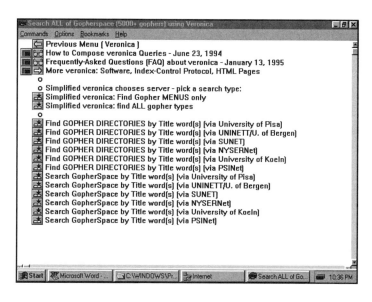

In the screen shown in Figure 17.8, notice two choices for a "simplified Veronica." This new program does not support the advanced search-phrasing options described later in this chapter. However, it does help you out by selecting the most appropriate Veronica server for you. As a new Veronica user, you may find Simplified Veronica a useful tool.

In the bottom half of the list are six different computers for Veronica searches. For each, there are two ways listed to search:

◆ **Find GOPHER DIRECTORIES....** These options search only for Gopher directories that contain the search term. Gopher *directories* are menus of items that lead to other Gopher menus.

◆ **Search GopherSpace....** These options search the Gopher directories, just like the preceding option, plus anything else stored and indexed on the local Gopher servers (even if it is not a Gopher menu). For example, this type of search locates text files and other files, FTP and Telnet sessions, and other items indexed on Gopher servers.

As a rule, when you're really just fishing for information, search for Gopher directories first.

One of the great problems with Veronica is that just a few servers have to handle all the Veronica searches in the world. As a result, it's very common to receive a message reading Too many connections—try again soon when you try to conduct a search on a particular server. In fact, it's not uncommon to find all the Veronica servers tied up.

## A Veronica Search

To start a Veronica search, choose one of the server options. As a rule, when you're really just fishing for information, search Gopher directories first. Searching directories is faster and may deliver a list of manageable size. Unless your search term is very specific, searching for titles in Gopherspace can return a *very* long list of responses that can be difficult to wade through.

When you select a Veronica server that is not overloaded, a dialog box like the one in Figure 17.9 appears.

**FIGURE 17.9.**

*Entering a search term for Veronica.*

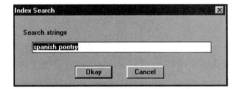

Enter your search term. Note that Veronica is not case sensitive; it makes no difference whether your search term is capitalized. When you've entered the search term you want, click Okay.

The search may take a few seconds or even a minute. When the search is finished, a new Gopher menu appears, showing any the items located by the search (see Figure 17.10). Select any item to follow where it leads, just as you do from any Gopher menu. After following any lead, you can use the back-arrow to navigate back to your list of Veronica hits so that you can try another lead. Remember that an item generated by the search may lead nowhere if the Veronica database on the server you selected is out of date.

**FIGURE 17.10.**

*Results of a search on Gopher directories.*

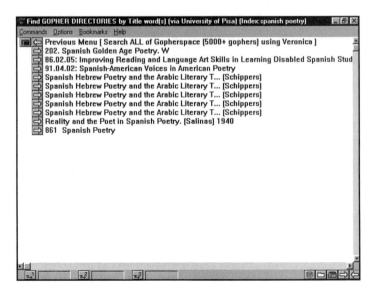

To show the difference between searching titles in Gopherspace and searching Gopher directories, Figure 17.11 shows the results you can expect if you searched Gopherspace for keywords in titles using the same search term that produced the results in Figure 17.10.

**FIGURE 17.11.**

*Results of a search of Gopherspace for keywords in titles, using the same term used to produce Figure 17.10.*

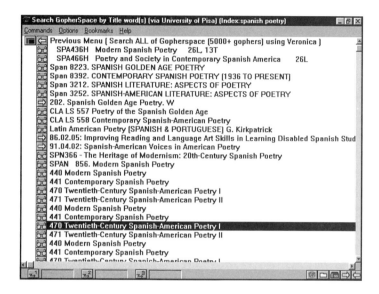

## Search-Term Options

Although Veronica queries are not case sensitive, you can use a number of other options for phrasing your search terms.

### Wild Cards

In addition to the options described in the following sections, you can use an asterisk (*) in Veronica to stand in for any character or number of characters. For example, the search term `cl*s` matches *clouds*, *clowns*, *classes*, *clips*, and many more. This asterisk "wild card" is especially useful for finding a particular type of file. The search term `w*.txt` matches any text file beginning with *w* and using the common text file extension, .TXT.

The asterisk is also handy as a stand-in for the letter *s*, to make sure that you pick up both singular and plural references. For example, `gopher*` picks up references to *Gopher* and *Gophers*.

### Boolean Phrasing

Veronica supports the Boolean operators AND, OR, and NOT for multiword search terms.

When a search term includes multiple words with no Boolean operator between them, Veronica assumes the AND operator. For example, the search term `history america` is read by Veronica as history AND america. This search selects only items that contain both the word *history* and the word *america*. To find all items that use either term, but not necessarily both, use the OR operator: history OR america.

To exclude certain references, use the NOT operator. For example, to produce a list that contains all references to *history* but discards any that also include the word *america*, use history NOT america.

# What Now?

Ever since the Web, Gopher gets no respect. But as you've learned in this chapter, Gopher remains an easy-to-use, powerful, and efficient means of navigating the Internet—especially when paired with its companion search tool, Veronica.

In the next chapter, you discover FTP, a file-downloading mechanism that's much more powerful—and only a little more difficult—than MSN's basic file-retrieval facilities.

# 18

# DOWNLOADING FILES WITH FTP

About FTP

Important FTP Sites for Windows Users

How to Use a Web Browser for FTP

How to Use Windows 95's FTP Client

A Third-Party FTP Client

How to Find FTP Files

What Now?

On its BBSs and in its libraries, MSN has a load of files for downloading (see Chapter 7, "Downloading and Uploading Files"). But MSN's file cache isn't equal to one percent of the Internet's. You tap that vast file mine with FTP, the Internet's standard file transfer facility.

The Internet is a treasure trove of computer files: freeware, shareware, and demo software; binary photos and artwork; sound, video, and animation; books, reference materials, and so much more. Much of this stuff can be downloaded to your PC through more than one resource. For example, Gopher and the Web both function as "front ends" to FTP file transfers so that you can download a file simply by choosing a menu item or clicking a hyperlink.

Sometimes, however, it's easier to go straight to the files through an *FTP client*, the PC software that enables you to download files from an *FTP server*, the computer on which the files reside.

Windows 95 has a built-in, somewhat spartan, FTP client. If that's not your style, you can choose from several popular third-party FTP clients, or you can access FTP resources through your Web browser.

In this chapter, you learn the following:

◆ How to access FTP servers and download files

◆ How to use Windows 95's built-in FTP client

◆ How to locate FTP files with the FTP search engine, Archie

> *Note*
>
> Although MSN has far fewer files for downloading than does the Internet, MSN offers one great advantage; almost everything you find on MSN runs in Windows 95. Remember that the Internet is populated by all types of computers—PCs, Macs, mainframes, various UNIX systems, and so on. Although a good proportion of the software on the Net is for Windows, much of it is written for other systems and may not run in Windows. Text files are universal, so you can download and read any text file you find. But programs, graphics, and other file types may not support Windows or Windows 95. When looking for FTP files, pay careful attention to descriptions that tell you which system the files are intended for.

# About FTP

FTP servers are prepared to display lists and directories of files available for downloading. These servers often accept "anonymous" FTP logins so that you don't need a special password or user ID to download files. Some FTP servers, however, are set up for the exclusive use of a specific group and require a username and password.

Even so-called "anonymous" servers require a username and password of sorts. Typically, you are required to enter **anonymous** (or sometimes **guest**) as the username and your e-mail address as your password. Good FTP clients do this for you, creating the illusion that no password or username is required for anonymous sites.

Using an FTP client to download a file typically involves two steps. The first step is logging in to the FTP server, which involves nothing more than supplying the FTP client with the address of the FTP server. In some cases (when anonymous login isn't supported), you may also have to supply a username and password.

After a successful login, you arrive at the top level of a hierarchical directory structure. Depending on the client you use, you may have to enter the **dir** command to see the list of files and directories (see Figure 18.1). The directory structure in most FTP servers is much like the DOS file structure: a root directory contains subdirectories and files; each subdirectory can contain other subdirectories and files; and so on. (You remember DOS, don't you?)

**FIGURE 18.1.**

*A list of files and directories on an FTP server.*

In Figure 18.1, the directory names appear to the far right of the list. As in DOS, to see what's in the current directory, you enter **dir**. To change directories, you enter **cd** */directoryname*.

To download a file, you must know its precise name and directory location. You can find this by browsing through the directory structure or by reading the contents of a *file index* available in the root directory of many FTP sites. The index is a text file that usually has a name like INDEX or README (README files may contain other useful tips, as well). When first visiting a particular FTP site, it's a good idea to download and read such files before doing anything else—they can save you time later by preventing mistakes.

After you log in, the second step to using an FTP site is navigating among the directories and file lists—and ultimately downloading files. When using command-oriented FTP clients like the one that comes with Windows 95, you perform all these actions by typing commands. In more Windows-oriented clients (see "A Third-Party FTP Client," later in this chapter), you can do almost anything by pointing and clicking—as you can by using a good Windows Web browser for FTP activities.

If you know, before you log in, the exact filename and directory location of the file you want to download, you can configure most FTP clients to log in, retrieve files, and log off all in one action without your intervention.

### Text Files Versus Binary Files

FTP transfers files in either of two modes. The two modes are required because simple text files, also known as *ASCII files*, use a smaller and less complicated character set than binary files, which include all files except simple text files. Any ASCII file is an unformatted text file of the kind you can edit in DOS or in Windows Notepad.

When downloading binary files, you must use binary mode. Although you can use binary mode for ASCII files, using ASCII mode for plain text is more efficient. ACSII mode cannot be used to transfer binary files.

Most FTP client software is pretty smart about choosing the right mode for the transfer. However, if you run into mode problems, switching between the modes is usually a simple matter of clicking a button or typing a simple command (see Table 18.1, later in this chapter).

# Important FTP Sites for Windows Users

The following list provides a small sample of the FTP sites you may want to visit:

| Site | Description |
| --- | --- |
| ftp.microsoft.com | You know who, with helpful instructional files, updated drivers and utilities, and more—all available for download. |
| ftp.cica.indiana.edu | The motherload of Windows software. |
| pkware.com | Creators of (and FTP source for) PKUNZIP and PKZIP, the most widely used compression/decompression utilities. |
| jpl.nasa.gov | Text and images from the Jet Propulsion Laboratory's NASA missions. |
| ftp.ncsa.uiuc.edu | Supplies a helpful guide to the Internet (among many other files). |
| ftp.merit.edu | Supplies PostScript-format maps (for printing on a PostScript printer) of the Internet. |
| sunsite.unc.edu | Offers most White House speeches and press releases (among many other files). |

# How to Use a Web Browser for FTP

FTP resources come through the Web in two ways. First, a Web link may point directly to an FTP file; click the link, and the file is downloaded to your computer. This method masks FTP behind the Web and requires no knowledge about FTP to use. Unfortunately, such simple links are set up for only a small fraction of the available FTP resources.

To get at the rest of the FTP world, you use your Web browser as an FTP client. As described in Chapter 16, "Browsing the World Wide Web," you access FTP sites by entering a URL (Universal Resource Locator) made up of the characters `ftp://` and the FTP address you ordinarily enter in an FTP client. For example, to reach Macmillan Computer Publishing's FTP server (`ftp.mcp.com`, which contains a great cache of Internet freeware and shareware), you enter this as the address in your FTP client software:

`ftp.mcp.com`

Alternatively, you enter this as the URL in your Web browser:

`ftp://ftp.mcp.com`

Once you reach the FTP server, you can click your way to files, as shown in Figure 18.2. Clicking a directory name displays the contents of a directory; clicking `Up one level` moves you back upward in the directory hierarchy by one level. Clicking a filename downloads the file. Cinch.

**FIGURE 18.2.**

*An FTP site seen through the Web browser, Internet Explorer.*

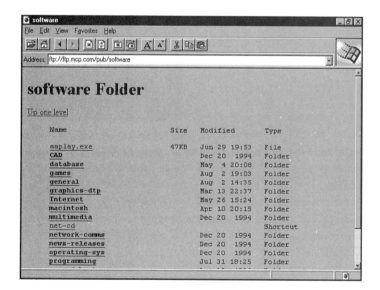

# How to Use Windows 95's FTP Client

Windows 95's built-in FTP client is one of its command-line programs. You execute command-line programs like DOS commands: by typing a command and any optional parameters at a *command prompt*. You reach the command prompt by choosing **R**un from the Start menu or by choosing MS-DOS Prompt from the Programs menu.

To download a file using the Windows FTP client, you connect to the Internet and then issue the FTP command (including the FTP site address in the **host** parameter, as described later) to access the FTP site. Once attached to the FTP site, you issue any of the commands listed in Table 18.1 to browse through the directories, download files, and quit the FTP session.

To use the Windows 95 FTP client to download a file, follow these steps:

1. Connect to the Internet.
2. Display the Windows 95 command prompt by choosing **R**un from the Start menu or by choosing MS-DOS Prompt from the Programs menu.
3. At the command prompt that appears, enter **ftp** to open the FTP window. When the prompt ftp> appears, type **open**, a space, and the address of the FTP server (see Figure 18.3); press Enter. (You can also choose Run from the Start menu and enter **ftp address**.)

**FIGURE 18.3.**

*Starting an FTP session with the Windows 95 FTP client.*

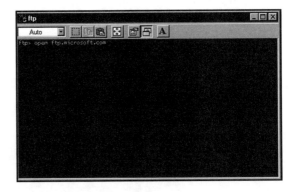

If the connection is successful, you are prompted for a username or you receive other instructions from the remote system. If you've connected to an "anonymous" FTP server, you don't need to know a special login name or password to use the server. Typically, you are prompted to enter a particular username (also called a *login name*) and password. If the login prompt offers no instructions, try **anonymous** or **guest** as your username and your e-mail address as your password. If the FTP server is not the anonymous type, you need a login name and password. That means this FTP site is set up for the exclusive use of those authorized to use it and is not for the general Internet public.

## FTP Command Syntax

The Windows 95 ftp command and its optional parameters are used only to log in to an FTP server. You can then use the commands in Table 18.1 to navigate the server and download files. Here's the syntax of the ftp command:

```
ftp [-v] [-n] [-i] [-d] [-g] [-s] [host]
```

In this syntax, the following, optional parameters can be used:

| Parameter | Description |
|---|---|
| -v | Turns off the display of remote server responses. |
| -n | Turns off automatic logging after connection to the FTP site. Logging keeps a running file of all your activity on the server for reference. |
| -i | Turns off the prompt that asks you for confirmation of each file during multiple-file transfers (all files selected are downloaded in succession without your involvement). |
| -d | Displays all FTP commands as they are exchanged between your PC and the FTP site. |
| -g | Prevents the use of wildcard characters in filenames. (You can also use the glob command, described in Table 18.1, to control wildcard use.) |
| -s: *filename* | Specifies a text file containing FTP commands to be run automatically after FTP starts. |
| *host* | The name or IP address of the FTP site. |

Table 18.1 details the effects of important FTP commands. You use these commands to navigate a server and collect files after you log in.

**Table 18.1. FTP commands.**

| Command | Description |
|---|---|
| ? *command* | Shows help information for the FTP *command* specified. |
| append | Appends a file on your PC to one on the remote computer. |
| ascii | Enables ASCII as the transfer type (this is the default mode). |
| bell | Turns on a bell that rings after each file transfer completes. |
| binary | Enables binary as the transfer type. |
| bye | Quits the FTP session and FTP. |
| cd *directoryname* | Changes the directory on the remote computer. |
| close | Quits the FTP session with the remote computer but keeps FTP active. |
| debug | Displays all commands sent to and received from the remote computer (aids in troubleshooting). |
| delete *filename* | Deletes files from the remote computer. |
| dir | Displays a list of files and subdirectories on the remote computer. |

*continues*

**Table 18.1. continued**

| Command | Description |
| --- | --- |
| disconnect | Disconnects from the remote computer; keeps FTP active. |
| get *filename* | Downloads one file. |
| glob | Turns globbing on or off. *Globbing* supports the use of wildcard characters in filenames and path names. |
| hash | Turns hash-mark printing for each 2,048-byte data block on or off. |
| help *command* | Shows help information for the FTP *command* specified. |
| lcd *directoryname* | Changes the working directory on your PC. (The current directory is the default.) |
| literal | Sends arguments to the remote FTP server. A single FTP reply code is expected in return. |
| ls | Shows an abbreviated list of a files and subdirectories in the current directory on the FTP server. |
| mdelete | Deletes multiple files on the FTP server. |
| mdir | Shows a detailed list of files and subdirectories on the FTP server; also lets you specify multiple directories. |
| mget | Downloads multiple files. |
| mkdir *directoryname* | Creates a new directory on the FTP server. |
| mls | Shows an abbreviated list of files and subdirectories on the FTP server; also lets you specify multiple directories. |
| mput | Uploads multiple files to the FTP server. |
| open | Connects to an FTP server. |
| prompt | Turns prompting on or off. When *prompting* is on, FTP pauses between multiple files being downloaded or up-loaded (using the mget and mput commands, respectively) so that you can choose to transfer each or skip to the next. |
| put *filename* | Uploads a file to the FTP server. |
| pwd | Prints the current FTP server directory. |
| quit | Quits the FTP session and exits FTP. |
| quote | Sends arguments to the remote FTP server. A single FTP reply code is expected in return. |
| recv *filename* | Downloads a file. Identical to get. |
| remotehelp *command* | Shows help for commands on the FTP server. |
| send *filename* | Uploads a file to the FTP server. Identical to put. |
| status | Shows the status of all FTP connections. |

| Command | Description |
|---------|-------------|
| trace | Turns packet tracing on or off. *Packet tracing* shows the route of each packet transferred by FTP. |
| type | Returns the file transfer type (binary or ASCII). |
| user | Names a user to the FTP server. |
| verbose | Turns verbose mode on or off. *Verbose mode* displays all FTP responses and a report of statistics following each file transfer. |

# A Third-Party FTP Client

WinSock-FTP (WS-FTP) is a popular shareware FTP client featured on the CD-ROM that accompanies this book. WS-FTP does a great deal to make FTP easier, mostly by making it more "Windows like" (see Figure 18.4). For example, you can navigate among lists of files and directories by clicking directory names and scrolling through lists, much as you navigate among files and folders with Windows 95's Explorer file/folder manager. When you see a file you want to download, double-click it to start the transfer.

**FIGURE 18.4.**

*WinSock-FTP, a more Windows-like way to download files.*

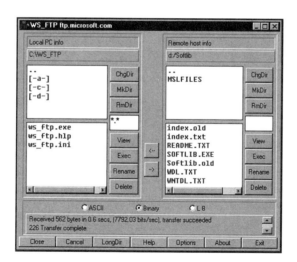

# How to Find FTP Files

You can find instructions all over the Internet and in Internet publications telling you a particularly cool file "is available via anonymous FTP at…" and then reporting the FTP address. The *addresses* reported are pretty reliable but *filenames* or *directory locations* change often. It's good practice to log in to the FTP server and download the README or INDEX file to make sure of the directory location and filename.

Web searches (see Chapter 16, "Browsing the World Wide Web") often come up with FTP files in response to your search term. Entering the type of program you're looking for as a search term—**gopher client**, for example—is a good way to find FTP sites that carry that type of software.

But the main way to find files available through FTP is to use Archie. Archie is a search engine that finds the names and locations of files stored on anonymous FTP servers. Because Archie finds only files accessible through anonymous FTP, you know that any file you locate through Archie is available without any special password or other restrictions.

A common misconception about Archie is that it, like some Web-based search engines, can search for a file by subject. Archie only searches through the text of file and directory names; it can find a file only if you can supply the filename (or at least part of the filename). Like most search engines, Archie doesn't really go out and search all the FTP servers when you request a search. Instead, each Archie server regularly polls FTP servers to update its database of filenames and locations. When you fire up your Archie client, connect to an Archie server, and search for a file, you're searching the database stored on the Archie server. This approach allows Archie to provide answers quickly, but also allows for the possibility that an Archie server may deliver inaccurate or outdated directions to a file.

*Note*

> Because the records of Archie servers can fall out of date, you may discover that the results of an Archie search lead to a dead end—the file you want is not where Archie said it would be. Fortunately, most Archie searches turn up directions to a file in several different locations. If one is a bust, you can try another. If all are a bust, you can try your Archie search again on a different server.

An Archie database must keep track of millions of files stored on thousands of FTP servers. Most Archie servers poll a small group of servers each night, working through the entire list of FTP sites in the course of a month or so. That means the information delivered by Archie in response to your search may be weeks old. It's probably still accurate, but there's no guarantee. Also, because each Archie server updates its database on its own schedule, there may be minor differences between the databases stored on different Archie servers.

After installing your Archie client (the examples in this chapter use WinSock Archie, a popular Windows client included on the CD-ROM that accompanies this book), all you need to know are the addresses of Archie servers. Good client software—including WinSock Archie—is preconfigured with several client addresses that can be selected from a drop-down list. Table 18.2 lists some Archie servers active at this writing.

**Table 18.2. North American Archie servers.**

| Server Address | Location |
|---|---|
| archie.rutgers.edu | New Jersey |
| archie.sura.net | Maryland |
| archie.unl.edu | Nevada |
| archie.ans.net | New York |
| archie.internic.net | New Jersey |
| archie.cs.mcgill.ca | California |

You can also reach Archie servers and perform searches using your Web browser. For example, you can reach the Rutgers Archie server through your Web browser at this URL:

```
http://www-ns.rutgers.edu/htbin/archie
```

*Tip*

Why do you need to know more than one Archie server address? *Aha!* You've found Archie's weak spot. Like Veronica servers (described in Chapter 17, "Browsing Gophers"), Archie servers can get overloaded with connections and requests. When trying to initiate an Archie search, you may have to try several different servers before finding one that's available. Traditionally, it's always been easier to get through to servers located where it's nighttime; for example, day-time users in the United States often try European Archie servers because it's night in Europe and those servers may not be tied up. However, given the small number of Archie servers and the burgeoning numbers of Internet users worldwide, this trick is not reliable. Today, any server can be tied up anytime. So keep trying.

## Using Archie

To locate a file with WinSock Archie, connect to the Internet and open WinSock Archie, as shown in Figure 18.5.

**FIGURE 18.5.**

*Starting a search in WinSock Archie.*

## Search Term

Enter a *search term* in the **S**earch For box. If possible, enter the exact name of the file you want. Otherwise, enter a substring of characters you believe make up a portion of the name of the file; for example, if you can't remember whether the file is called winmaker or winmonkey, enter the substring winm and see what Archie finds. (Obviously, the closer you can come to the actual name, the better Archie's results.)

Use the radio buttons to the right of the **S**earch For text box to tell the client how to treat the search term:

| Option | Meaning |
|--------|---------|
| Su**b**string | The search term represents a set of characters that may make up the whole filename, only a portion of the filename, or a portion of a directory name. Click this button when your search term is not the exact filename. |
| Substring (**C**ase Sensitive) | The same as Su**b**string, except that Archie delivers only references that not only match the search term but also match the exact capitalization of the search term. If you type **Win** for your search term, Archie regards as matches any filenames or directory names containing *Win* but ignores any names containing *win, WIN, wIN,* and so on. Most FTP servers are case sensitive, so it's important to note the exact capitalization of any file you locate through Archie. However, for searches, it's typically best to leave case sensitivity off, to increase your chances of finding a file, regardless of how its name is capitalized on the server. |

| Option | Meaning |
| --- | --- |
| **Ex**act | The search term represents the exact and entire filename. Archie's search returns only the directory locations in which that precise filename can be found. |
| **R**egex | Short for *regular expression*, Regex is a system for phrasing search strings with wildcard characters and operators borrowed from the UNIX operating system. Also known as *ed(1)* expressions, Regex search strings allow you to phrase substrings that search for filenames that exclude certain characters or include certain sets of characters that may be separated by any other characters. That's useful if you know several parts of the filename but not the whole thing. |
| | To learn more about Regex expressions, see WinSock Archie's Help system. |

Below the radio buttons that define the search term is the Exact First checkbox. If you enter a substring as a search term and click either of the Substring radio buttons, clicking the Exact First box asks Archie to first try using the search term as an exact term (that is, as a complete filename). If that search comes up with nothing, Archie should search again, using the search terms as a substring. The Exact First checkbox is useful when you *think* your search term is the correct filename, but you're not sure. Note that the Exact First checkbox has no effect when the Exact radio button is selected.

## Server and Domain Selection

After choosing your search term and selecting how it should be treated, enter the address of an Archie server or select one from the **A**rchie Server drop-down list. (***Note:*** With WinSock Archie, you must select the address of an Archie server from the drop-down list; no provision is made to allow you to type a server address.) Note that the list tells you where the server is physically located. As a rule, choose one geographically close to you to minimize network delays (and to minimize your contribution to network delays). If the nearest servers are tied up, try the farther ones or wait and try your search later.

Below the **A**rchie Server box is the optional **D**omain text box. If you want to restrict your search to one particular FTP server, enter its address here. You can also enter a domain that restricts the search to servers in a particular type of organization; for example, entering `edu` restricts the search to FTP servers whose addresses end in `.edu` (which means they are located at colleges and universities).

## Searching

After entering your search term and server address, click the Search button to connect to the Archie server and initiate the search. Be prepared for the server to return a message rejecting your connection because it's too busy. If that happens, enter or select another server in the Archie Server text box and click the Search button again.

If all goes well, Archie puts information in the **Hosts** (FTP server addresses), **Directories** (the directory location), and Files (exact filenames) boxes below your search instructions (see Figure 18.6). These three boxes provide you with all the information you need for downloading a file through anonymous FTP. Note that the **Directories** list shows directories only for the currently selected host; the **Files** list shows only the files in the selected directory. To review all of Archie's finds, select each host in the **Hosts** list, and then select each directory within each host, to see the filenames that were found.

Of course, if you don't see the desired file in the results returned by the first Archie search, modify your search term and try again. If, after several attempts, you can't find a file, either the file doesn't exist or your best guess about its name or possible substrings are too far off the mark. Try using another search engine (such as a Web search tool) or post a query in a related newsgroup.

**FIGURE 18.6.**
*Search results.*

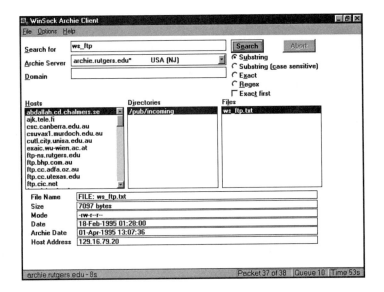

## Retrieving a File

Once you identify the FTP server, directory location, and filename of a file you want to download, acquiring the file is a simple matter of firing up your FTP client and supplying it with that information. If your search returned multiple instances of the same file, you may have to try more than one. Because Archie databases can fall out of date, your first attempt to download a file can come up empty if the file was moved or renamed on the FTP server since the last time the Archie database was updated. If Archie found multiple copies of a file, however, it's unlikely that they're all wrong. Move from one file location to another until you find one that downloads successfully.

Some Archie clients—WinSock Archie included—can fire up your FTP client automatically and can pass to the FTP client the server address, directory location, and filename of a file you select from the Archie search results. When WinSock Archie is properly configured, double-clicking a filename in the search results dialog box automatically fires up an FTP client.

To configure an FTP client for WinSock Archie, choose **O**ptions, **F**TP Setup. A dialog box like the one in Figure 18.7 appears.

**FIGURE 18.7.**

*Configuring an FTP client*
*for WinSock Archie.*

Fill in the options in the FTP Setup dialog box as follows:

| *Field Name* | *Meaning* |
| --- | --- |
| Command | Enter the command (including the full path) required to open your FTP program. In the example in Figure 18.7, the FTP program is WS_FTP.EXE (WinSock FTP), in the directory C:\NETWORK\WINSOCK. Following the program filename, type a space and **%h:%d\%f**. These arguments pass the FTP server address (**%h:**, from the **H**osts box), directory location (**%d\**, from the **D**irectories box), and filename (**%f**, from the Fi**l**es box) to the FTP server so that it can initiate the downloading procedure automatically. |
| User Name, Password | Leave the default anonymous choices in these two text boxes because Archie lists only files available from anonymous FTP servers. |
| Directory | The disk and directory location where you want to store the downloaded files on your PC. |

# What Now?

FTP is enormously powerful, not simply because of what it can do, but because of the size of the libraries it taps—gigabyte after gigabyte of publicly accessible FTP files.

All that remains now in your MSN/Internet education is a little group of lesser-used Internet facilities I file under the ever-popular category *misc.* But *misc.* doesn't look very impressive on a table of contents; more importantly, I was always told every book, play, and movie had to have a Big Finish, and *misc.* ain't it.

So, because the last Internet facilities demand the greatest skill, this book concludes with Chapter 19, "Advanced Internet Techniques." My Big Finish. So there.

# 19

# ADVANCED INTERNET TECHNIQUES

Telnet

Internet Relay Chat (IRC)

MUDs

Mailing Lists

What Now?

More and more, if something isn't a Web page, folks don't bother with it. Oh, sure, people make little detours off the beaten path into Gopherspace and to FTP sites, but they quickly return to the Web—before night falls.

But if you're really interested in reaching all of the Internet, you should know that there's a lot more to it than e-mail, the Web, Gopher, and FTP. As a group, these other types of Internet resources are more difficult to use and require more technical expertise than the Web—hence the title of this chapter. These resources are all accessible, at least in part, from the Web or through e-mail, however, and are not all that difficult to master, especially if you've already wet your feet in the Web.

In this chapter, you learn the following:

  ◆ How to access and operate remote computers through Telnet

  ◆ How to converse on IRC channels, the Internet version of MSN's chat rooms

  ◆ How to play interactive, real-time, role-playing games

  ◆ How to sign up for mailing lists that deliver to you a steady stream of e-mail on any subject

# Telnet

Telnet allows you to dial into a remote computer and use it as if you were a local user—real old-fashioned hacking. As a rule, you use Telnet to access resources not available through Gophers and Web pages.

It's important to understand right up front that Gopher and the Web provide access to Telnet resources in two different ways:

  ◆ A Gopher menu or Web page may provide access to the same information previously offered only through the Telnet site—in effect, replacing a Telnet resource with a friendlier Gopher or Web resource.

  ◆ A Gopher menu or Web page can offer a menu item or link that, when activated, instructs your Gopher or Web client to open the Telnet session for you, using your own Telnet client as a "helper" application. This second scenario offers little advantage over plain-vanilla Telnet, except that Gopher and the Web may make the Telnet resource easier to find and, in many cases, easier to sign on to.

Telnet's Achilles' heel is that every computer system is different, and Telnet does nothing to make differing computers work more consistently the way Gopher and the Web do. Telnet simply gets you connected to a remote computer—figuring out how to use it is your problem.

When a Telnet client is set up on your PC, and the remote computer is configured as a Telnet server, you can connect to the remote computer and send it commands and menu selections. The remote, in turn, sends its screen output across the Internet to your PC, so that you see on your screen exactly what you would see if you were using a terminal directly connected to that computer.

That screen display is usually *very* simple—text only, no colors, and no fancy fonts (see Figure 19.1). It's the simplicity of the display parameters used that helps ensure that any type of computer can communicate with any other—as long as TCP/IP and Telnet run the show. Fancy formatting can cause incompatibilities.

**FIGURE 19.1.**

*A typical Telnet session.*

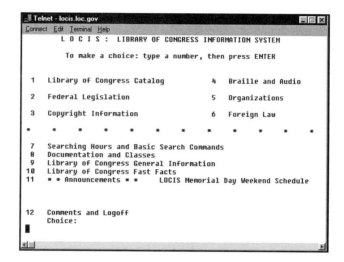

## Connecting and Logging In

All you need to use a Telnet site are the following:

◆ The Telnet host's Internet address, typically a domain name but sometimes a numeric IP address.

◆ A *port* number (not always required). Some Telnet servers run more than one Telnet activity on the same server. Ports allow people to connect directly to the activity they want. A port is not always required; most of the time, when it is required, the standard Telnet port (23) does the job.

◆ Whatever specific login information the given system requires.

You enter the Telnet site's address (and port number, if necessary) in your Telnet client to establish the connection. Figure 19.2 shows the Connect dialog box in Windows 95's Telnet client, filled out to connect to the Library of Congress's card catalog database (LOCIS.LOC.GOV). Note that, for the port setting, `telnet` is shown; this represents the default Telnet port of 23. Note also that a terminal type (in the **T**erm Type field) appears; this is the terminal emulation setting (see "About Terminal Emulation," later in this chapter.)

**FIGURE 19.2.**

*Connecting to a Telnet server.*

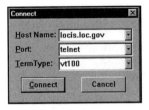

The login steps for a Telnet computer vary based on how happy it is to be visited by the Internet world at large. Friendly systems simply log you in when you connect. Others display messages at connection, telling you the "guest" username and password for the system. The most restrictive systems require a username *and* a password, and don't tell you what they are—you have to know them before you log in. (In many cases, Gopher menus or Web pages can supply you with login information if you use them to access the Telnet session.)

Once you connect to the remote computer, you must log in. Some systems that supply guest logins require you to move through a procedure after you log in to choose a personal username and password for the next time you log in. Others allow you to use the guest login every time.

Once you log in, every system is different. Most systems available through Telnet are designed and maintained primarily for the benefit of their regular users—typically employees of a company, university, or government agency. Internet users are guests, and although a system may offer visitors a little assistance, the system's administrator feels no great need to retool the system just to make Internet visitors happy.

After you log in, most systems display menus on-screen (refer back to Figure 19.1). Some tell you right away how to get help; for example, the system may display the message, For help, press ? at any menu. Be sure to jot down any such messages—you may need them later. Especially important is the command or procedure for logging off. You must log off the remote computer before quitting Telnet. If you forget to log off before quitting Telnet or disconnecting, don't worry; most Telnet computers are smart enough to terminate your login when they sense the broken connection or after a few minutes of inactivity.

To use most menus you'll see in Telnet sessions, press the number or letter of the menu item you want and then press Enter to transmit your selection to the remote computer. When you use a remote system, push your mouse aside; you use Telnet systems with your keyboard. Most of the time, your cursor keys are useless as well. Most Telnet systems operate like all computer systems did 20 years ago. Enjoy the nostalgia.

## About Terminal Emulation

When a Telnet client negotiates a connection with a Telnet server, one of the first things the two must agree on is the terminal type of the client. Telnet servers are set up to interface with one or more specific types of terminals; your PC must be able to emulate one of those if it is to use the remote computer. Otherwise, screen information may appear garbled, or the remote may not understand your commands.

Fortunately, most Telnet clients and servers support either of two widely used types: VT*x* or TTY. Ideally, if the server requires a VT*x* terminal, your PC should be able to emulate the specific model: VT52, VT100, VT200, or VT220. If the remote wants a VT100, and your PC emulates only VT200, try it—it will probably work. Some remotes ask you to specify the type of terminal you use (or, rather, the terminal your PC is emulating) when setting up the connection. When all else fails, look for choices like dumb, generic, or hardcopy terminal; these emulations sacrifice screen formatting in order to be as universally compatible as possible.

# Using Windows 95's Telnet Client

Windows 95's built-in Telnet client is one of its command-line programs. You start command-line programs the way you enter DOS commands: by typing a command at a prompt (plus any optional parameters). In Windows 95, you reach the command prompt by choosing **R**un from the Start menu or by choosing MS-DOS Prompt from the Programs menu.

Although it isn't flashy, Windows 95's command-line Telnet client gets the job done. And to be frank, Telnet is not a flashy occupation. In fact, Windows 95's Telnet offers some distinct advantages:

◆ It saves you from bothering with a third-party Telnet client.

◆ It's easy to anoint as the Telnet client automatically opened by a Gopher or Web client when starting a Telnet session because Windows 95 can always find its command-line programs without any disk or path information. To configure your Gopher and Web clients, you need only enter the word **telnet** where the name and path of the Telnet client are required.

◆ It's a 32-bit Windows program, so it performs well under Windows 95.

By default, Internet Explorer uses Windows Telnet to access Telnet resources called by Web links.

## Starting a Windows Telnet Session

To use Windows 95's Telnet client to connect and log into a Telnet site, follow these steps:

1. Connect to the Internet.

2. Display the Windows 95 command prompt by choosing **R**un from the Start menu or by choosing MS-DOS Prompt from the Programs menu.

3. At the command prompt, enter the word **telnet** to open the Telnet window. From the window, choose **C**onnect, **R**emote System. In the dialog box that appears, type the host name (and port number, if required). If no port number is required, or if port 23 is required, leave the word *telnet* in the **P**ort box, which indicates the default Telnet port, 23.

4. To start the connection, click **C**onnect.

If the connection is successful, the remote system prompts you for a username or offers other instructions for logging on.

### Ending a Session

To end a Telnet session, first log off the remote computer, if possible. If you've forgotten how to log off a given system, try to display its command help. Failing that, good entries to try are q (for *quit*), x (for *exit*), or the commands logoff or just log. Once you log off the remote system, Windows Telnet usually detects the disconnection and reports that the connection has been lost. If Telnet does not disconnect automatically, choose **C**onnect, **D**isconnect to disconnect manually. You can then connect to another Telnet host, or choose **C**onnect, E**x**it to quit Telnet.

# Internet Relay Chat (IRC)

If you've already read Chapter 6, "Hanging Out in Chat Rooms," Internet Relay Chat is going to look pretty familiar. Chat was modeled on Internet Relay Chat, also known as IRC. IRC allows any number of Internet users to collectively participate in a live, real-time, online discussion.

---

### A Lag in the Conversation

Although it affects all Internet tools in one way or another, and it affects MSN slightly, *Net lag* afflicts IRC especially heavily. Net lag is the varying time it takes for a message to travel from your PC to another computer, and the time required for the reverse trip.

In IRC, Net lag prevents the conversation shown on the screen from appearing in a precise, logical order. For example, when you respond to another's comment, your response does not show up on the screen directly below the comment you're responding to—by the time you type your response, several other responses are already on their way. When you ask a question, the response may not show up until several exchanges later. With a little experience, you'll soon learn to follow the flow.

---

IRC is a client/server system. The IRC server program runs on a server connected to the IRC network; you must run an IRC client to interact with the server. Several good clients are available for Windows. The examples in this chapter were created with WinIRC, a shareware IRC client for Windows that makes IRC a near ringer for MSN Chat, both in appearance and in operation. WinIRC is included on the CD-ROM that accompanies this book.

After you install an IRC client, you must connect to a server on the IRC network, using the IRC server's domain name and a port number. Following are several IRC servers in operation at this writing:

```
irc.bu.edu
irc.colorado.edu
```

```
irc.uiuc.edu
ug.cs.dal.ca
```

*Tip*

To connect to a server through WinIRC, choose **File**, **S**etup to display the dialog box shown in Figure 19.3.

**FIGURE 19.3.**

*Connecting to an IRC server.*

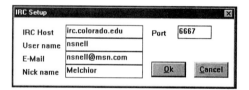

If the elements of this dialog box look familiar, it's because Telnet is the technology underlying IRC. As with Telnet, you supply the Internet address of an IRC host and a port number. (Windows IRC clients generally supply a default port number; if you have trouble connecting, change the port number setting in the IRC Setup dialog box.) The other information in the dialog box shown in Figure 19.3 is required by the IRC server program: your full name, your complete e-mail address, and the nickname you want to use in Chat sessions.

After you connect to a server, you immediately see various messages pertaining to the version of the IRC server software, system maintenance, and so on. This "message of the day" is important because it announces any anticipated problems with the server or current restrictions. Once you review the message of the day, you can select a *channel*, or particular Chat session in which to engage.

## Choosing a Channel

A *channel* is a particular discussion—just as a particular chat room is a discrete discussion area on MSN. To see a list of channels available, choose **L**ist from the menu bar. A list of all available channels appears (see Figure 19.4). The actual channel name appears on the left, followed by the number of people currently participating in the discussion. Observe that the channel name is preceded by a hash mark (#). To the right of each channel name is a description of the current topic of discussion within that channel, if there is one.

**FIGURE 19.4.**

*A listing of IRC channels.*

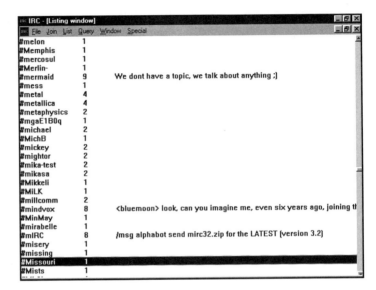

IRC is operated by a standard set of commands. User-friendly Windows clients issue commands when you select menu items so that the most commonly used commands—join, list, and so on—are easy to use. But you can enter any IRC command yourself, using the same text window you use for typing your part of the conversation. All IRC commands are preceded by a slash (/). When you type a slash, the IRC server knows that what follows the slash is a command. (Once you join a channel, IRC automatically treats everything you type as a statement to be added to the conversation unless it is preceded by a slash character.) IRC commands are not case sensitive.

For example, entering /**help** or /**HELP** displays IRC help; entering /**list** displays the channel list.

The subject of many channels is easy to identify by the channel names. Some channels have no real subject; they're just free-form places to hang out and rap. Other channels have not only a subject, but a given topic for the conversation of the moment.

Although most IRC channels have purely social purposes (for example, #hottub for casual chatting or #jeopardy for trivia exchange), some are set up as forums for serious discussion. IRC gained fame during the 1991 Persian Gulf War, during which it was used to distribute important news to users in areas where news was blacked out. IRC served the same function two years later, when Internet users in Russia and surrounding countries gathered in IRC channels to exchange news about the coup against Boris Yeltsin.

Most channels you'll find are created for various styles of purely social fun. Still, you'll see some dedicated to scientific disciplines (#biochemistry), culture (#bible), and countries (#belgium). In most channels, the dominant language is English, but there are channels where the dominant language is another. This is particularly true of channels named after countries and languages (#polska, #español), and those that you may see near the top of your channel list in seemingly garbled characters. These are mostly Japanese channels, whose names appear garbled on your Windows screen because the channels require a terminal designed for the Kanji alphabet.

Some channels are the Internet equivalent of phone-sex party lines; bored, lonely people chat there for a cheap turn-on. If that's not your bag, steer clear of channels with names like SEXXXY-CHAT.

In WinIRC, you join a channel by double-clicking it in the list or selecting it and then choosing Join from the menu bar. In another client, you might choose a Join menu item or type the command /**join** followed by the channel name (for example, /**join #jeopardy**). As soon as you join a channel, a window opens to display the conversation as it progresses. You may not see anything for a few moments because IRC shows you only the statements that come into the channel after you join. When you join, IRC automatically announces your presence to others in the channel with a message.

In WinIRC, a small box, one line high, appears at the bottom of the window and serves the same role as MSN Chat's compose pane. Anything you type appears here, but it does not go out to the discussion until you press Enter. That gives you a chance to fix your spelling and consider your statements carefully before they hit the group. Note that this is also where you type IRC commands, always preceded by a slash (/), so that the IRC server knows your entry is a command and not a contribution to the conversation.

To leave a channel, enter the command /**leave**. You leave the channel, but retain your IRC connection, so you can immediately join another channel. To quit IRC completely, close your client or enter the command /**quit**.

Each channel on IRC has a "channel operator," or *chanop*, who is the king or queen of the channel. You can identify chanops easily because their nicknames are preceded by the "at" character (@).In general, the chanop is the person who creates or first joins a given channel; that chanop has the power to bestow chanop status on other users (even multiple users at once), so that a chanop remains even if the original chanop leaves. If a participant in a channel harasses other users, refuses to stick to the topic, or misbehaves in another way, the chanop can kick the offender off the channel. Note that chanops can't kick a user off the IRC server altogether; kicked-out users can join other channels or start their own channels.

# MUDs

MUDs are Internet role-playing scenarios that allow users to interact with one another, and with an imaginary online environment, in real time. Mudding is a lot like using IRC or Chat, except that the following are true with MUDs:

◆ Everybody in the conversation is pretending to be someone else, playing a role or *character*

◆ Everybody in the conversation is pretending to be in a particular environment or situation, such as fighting a battle or exploring a castle or recreating some scientific experiment

◆ The environment itself plays a part, displaying descriptions of the surroundings and events, responding to the actions and commands of players, and enforcing the rules of game

Originally, the MUD acronym stood for *multi-user dungeon* because the early MUDs resembled *Dungeons and Dragons*, the fantasy role-playing game popular on college campuses when geeks had lots of free time because they weren't on the Internet yet. Because MUDs have long since expanded into many other styles of environments and games, the source of the acronym has been backformed to *multi-user dimensions*, *multi-user domains*, and *multi-user dialogs*. No matter. In the end, it's all just MUD, and players are often known as *mudders*.

Although *MUD* is the accepted generic term, there are variations. Each variation is actually a different program running on a MUD server. You'll see MUSHes (*multi-user shared hallucinations*), MOOs (*multi-user object oriented*—nobody knows where the *U* went), and MUCKs, so named because designated users have the authority to manipulate the environment, or "muck" around in it.

Each MUD is created and controlled by a program running on a MUD server. You can often run these programs through Telnet, and so require no special software. (You can even run them through your Web browser, through its Telnet support.) MUDs have become more sophisticated of late, however; some can display graphics and play other tricks that can greatly enhance the role-playing experience. These advanced features require client software—and each special server program requires a different client. There are few such MUDs for which a Windows client is available. Nearly all are for various flavors of the UNIX operating system, common at colleges.

MUDs look like fun, and they often are. They are also, surprisingly, the Internet resource that requires the most skill and experience to master. When you join a MUD, you usually enter an elaborate world with precise gaming rules, populated by experienced players who take it *very* seriously (*way too* seriously, at times—but then, it's their game). Do something dumb and they'll let you know it.

## MUD Rules

Every MUD, like any game, has rules. When you first connect to a MUD server, you almost always receive information about displaying instructions or for acquiring them with FTP. If you don't see instructions, enter **help** after connecting.

Some MUDs allow you to create your own character right away; others require that you send an e-mail message to the MUD God or Wizard (as the leaders of MUDs are known) before playing, and wait for an e-mail response. When it comes, the response includes information about your character and, usually, complete rules and instructions for playing the game.

## Finding a MUD

Finding lists of available MUDs is simple. On the World Wide Web, you can find lists of MUDs and other MUD information at the MUD Connector (see Figure 19.5), which also includes direct Telnet links to MUDs that don't require special client software. The MUD Connector's URL is shown here:

```
http://www.magicnet.net/~cowana/mud.html
```

**FIGURE 19.5.**

*The MUD Connector, a good source for information about MUDs and links to MUDs.*

Another useful Web page about MUDs is called the MUD Home Page, located at this URL:

```
http://www.shef.ac.uk/uni/academic/I-M/is/studwork/groupe/home.html
```

On the Web, you'll find links to many Telnet-accessible MUDs. These links open the Telnet client used by your Web browser and supply the proper address, port number, and login information to take you directly into the MUD's opening dialog boxes. There, you choose a character and learn about the rules of the game.

A good place to find links to Telnet MUDs is the MUD Connector Page (shown in Figure 19.5) at this URL:

```
http://www.magicnet.net/~cowana/mud.html
```

## Playing a MUD

When you join a MUD through Telnet, what you see is a lot like what you see on IRC: The statements and actions of other players appear on-screen, preceded by their character names. You'll also see *descriptions* displayed by the MUD program. Descriptions detail the environment around you as you move through the game; they also itemize the events around you and even facts about you, such as how you are dressed or what you are holding (see Figure 19.6).

**FIGURE 19.6.**

*Playing a MUD through Telnet.*

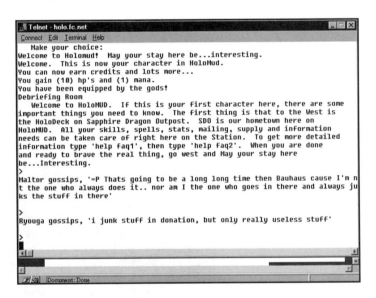

Because every MUD program is different, the commands used to navigate within MUDs also differ. A few common commands, such as those listed in the following chart, are available in many types of MUD environments.

| MUD Command | Function |
| --- | --- |
| who | Displays a list of the character names of the other players. |
| look | Displays a description of the current environment; a "look around," so to speak. |
| go | Moves you in a direction (go east), into or out of a room (go in), or toward an object or player (go fredo). |

| MUD Command | Function |
| --- | --- |
| say | Displays whatever you type next as a quote, so that others can see what you're saying. Suppose that my character is Melchior and I enter this command: `say Where the hell are we?` Every other player sees this message: `Melchior says, "Where the hell are we?"` The say command can often be replaced with a quotation mark (") for faster typing. |
| act | Displays whatever you type next as an action of your character. If I enter this command: `act kicks the ball` Every player sees this message: `Melchior kicks the ball` The act command can often be replaced with a colon (:) for faster typing. |
| get, drop | Enable you to manipulate objects. Use get to pick something up (`get knife`); use drop to put something down (`drop money`). |
| whisper | Lets you say something privately to another player; the statement you type following the whisper command appears only on his or her screen. If I type this command: `whisper suzy=Let's get out of here!` The player nicknamed Suzy—and only Suzy—sees this message: `Melchior whispers, "Let's get out of here!"` |

# Mailing Lists

The principle of mailing lists, sometimes also known as *discussion groups*, is simple: Someone sets up an Internet account as a central repository for the list (a kind of post office) and puts out the word that this is the address for a discussion list covering, say, botany. A separate account is set up for the administration of the list; botanists and botany buffs send subscription requests to the administration account so that they can be added to the list.

Subscribers send e-mail containing news, comments, questions, answers, and any other botany-related information to the list address. (The folks who run the list, its *owners*, typically also collect and supply information to the list.) All e-mail received by the list account is forwarded by e-mail to every person on the list.

This is all accomplished in one of two ways: manually (some poor soul maintains the list of subscribers and performs the forwarding) or automatically, through one of several programs that can accept subscriptions and do the forwarding with little or no human involvement. Several such programs are available, but by far the most common is a family of programs called *Listservs*. In fact, you're more likely to encounter a Listserv list today than any other type.

Beyond subscribing and maintaining your subscription, the processes of using manual and automated lists are identical. You send news in e-mail messages to the list address; you receive the latest messages each time you retrieve your e-mail.

---

### Keep Your Addresses Straight

The most common mistake made by mailing list newbies is failing to remember the distinction between the *subscription* address and the *list* address.

◆ The **subscription address** is the one to which you send your subscription requests and any other mail related to the maintenance of your subscription. For automated lists, the subscription address is often informally called by the name of the list processor. For example, you might be instructed to send subscription requests "to the Listserv."

◆ The **list address** is only for postings of information, questions, or comments intended for all subscribers.

If you send news to the subscription address, it won't reach the other subscribers. Worse, if you send a message about your subscription to the list address, the message will probably wind up in the mailbox of every subscriber (unless it is helpfully intercepted by a moderator). The inevitable result: at least embarrassment, at worst a torrent of flames from annoyed subscribers who learn your e-mail address from the header on your message.

---

## Where to Find Lists

A good way to find a list is through colleagues or friends with similar interests. Failing that, there are ways to locate lists through the Internet itself.

A master index of Internet mailing lists, which includes all types of lists—manual lists, Listserv lists, and lists maintained by other programs—is available. Each entry in the alphabetical list includes the list's name, a complete description of the list, and instructions for subscribing.

You can acquire this master index in three ways:

◆ The list is posted in the newsgroup `news.lists`.

◆ Use anonymous FTP at address `rtfm.mit.edu`. Download the group of files stored as `/pub/usenet-by-group/news.answers/mail/mailing-lists`.

◆ Use the list on the Web at `http://www.neosoft.com/internet/paml` (see Figure 19.7). When you access the list through the Web, you can search for mailing lists by name or subject.

**FIGURE 19.7.**

*A master index of mailing lists on the World Wide Web.*

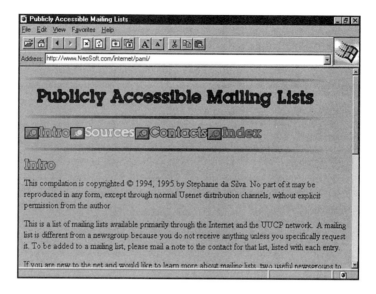

In fact, a range of search tools is available on the Web to hunt down all types of Internet resources related to a topic. Although they run on the Web, many of these tools can find the names and addresses of mailing lists related to a topic as well.

## Subscribing to a List

The exact steps required to subscribe to mailing lists vary. Subscribing to a manual list is different from subscribing to a Listserv list—and even Listservs vary a little. Three facts mean this isn't such a big problem:

◆ When you locate the name and address of a list, you almost always find subscription information mentioned along with it.

◆ Most lists today are controlled by a Listserv and accept the standard Listserv subscription commands. The lists automated by other list processors usually accept Listserv subscription commands, or minor variations thereof.

◆ As long as you send your subscription request to the correct address, if you send an incorrectly phrased request, you usually get a return message detailing the proper phrasing. Try to get it right the first time, but rest assured that you'll probably receive a little coaching if you mess up.

The important thing to remember is that any mailing list really needs only three pieces of information, no matter how it's administered: your e-mail address, your name, and the name of the list to which you want to subscribe.

Because *manual* mailing lists are managed by people who can read, all you have to do is send a cordial letter to the subscription address (not the list address!), requesting a subscription and including your full name and e-mail address.

To explain how to subscribe to an *automated* list, I'll describe the usual steps for subscribing to a Listserv because they're the most common type. Be aware, though, that different list processors require different commands.

When you send e-mail to a Listserv, you're running a computer program by remote control. As with any computer program, you must phrase and format your commands the way the program wants you to. When you send an e-mail message to a Listserv, it reads the body of the message for valid commands and ignores anything else it finds.

The most important command a Listserv understands is SUB, the command to subscribe. The command has this syntax:

```
SUB listname firstname lastname
```

For example, to subscribe to a Listserv list about Windows 95 (called WIN95-L), I sent this command to the e-mail address of the Listserv:

```
SUB WIN95-L ned snell
```

If you know the address of the Listserv, but not the name of the list, use the LIST command (described later in this chapter) to find the names of all lists served by a given Listserv.

> The instructions for subscribing to a Listserv list sometimes show the command SUB; at other times, the command is SUBSCRIBE. Even if you see SUBSCRIBE, SUB will probably work. Nevertheless, because there are variations among list programs and among versions of Listserv, always follow any subscription instructions to the letter.

Instructions for subscribing to Listserv lists often tell you to leave blank the subject line of the e-mail message, but it really doesn't matter. At worst, typing a subject line causes the Listserv to spit back an error message, but it won't prevent your subscription from going through.

## Confirming Your Subscription

After you send your subscription request, check your e-mail from time to time for a response. How long it takes to get a response depends on the list; most Listserv lists respond within hours (sometimes minutes); manual lists may take days to get back to you.

When a response arrives, it contains one of the following:

◆ A notice that your subscription has been accepted, followed by your first batch of messages. Often, the acceptance notice includes important information, such as any special rules of etiquette and instructions for canceling your subscription. You may want to delete old messages from time to time, but hold onto the confirmation message for future reference.

◆ A request to confirm your subscription. When issued by a Listserv, confirmation requests instruct you to follow specific steps to confirm. Typically, you're asked to reply to the confirmation message, using the words OK or CONFIRM as the body of the message. Shortly after you confirm, you receive your subscription notice and your first messages.

◆ A notice that your request was improperly phrased or did not include all the required information. These error messages usually contain instructions for resubmitting your request correctly. If the list is limited, you may also receive a message denying your subscription, usually with an explanation. Denials are rare, especially on Listserv lists.

---

### Keep Those Confirmation Messages

The first message or two you receive from a mailing list—especially your subscription confirmation—usually contain valuable information such as commands for subscription maintenance, codes of conduct, and instructions for canceling your subscriptions.

Make sure that you save such messages; don't clean them out when you clean out old e-mail messages. You'll need this information later on. You may also receive other administrative messages from time to time, informing you of changes to the list address or other important information. Keep these as well. They'll save you headaches later on.

---

## Using Your Subscription

Once you sign up, there's nothing to do except check your e-mail regularly to collect the latest messages.

To post news or a message for others on the list, simply send e-mail to the list address. Again, be sure to send it to the *list address*, not to the address you used to subscribe—the list administration and the list itself are handled in separate accounts.

You can also use Exchange's Reply function (described in Chapter 8, "Composing, Sending, and Receiving E-Mail") while reading any message from the list; Exchange automatically addresses your reply to the list. If you use Reply to automatically address your mail, but you're sending something new instead of responding to another message, be sure to write a new subject line and delete the quotes to avoid confusing other subscribers.

---

*Tip*

Sometimes, an ongoing conversation through a list may lead to the need to communicate directly with another subscriber—*outside* the list. For example, you may want to ask a question that falls outside the boundaries of the list's topic, but one that you suspect a certain subscriber can answer.

To communicate privately with another subscriber, use the address in the From: line of the header on a message from that person. Don't use Reply for this because the Reply feature addresses mail back to the list, not to the original sender.

## Unsubscribing

When you no longer want or need a list, unsubscribe from it. You should receive complete instructions for unsubscribing in the acknowledgment message you receive when you subscribe (another reason to save that message). Typically, you send exactly what you sent to subscribe, replacing SUB with UNSUB (simple, *n'est pas?*). For a one-list Listserv, send this message:

UNSUB

For a multilist Listserv, send this message:

UNSUB *listname*

When in doubt, include the list name.

# What Now?

Go wild. You have arrived at the end of this book, which means you have arrived at the end of the skill set you need to make the most of The Microsoft Network and its Internet access. I hope the experience has been a productive and pleasant one.

See you online.

# PART V

# REFERENCES

A        Go Word Directory        333

B        Web Highlights        343

Glossary        353

Index        361

# APPENDIX A

# GO WORD DIRECTORY

This appendix lists the Go words used to reach the major category folders and forums on MSN. Although you can reach any of the folders and forums listed in this appendix by opening a series of folders in MSN (see Chapter 4, "Basic Navigation Techniques"), using a Go word usually takes you to a given folder or forum more quickly.

The Go words in this appendix are organized by major category folder. Each of the headings represents an icon in MSN's Categories folder and its Go word; beneath each heading are listed the major folders and forums within that category as well as their Go words.

To use a Go word, follow these steps:

1. From the **E**dit menu on MSN Central (the MSN home page) or from any open folder in MSN, select **E**dit, **G**o To, **O**ther Location to display the Go To Service dialog box.
2. Type the Go word and press Enter (or click OK).

When you type the Go word, capitalization does not matter. For example, the Go word `SciFi` takes you to the Science Fiction and Fanstasy forum whether you enter `SciFi`, `SCIFI`, `scifi`, or `scIfI` in the Go To Service dialog box. In this appendix, Go words are capitalized as they are only to help you remember them.

Note that this list does not include every Go word that may be available to you on MSN. The Go words in this list are the most useful for taking you from one region of MSN to another. But in addition to these Go words, many individual services (BBSs, titles, and so on) and folders within folders have their own Go words.

To learn the Go word for a folder icon or service icon in MSN, right-click the icon and choose Properties from the context menu. The Go word, if there is one, is listed on the Properties sheet that appears.

Arts and
Entertainment

# Arts & Entertainment (Go Word = Entertainment)

| Folder/Forum | Go Word |
| --- | --- |
| Art & Design | Design |
| Books & Writing | Books |
| Comedy | Comedy |
| Comics & Animation | Comics |
| Movies | Movies |
| Music | Music |
| Newspapers & Magazines | Magazines |
| Science Fiction & Fantasy | SciFi |
| Television & Radio | TV |
| Theater & Performance | Theater |

# Business & Finance (Go Word = Business)

Business and
Finance

| *Folder/Forum* | *Go Word* |
|---|---|
| Business & Finance Directory | B&FDirectory |
| Business News & Reference | BusinessNews |
| Business Services | BusinessServices |
| Career Connection | CareerConnect |
| International Trade | IntTrade |
| Investing | Investing |
| Personal Finance | PersonalFinance |
| Professions & Industries | Professions |
| Small Office/Home Office | SOHO |

# Chat World (Go Word = ChatWorld)

Chat World

| *Folder/Forum* | *Go Word* |
|---|---|
| Atrium Restaurant | cwAtrium |
| Chat Garden | ChatGarden |
| Chat World Foyer | cwFoyer |
| Chat World Front Desk | cwbbs |
| Chat World Elevator | Elevator |
| Chat World Lobby | cwChat |
| Games & Casino | cwCasino |
| Lobby Photo Gallery | cwLibrary |
| Pool & Spa | cwPool |

# Computers & Software (Go Word = Computing)

Computers and
Software

| *Folder/Forum* | *Go Word* |
|---|---|
| Computer Classified Ads | CompClass |
| Computer Companies & Organizations | ComputerCompanies |
| Computer Industry News | ComputerNews |
| Computer Publications | ComputerPubs |

*continues*

| Folder/Forum | Go Word |
|---|---|
| Computer Training & Support | ComputerSupport |
| Emerging Computer Technologies | EmergingTech |
| Hardware | Hardware |
| Multimedia & CD-ROM | Multimedia |
| Networking | Network |
| Safe Computing | SafeComputing |
| Software | Software |
| Software Development | Development |

Education and Reference

# Education & Reference (Go Word = Education)

| Folder/Forum | Go Word |
|---|---|
| Colleges & Universities | University |
| Technology in Education | EdTech |
| Educator to Educator | Educator |
| Fields of Study | Fields |
| International Students | IntStudents |
| Primary & Secondary Education | PrimaryEd |
| Reference | Reference |
| Student to Student | Students |

# Health & Fitness (Go Word = Health)

| Folder/Forum | Go Word |
|---|---|
| Exercise & Physical Fitness | Exercise |
| Healthcare Professionals | HealthProf |
| Medicine | Medicine |
| Mental Wellness & Counseling | Counseling |
| Nutrition | Nutrition |
| Preventive Medicine | PreventMedicine |
| Public Health | PublicHealth |

# Home & Family (Go Word = Home)

| Folder/Forum | Go Word |
| --- | --- |
| Family Health & Wellbeing | FamilyHealth |
| Family Interests & Recreation | FamilyInterests |
| For Kids | Kids |
| Home & Family Media | HomeMedia |
| Home & Garden | HomeGarden |
| In the Kitchen | InTheKitchen |
| Parenting | Parents |
| Teen to Teen | Teens |

Home and Family

# Interests, Leisure, & Hobbies (Go Word = Interests)

| Folder/Forum | Go Word |
| --- | --- |
| Arts & Crafts | Craft |
| Automotive Interests | Automotive |
| Collecting | Collecting |
| Games & Gaming | Games |
| Holidays & Special Occasions | Holidays |
| Home Interests | HomeInterests |
| Indoor Sports & Recreation | IndoorSports |
| Models & Radio Control | Models |
| Mysteries, Magic, & Phenomena | Mystery |
| Outdoor Interests & Activities | OutdoorInterests |
| Science & Electronics Hobbies | ScienceHobbies |
| Travel | Travel |

Interests, Leisure, and Hobbies

# Internet Center (Go Word = Internet)

| Folder/Forum | Go Word |
| --- | --- |
| Core Rules of Netiquette | CoreRules |
| Getting on the Internet | GetOnInternet |

The Internet Center

*continues*

| Folder/Forum | Go Word |
|---|---|
| Internet Newsgroups | newsgroups |
| World Wide Web | www |

# MSN Passport (Go Word = Passport)

MSN Passport

| Folder/Forum | Go Word |
|---|---|
| Australian Passport | PassportAustralia |
| Canadian Passport | PassportCanada |
| Deutscher Reisepass | PassportGermany |
| Passeport pour la France | PassportFrance |
| United Kingdom Passport | PassportUK |

# News & Weather (Go Word = w)

| Folder/Forum | Go Word |
|---|---|
| MSN News | MSNnews |
| The Weather Lab | TheWeatherLab |

# People & Communities (Go Word = Community)

People and
Communities

| Folder/Forum | Go Word |
|---|---|
| Advice & Support | Advice |
| Cultures | Culture |
| Genealogy | Genealogy |
| Holidays & Special Occasions | Holidays |
| Men | Men |
| People to People | People |
| Religion | Religion |
| Women | Women |

# Public Affairs (Go Word = Public)

Public Affairs

| *Folder/Forum* | *Go Word* |
|---|---|
| Consumer Services & Information | ConsumerServices |
| Government Agencies & Departments | Government |
| Interest Groups & Non-Profits | InterestGroups |
| Media Affairs | Media |
| Politics | Politics |
| Public Health | PublicHealth |
| Public Safety | PublicSafety |

# Science & Technology (Go Word = Science)

Science and Technology

| *Folder/Forum* | *Go Word* |
|---|---|
| Astronomy & Space | Astronomy |
| Biology & Life Sciences | Biology |
| Chemistry Forum | Chemistry |
| Communications Technology | CommTech |
| Computers & Electronics | ComputerElectronic |
| Edison Auditorium | ScienceEvents |
| Engineering Forum | Engineering |
| Environment | Environment |
| The Futurist | Futurist |
| Geology & Geography | Geology |
| Industry & Infrastructure | Industry |
| Math | Math |
| Medicine | Medicine |
| Physics | Physics |
| Transportation | Transportation |

Special Events

# Special Events (Go Word = Events)

| Folder/Forum | Go Word |
|---|---|
| Babbage Auditorium | Babbage |
| Ask Questions Here | AskBabbage |

# Sports & Recreation (Go Word = Sports)

| Folder/Forum | Go Word |
|---|---|
| Field & Court Sports | FieldSports |
| Indoor Sports & Recreation | IndoorSports |
| Motorsports | MotorSports |
| Outdoor Sports & Recreation | OutdoorSports |
| Snow & Winter Sports | SnowSports |
| Special Sports | SpecialSports |
| Sports Media | SportsMedia |
| Sports Psychology & Medicine | SportsMedicine |
| Water Sports | WaterSports |

The MSN Member Lobby

# Member Lobby (Go Word = Lobby)

Unlike the rest of the folders and forums listed in this appendix, those in this section are not located under the Categories folder. The following folders can be found under Member Assistance on MSN Central (the MSN home page). However, the Go words for these items can still be used from any open folder (including any open category folder) and from MSN Central as described at the beginning of this appendix.

| Folder/Forum | Go Word |
|---|---|
| Accounts & Billing | MSNaccounts |
| Lobby Newsstand | newsstand |
| Maps & Information | MSNmaps |
| Member Activities | MSNactivities |
| Member Directory | MSNdirectory |

| Folder/Forum | Go Word |
| --- | --- |
| Member Support | usSupport |
| MSN Gift Shop | MSNgifts |
| Reception Desk | Reception |

# APPENDIX B

# WEB HIGHLIGHTS

This appendix lists a range of interesting Internet sites you may want to visit. Because there are millions of pages of information on the Internet, this list is only a sampling. But its entries offer an excellent introduction to the resources on the Net, and many pages listed here contain links to other Internet resources related to the same subject.

The addresses in this section are all entered in Universal Resource Locator (URL) format, the address format used to navigate to Internet resources through a Web browser such as Internet Explorer. In your Web browser, enter each address exactly as shown (observe any capitalization exactly as shown).

For more about the World Wide Web, links, and URLs, see Chapter 16, "Browsing the World Wide Web."

# Internet Directories and Search Tools

◆ **Yahoo** (http://www.yahoo.com)

An easy-to-use, subject-sorted directory and search engine for Web and other resources.

◆ **EINet Galaxy** (http://galaxy.einet.net)

Another solid index of Web sites with a companion search tool.

◆ **SavvySearch** (http://www.cs.colostate.edu/~dreiling/smartform.html)

A simple but powerful search engine that searches multiple directories at once.

◆ **WebCrawler** (http://webcrawler.cs.washington.edu)

An extremely powerful Web search engine.

◆ **OpenText** (http://www.opentext.com:8080)

A facility that can perform a full text search of the contents of over one million Web pages.

# Business Pages

The following sections list sites that are of interest to the various "subcategories" of the huge topic called *business*.

## Starting an Internet Business

◆ **Internet Plaza** (http://plaza.xor.com/plaza/index.html)

Internet Plaza offers a range of business services to help companies get started in online business.

◆ **Digital Future** (gopher://marketplace.com)

An online newsletter about Internet-based commerce.

◆ **Internet Business Center** (http://www.tig.com/ibc)

A Web server specializing in providing information about business uses of the Internet.

◆ **Commercial Use Strategies Home Page** (http://www.netrex.com/business/usage.html)

More strategies and tips for online businesses.

◆ **Small Business Administration** (http://www.sbaonline.sba.gov)

A Web page for the U.S. Small Business Administration, created to help new and existing small businesses compete. Includes business development services and links to other resources.

◆ **Open Market Commercial Sites Index** (http://www.directory.net)

A pile of links to economic information, such as the files of the Financial Services Technology Consortium and the customer support pages of major corporations. A great place for ideas.

## Economic/Financial Data

◆ **Financial Economics Network** (http://www.crimson.com/fen/)

Created by the editor of the *Journal of Financial Economics*, this home page features abstracts of forthcoming papers and articles and also includes listings of jobs and job-seekers in the field.

◆ **QuoteCom** (http://www.quote.com)

QuoteCom displays stock quotes (delayed 15 minutes) plus a wealth of information from newswires, market data, and more.

## Advertising

◆ **Chiat-Day Idea Factory** (http://www.chiatday.com/factory)

Chiat-Day is a former ad agency (now specializing in "brand promotion") whose Web site, a "virtual office," shows off splendidly what a little imagination can do on the Web. Whether you do business with Chiat-Day or not, the company's Web pages are a guide to the possibilities.

◆ *Advertising Age* (http://www.adage.com)

The venerable advertising magazine and sourcebook, now in an online version.

# Education Pages

Following are Web sites to visit if you are involved in any aspect of education.

# General Education Resources

◆ **AskERIC** (http://ericir.syr.edu)

AskERIC is a venerable educator's resource of the Educational Resources Information Center (ERIC), long available through Telnet and now available on the Web. It features extensive holdings of federally funded education information.

◆ **Center for Excellence in Education** (http://rsi.cee.org)

Information about programs for keeping U.S. students competitive in science and technology; also has information on other education initiatives.

◆ **Educational Online Sources** (http://netspace.students.brown.edu/eos1)

Links to all kinds of educational resources all over the Net, courtesy of Brown University.

◆ **Web Lecture Hall** (http://www.utexas.edu:80/world/instruction)

A collection of materials about using the Web as a teaching tool. Resources include course syllabi, notes, textbooks, and more.

◆ **Galaxy Education** (http://galaxy.einet.net/galaxy/Social-Sciences/Education.html)

Materials and pointers to educational resources.

◆ **Educational Technology** (http://tecfa.unige.ch/info-edu-comp.html)

Education-related links in the World Wide Web Virtual Library (see Chapter 16, "Browsing the World Wide Web").

◆ **CoVis: Learning through Collaborative Visualization** (http://www.covis.nwu.edu)

A project at Northwestern University to explore the unique ways the Web can be used in teaching applications.

◆ **Teacher Education** (http://curry.edschool.virginia.edu/teis)

A service of the Society for Technology and Teacher Education, this site contains documents and links to teacher educational resources.

◆ **U.S. Department of Education** (http://www.ed.gov)

At this writing, Congress is considering a proposal to abolish the Department of Education. But for as long as it survives, you'll find information about its programs here.

# K–12 Resources

The resources listed here may be useful in K through 12 classrooms. They also serve as models for programs teachers can create themselves.

◆ **Empire Internet Schoolhouse** (gopher://nysernet.org:3000/11)

A rich set of documents and links to K through 12 resources, projects, and discussion groups.

◆ **Exploratorium** (http://www.exploratorium.edu)

Hundreds of interactive exhibits about science, art, and human perception.

◆ **Travels with Samantha** (http://www-swiss.ai.mit.edu/samantha/travels-with-samantha.html)

Travels with Samantha is a travel show on the Internet that takes students to interesting destinations all over North America.

◆ **The Jason Project** (http://seawifs.gsfc.nasa.gov/scripts/JASON.html)

A collaborative effort of NASA and scientists to provide an interactive learning environment about science. Jason takes students to the rain forest, outer space, and more; it's an excellent showcase for the potential of Web-based teaching.

◆ **NASA** (http://www.nasa.gov)

Documents, graphics, and links to an array of space-related resources, including a K–12 education program.

◆ **Children's Literature Web Guide** (http://www.ucalgary.ca/~dkbrown/index.html)

Provides abstracts and other information about winners of the Newbery and Caldecott medals for children's literature, plus the *Publishers Weekly* Children's Bestsellers list.

◆ **The Smithsonian Natural History Gopher** (gopher://nmnhgoph.si.edu)

Offers a treasure of news and information about projects underway at the Smithsonian, divided by Natural History disciplines. This Gopher also offers links to other Natural History Gophers.

◆ **The White House** (http://www.whitehouse.gov)

Pictures of White House interiors; access to speeches, press releases, and other documents; and personal information about the First Family, right down to Socks, the cat.

◆ **CapWeb** (http://policy.net)

Unofficial information about events on Capitol Hill, including documents of pending legislation.

◆ **The Cornell Theory Center Math and Science Gateway** (http://www.tc.cornell.edu:80/Edu/MathSciGateway)

A great clearinghouse of sorts, containing links to dozens of math and science education-related Internet resources for grades K–12.

## Post-Secondary Resources

The resources listed here can be of special interest to college students—or those heading for college.

◆ **Money for College Directory** (`http://www.studentservices.com/mfc`)

This page offers a searchable database of thousands of scholarships, grants, and special loans to help students locate all the financial resources for which they may be eligible.

◆ **CNU Online** (`http://cnuonline.cnu.edu`)

A project of Christopher Newport University (CNU), CNU Online offers credit-bearing courses from CNU, plus links to credit-bearing online courses at other universities, to allow students to acquire a bachelor's degree online. CNU Online is still under construction, but you can check it out to see what courses and degrees are offered, or will be offered.

# Entertainment and Leisure Pages

Although you could say that a good percentage of the Internet is devoted to "entertainment and leisure," the following sections divide this huge category into more specific areas.

## Shopping

◆ **Internet Shopping Network** (`http://shop.internet.net`)

Owned by TV's Home Shopping Network, the ISN is one of the first Web-based marketplaces. You can shop the catalogs of major mail-order houses and place orders online. Note that the opening page of the Shopping Network requires a registration procedure for new users. This is part of the Shopping Club's security system, designed to prevent unauthorized users from accessing the credit-card information you supply to make purchases online.

◆ **Deep Space Mall** (`http://www.deepspace.com/deepspace.html`)

An odd combination of shopping sites and links to space pictures. To each his own.

◆ **One World Plaza** (`http://www.digimark.net/windata`)

Over 100 shops to browse. Bring lunch.

◆ **Burlington Coat Factory** (`http://www.coat.com`)

Order anything from the bargain outlet clothing shop. (Remember: *Not* affiliated with Burlington Industries!)

◆ **Download Bookstore** (`http://dab.psi.net/downloadbookstore`)

An innovative online bookstore that lets you "try before you buy" by downloading excerpts or tables of contents from books before ordering.

◆ **CDnow!** (`http://cdnow.com`)

An online CD store offering 140,000 recordings plus online copies of articles and reviews from music industry magazines.

## Entertainment

◆ **Top Ten Lists from** *The Late Show with David Letterman* (`http://www.cbs.com/lateshow/ttlist.html`)

The latest lists, plus archives of *all* the lists—even the ones that weren't funny.

◆ **The Internet Movie Database** (`http://www.msstate.edu/Movies`)

Formerly known as the Cardiff Movie Database, this is an elaborate database of *professional* film reviews ("Keanu Reeves can't talk"), film writing, graphics, and much more. A great place to learn anything about the movies.

◆ **Amateur Movie Reviews** (newsgroup `rec.art.movies.reviews`)

The opinions of your fellow movie fans plus the counter-points of their colleagues. ("Keanu Reeves *can so* talk!")

◆ **Buena Vista** (`http://bvp.wdp.com`)

Information, graphics, clips, and more about the Disney empire: Disney Pictures, Touchstone Pictures, and Hollywood Pictures.

◆ **Fox Broadcasting** (`http://www.eden.com/users/my-html/fox.html`)

Everything about the rebel fourth network, including the latest about *The Simpsons* and *Melrose Place*. The site is not created and maintained by Fox but by *fans*—which can be for the better or worse, depending on how you look at it.

◆ **Warner Brothers Records** (`http://www.iuma.com/warner`)

Complete information on the Warner's label, including tour dates of its artists, new CD releases, and even video clips of stars such as Madonna.

◆ **The Rolling Stones** (`http://www.stones.com`)

Yes, the world's oldest working rock band has its own Web site to keep you informed about tour dates and to sell you licensed Stones merchandise.

◆ **Ultimate TV List** (`http://tvnet.com/TVnet.html`)

A list of links to much of the TV-related stuff all over the Net, including Web sites, Gophers, FTP files, and newsgroups. A great starting place for finding information about your favorite show.

◆ **Cinema Sites** (`http://www.webcom.com/~davidaug/Movie_Sites.html`)

A great directory of links to dozens of Internet sites offering movie information; it's a good starting place for film browsing.

◆ **Wiretap Archive** (`gopher://wiretap.spies.com:70/11/Library/Media/Film`)

A "pop culture" archive from which you can extract information about movies, music, and more.

◆ **Paramount Pictures** (`http://www.paramount.com`)

Information, clips, and more from the studio that gave us *The Godfather* films, the *Star Trek* films, the *Indiana Jones* films, and more.

◆ **Cannes Film Festival** (http://www.mhm.fr/cannes/eng/index.html)

News about awards, personalities, and seminars at the glitziest annual film extravaganza.

◆ **The Sundance Film Festival** (http://cybermart.com/sundance/institute/institute.html)

News about the goings-on at the festival Robert Redford founded to support independent film.

◆ *ER* (http://sunsite.doc.ic.ac.uk/public/media/tv/collections/tardis/us/drama/ER)

All about the actors, plotlines, and more of everybody's favorite show about overly skinny, angst-ridden doctors.

◆ *Friends* (http://geminga.dartmouth.edu/~andyjw/friends)

All about the actors, plotlines, and more of everybody's favorite comedy about overly skinny, angst-ridden, self-involved, overpaid, white twenty-somethings.

◆ *The Rockford Files* (http://falcon.cc.ukans.edu/~asumner/rockford)

Trivia, lore, photos, and more about the long-dead, best private-eye show ever, featuring a great ensemble cast (headed by James Garner) in which no regular was overly skinny.

◆ **Classical Music on the Net** (http://www.einet.net/galaxy/Leisure-and-Recreation/Music/douglas-bell/Index.html)

A great source for links to the many classical music resources on the Web.

## Sports

◆ **ESPNET SportsZone** (http://espnet.sportszone.com)

A great source for up-to-date sports information.

◆ **Highlights** (http://tns-www.lcs.mit.edu/cgi-bin/sports/mlb/highlights)

A page that publishes highlights of the previous day's games.

◆ **WWW/Sports** (http://tns-www.lcs.mit.edu/cgi-bin/sports)

Links and updates about sporting events all over the world.

◆ **Sports Server** (http://www.nando.net/sptsserv.html)

Complete coverage of scores, stats, standings, and injuries for professional and college basketball, football, and baseball teams.

◆ **Americas Cup** (http://www.ac95.org)

Everything about the world's biggest sailboat race and national pride surrogate, including photos, history, and more.

◆ **The 19th Hole** (http://zodiac.tr-riscs/panam.edu/golf/19thhole.html)

A complete golfer's resource.

◆ **The Internet Ski Guide** (http://cybil.kplus.bc.ca/www/ski_net/ski_na.htm)

Complete information about major ski resorts, including conditions.

◆ **Tour De France** (http://www.velonews.com/VeloNews)

Everything about the world's biggest bike race and national pride surrogate, including results, course maps, and more.

◆ **Water Skiing** (http://www.primenet.com:80/~jodell)

Tournament schedules and results, pictures, and more about a sport I tried once and won't try again unless I become suicidally depressed.

# Miscellaneous Interesting Stuff

◆ **Vegetarian Pages** (http://catless.ncl.ac.uk/Vegetarian)

A great place to learn about veggie techniques, recipes, nutritional information, and events. Bring celery.

◆ **Bookwire** (http://www.bookwire.com)

The first stop for information about books, Bookwire features *Publishers Weekly* bestseller lists, a title database, and hundreds of links to book-related resources elsewhere on the Internet.

◆ **Westin Travel Guide** (http://www.westin.com)

An international travel guide with advisories, destination attractions, business and family travel planning, and, of course, Westin hotel reservations.

◆ **The First Church of Cyberspace** (http://execpc.com/~chender)

Founded by a Presbyterian pastor in New Jersey, the First Church of Cyberspace features a sanctuary, a library, a gallery, a gathering place, and a multimedia bible. Other features include Sunday school classes and files of sermons from ministers across the country. Visitors are encouraged to practice "active worship" by responding to sermons and other material offered through the Church. Obviously, the materials and activities are heavily Presbyterian—but everyone's welcome.

◆ **Internal Revenue Service** (http://www.ustreas.gov/treasury/bureaus/irs/irs.html)

Yes, the IRS. You can get forms, look up rules, and communicate with the tax commissioner. (My dog ate the receipts, I swear.)

◆ **Genealogy Home Page** (http://ftp.cac.psu.edu/~saw/genealogy.html)

Look up your family tree.

◆ **The Wine Page** (http://augustus.csscr.washington.edu/personal/bigstar-mosaic/wine.html)

Everything about wine, including tasting notes and "virtual tasting" of online wine.

◆ **Consumer Information Center** (http://www.gsa.gov/staff/pa/cic/cic.htm)

The U.S. government's incredible database of consumer information, including guides to personal finance.

◆ **Self-Help Psychology Magazine** (http://www.well.com/user/selfhelp)

A Web page featuring helpful articles written by mental-health experts for lay people who have problems (or think they have problems).

GLOSSARY

**address**    A general way of describing the information required to locate a computer or person on a network. MSN **member IDs**, Internet e-mail addresses, and **URL**s are all examples of addresses.

**Archie**    An Internet facility that helps users locate files available for download from the Internet with **FTP**. See Chapter 18, "Downloading Files with FTP."

**BBS**    A public message board on MSN to which users post messages and files related to a given topic, and from which users can read messages and download files posted by others. See Chapter 5, "Reading and Contributing to Bulletin Boards and Newsgroups."

**browse**    To wander around MSN or the Internet, screen by screen, looking for items of interest. Also known as *surfing* or *cruising*.

**browser**    A software **client** that enables users to **browse**.

**bulletin board**    A general term referring to computer services for public message exchanges. **BBS**s and **newsgroups** are examples.

**category**    A folder on MSN containing other folders, documents, and **forums** related to a given topic.

**Chat room**    An MSN service that allows members to participate in a live, real-time online discussion carried out through typed messages. See Chapter 6, "Hanging Out in Chat Rooms."

**client**    A software tool for using a particular type of computer resource located on a **server** computer. See also **MSN Client** and **browser**.

**compression**    The process of making a computer file smaller so that it can be copied more quickly between computers. Compressed files, sometimes called *ZIP files*, must be decompressed on the receiving computer before they can be used. See Chapter 7, "Downloading and Uploading Files."

**content tree**    A metaphor used to describe the hierarchical organization of folders, files, and services on MSN.

**context menu**    A menu that pops up when you right-click any icon in Windows or MSN, the taskbar, or any empty area of the desktop. From the context menu, you can initiate most activities available for the item you right-clicked.

**cyberspace**    A broad expression used (perhaps overused, but it's all we have) to describe the activity, communication, and culture happening on the Internet and online services.

| | |
|---|---|
| **dial-up account** | An Internet account, accessed through a modem and telephone line, that offers complete access to the Internet through **TCP/IP** communications. |
| **domain** | The address of a computer on the Internet. A user's Internet address is made up of a username and a domain name. See Chapter 8, "Composing, Sending, and Receiving E-Mail," and Chapter 15, "Understanding the Internet." |
| **download/upload** | Two terms for the act of copying a file from one computer to another. When the computer receiving the file initiates the copying, it's downloading; when the computer sending the file initiates the copying, it's uploading. See Chapter 7, "Downloading and Uploading Files." |
| **e-mail** | Short for electronic mail, a system that enables a person to compose a message on a computer and transmit that message through a computer network, such as MSN or the Internet, to another computer user. All e-mail activity on MSN is conducted through **Microsoft Exchange**. |
| **emoticon** | *See* **smiley**. |
| **Exchange** | *See* **Microsoft Exchange**. |
| **Explorer** | *See* **Microsoft Explorer** or **Internet Explorer**. |
| **FAQ file** | Short for Frequently Asked Questions file, a computer file containing the answers to frequently asked questions about a particular Internet resource. |
| **Favorite Places** | A special folder containing **shortcut**s to MSN services. The shortcuts are created by an MSN user to provide a convenient way to navigate to the MSN resources he or she uses often. |
| **flame** | Hostile messages, often sent through **e-mail** or posted in **BBS**s or **newsgroups,** from MSN or Internet users in reaction to breaches of **netiquette**. |
| **forum** | A folder in MSN containing a group of services (BBS, chat room, and so on) related to a specific topic. |
| **forum manager** | A Microsoft employee in charge of a **forum**. The forum manager is responsible for approving all files uploaded to the forum's **BBS**s and **libraries**, and for managing overall forum activity. |
| **freeware** | Software available to anyone, free of charge; unlike **shareware**, which requires payment. |

| | |
|---|---|
| **FTP** | Short for File Transfer Protocol, the basic method for copying a file from one computer to another through the Internet. See Chapter 18, "Downloading Files with FTP." |
| **Go** or **Go word** | Go is a special dialog box that allows you to quickly navigate to any service or resource on MSN. A Go word is the word you enter in the dialog box to select the desired resource. See Chapter 4, "Basic Navigation Techniques." |
| **Gopher** | A system of menus layered on top of existing Internet **resources** that makes locating information and using services easier. See Chapter 17, "Browsing Gophers." |
| **home** or **home page** | A general term for a top-level page or screen, or a user-selected page or screen, to which you can return quickly from any activity by clicking a house-shaped button or choosing a Home menu item. Home on MSN is **MSN Central**. The "home" concept is also used by **browsers** for the **World Wide Web** and **Gopher**. |
| **HTML** | HyperText Markup Language, the document-formatting language used to create pages on the **World Wide Web**. |
| **HTTP** | HyperText Transfer Protocol, the standard protocol used for communications between servers and clients on the **World Wide Web**. |
| **hypermedia** and **hypertext** | Methods for allowing users to jump spontaneously among on-screen documents and other **resources** by selecting highlighted keywords that appear on each screen. Hypermedia and hypertext appear most often on the **World Wide Web**. See Chapter 16, "Browsing the World Wide Web." |
| **Internet** | A large, loosely organized **internetwork** connecting universities, research institutions, governments, businesses, and other organizations so that they can exchange messages and share information. |
| **Internet Explorer** | A **browser** for the **World Wide Web**, created by Microsoft. Can be confused with **Microsoft Explorer**, which is the basic file/folder management system in Windows 95. |
| **internetwork** | A set of **networks** and individual computers connected so that they can communicate and share information. The Internet is a very large internetwork. |
| **IRC** | Short for Internet Relay Chat, an Internet tool, similar to MSN's **Chat**, that allows two or more Internet users to participate in a live conversation by typing messages. See Chapter 19, "Advanced Internet Techniques." |

| | |
|---|---|
| **kiosk** | A document file located in an MSN **category** folder or **forum**, containing valuable instructions, information, or news about the folder or forum. |
| **link** | An area of text or a graphic you can click to navigate somewhere else. Links are used in **MSN titles** and on the **World Wide Web**. |
| **library** | A special type of MSN **BBS** set up exclusively to allow members to download useful files. See Chapter 5, "Reading and Contributing to Bulletin Boards and Newsgroups." |
| **mailing list** | An Internet **resource** that automatically sends **e-mail** messages related to a particular topic to people who have indicated an interest in that topic. See Chapter 19, "Advanced Internet Techniques." |
| **member ID** | The unique identifying name used to identify an MSN member. Members choose their own IDs, which they use to sign in to MSN. To send **e-mail** to an MSN member, you address it to his or her member ID. |
| **Microsoft Exchange** | The universal messaging client built into Windows 95. Exchange is the required program for sending and receiving MSN **e-mail**. |
| **Microsoft Explorer** | The basic file/folder management system in Windows 95. Can be used to navigate MSN and view the MSN **content tree**. Because of its name, Microsoft Explorer may be confused with **Internet Explorer**, a **browser** for the **World Wide Web**. |
| **Microsoft Plus!** | An add-in package for Windows 95 that includes a number of accessories, including a **wizard** for configuring Windows 95 for the Internet. |
| **MIME** | Multipurpose Internet Mail Extensions, a standard that allows graphics and multimedia information to be included in Internet documents such as e-mail messages. |
| **modem** | A device that allows a computer to communicate with another computer through telephone lines. A modem is required to use MSN. |
| **Mosaic** | A software **browser** that helps users navigate the **World Wide Web**. See Chapter 16, "Browsing the World Wide Web." |
| **MSN Central** | The **home page** from which all MSN navigation begins. |
| **MSN Client** | The Windows software on your PC you use to access MSN. This **client** software interacts with **server**s at Microsoft's MSN data center. |

| | |
|---|---|
| **MSN Today** | An **MSN title**, updated daily, that describes important events of the day on MSN and provides **links** for navigating to them. You reach MSN Today from **MSN Central**; MSN Today can also be displayed automatically every time you sign in to MSN. |
| **MSN title** | A graphical document on MSN that is played by MSN through a program called the Online Viewer. Titles serve as magazines, guidebooks, or instructional manuals, and typically feature graphics and **links**. See Chapter 9, "Viewing and Operating Titles." |
| **MUD** | Short for Multi-User Dungeon, Multi-User Dimension, or Multi-User Dialog, an Internet resource in which users role-play by interacting within an imagined environment created through on-screen messages. See Chapter 19, "Advanced Internet Techniques." |
| **multitasking** and **multithreading** | Two advanced techniques supplied by Windows 95 and 32-bit applications that allow multiple applications to run together more quickly, smoothly, and reliably. |
| **netiquette** | The code of proper conduct (etiquette) on the Internet and MSN. See Chapter 3, "Member Rules and Etiquette." |
| **Netscape** | Short for Netscape Communications, a software company that developed and markets a popular **browser** for the **World Wide Web** called Navigator. Some people refer to Navigator casually as Netscape. |
| **network** | A set of computers interconnected so that they can communicate and share information. Connected networks together form an **internetwork**. |
| **newsgroup** | An Internet resource through which people post and read messages related to a specific topic. Similar to MSN's **BBS**s, newsgroups are accessible through the **MSN Client**. |
| **password** | A secret code, known only to the user, that allows the user to access a computer protected by a security system. |
| **Properties sheet** | A special Windows 95 screen that supplies detailed information about almost anything in Windows or on MSN. You display the Properties sheet for a file, folder, program, or shortcut by right-clicking it to display its context menu and then choosing Properties. Most Properties sheets are made up of several pages, or *tabs*. |
| **resource** | A generic term to describe the varied information and activities available online through MSN and the Internet. |

| | |
|---|---|
| **search engine** | A program that provides a way to search for specific information. |
| **server** | A networked computer that "serves" a particular type of information to users or performs a particular function. Users run **client** software to access servers controlling certain types of resources such as MSN and the **World Wide Web**. |
| **shareware** | Software programs users are permitted to acquire and evaluate for free. Shareware is different from **freeware** in that, if a person likes the shareware program and plans to use it on a regular basis, he or she is expected to send a fee to the programmer. |
| **shortcut** | A feature of Windows 95 that allows you to place an icon anywhere in Windows, even on the desktop, that you can click to open a file or program. You can create Windows 95 shortcuts to resources located on MSN. |
| **shorthand** | A system of letter abbreviations used to efficiently express certain ideas in **e-mail** messages, **BBS** and **newsgroup** postings, and **Chat** sessions. See Chapter 3, "Member Rules and Etiquette." |
| **signing in** | The act of connecting to MSN and entering your **member ID** and **password** so that MSN can verify that you are authorized to go online. |
| **signing out** | The act of disconnecting from MSN. |
| **smiley** | A picture created from typed characters (often punctuation marks), used by MSN members and Internet users to express emotions or other abstract ideas in messages. See Chapter 3, "Member Rules and Etiquette." |
| **spider** | A program that searches methodically through a portion of the Internet to build a database that can be searched by a **search engine**. See Chapter 16, "Browsing the World Wide Web." |
| **TCP/IP** | Transmission Control Protocol/Internet Protocol, the fundamental internetworking protocol that makes the Internet work. See Chapter 15, "Understanding the Internet." |
| **Telnet** | A facility for accessing other computers on the Internet and for using the **resources** that are there. See Chapter 19, "Advanced Internet Techniques." |
| **title** | *See* **MSN title**. |

**URL**

Short for Universal Resource Locator, a method of standardizing the addresses of different types of Internet **resources** so that they can all be accessed easily from within a **browser** for the **World Wide Web**. See Chapter 16, "Browsing the World Wide Web."

**Usenet**

A loose affiliation of sites that together control the majority of Internet **newsgroups**.

**Veronica**

A facility that helps users search for and locate information available through **Gopher**. See Chapter 17, "Browsing Gophers."

**Web**

*See* **World Wide Web**.

**wizard**

Automated routines, used throughout Windows 95, for conveniently performing a step-by-step procedure, such as setting up Windows 95 or configuring it for the Internet.

**World Wide Web, WWW**, or **Web**

A set of Internet computers and services that provide an easy-to-use system for finding information and moving among **resources**. Web services feature **hypertext** and **hypermedia** information, which can be explored through **browsers** such as **Internet Explorer** and **Mosaic**.

# INDEX

## Symbols

" " (quotation marks) in multiple word matches, 175

, (commas) in multiple word matches, 175

* (asterisks)
    partial word matches, 176
    Veronica, 295

? (question marks) and partial word matches, 176

32-bit access
    performance, 224
    Windows 95, 228-230

## A

access
    Internet, 19, 236-237
    newsgroups, 103-105
access numbers, 6-7, 18
    Connection Settings dialog box, 31-32
account information, 189
Address Book, 204-210
    e-mail, 209-210
    Member Directory, 207-209
    member properties, 188

MSN members and non-members, 206-207
    people searches, 176-179
Address Book command (Tools menu), 205
addresses
    domains, 242-243
    e-mail, 204
    Internet, 242-243
    mailing lists, 326
    Personal Address Book, 204-210
    usernames, 242
Advanced Graphics Settings dialog box, 231
advertising (netiquette), 54-55
All the Gopher Servers in the World, 287-288
alt newsgroups, 101
America Online
    e-mail, 155
    performance, 220
anchoring links, 254
anonymous FTP, 302
Archie
    domains, 309
    FTP, 306-311
    search terms, 308-309

searches, 180
servers, 307, 309
**articles**
authorship, 92
BBSs, 86-92
composing, 93-94
posting, 93-94
reading, 90-92
replying to, 94-95
*by mail, 95-97*
views, 87-90
writing, 93-97
**ASCII files (FTP), 300**
**asterisks (*)**
partial word matches, 176
Veronica, 295
**attached files**
BBSs, 83
e-mail, 150, 212-216
**audio files, 125**
**authorship of BBS messages, 92**
**auto-disconnect**
Internet, 241
MSN Today, 37
**auto-display (MSN Today), 225**
**AutoDial (Internet), 240**

# B

**Back function (titles), 163**
**backing up hard disks (Windows 95), 230**
**BBSs (bulletin board systems), 65, 82-105**
attached files, 83
authorship, 92
composing messages, 93-94
*offline, 196*
conversations, 87-88
downloading files, 128-133
Favorite Places folder, 85
File view, 89-90
finding, 83-86
forums, 85
kiosks, 86
List view, 89
marked messages, 92
messages (articles), 86-92

opening, 83-86
posting messages, 93-94
reading messages, 90-92
replying to messages, 94-95
*by mail, 95-97*
shortcuts, 193
Suggestion Box, 84
updating, 89
uploading files, 134-136
views, 87-90
writing messages, 93-97
**billing, 38-41**
multiple accounts, 189
Notify Me When Any One
Charge Would Exceed...
option, 41
Online Statement, 39
Payment Method option,
38-39
subscriptions, 40
**Billing command (Tools menu), 38**
**binary files (FTP), 300**
**BINHEX, 212**
**blank lines (Chat), 117**
**blind carbon copies (e-mail), 145**
**body (e-mail), 145**
**bookmarks**
All the Gopher Servers in the
World, 288
Gopherspace, 286-287
World Wide Web, 262
**Bookmarks menu commands**
Mark Item, 288
Save Bookmarks, 288
**Boolean phrasing (Veronica), 295**
**browsers, 250, 263-268**
caching, 261
Explorer, 263-265
FTP, 300-301
Mosaic, 265-267
navigation, 62
Netscape, 267-268
toolbar tools, 261-262
**browsing, 69-74, 170-180**
content tree, 71-74
Explorer, 75

Folder tab (Options dialog
box), 35-36
Gopher, 282-296
Gopherspace, 288-289
Internet, 179-180
people, 176-179
services, 171-176
World Wide Web, 249-280
**bulletin board systems, *see*
BBSs**
**business issues on the Internet,
54-55**

# C

**caching**
Explorer, 261
VCACHE (virtual cache), 230
World Wide Web, 261
**Calendar of Events, 24**
Chat, 109
**call waiting, disabling, 34**
**capitalization (netiquette), 53**
**carbon copies (e-mail), 145**
**Cascade menu commands**
Tile Horizontally, 74
**case sensitivity**
Find utility, 174
member IDs, 10
Veronica, 294
Web servers, 260
**Categories folder, 26, 65, 71**
**censorship**
e-forms, 47
e-mail, 48
newsgroups, 103-105
**channels**
IRC, 319-321
WinIRC, 321
**chanops (IRC), 321**
**Chat, 66, 108-120**
blank lines, 117
clearing Chat histories, 116
compose pane, 111
*cut and paste, 115*
entering chats, 109
hiding spectators, 116
history pane, 111-112, 115

hosts, 113
ignoring members, 117
IRC, 318-321
Join the Chat option, 116
kiosks, 113
Leave the Chat option, 116
lurking, 113
Member Guidelines, 113
member list pane, 111
navigation, 109
netiquette, 113
participation, 113-115
properties, 109
saving Chat histories, 116
shortcuts, 193
shorthand, 114
smileys, 114
spectators, 113
statement order, 112
**Chat World, 120**
**Clear History command (Edit menu), 116**
**Clearinghouse for Subject-Oriented Internet Resource Guides, 270**
**client/server computing**
Internet, 244
IRC, 318
**clients**
FTP, 299, 301-305
Gopher, 284-290
Gopher+, 289-290
MUDs, 322
software (Internet), 244-246
Telnet, 317-318
**color**
e-mail, 152
links, 253
**commas in multiple word matches, 175**
**commands**
Bookmarks menu
*Mark Item, 288*
*Save Bookmarks, 288*
Cascade menu
*Tile Horizontally, 74*
Compose menu
*Forward by E-Mail, 96*
*New Message, 93, 150, 196*

*Reply by E-Mail, 96*
*Reply to BBS, 94*
Edit menu
*Clear History, 116*
*Copy, 196*
*Go To, 78*
*Links, 195*
*Mark as Read or Edit, 147*
File menu
*Create Shortcut, 164, 192*
*Decode, 139*
*Explore, 75*
*Post Message, 94, 134*
*Save As, 133*
*Save History, 116*
*Send, 196, 216*
*Sign Out, 27*
*Transfer and Disconnect, 132*
*Up One Level, 73*
FTP, 302-305
Insert menu
*File, 134, 213*
*Object, 215*
IRC, 320
Options menu
*FTP Setup, 311*
Start menu
*Help, 41*
Tools menu
*Address Book, 205*
*Billing, 38*
*Deliver Mail Now, 196*
*Deliver Now, 148*
*Find, 171*
*Member Properties, 92*
*Options, 200*
*Select Members, 117*
View menu
*Details, 67*
*Ignore Members, 117*
*Member Properties, 119*
*Options, 35*
*Show Spectators, 116*
**commercial issues (netiquette), 54-55**
**commercial online services (e-mail), 154-155**

**commercial software, 245**
**communications, 54**
**Communications Decency Act, 46**
**compatibility mode (Windows 95), 228**
**Compose menu commands**
Forward by E-Mail, 96
New Message, 93, 150, 196
Reply by E-Mail, 96
Reply to BBS, 94
**compose pane (Chat), 111**
cut and paste, 115
**composing**
BBS messages, 93-94
e-mail, 150-152
*offline, 196*
**compression, 127**
e-mail, 214
files, 132
Windows 95, 231
**CompuServe (e-mail), 155**
**configuration, 182-190**
file type registration, 182-185
Gopher+ clients, 289-290
languages, 185-187
member properties, 187-188
multiple accounts, 189
**confirmation messages (mailing lists), 328-329**
**Connection Settings dialog box, 30, 238**
access numbers, 31-32
dialing properties, 33-34
**connections**
Internet, 240
IRC, 319
MSN, 21-27
Telnet, 315-318
**content tree, 68-69**
backing up, 73-74
navigating down, 71-73
**Content View (MSN Today), 38**
**context menus (Windows 95), 63**
**conversations on BBSs, 87-88**
**Copy command (Edit menu), 196**

copying files, 122-140
crawlers, 269, 277-279
Create Shortcut command (File menu), 164, 192
customs, 46-58
 cybersleaze, 46-49
 emoticons, 56-58
 Member Guidelines, 50-51
 netiquette, 52-55
 shorthand, 55-56
cut and paste (compose pane), 115
cybersleaze, 46-49

## D

Decode command (File menu), 139
decoding newsgroup files, 128, 139-140
decompression, 127
 files, 132
defragmenting hard disks (Windows 95), 231
Deliver Mail Now command (Tools menu), 196
Deliver Now command (Tools menu), 148
demo software, 245
desktop shortcuts, 192-193
Details command (View menu), 67
DHCP (Dynamic Host Configuration Protocol), 242
dialing properties (Connection Settings dialog box), 33-34
dialog boxes
 Advanced Graphics Settings, 231
 Connection Settings, 30, 238
 Exchange Options, 200
 Find, 172
 FTP Setup, 311
 Go To Service, 78
 Insert File, 213
 Insert Object, 216
 Internet Properties, 240
 MSN Sign In, 239

Options, 35-38
 Properties, 129
 Sign In, 21
direct-marketing lists, 15
directories
 FTP, 299
 World Wide Web, 253, 269, 272-277
discretion (netiquette), 53-54
discussion groups, 244, 325-330
 addresses, 326
 confirmation messages, 328-329
 finding, 326-327
 Listservs, 326
 master index, 326
 subscriptions, 327-330
 unsubscribing, 330
disk tuning (Windows 95), 228
documents
 online documents, 66
 retrieving with Gopher, 283
domains
 addresses, 242-243
 Archie, 309
DOS disk tuning (Windows 95), 228
double-clicking shortcuts, 193
downloading files, 122-140
 BBSs, 128-133
 Gopher, 283
 libraries, 128-133
 newsgroups, 136-140
 performance, 225
DriveSpace (compression), 231
Dynamic Host Configuration Protocol (DHCP), 242

## E

e-forms (censorship), 47
e-mail (electronic mail), 26, 142-156, 200-218
 addresses, 204, 242-243
 America Online, 155
 attached files, 150, 212-216
 BBS messages, 95-97

BINHEX, 212
blind carbon copies, 145
body, 145
carbon copies, 145
censorship, 48
color, 152
composing, 150-152
 *offline, 196*
compression, 214
CompuServe, 155
embedded links, 150
Exchange, 146-148
faxes, 218
files, 213-214
fonts, 152
formatting, 152-153
forwarding, 153-154
headers, 144-145
Inbox folder, 148
Internet, 143, 155
Listserv, 328
mailing lists, 325-330
MAPI (Messaging Application Program Interface), 217
marking messages, 147
MIME (Multipurpose Internet Mail Extensions), 212
MSN, 23
netiquette, 53
objects, 214-216
online services, 154-155
paragraphs, 152
Personal Address Book, 204-210
Personal Distribution List, 210-211
printing, 149
Prodigy, 155
Read option, 200-201
reading offline, 196
receiving, 148-149, 202
reply separators, 153
replying to, 153-154
sending, 150-152, 202-204
 *from Windows, 216-217*
sensitivity options, 203
Sent Items folder, 152, 204

services, 204, 217-218
Set Importance options, 203
shortcuts, 63, 150, 193, 195-196
signatures, 146
Spelling option, 201-202
store and forward, 143
voice mail, 216
**Edit menu commands**
Clear History, 116
Copy, 196
Go To, 78
Links, 195
Mark as Read or Edit, 147
**editing registered actions, 184-185**
**electronic mail,** *see* **e-mail**
**embedding**
links (e-mail), 150
MSN content, 194-195
**emoticons, 56-58**
**etiquette, 46-58**
cybersleaze, 46-49
emoticons, 56-58
Member Guidelines, 50-51
netiquette, 52-55
shorthand, 55-56
**Exchange, 146-148**
e-mail, 142-156
marking messages, 147
printing e-mail, 149
**Exchange Options dialog box, 200**
**Explore command (File menu), 75**
**Explorer, 263-265**
browsing, 75
caching, 261
content tree, 68
picture files, 127
progressive rendering, 263
World Wide Web, 251

**F**

**FAQs (Frequently Asked Questions) and IRC, 319**
**Favorite Places, 26, 76-77, 262**
BBSs, 85

restrictions for children, 48
**faxes, 218**
**File command (Insert menu), 134, 213**
**File menu commands**
Create Shortcut, 164, 192
Decode, 139
Explore, 75
Post Message, 94, 134
Save As, 133
Save History, 116
Send, 196, 216
Sign Out, 27
Transfer and Disconnect, 132
Up One Level, 73
**file transfer protocol,** *see* **FTP**
**File Types registry, 78-80, 124, 182-185**
Windows 95, 182
**File view (BBSs), 89-90**
**file viewers, 256-257**
**files**
audio, 125
compression, 127, 132
decompression, 127, 132
downloading, 122-140
*BBSs, 128-133*
*Gopher, 283*
*libraries, 128-133*
*newsgroups, 136-140*
*performance, 225*
inserting in e-mail, 213-214
opening, 78-80
picture files, 126
players, 125-127
save paths, 133
transferring, 131-132
uploading, 122-140
*to BBSs, 134-136*
video, 125-126
viewers, 125-127
**Find command (Tools menu), 171**
**Find dialog box, 172**
**Find GOPHER DIRECTO-RIES... options (Veronica), 293**
**Find utility, 170-180**
case sensitivity, 174

**finding**
BBSs, 83-86
chats, 109
FTP files, 305-311
Internet services, 179-180
mailing lists, 326-327
MUDs, 323-324
newsgroups, 98-105
people, 176-179
services, 171-176
titles, 160
Web resources, 269-279
**flaming (netiquette), 54**
**folder icons, 67**
**folders**
Options dialog box, 35-36
Windows 95, 63
**fonts (e-mail), 152**
**formatting e-mail, 152-153**
**forums, 65**
BBSs, 85
**Forward by E-Mail command (Compose menu), 96**
**forwarding**
BBS messages by mail, 95-97
e-mail, 153-154
**fragmenting hard disks (Windows 95), 231**
**freeware, 245**
**Frequent User Monthly Plan, 11**
**Frequently Asked Questions,** *see* **FAQs**
**FTP (file transfer protocol), 244, 298-312**
anonymous FTP, 302
Archie, 306-311
binary files, 300
clients, 299, 301-305
commands, 302-305
directories, 299
finding files, 305-311
passwords, 298
text files, 300
Web browsers, 300-301
WinSock-FTP, 305
**FTP Setup command (Options menu), 311**
**FTP Setup dialog box, 311**

# G

**General tab (Options dialog box)**, 36-38

**Go To command (Edit menu)**, 78

**Go To Service dialog box**, 78

**Go word**, 77-78

**Gopher**, 244, 282-296
All the Gopher Servers in the World, 287-288
clients, 284-290
*setup, 285*
*startup servers, 285*
downloading files, 283
navigation, 283
retrieving documents, 283
searches, 180, 292-296
sites, 290-291
Telnet, 284, 314
University of Minnesota, 282
Veronica, 292-296

**Gopher+**
clients
*configuring, 289-290*
*Telnet, 290*
multimedia, 284

**Gopherspace**, 282
bookmarks, 286-287
browsing, 288-289
navigating, 285-287

**graphics**, 8, 126
links, 254
performance, 220
Windows 95, 231-232

**graphics adapters**, 223

**guidebooks**, 160, 163-164

# H

**hard disks (Windows 95)**, 223
backups, 230
compression, 231
fragmentation/defragmentation, 231
storage space, 230-231
tuning, 228

**hardware**, 7-9, 221-223
graphics adapters, 223
hard disks, 223
memory, 222
modems, 222
processors, 222
speed, 221

**headers (e-mail)**, 144-145

**help**, 41
offline help, 195

**Help command (Start menu)**, 41

**helpers**, 256-257

**HGopher 2.3c (Gopher client)**, 285-290

**hiding**
MSN Today, 37
spectators (Chat), 116

**history lists**, 262

**history pane (Chat)**, 111-112, 115

**home pages**
MSN home page, 69, 74
World Wide Web, 257

**hosts (Chat)**, 113

**hotlinks**, 251

**hotlists**, 262

**HTML (HyperText Markup Language)**, 251
hypermedia, 251-256
hypertext, 251-256

**HTTP (HyperText Transfer Protocol)**, 251

**hyperlinks**, 251

**hypermedia**, 251-256

**hypertext**, 251-256

# I

**icons**
folder icons, 67
title icons, 159

**identifying titles**, 159-160

**Ignore Members command (View menu)**, 117

**ignoring Chat members**, 117

**importance options (e-mail)**, 203

**Inbox folder (e-mail)**, 148

**InfoSeek**, 270

**Insert File dialog box**, 213

**Insert menu commands**
File, 134, 213
Object, 215

**Insert Object dialog box**, 216

**inserting**
files in e-mail, 213-214
objects in e-mail, 214-216
shortcuts in documents, 193

**Internet**, 236-247
access, 19, 236-237
addresses, 242-243
auto-disconnect, 241
AutoDial, 240
client software, 244-246
client/server computing, 244
commercial software, 245
connections, 240
demo software, 245
e-mail, 143, 155
emoticons, 56-58
freeware, 245
FTP, 244
Gopher, 244
IRC, 244
mailing lists, 244, 325-330
MUDs, 244, 322-325
netiquette, 52-55
newsgroups, 69
PPP, 236-237
proxy servers, 241
publications, 246-247
searching, 179-180
security, 237
shareware, 245
shorthand, 55-56
signing up for Internet access, 237-241
TCP/IP, 236
Telnet, 244, 314-318
threads, 88
tools, 243-244
WinSock, 245
World Wide Web, 243

**Internet Control Panel**, 240-241

Internet Explorer, *see* Explorer
Internet Properties dialog box, 240
Internet Wizard, 238-240
IP addresses, 242-243
IRC (Internet Relay Chat), 244, 318-321
   channels, 319-321
   chanops, 321
   client/server computing, 318
   commands, 320
   connections, 319
   FAQs (Frequently Asked Questions), 319
   Net lag, 318
   servers, 318

## J-K

Join the Chat option, 116

kiosks
   BBSs, 86
   Chat, 113
   member support, 42

## L

language (netiquette), 53
languages, 185-187
   Content View, 38
Leave the Chat option, 116
libraries, 66
   downloading files, 128-133
links, 66
   anchoring, 254
   color, 253
   graphical links, 254
   hypertext, 251-256
   magazine titles, 164
   MSN content, 194-195
   thumbnails, 254
   titles, 162-163
   updating, 195
   Web pages, 163
Links command (Edit menu), 195
List view (BBSs), 89

Listserv
   e-mail, 328
   mailing lists, 326
   subscriptions, 327-330
logins, Telnet, 315-318
logoffs, Telnet, 316, 318
long filenames (Windows 95), 63
lurking (Chat), 113
Lycos, 270, 277-279

## M

magazine titles, 161, 164-166
   links, 164
mailing lists, 244, 325-330
   addresses, 326
   confirmation messages, 328-329
   finding, 326-327
   Listservs, 326
   master index, 326
   subscriptions, 327-330
   unsubscribing, 330
maintenance
   billing, 38-41
   MSN, 30-44
   Options dialog box, 35-38
   passwords, 34-35
   settings, 30-34
   support, 41-44
MAPI (Messaging Application Program Interface), 217
Mark as Read or Edit command (Edit menu), 147
Mark Item command (Bookmarks menu), 288
marked messages
   BBSs, 92
   Exchange, 147
master index (mailing lists), 326
matching
   multiple words in searches, 175
   partial words in searches, 176
Member Agreement, 16-17
   Member Guidelines, 50-51

Member Directory (Personal Address Book), 207-209
Member Guidelines, 47, 50-51
   Chat, 113
member IDs, 9-11, 18
   case sensitivity, 10
   signing in, 22
member list pane (Chat), 111
Member Lobby folder, 27
member properties, 187-188
Member Properties command
   Tools menu, 92
   View menu, 119
member searches, 176-179
member support, 41-42
memory, 222
   paging, 8
   Windows 95, 226-232
menus
   context menus (Windows 95), 63
   Gopher, 282-296
messages
   authorship, 92
   BBSs, 86-92
   composing, 93-94
   posting, 93-94
   reading, 90-92
   replying to, 94-95
   *by mail,* 95-97
   views, 87-90
   writing, 93-97
Microsoft Network, *see* MSN
MIME (Multipurpose Internet Mail Extensions), 212
modems
   dialing properties, 33-34
   speed, 8, 222
   Windows 95, 6
moderated newsgroups, 102
Mosaic, 250, 265-267
   multithreading, 266
   performance, 220
MOV (video) files, 125-126
MPEG (video) files, 125-126
MSN (Microsoft Network)
   32-bit applications, 224
   access numbers, 6-7, 18

advertising, 54-55
BBSs (bulletin board systems), 65, 82-105
billing, 38-41
browsing, 69-74
categories, 65
Categories folder, 26, 71
Chat, 66, 108-120
configuration, 182-190
content tree, 68-69
cybersleaze, 46-49
direct-marketing lists, 15
downloading files, 122-140, 225
e-mail, 23, 26, 142-156, 200-218
    *shortcuts, 195-196*
Explorer, 75
Favorite Places, 26, 76-77
faxes, 218
file type registration, 78-80, 182-185
Find utility, 170-180
FTP, 298
Go word, 77-78
Gopher, 282-296
hardware, 7-9, 221-223
Internet
    *access, 236-247*
    *searches, 179-180*
languages, 185-187
libraries, 66
links, 66
maintenance, 30-44
Member Agreement, 16-17
member IDs, 9-11, 18
Member Lobby folder, 27
member properties, 187-188
modems, 6
multiple accounts, 189
multitasking, 130, 223
navigation, 62-80, 224
Net lag, 318
netiquette, 52-55
newsgroups, 69, 82-105
obscenity, 47-49
offline help, 195
offline work, 224

OLE (Object Linking and Embedding), 194-195
online documents, 66
opening files, 78-80
Options dialog box, 35-38
passwords, 9-11, 18, 34-35
people searches, 176-179
performance, 220-232
Personal Address Book, 204-210
Personal Distribution List, 210-211
Plus!, 224
policies, 136
pricing, 11-12
security, 237
service searches, 171-176
settings, 30-34
shortcuts, 63, 192-193
sign-up routine, 4-20
    *Internet access, 237*
signing in, 21-27
signing out, 27-28
software requirements, 5-6
support, 41-44
time savers, 192-197
titles, 66, 158-166
tuning, 221-225
updating links, 195
uploading files, 122-140
Visual Basic, 123
World Wide Web, 249-280
**MSN Central (MSN home page), 22, 69, 74**
**MSN data center, 179**
**MSN Member Agreement, 47**
**MSN Shareware Forum, 124**
**MSN Sign In dialog box, 239**
**MSN Today, 23-24**
    auto-disconnect, 37
    auto-display, 225
    Chat, 109
    Content View, 38
    General tab (Options dialog box), 36-38
    hiding, 37
**MUDs (multi-user dungeons), 244, 322-325**
    clients, 322

    finding, 323-324
    playing, 324-325
    rules, 323
**multimedia (Gopher+), 284**
    client configuration, 289-290
**multiple accounts, 189**
**multiple user profiles, 224**
**multiple word matching (searches), 175**
**Multipurpose Internet Mail Extensions (MIME), 212**
**multitasking, 130**
    performance, 223
**multithreading (Mosaic), 266**

# N

navigation, 62-80
    browsers, 62
    chats, 109
    content tree, 68-69, 71-74
    Explorer, 75
    Favorite Places folder, 76-77
    Go word, 77-78
    Gopher, 283
    Gopherspace, 285-287
    MSN home page, 69, 74
    opening files, 78-80
    performance, 224
    Windows 95, 62-64, 74
    World Wide Web, 259-262
**NCSA Mosaic,** *see* **Mosaic**
**Net lag, 318**
**netiquette, 52-55**
    advertising, 54-55
    capitalization, 53
    Chat, 113
    communication, 54
    discretion, 53-54
    flaming, 54
    language, 53
    politeness, 54
    quoting, 53
**Netscape, 267-268**
**New Message command (Compose menu), 93, 150, 196**

newsgroups, 69, 82-105
  access, 103-105
  alt newsgroups, 101
  censorship, 103-105
  composing messages off-
    line, 196
  decoding newsgroup files,
    128, 139-140
  downloading files, 136-140
  finding, 98-105
  moderated newsgroups, 102
  non-Usenet newsgroups,
    101-102
  opening, 98-105
  saving message files, 138
  Usenet, 99-100
  ZIP files, 138
NNTP (network news transfer
  protocol), 136
non-Usenet newsgroups,
  101-102
Notify Me When Any One
  Charge Would Exceed...
  option (billing), 41

O

Object command (Insert
  menu), 215
objects (e-mail), 214-216
obscenity, 47-49
offline help, 195
offline work (performance),
  224
OLE (Object Linking and
  Embedding), 194-195
online communication
  graphics, 220
  performance, 220
online documents, 66
online help, 41
online e-mail services, 154-155
Online Statement (billing), 39
Online Viewer (titles), 162
opening
  BBSs, 83-86
  files, 78-80
  newsgroups, 98-105

Options command
  Tools menu, 200
  View menu, 35
Options dialog box, 35-38
  Folder tab, 35-36
  General tab, 36-38
Options menu commands
  FTP Setup, 311

P

paging (memory), 8
paragraphs (e-mail), 152
partial word matches, 176
participation (Chat), 113-115
passwords, 9-11, 18, 34-35
  FTP servers, 298
  security, 48
  signing in, 21
Payment Method option
  (billing), 38-39
people searches, 176-179
performance, 220-232
  32-bit applications, 224
  America Online, 220
  downloading files, 225
  graphics, 220
  Mosaic, 220
  MSN tuning, 221-225
  MSN Today auto-display, 225
  multitasking, 223
  navigation, 224
  offline work, 224
  online communication, 220
  Plus!, 224
  Prodigy, 220
  productivity, 221
  responsiveness, 221
  Windows 95, 232
  *tuning, 225-232*
Personal Address Book,
  204-210
  e-mail, 209-210
  Member Directory, 207-209
  member properties, 188
  MSN members and non-
    members, 206-207
  people searches, 176-179

Personal Distribution List,
  210-211
pictures, 8, 126
PKUNZIP (decompression),
  127
PKZIP (compression), 127
players, 125-127
playing MUDs, 324-325
Plus!
  performance, 224
  Setup Wizard, 238-240
policies of MSN, 136
politeness (netiquette), 54
pornography, 47-49
Post Message command (File
  menu), 94, 134
posting BBS messages, 93-94
PPP (Point-to-Point Protocol),
  236-237
pricing MSN, 11-12
printing e-mail, 149
privacy (netiquette), 53
processors, 222
Prodigy
  e-mail, 155
  performance, 220
productivity, 221
progressive rendering
  Explorer, 263
  titles, 164
Properties dialog box, 129
Properties sheets
  member properties, 187-188
  Windows 95, 63
proxy servers, 241
public domain software, 245
publications, Internet, 246-247

Q

question marks in partial word
  matches, 176
quitting Telnet, 318
quotation marks in multiple
  word matches, 175
quoting netiquette, 53

# R

**RAM and Windows 95, 226**
**Read option (e-mail), 200-201**
**reading**
  BBS messages, 90-92
  e-mail offline, 196
**receiving e-mail, 148-149, 202**
**registered actions, editing,
  184-185**
**registering file types, 182-185**
**remote access (Telnet), 314-318**
**Reply by E-Mail command
  (Compose menu), 96**
**reply separators (e-mail), 153**
**Reply to BBS command
  (Compose menu), 94**
**replying to**
  BBS messages, 94-95
    *by mail,* 95-97
  e-mail, 153-154
**responsiveness (perfor-
  mance), 221**
**retrieving documents with
  Gopher, 283**
**rules, 46-58, 136**
  cybersleaze, 46-49
  emoticons, 56-58
  Member Guidelines, 50-51
  MUDs, 323
  netiquette, 52-55
  shorthand, 55-56

# S

**Save As command (File
  menu), 133**
**Save Bookmarks command
  (Bookmarks menu), 288**
**Save History command (File
  menu), 116**
**save paths, 133**
**saving**
  Chat histories, 116
  newsgroup message files, 138
**search engines, 269**
**Search GopherSpace... options
  (Veronica), 293**

**search terms**
  Archie, 308-309
  Veronica, 294-296
**searches, 170-180**
  BBSs, 83-86
  FTP files, 305-311
  Gopher, 292-296
  Internet, 179-180
  mailing lists, 326-327
  MUDs, 323-324
  people, 176-179
  services, 171-176
  titles, 160
  Veronica, 292-296
  Web resources, 269-279
**security, 237**
  passwords, 48
**Select Members command
  (Tools menu), 117**
**selling products (netiquette),
  54-55**
**Send command (File menu),
  196, 216**
**sending e-mail, 150-152,
  202-204**
**sensitivity options (e-mail), 203**
**Sent Items folder (e-mail),
  152, 204**
**servers**
  Archie, 307, 309
  FTP, 298
  Gopher, 287-288
  IRC, 318
  Web, 259
**services**
  e-mail, 204, 217-218
  finding, 171-176
**Set Importance options
  (e-mail), 203**
**settings, 30-34**
  access numbers, 31-32
  auto-disconnect (MSN
    Today), 37
  Connection Settings dialog
    box, 30
  dialing properties, 33-34
**Setup Wizard (Internet access),
  238-241**

**shareware, 245**
**Shareware Forum, 124**
**shortcuts, 192-193**
  BBSs, 193
  Chat, 193
  double-clicking, 193
  e-mail, 63, 150, 193, 195-196
  Favorite Places folder, 76-77
  inserting in documents, 193
  MSN, 63
  offline help, 195
  OLE (Object Linking and
    Embedding), 194-195
  titles, 162
  Windows 95, 63
**shorthand, 55-56**
  Chat, 114
**Show Spectators command
  (View menu), 116**
**Sign In dialog box, 21**
**Sign Out command (File
  menu), 27**
**sign-up routine**
  Internet access, 237-241
  MSN, 4-20
  multiple accounts, 189
**signatures (e-mail), 146**
**signing in, 21-27**
  member IDs, 22
  passwords, 21
**signing out, 27-28**
**Simplified Veronica, 293**
**smileys, 56-58**
  Chat, 114
**software, 5-6**
  Internet client software,
    244-246
**sound files, 125**
**spectators**
  Chat, 113
  hiding, 116
**speed**
  hardware, 221
  modems, 8, 222
  processors, 222
**Spelling option (e-mail),
  201-202**
**spiders, 269, 277-279**

Standard Monthly Plan, 11
Start menu commands
    Help, 41
startup servers (Gopher clients),
    285
statement order (Chat), 112
storage space (Windows 95),
    230-231
store and forward (e-mail), 143
subscriptions
    billing, 11-12, 40
    mailing lists, 327-330
Suggestion Box (BBSs), 84
support, 41-44
    help, 41
    member support, 41-42
    telephone support, 42-44
swapfiles (Windows 95), 226
sysop IDs, 42

**T**

TCP/IP (Transmission Control
    Protocol/Internet Protocol),
    236
technical support, 41-44
telephone support, 42-44
Telnet, 244, 314-318
    connections, 315-318
    Gopher, 284, 314
    Gopher+ clients, 290
    logins, 315-318
    logoffs, 316, 318
    quitting, 318
    starting, 317
    terminal emulation, 316-317
    World Wide Web, 314
Telnet client, 317-318
terminal emulation (Telnet),
    316-317
text files (FTP), 300
threads, 88
thumbnails, 254
Tile Horizontally command
    (Cascade menu), 74
time savers, 192-197
    shortcuts, 192-193
title icons, 159

titles, 66, 158-166
    Back function, 163
    compared to Web pages, 158
    finding, 160
    guidebooks, 160, 163-164
    identifying, 159-160
    links, 162-163
    magazine titles, 161, 164-166
    Online Viewer, 162
    progressive rendering, 164
    shortcuts, 162
toolbars
    Windows 95, 64
    World Wide Web, 261-262
Tools menu commands
    Address Book, 205
    Billing, 38
    Deliver Mail Now, 196
    Deliver Now, 148
    Find, 171
    Member Properties, 92
    Options, 200
    Select Members, 117
Transfer and Disconnect
    command (File menu), 132
transferring files, 131-132
tuning
    hard disks (Windows 95), 228
    MSN, 221-225
    Windows 95, 225-232

**U**

Uniform Resource Locators, *see*
    URLs
University of Minnesota
    (Gopher), 282
unmoderated newsgroups, 102
unsubscribing to mailing lists,
    330
Up One Level command (File
    menu), 73
updating
    BBSs, 89
    links, 195
uploading files, 122-140
    to BBSs, 134-136
uppercase (netiquette), 53

URLs (Uniform Resource
    Locators), 258-260
Usenet newsgroups, 99-100
user profiles, multiple, 224
user searches, 176-179
usernames (addresses), 242
UUENCODE/UUDECODE,
    139-140

**V**

VCACHE (virtual cache), 230
Veronica, 292-296
    asterisk (*), 295
    Boolean phrasing, 295
    case sensitivity, 294
    Find GOPHER DIRECTO-
        RIES... options, 293
    Search GopherSpace...
        options, 293
    search terms, 294-296
    searches, 180
    Simplified Veronica, 293
video files, 125-126
View menu commands
    Details, 67
    Ignore Members, 117
    Member Properties, 119
    Options, 35
    Show Spectators, 116
viewers, 125-127, 256-257
views
    BBSs, 87-90
    Windows 95, 64
Virtual Library (World Wide
    Web), 271, 274-276
virtual memory management
    (Windows 95), 226-228
Visual Basic, 123
voice mail, 216

**W**

Web pages
    compared to titles, 158
    links, 163
WebCrawler, 279
Whole Internet Catalog, 277

**wildcards**
  partial word matches, 176
  Veronica, 295
**WinCode, 128**
**Windows**
  e-mail, 216-217
  Visual Basic, 123
**Windows 95**
  32-bit access, 228-230
  compatibility mode, 228
  compression, 231
  context menus, 63
  disk tuning, 228
  Explorer, 75
    *content tree, 68*
  File Types registry, 182
  folder icons, 67
  folders, 63
  forums, 65
  graphics, 231-232
  hard disks
    *backups, 230*
    *fragmentation/*
      *defragmentation, 231*
  long filenames, 63
  memory management,
    226-232
  modems, 6
  navigation, 62-64, 74
  performance, 232
  Properties sheets, 63
  RAM, 226
  servers (case sensitivity), 260
  shortcuts, 63
  storage space, 230-231
  swapfile, 226
  toolbars, 64
  tuning, 225-232
  VCACHE (virtual cache), 230
  views, 64
  virtual memory management,
    226-228
**WinIRC channels, 321**
**WinSock, 245**
**WinSock-FTP, 305**
**World Wide Web, 243,**
  **249-280**
  bookmarks, 262

  browsers, 250, 263-268
    *FTP, 300-301*
  caching, 261
  Clearinghouse for Subject-
    Oriented Internet Resource
    Guides, 270
  directories, 253, 269, 272-277
  Explorer, 251, 263-265
  file viewers, 256-257
  home pages, 257
  HTML (HyperText Markup
    Language), 251
  HTTP (HyperText Transfer
    Protocol), 251
  hypermedia, 251-256
  hypertext, 251-256
  InfoSeek, 270
  Lycos, 270, 277-279
  Mosaic, 250, 265-267
  navigation, 259-262
  Netscape, 267-268
  searches, 180, 269-279
  spiders, 269, 277-279
  Telnet, 314
  toolbar tools, 261-262
  URLs (Uniform Resource
    Locators), 258-260
  Web pages, 158, 163
  Web servers, 259
  WebCrawler, 279
  Whole Internet Catalog, 277
  Yahoo, 270, 272-274
**World Wide Web Virtual**
  **Library, 271, 274-276**
**World Wide Web Worm, 279**
**worms, 269, 277-279**
**writing BBS messages, 93-97**

# X-Y-Z

**Yahoo, 270, 272-274**

**ZIP files (newsgroups), 138**

# Add to Your Sams Library Today with the Best Books for Programming, Operating Systems, and New Technologies

## The easiest way to order is to pick up the phone and call

# 1-800-428-5331

## between 9:00 a.m. and 5:00 p.m. EST.
## For faster service please have your credit card available.

| ISBN | Quantity | Description of Item | Unit Cost | Total Cost |
|---|---|---|---|---|
| 0-672-30737-5 | | The World Wide Web Unleashed, Second Edition | $39.99 | |
| 0-672-30714-6 | | The Internet Unleashed, Second Edition | $39.99 | |
| 1-57521-014-2 | | Teach Yourself Web Publishing with HTML in a Week, Premier Edition | $35.00 | |
| 0-672-30745-6 | | HTML and CGI Unleashed | $49.99 | |
| 0-672-30764-2 | | Teach Yourself Web Publishing with Microsoft Word in a Week | $29.99 | |
| 1-57521-039-8 | | Presenting Java | $19.99 | |
| 1-57521-004-5 | | The Internet Business Guide, Second Edition | $25.00 | |
| 0-672-30595-X | | Education on the Internet | $25.00 | |
| 0-672-30718-9 | | Navigating the Internet, Third Edition | $22.50 | |
| 0-672-30765-0 | | Navigating the Internet with Windows 95 | $25.00 | |
| 0-672-30761-8 | | Navigating the Internet with CompuServe | $25.00 | |
| 0-672-30740-5 | | Navigating the Internet with Prodigy | $19.99 | |
| 0-672-30669-7 | | Plug-n-Play Internet for Windows | $35.00 | |
| 1-57521-010-X | | Plug-n-Play Netscape for Windows | $29.99 | |
| 0-672-30723-5 | | Secrets of the MUD Wizards | $25.00 | |
| ❏ 3 ½" Disk | | Shipping and Handling: See information below. | | |
| ❏ 5 ¼" Disk | | TOTAL | | |

Shipping and Handling: $4.00 for the first book, and $1.75 for each additional book. Floppy disk: add $1.75 for shipping and handling. If you need to have it NOW, we can ship product to you in 24 hours for an additional charge of approximately $18.00, and you will receive your item overnight or in two days. Overseas shipping and handling adds $2.00 per book and $8.00 for up to three disks. Prices subject to change. Call for availability and pricing information on latest editions.

## 201 W. 103rd Street, Indianapolis, Indiana 46290

## 1-800-428-5331 — Orders    1-800-835-3202 — FAX    1-800-858-7674 — Customer Service

Book ISBN 0-672-30778-2

# PLUG YOURSELF INTO...

# THE MACMILLAN INFORMATION SUPERLIBRARY™

## Free information and vast computer resources from the world's leading computer book publisher—online!

### *FIND THE BOOKS THAT ARE RIGHT FOR YOU!*

A complete online catalog, plus sample chapters and tables of contents give you an in-depth look at *all* of our books, including hard-to-find titles. It's the best way to find the books you need!

- **STAY INFORMED** with the latest computer industry news through our online newsletter, press releases, and customized Information SuperLibrary Reports.

- **GET FAST ANSWERS** to your questions about MCP books and software.

- **VISIT** our online bookstore for the latest information and editions!

- **COMMUNICATE** with our expert authors through e-mail and conferences.

- **DOWNLOAD SOFTWARE** from the immense MCP library:
    - Source code and files from MCP books
    - The best shareware, freeware, and demos

- **DISCOVER HOT SPOTS** on other parts of the Internet.

- **WIN BOOKS** in ongoing contests and giveaways!

**TO PLUG INTO MCP:** ➔  WORLD WIDE WEB: **http://www.mcp.com**

GOPHER: gopher.mcp.com

FTP: ftp.mcp.com